Martin Heidegger

Key Concepts

Key Concepts

Martin Heidegger

Key Concepts

Edited by Bret W. Davis

First published in 2010 by Acumen

Acumen Publishing Limited
4 Saddler Street
Durham
DH1 3NP
www.acumenpublishing.co.uk

ISBN: 978-1-84465-198-6 (hardcover)
ISBN: 978-1-84465-199-3 (paperback)

British Library Cataloguing-in-Publication Data
A catalogue record for this book is available
from the British Library.

Designed and typeset in Classical Garamond and Myriad.
Printed and bound in the UK by Cromwell Press Group, Trowbridge,
Wiltshire

Contents

Contributors

Charles Bambach is Professor of Philosophy at the University of Texas at Dallas. His books include *Heidegger's Roots: Nietzsche, National Socialism, and the Greeks* (2003) and *Heidegger, Dilthey, and the Crisis of Historicism* (1995). He has also written variously on hermeneutics, phenomenology, ethics and the history of German philosophy. Bambach's current book project, *Doing Justice to Poetry: Heidegger, Hölderlin, Celan, and the Greek Experience of dikē*, deals with the tragic aporia between ethics and justice in modern German philosophy, specifically Heidegger's dialogue with the poetry of Friedrich Hölderlin (1770–1843) and Paul Celan (1920–1970).

Daniel O. Dahlstrom, Professor and Chair of the Department of Philosophy, Boston University, is the author of *Philosophical Legacies* (2008), *Heidegger's Concept of Truth* (2001) and *Das logische Vorurteil: Untersuchungen zur Wahrheitstheorie des frühen Heidegger* (1994). He is the translator of Heidegger's first Marburg lectures, *Introduction to Phenomenological Research* (2005). His recent articles on Heidegger's thought include "Transcendental Truth and the Truth that Prevails" in *Transcendental Heidegger* (2007) and "Feenberg on Heidegger and Marcuse" in *Techne* (2006).

Bret W. Davis is Associate Professor of Philosophy at Loyola University Maryland. In addition to numerous journal articles and book chapters, he is the author of *Heidegger and the Will: On the Way to Gelassenheit* (2007), translator of Martin Heidegger, *Country Path Conversations* (2010), co-editor of *Japanese and Continental Philosophy: Conversations with the Kyoto School* (with Brian Schroeder and Jason Wirth,

2010), and co-editor of *Japanese Philosophy in the World* (with Fujita Masakatsu, 2005 [in Japanese]).

Jonathan Dronsfield is Reader in Theory and Philosophy of Art at the University of Reading and sits on the Executive Committee of the Forum for European Philosophy, European Institute, London School of Economics. He is currently writing a book, *Derrida and the Visual*, and has published mainly on art and ethics, including most recently "Between Heidegger and Deleuze There is Never any Difference", in *French Interpretations of Heidegger* (Raffoul & Pettigrew [eds], 2009); "Philosophies of Art", in *The Continuum Companion to Continental Philosophy* (Mullarkey & Lord [eds], 2009); and "Nowhere is Aesthetics contra Ethics: Rancière the Other Side of Lyotard" in *Art&Research* (2008).

Günter Figal is Professor of Philosophy at the University of Freiburg, Germany, where he holds the chair previously occupied by Martin Heidegger. His many books include *The Heidegger Reader* (2009), *Verstehensfragen: Studien zur phänomenologisch-hermeneutischen Philosophie* (2009), *Zu Heidegger: Antworten und Fragen* (2009), *Gegenständlichkeit* (currently being translated into English) (2006), *For a Philosophy of Freedom and Strife* (1998), *Der Sinn des Verstehens* (1996), *Heidegger zur Einführung* (1992) and *Martin Heidegger: Phänomenologie der Freiheit* (1988).

Theodore Kisiel is Distinguished Research Professor Emeritus of Philosophy at Northern Illinois University. His books include *Heidegger's Way of Thought: Critical and Interpretative Essays* (2002), *The Genesis of Heidegger's "Being and Time"* (1993) and *Phenomenology and the Natural Sciences* (with Joseph Kockelmans, 1970). Editions include *Becoming Heidegger: On the Trail of His Early Occasional Writings, 1910–1927* (with Thomas Sheehan, 2007) and *Reading Heidegger from the Start: Essays in His Earliest Thought* (with John van Buren, 1994). Translations include Martin Heidegger, *History of the Concept of Time: Prolegomena* (1985) and Werner Marx, *Heidegger and the Tradition* (1971).

John T. Lysaker is Professor of Philosophy at Emory University, Georgia. He is the author of *Emerson and Self-Culture* (2008) and *You Must Change Your Life: Poetry, Philosophy, and the Birth of Sense* (2002), and the co-author of *Schizophrenia and the Fate of the Self* (2008). Current interests include the nature of the self, the social function of art and the intersections of phenomenology, pragmatism and social theory.

Andrew J. Mitchell is Assistant Professor of Philosophy at Emory University, Georgia. He is the author of *Heidegger Among the Sculptors:*

Body, Space, and the Art of Dwelling (forthcoming) as well as essays on Heidegger, Nietzsche, Derrida, James Joyce and Rainer Werner Fassbinder. He is currently revising a manuscript exploring the conception of things in Heidegger's later period, entitled *The Fourfold: Thing and World in Late Heidegger*. He is co-editor (with Jason Winfree) of *Community and Communication: The Thought of Georges Bataille* (2009), and co-translator (with François Raffoul) of Heidegger's *Four Seminars* (2003).

Richard Polt is Professor of Philosophy at Xavier University, Ohio. He is the author of *The Emergency of Being: On Heidegger's "Contributions to Philosophy"* (2006) and *Heidegger: An Introduction* (1999) and editor of *Heidegger's "Being and Time": Critical Essays* (2006). With Gregory Fried, he has translated Heidegger's *Being and Truth* (2010) and *Introduction to Metaphysics* (2000) and edited *A Companion to Heidegger's "Introduction to Metaphysics"* (2001).

Hans Ruin is Professor of Philosophy at Södertörn University College, Sweden. He is the author of *Inledning till Heideggers Varat och tiden* (2006), *Herakleitos Fragment* (1997) and *Enigmatic Origins: Tracing the Theme of Historicity through Heidegger's Works* (1994). He is co-editor of *The Past's Presence* (with M. Sá Cavalcante, 2006), *Metaphysics, Facticity, Interpretation: Phenomenology in the Nordic Countries* (with D. Zahavi and S. Heinämaa, 2003) and *Fenomenologiska Perspektiv* (1997). He is co-founder of the Nordic Society for Phenomenology and co-editor of Nietzsche's collected works in Swedish. He has also translated works by Derrida, Husserl and Heidegger into Swedish.

Charles E. Scott is Distinguished Professor of Philosophy at Vanderbilt University, Tennessee. His recent books include *Living With Indifference* (2007), *The Lives of Things* (2002) and *The Time of Memory* (1999). He also co-edited *A Companion to Heidegger's Contributions to Philosophy* (2001).

Thomas Sheehan is Professor of Religious Studies at Stanford University and Professor of Philosophy Emeritus at Loyola University Chicago. Among his books and editions are his edition and translation of Heidegger's *Logic: The Question of Truth* (2010); *Becoming Heidegger: On the Trail of his Early Occasional Writings, 1910–1927* (with Theodore Kisiel, 2007); *Edmund Husserl: Psychological and Transcendental Phenomenology and the Confrontation with Heidegger (1927–1931)* (with Richard Palmer, 1997); *Karl Rahner: The Philosophical Foundations* (1987); and *The First Coming: How the Kingdom of God Became Christianity* (1986).

Timothy Stapleton is Associate Professor of Philosophy at Loyola University Maryland. He is the author of *Husserl and Heidegger: The Question of a Phenomenological Beginning* (1984) and editor of *The Question of Hermeneutics* (1994).

Daniela Vallega-Neu is Associate Professor of Philosophy at California State University Stanislaus. She is the author of *The Bodily Dimension in Thinking* (2005) and *Heidegger's Contributions to Philosophy: An Introduction* (2003), and co-editor of *A Companion to Heidegger's Contributions to Philosophy* (2001).

Ben Vedder is Professor of Metaphysics and Philosophy of Religion at the Radboud Universiteit Nijmegen, the Netherlands. He publishes especially in the fields of hermeneutics, metaphysics and philosophy of religion. His works include *Heidegger's Philosophy of Religion: From God to the Gods* (2007) and *Was ist Hermeneutik? Ein Weg von der Textdeutung zur Interpretation der Wirklichkeit* (2000).

Peter Warnek is Associate Professor of Philosophy at the University of Oregon. He is the author of *The Descent of Socrates: Self-knowledge and Cryptic Nature in the Platonic Dialogues* (2006), and co-translator (with Walter Brogan) of Martin Heidegger, *Aristotle's Metaphysics, Theta 1–3: On the Essence and Actuality of Force* (1995).

Acknowledgements

Let me begin by thanking the contributors to this volume. While there are a number of introductory level books on Heidegger (which run the risk of superficiality and even distortion), and while there is an abundance of more scholarly level treatises (which run the risk of inaccessibility and even obfuscation), this volume was conceived with the intent of bridging the gap between these levels. The chapters are meant to explicate the key concepts of Heidegger's thought in a way that is *both rigorous and accessible*. The only way this can done, in my mind, is if some of the very best scholars in the field, who have all published at the highest level of scholarship, are willing to take a step back and attempt to clearly and concisely articulate, with ample and precise textual references, their understanding of the key concepts of their particular areas of expertise. I thank the contributors for their willingness to take on this daunting balancing act, and for managing to find the middle way with such care and acumen. Owing to their reservoirs of research and facilities of elucidation, I believe that this book will be useful to students looking for a reliable, discerning and comprehensive introduction to the conceptual contours of Heidegger's thought, in all its phases, as well as to scholars looking to focus their attention on, and deepen their understanding of, this or that particular Heideggerian concept.

Heidegger's thought has elicited a diverse array of responses, even at the level of explication and interpretation. One advantage that a collection has over a monograph is that the reader is exposed to some of this variety. While certain conventions of citation and translation have been coordinated, and while I have requested of all authors that they focus on *elucidation* rather than development or critique of Heidegger's concepts, I have not wanted to unduly restrict the individual approaches and styles of the chapters. In part owing to the concepts treated, students may find some chapters (such as 1, 6, 8 and 10) more challenging, other chapters (such as 3, 4, 7, 14 and 16) more accessible, and the rest somewhere in between. While the book can be read from start to finish as a comprehensive and roughly chronological account of Heidegger's thought, each of the chapters can also be read independently; and so even the beginning student should feel free to pick and choose chapters according to his or her interests.

Having thanked the contributors, I want also to express my gratitude to Tristan Palmer and Kate Williams for the professionalism and skill with which they have escorted the manuscript through its various stages from planning to production. It has been a pleasure to work with them and their colleagues at Acumen on this project. I would also like to use this occasion to thank all those who have helped me find my way into and along Heidegger's way of thought. These include, first and foremost, my former teachers at Vanderbilt University, Charles Scott, John Sallis and David Wood. Also included are teachers and colleagues in Japan, at the Collegium Phaenomenologicum in Italy, and at conferences such as those of SPEP, CCPC and the Heidegger Circle. At Loyola University Maryland I would like to thank my colleagues, especially those participating in our Heidegger study group, and my students, especially those who took my seminars on Heidegger's thought. I am grateful to Loyola for a summer research grant that enabled me to spend a summer in Freiburg working on this project.

Let me end by thanking, as always, my family, starting with my wife Naomi, my son Toshi and my daughter Koto, for making it all worthwhile each and every day. Although I regret not being able to share the fruition of this project – and so much more – with my mother, Barbara Davis (1938–2009), I am grateful that she lived long enough to share in the many wanderings and homecomings of her sons, and to laugh and sing for a few years with her grandchildren. I would like to dedicate this volume to my brothers, Peter, Chris and Sean. I am deeply grateful for their fraternal companionship (and WML) in times of sadness as well as in times of joy.

Bret W. Davis

Abbreviations

FCM   *The Fundamental Concepts of Metaphysics: World, Finitude, Solitude* (1995; written 1929–30)
 FS   *Four Seminars* (2003; written 1966–73)
  G   *Gelassenheit*, 10th edn (1992; written 1944–55)
 GA   *Gesamtausgabe* (1975–) [cited by volume number; see Bibliography for details]
HBB   *Martin Heidegger/Elisabeth Blochmann Briefwechsel* (1990)
 HC   *The Heidegger Controversy: A Critical Reader* (1993)
HCT   *History of the Concept of Time: Prolegomena* (1985; written 1925)
HHI   *Hölderlin's Hymn "The Ister"* (1996; written 1942)
HJB   *Martin Heidegger/Karl Jaspers: Briefwechsel 1920–1963* (1990)
 HK   "Die Herkunft der Kunst und die Bestimmung des Denkens" (1983; written 1967)
HPS   *Hegel's Phenomenology of Spirit* (1988); written 1930–31)
 ID   *Identität und Differenz*, 11th edn (1999; written 1956–7)
IDS   *Identity and Difference* (1969; written 1956–7)
IHS   "Phenomenological Interpretations with Respect to Aristotle: Indication of the Hermeneutical Situation", in *BH* (written 1922)
 IM   *Introduction to Metaphysics* (2000; written 1935)
KPM   *Kant and the Problem of Metaphysics*, 4th enlarged edn (1990; written 1929)
 LW   *Letters to His Wife: 1915–1970* (2008)
  M   *Mindfulness* (2006; written 1938–9)
MFL   *The Metaphysical Foundations of Logic* (1984; written 1928)
MHC   "Martin Heidegger in Conversation", in *MHNS* (written 1969)
MHNS *Martin Heidegger and National Socialism: Questions and Answers* (1990)
MLS   *"Mein liebes Seelchen!": Briefe Martin Heideggers an seine Frau Elfride 1915–1970* (2005)
 NI   *Nietzsche: Erster Band*, 5th edn (1989; written 1936–46)
NII   *Nietzsche: Zweiter Band*, 5th edn (1989; written 1939–46)
 N1   *Nietzsche: Vol. I, The Will to Power as Art* (1979; written 1936–7)
 N2   *Nietzsche: Vol. II, The Eternal Recurrence of the Same* (1984; written 1937, 1953)
 N3   *Nietzsche: Vol. III, The Will to Power as Knowledge and as Metaphysics* (1987; written 1939–40)

N4   *Nietzsche: Vol. IV, Nihilism* (1982; written 1940–46)

OBT   *Off the Beaten Track* (2002; written 1935–46)

OG   "'Only a God can Save Us': *Der Spiegel*'s Interview with Martin Heidegger", in *HC* (written 1966)

OHF   *Ontology: The Hermeneutics of Facticity* (1999; written 1923)

OWAF "Of the Origin of the Work of Art (first elaboration)" (2008; written 1935)

OWL   *On the Way to Language* (1971; written 1950–59)

PIA   *Phenomenological Interpretations of Aristotle: Initiation into Phenomenological Research* (2001; written 1921–2)

PLT   *Poetry, Language, Thought* (2001; written 1936–54)

PM   *Pathmarks* (1998; written 1919–61)

PMH   "Preface by Martin Heidegger", in William J. Richardson, *Heidegger: Through Phenomenology to Thought* (2003; written 1962)

PR   *The Principle of Reason* (1991; written 1955–6)

PRL   *The Phenomenology of Religious Life* (2004; written 1918–21)

PRM   *Parmenides* (1992; written 1942–3)

PT   *The Piety of Thinking* (1976)

QCT   *The Question Concerning Technology and Other Essays* (1977; written 1936–54)

R   *Die Selbstbehauptung der deutschen Universität: Das Rektorat 1933/34* (1990; written 1933, 1945)

RFT   "The Rectorate 1933/34: Facts and Thoughts", in *MHNS* (written 1945)

SA   *Schellings Abhandlung Über das Wesen der menschlichen Freiheit (1809)*, 2nd edn (1995; written 1936, 1941–3)

SG   *Der Satz vom Grund*, 7th edn (1992; written 1955–6)

SJG   *Sojourns: The Journey to Greece* (2005; written 1962)

ST   *Schelling's Treatise on the Essence of Human Freedom* (1985; written 1936, 1941–3)

SU   "The Self-Assertion of the German University", in *HC* (written 1933)

SUP   *Supplements: From the Earliest Essays to Being and Time and Beyond* (2002; written 1910–25)

SZ   *Sein und Zeit*, 17th edn (1993; written 1927); both *BT* and *BTS* include references to the pagination of *SZ*

TB   *On Time and Being* (1972; written 1962–4)

TDP   *Towards the Definition of Philosophy* (2000; written 1919)

UKE   *"Vom Ursprung des Kunstwerks: Erste Ausarbeitung"* (1989; written 1935)

UV   "Unbenutzte Vorarbeiten zur Vorlesung vom Wintersemes-
     ter 1929/1930: *Die Grundbegriffe der Metaphysik: Welt,
     Endlichkeit, Einsamkeit*" (1991; written 1929–30)
VA   *Vorträge und Aufsätze*, 7th edn (1994; written 1936–53)
WCT *What is Called Thinking?* (1968; written 1951–2)
WhD *Was heißt Denken?*, 4th edn (1984; written 1951–2)
WP   *What is Philosophy?* (bilingual edition) (1958; written
     1955)
WT   *What is a Thing?* (1967; written 1935–6)
Z   *Zollikoner Seminare: Protokolle – Zwiegespräche – Briefe*
     (1987; written 1959–71)
ZS   *Zollikon Seminars: Protocols – Conversations – Letters*
     (2001; written 1959–71)
ZSD *Zur Sache des Denkens*, 3rd edn (1988; written 1962–4)

Citations of Heidegger's texts will generally list both the English translation and the corresponding original German source. In cases where
the translation has been modified, this will be noted. In cases where
only the German source is cited for a quotation, the translation is the
author's own.

Key concepts in Heidegger's thinking of being

Bret W. Davis

"Basic concepts" or Ground-Concepts" *[Grundbegriffe]* means for us here: grasping *[begreifen]* the ground *[Grund]* of beings as a whole. ... When we have grasped something we also say something has opened up to us. ... Thus "to grasp" *[Be-greifen]* the ground means above all that the "essence" of the ground embraces us into itself *[ein-begriffen]*, and that it speaks to us in our knowing about it.   (*BC* 18–19 = *GA* 51: 21, trans. mod.)

Martin Heidegger (1889–1976) is widely considered to be the most famous, influential and controversial philosopher of the twentieth century. His writings are also among the most formidable. The fundamental concepts of his thought are for many the source of both fascination and frustration. Yet any student of philosophy – or of contemporary thought in general – needs to become acquainted with Heidegger's main ideas. This book is designed to facilitate this process. Each chapter introduces and explains a key concept – or a cluster of closely related concepts – in Heidegger's thought. Together, the chapters cover the full range of his path of thought in its early, middle and later periods.

What are the key concepts of Heidegger's thought? A selection of the most important of these appear in the chapter titles of this book: the thinking of being; the hermeneutics of facticity; phenomenology; Dasein as being-in-the-world; care and authenticity; being and time; the turn; the German People; truth as *alētheia* and the clearing of beyng; the work of art; *Ereignis* (the event of appropriation); the history of being; will and *Gelassenheit* (releasement); *Ge-stell* (enframing as the essence of technology); language and poetry; the fourfold; and ontotheology

1

(along with Heidegger's conceptions of divinity). I shall let the chapter authors, each an expert in the area of his or her chapter topic, explain these key concepts in depth.

In this introductory chapter, I wish to orient the reader by addressing the following questions: who is Heidegger and how is his personal life related to his thought? What is "the question of being", Heidegger's central issue of concern, and what are the distinguishing character-istics of Heidegger's thinking of being? And, finally, what are "basic concepts" according to Heidegger? I shall conclude with some brief reflections on the legacies of Heidegger's thought.

Life, death and thought

Is a philosopher's biography philosophically significant? Or is it the case that, as Heidegger once claimed, "when a thinker's work ... [is] ... available, the 'life' of a philosopher is unimportant for the public. We never get to know what is essential in a philosophical life through bio-graphical descriptions anyhow" (*ST* 5 = *SA* 5)? In his opening remarks to a lecture course on Aristotle, Heidegger once stated: "The only thing of interest regarding the person of a philosopher is this: He was born on such and such a date, he worked, and he died" (*GA* 18: 5).[1] Heidegger may well have wished the same to be said about himself. To be sure, few philosophers have devoted their lives so single-mindedly to the task of thinking. Nevertheless, there are several compelling *Heideg-gerian* reasons why it would not be entirely appropriate to simply say of Heidegger that he was born, worked and then died.

The first reason why we should not isolate Heidegger's thought from his life is that, from early on, his thought is specifically about returning to the concreteness – the "facticity" – of human existence, and this return has to be a hermeneutical as well as a phenomenological endeavour given the historical embeddedness of human beings. Accord-ing to Heidegger, the philosopher must start with and return to the concrete situation of his or her own historical life. "The problem of the self-understanding of philosophy", Heidegger says in an early lecture course from 1920, "has always been taken too lightly. If one grasps this problem more radically, one finds that philosophy arises from factical life experience. And within factical life experience philosophy returns back into factical life experience" (*PRL* 6–7 = *GA* 60: 8). As he argues in *Being and Time* (1927), the life projects of an individual are embedded in the historical and social context into which one is "thrown". One can authentically choose to modify one's existential "situation" only by first awakening to it. This not only means that we should attend to the situation in which we ourselves stand as we read Heidegger, but it also means that we should take into consideration the life context in which he wrote.

Hence it is not irrelevant for understanding Heidegger's thought to know that he was born in 1889 and died in 1976; that he was raised in Messkirch, a small conservative Catholic town in southwest Germany; that he intended to become a priest and studied theology before devoting himself fully to philosophy and leaving the Church; that he lived through both world wars, and notably through the Nazi era (more on this below); that he was German and wrote in the German language; that he lived and taught for most of his career in Freiburg; that he rarely travelled, other than a few trips to other European countries (such as Austria, Italy, France, Switzerland, the Netherlands and Greece), and yet frequently conversed with visiting scholars from around the world, including seminal exchanges with visitors from China and Japan (see May 1996); that he spent much time at his beloved cabin in Todtnauberg, a mountain village in the Black Forest; and that he lived in an age of the rapid development and increasingly pervasive spread of modern technology.[2]

A major reason why we cannot ignore Heidegger's personal (or "existentiell") history is his infamous official involvement with National Socialism in the first years of Hitler's regime. Indeed, this entanglement with Nazism was not merely personal, in so far as Heidegger was, at the time, convinced that it was his philosophical calling to take a leading role in the formation of the movement. While his political role as rector of Freiburg University lasted only from 1933 to 1934, while his own version of what the movement *should* be about – his failed attempt to philosophically orient the movement, which he later claims was dismissively referred to as his own "private National Socialism" (*RFT* 23 = R 30) – was essentially untainted by biological racism, and while he increasingly became sharply (albeit often cryptically) critical of Hitler and Nazism in his public lectures and private writings and correspondence, nevertheless his short-lived political involvement as well as the more lasting political implications of his thought remain a troubling and fiercely debated topic to this day.

Finally, it would be inappropriate to abstract Heidegger's thought from his historical situatedness in so far as, in his later period, he comes to hold that the historical existence of the individual is located within an epoch of the "history of being" itself. Accordingly, in studying any philosopher we need to know when – in which epoch of the history of being – he or she wrote. It is not enough, therefore, to say that a thinker

MARTIN HEIDEGGER: KEY CONCEPTS

was born on such and such a date, in so far as his or her thought arises out of and helps determine a historical context of meaning. The great philosophers are thought to play crucial roles in the shifts between epochs, and Heidegger saw his own thought as pivotally situated at the end of the history of philosophy as metaphysics and at the beginning of what he called "the task of thinking" (see *BW* 431ff. = *ZSD* 61ff.).

For Heidegger, it would also be insufficient to simply say that a thinker "died", at least in so far as this would imply that death is merely a biological event that happens at the end of one's life. As Heidegger explains in *Being and Time*, human existence (which he calls "Dasein") is essentially determined as "being-toward-death" from the moment of its birth (*BTS* 228 = *SZ* 245). Our being is always confronted with its impending non-being, even though we for the most part inauthentically flee from this most certain truth. Authentically anticipating this inevitable non-being, however, is not simply a gloomy looking ahead to the annihilation of life and meaningful existence; rather, facing up to our mortality allows us to properly take on the responsibility of embracing this or that possibility of existence, which is in turn what makes life meaningful. Later, Heidegger will say that death is "the shrine of the nothing" (*PLT* 176 = *VA* 171), and that "the nothing, as other than beings, is the veil of being" (*PM* 238 = *GA* 9: 312), implying that authentically facing up to our mortality is also what opens us up to an attentive correspondence with being, which, in its "ontological difference" from beings, must be approached as itself no-thing (see *PM* 233 = *GA* 9: 306; *PM* 290 = *GA* 9: 382). Thus, far from being a philosophically irrelevant biographical or biological event, death, or the being-toward-death of mortal human existence, would be a fundamental experience that opens and sustains Heidegger's philosophy as a thinking of being.

A final objection to summing up Heidegger's life by saying that he "was born, worked, and then died" is that, strictly speaking, he did not understand his efforts at thinking in terms of "working" or his writings in terms of "works". There are two reasons for this. One is that Heidegger considered his thought to be essentially "on the way". His motto for his *Collected Edition* (*Gesamtausgabe*) was "ways, not works" (*Wege, nicht Werke*), and he tell us that his books, essays and lectures should be read as "pathmarks" (*Wegmarken*) rather than as completed works. Another reason is that Heidegger contrasted the "work" done in the sciences with the "thinking" done in philosophy. While the former aims at "progress", the latter aims at "re-gress", that is to say, at taking a radical "step back". "Science does not think" (*WCT* 8 = *WhD* 4), Heidegger was fond of provocatively stating. What he meant by this "shocking statement" is that science for the most part does not radically question its presuppositions, but rather carries out the work of research within certain given parameters. Heidegger is interested in how those parameters are given in the first place. (In Thomas Kuhn's terms, Heidegger would be more interested in "revolutionary science", which brings about "paradigm shifts", than in "normal science", which works within established paradigms [see *BTS* 7–8 = *SZ* 9; *BW* 271–305; Kuhn 1970].) Thinking, Heidegger says, is not a matter of "work and achievement" within given horizons of intelligibility, but rather a kind of "thanking and attentiveness" through which such horizons are first delimited within the open-region of being (see *GA* 77: 99–100). In contrast to the work of the sciences, with its measurable achievements and technological effectiveness, the meditative thinking of philosophy is "the immediately useless, though sovereign, knowledge of the essence of things" (*BQP* 5 = *GA* 45: 5).

The question of being

Heidegger's chief concern is not with how this particular thing *X* relates to that particular thing *Y*, but rather how it is that the meaning of *X*s and *Y*s and their possible relations gets determined in the first place. What does it mean for such things *to be*; what does it mean to say that they *are*? This question of "ontology" (the study of being), rather than questions regarding the "ontic" relations between particular beings, is what primarily interests Heidegger. Moreover, his central concern is not just with "regional ontologies", that is, with the meaning of the being of, for example, biological things, artificial things, mental things, social things or imaginary things. Rather, following Aristotle's understanding of ontology as "first philosophy", Heidegger wants to know first and foremost about "being as such". What is the sense of being that all entities share? What is the being of all beings?

"For manifestly you have long been aware of what you mean when you use the expression '*being*.' We, however, who used to think we understood it, have now become perplexed." Heidegger opens his first great book, *Being and Time* (1927), with this quotation from Plato (*Sophist* 244a). He goes on to say that not only do we in our time not have an answer to this question of the meaning of being, but we are no longer even perplexed about this most fundamental of philosophical concerns. We have forgotten the *question* of being. After Plato, Aristotle wondered about the question of "being *qua* being" (*on hēi on*), that is, the question of what it means for anything to be, irrespective of whatever other qualities it may have. While an ontological enquiry might go on to ask, for example, what makes the being of an animal different from the being of an artefact, the foundational question of ontology asks: what does it mean for anything at all to be?

As Heidegger points out, later philosophers such as Leibniz and Schelling rephrase the fundamental question of ontology as: "Why are there beings at all, and not rather nothing?" (see *IM* 1 = *EM* 1; *PM* 290 = *GA* 9: 382). But this way of framing the question of being can be misleading, in so far as it would lead us to think of being (*das Sein*) as the highest being or entity (*das höchste Seiende*), and to think of the relation between being and beings in terms of causality (in the sense in which one entity gives rise to another). In this manner, theologians might answer the question of being by saying that God is the highest being who creates the world, and that is why there are beings rather than nothing. For Heidegger, such answers evade rather than address the question of being, in that they fail to see what he calls the "ontological difference" between being and beings. "The being of beings 'is' itself not a being", and so the "first philosophical step in understanding the problem of being consists in … not determining beings as beings by tracing them back in their origins to another being – as if being had the character of a possible being" (*BTS* 5 = *SZ* 6).

Being is not one being among others; being is not this or that entity. It is not even the highest being from which lower levels of beings derive their privative measure of being, as is thought in the many versions of the "great chain of being" (see Lovejoy 1964). Nor is being to be derived from beings by way of generalization, for example in the following manner: dogs and cats are animals, animals and plants are animate entities, animate and inanimate bodies are material entities, material and mental entities are both substances, and they are all that is; thus substance is the being of all beings. For Heidegger, when being is thought either in terms of the highest being (as it often is in theology), or in terms of the most universal category of entities (as it often is in ontology), it is thought from or in terms of beings or entities, the ontological difference is missed, and the question of being as such is forgotten. This oblivion of the question of being is said to pervade the history of Western metaphysics, which is dominated by what Heidegger calls "ontotheology".

Being (*das Sein*) is not itself a being or something that is (*das Seiende*), but rather what determines beings as beings, or what it means for a being or an entity to be (see *BTS* 4–5 = *SZ* 6). Ultimately, for Heidegger, being – or rather, as he sometimes writes, "beyng" (*Seyn*) – is the appropriating event (*Ereignis*) through which the meaning of the being of beings gets determined (see *CP = GA* 65: pt VIII). Although he does not always clearly mark this distinction in his terminology, Heidegger is increasingly concerned not just with the difference between being and beings, but also with the difference between the being of beings (what it means for beings to be, the horizon of their intelligibility) and beyng itself (the originary event through which the being of beings gets determined). While the question of being and the ontological difference between being and beings have fallen into oblivion over the course of the history of Western metaphysics, beyng itself was intimated yet remained largely "unthought" even in the Greek beginning of Occidental thinking.

Rethinking being, together with time, humans and truth

For Aristotle, although "being is spoken of in many ways", the primary meaning of being is "substance" (*Categories* 4–5; *Metaphysics* VII).[3] Substance (*ousia*) is the enduring substratum (*hupokeimenon*) of something that underlies changes in its qualities, location and so on. The substance of something remains *constantly present* despite whatever else changes through time. Heidegger's dismantling (*Abbau* or *Destruktion*) of the Western tradition of metaphysics proceeds by pointing out the *temporal* determination of being implied in this thinking of being in terms of "constant presence". Thus, in *Being and Time* he writes that "time is that from which Da-sein tacitly understands and interprets something like being at all", and so time must now "be brought to light and genuinely grasped as the horizon of every understanding of and interpretation of being" (*BTS* 15 = *SZ* 17).

The following quotation from a transcript of lectures Heidegger delivered in 1925 gives a particularly clear formulation of Heidegger's decisive critique of "a certain interpretation of being [that] pervades the history of philosophy and determines its whole conceptuality":

> What is striking here is how the Greeks interpreted being in terms of time: *ousia* [being] means presence, the present. If this is what being signifies, then authentic being is that which is never not there, i.e., what is always there (*aei on* [perpetual being]). Within the tradition, this concept of being was employed to understand historical reality, a reality that, however, is not always there. It is clear that if the Greek doctrine of being is uncritically accepted as absolute, then it becomes impossible for research to understand a reality such as historical Dasein. (*SUP* 175; see also *BH* 273)

Heidegger goes on to claim that Descartes and Husserl, for example, fail to ask about the being of the "I am" and, using unawares a temporally restricted conception of being as constant presence, fail to give an adequate account of human being. Such an account would have to take into consideration the temporal "ek-stasis" (literally "standing outside oneself") of human being: human existence is not simply immersed in the present, but also lives out towards the future and back towards the past.

Yet Heidegger's call for a rethinking of the temporal dimension of being is not restricted to questions of philosophical anthropology. From his early analysis of the temporality of Dasein (human existence) to his later "being-historical thinking" (*seinsgeschichtliches Denken*), one of Heidegger's central and most decisive philosophical claims is that *being itself essentially occurs temporally and historically*. Indeed, *Being and Time* not only begins with the hypothesis that the "meaning of the being of that being we call Da-sein proves to be *temporality*" (*BTS* 15 = *SZ* 17), but also ends with the question of whether time can be considered the horizon of being as such (*BTS* 398 = *SZ* 437). In the final chapters of *Being and Time*, Dasein's temporality is shown to be involved in a shared "historicity" (*BTS* = *SZ* §§72–7), and in later texts Heidegger begins to speak of the occidental "history of being". Indeed, in places he goes so far as to say that "the history of being is being itself" (*EP* 82 = *NII* 489; see also *N4* 221 = *NII* 362).

Another crucial claim Heidegger makes is that *human being* – as Da-sein (literally "being-there") – *is the site of the occurrence of being*. In his later thought Heidegger comes to say that humans are required (*gebraucht*) for the appropriating event (*Ereignis*) that opens up a meaningful world, and it is only in such a world that beings can be the beings that they are (see *CP* = *GA* 65: §§194–5; *EGT* 53 = *GA* 5: 367–8; *PM* 308 = *GA* 9: 407). Hence, Heidegger often stresses that his question of being must be understood as a question of the *relation* between being and human being, a relation he characterizes as a "belonging together" (see *WCT* 79 = *WhD* 74; *IDS* 30–32 = *ID* 17–19). This relation was in one way or another at the centre of his thought-path from beginning to end, and all the "turns" in his thinking of being – both those of his thinking and those of being – must be understood in terms of his abiding concern with this pivotal relation between being and human being. The question of being is thus at once the question of the place and role of human being in the temporal–historical event that lets beings be the meaningful beings they appear to be. While an important shift does occur in the course of Heidegger's path of thought with regard to his idea of the proper comportment of human being to being – a shift from an ambivalent tendency towards voluntarism in his early and middle periods to a fundamental attunement of "releasement" (*Gelassenheit*) and an explicit attempt to think non-willing(ly), which is not to say passively, in his later period (see *DT* = *G*; *CPC* = *GA* 77; Davis 2007) – the question of being for Heidegger remains throughout all the phases of his thought a question about the relation between being and human being.

A third crucial claim Heidegger makes is that *being never reveals* (or "de-conceals", *entbirgt*) *itself completely*. As Heraclitus wrote, "*physis* [nature or being] loves to hide" (fr. 123). The epistemological demand for certainty and the omniscience of "unbounded unconcealment" belongs to the metaphysical misrepresentation of being as constant presence. Heidegger is not a sceptic, since he does not relinquish the quest for truth; nor is he a relativist (or even a pragmatist), in so far as that would mean that truth varies according to mere subjective opinion or instrumental usefulness. Truth for Heidegger is not arbitrary; it is not subject to our individual or collective whims. Events of truth do take place – events that open up a "clearing" (*Lichtung*) or a space of intelligibility wherein knowledge of beings first becomes possible – and we are called on to take part in these events, which appropriate us into the world as a place of significant relations wherein we belong. Meaningful configurations of the world do come about, but such events of "unconcealment" (Heidegger's literal translation of the Greek word for "truth", *alētheia*) always entail at the same time a withdrawal into concealment. Truth is always coupled with untruth, openness with seclusion, clarity with mystery. Being withdraws as it comes to presence; it expropriates as it appropriates; it holds back as it gives. This understanding of truth as a twofold event of the revealing/concealing of being is a central thread running through Heidegger's path of thought (see esp. *BTS* = *SZ* §44; *PM* 136–54 = *GA* 9: 177–202).

Given these three basic characteristics of Heidegger's thinking of being – namely being's essential temporality/historicity, its requirement of human being, and its truth as an event of revealing/concealing – it is not surprising that Heidegger considered his own path of thought to be always on the way towards a more appropriate conception of, and relation to, being. When approaching the key concepts of his thinking, it is thus generally advisable to proceed chronologically; and so the chapter topics of this book are arranged roughly according to the order in which they appear as specific foci of his thinking. It should immediately be added, however, that the earlier concepts usually carry over into later periods, even as they get recontextualized and rethought along the way. While some readers may end up preferring (aspects of)

Heidegger's earlier thought to his later thought, Heidegger himself, as one would expect, maintained that his journey brought him ever nearer to a proper thinking of being. But he also stressed the necessity of retracing all the steps along the way. The reader will find that key concepts first formulated in earlier way-stations can often be heard still resounding in the "clearings" in the forest of being to which the winding "wood paths" (*Holzwege*) of Heidegger's thought later lead. Heidegger might have characterized his pathway of thinking in terms of a deepening spiral rather than a linear progression, a spiral that always circles around the central question of being and its proper relation with human being.

Language and basic concepts

Before allowing the reader to study in greater depth the key concepts selected as chapter topics for this volume, there is one other central aspect of Heidegger's thought that deserves special comment in this introduction. In all periods of his thought, *language* is vitally import-ant for Heidegger. As he famously wrote in the "Letter on Humanism" (1947), "language is the house of being" (*PM* 239 = *GA* 9: 313); that is to say, language demarcates the parameters of a realm wherein humans can meaningfully dwell. Language domesticates being: it makes the world liveable for us. In *Being and Time*, Heidegger spoke of the "as structure" of experience, meaning that when I hear a sound I hear it *as* a "motorcycle" or *as* a "baby's cry" (*BTS* = *SZ* §32). It is lan-guage that allows us to perceive and understand things as the things that they appear to us to be. In a later text, commenting on the poet Stefan George's lines, "Where the word breaks off no thing may be", Heidegger writes: "Only where the word for the thing has been found is the thing a thing. Only thus *is* it" (*OWL* 62 = *GA* 12: 154). In his later accounts of the history of being, Heidegger goes so far as to claim that the horizon of intelligibility of an entire epoch is founded on a single term or cluster of terms: such words as *physis* (nature as what emerges of itself), *ousia* (substance as what permanently endures), *actualitas* (actuality), subject and will to power determine the manner in which the being of beings is revealed (and concealed) in the various epochs of Western civilization (see *EP* = *NII*).

Heidegger's accounts of the history of metaphysics, as well as his own attempts to think otherwise, often focus on certain basic or funda-mental concepts (*Grundbegriffe*). A number of titles of his texts testify to the centrality of such concepts: for example, *Fundamental Concepts* of *Ancient Philosophy* (1926, *FCAP = GA* 22), *Fundamental Concepts of Metaphysics* (1929/30, *FCM = GA* 29/30) and *Basic Concepts* (1941, *BC = GA* 51). Although in his earlier texts, such as *Being and Time*, Heidegger often attempts to fashion a new philosophical vocabulary with such neologisms as "thrownness", "readiness-to-hand" and "being-in-the-world", in his later writings Heidegger more often attempts to draw on etymology and cognate connections to retrieve a more original sense from accustomed locutions, letting words speak anew from their origins. For example, Heidegger attempts to let the everyday word for event, *Ereignis*, name the "event of appropriation" in which humans rediscover their proper (*eigentliche*) relation of belonging to being, and through which beings are brought back into their proper interrelational place in the world. It is also the case, however, that even in his earliest writings Heidegger is concerned with uncovering profounder implications of everyday words (for example, see his emphatic use of this very same word, *Ereignis*, in *TDP* 63 = *GA* 56/57: 75). Indeed, it should be borne in mind that when in *Being and Time* he speaks of the "destructuring of the tradition", his aim is to recover access to "those original 'wellsprings' out of which the traditional categories and concepts were in part genuinely drawn" (*BTS* 19 = *SZ* 21). It is also the case that we often find him composing neologisms even in his later period, such as the "fourfold" (*Geviert*) of earth and sky, mortals and divinities.

In his later writings on language, Heidegger famously claims that "Language speaks" (*Die Sprache spricht*), while "humans speak in that they correspond [*entspricht*] to language" (*PLT* 207 = *GA* 12: 30, trans. mod.). In the course of his thinking, Heidegger became increasingly concerned with *letting* language speak, with "undergoing an experience with language" (*OWL* 57 = *GA* 12: 149), in contrast to a voluntaristic "grasping" (*begreifen*) of concepts (*Begriffe*) (*WCT* 211 = *WhD* 128). Already in *Being and Time*, in fact, Heidegger had defined his method of hermeneutical phenomenology as an attempt to "let what shows itself be seen from itself, just as it shows itself from itself", as opposed to a theoretical imposition of subjective categories on things (*BTS* 30 = *SZ* 34). Later, he sharply distinguishes his approach to language from logical positivism's project of constructing a "metalanguage" in order to supposedly clear up the obscurities of everyday language and philosophy. In so far as "Analytical philosophy ... is set on producing this super-language", it is, as "metalinguistics", "the thoroughgoing technicalization of all languages into the sole operative instrument of interplanetary information" (*OWL* 58 = *GA* 12: 150). Such attempts to "master language" are, Heidegger thinks, one of the greatest hubristic follies of modern humanity. "Humans act as though they were the shaper and master of language, while in fact language remains the master of humans" (*PLT* 213 = *VA* 184, trans. mod.).

Nevertheless, and despite Heidegger's penchant for rhetorical reversals, it is crucial to recognize that for him the task of thinking, as letting language speak, is not simply passive. Rather, it involves a non-willing corresponding – a listening and a responding – to the address of being. The fundamental words of our historical worlds arise in the conversation that takes place between the address (*Zuspruch*) of being (*Sein*) and the correspondence (*Entsprechung*) of human Dasein. With their basic concepts, according to Heidegger, great thinkers should aspire to nothing less than such historically determined and determining words of being. Thinkers can also aspire to nothing more, unless perhaps, as in the case of Heidegger's own basic concepts, they attempt to articulate the abiding relations involved in this always finitely word- and world-bestowing event.

Heidegger's legacies

As this introductory chapter has begun to reveal, and as the remaining chapters in this volume will explicate in more detail and depth, in his attempt to rethink the most fundamental issue of ontology, the question of "being" as such, Heidegger radically rethought such basic philosophical concepts as time, space, the self (Dasein), interpersonal relations, things, the world, language, truth, art, technology and the divine. The originality of Heidegger's ideas is matched only by the thoroughness of his engagement with the texts of the history of philosophy, and the radicality of his reinterpretations of their key concepts. As a result of its originality and radicality, the influence Heidegger's thought has exerted – and continues to exert – on subsequent developments in philosophy and in related disciplines of intellectual enquiry is arguably on a par with such landmark figures in the history of philosophy as Plato, Augustine, Descartes, Kant and Nietzsche.

While it would be an exaggeration to claim that, for the past three-quarters of a century, the history of philosophy has now become "a series of footnotes to Heidegger", the legacies of his thought, especially in Europe and in "continental philosophy" around the globe, have been extensive and profound. As his reputation as a lecturer spread in a manner Hannah Arendt compared to "the rumor of the hidden king", Heidegger's name became well known in German universities years before the publication of *Being and Time* launched him on to the world stage in 1927. Since that time, and on account of his prolific writing and continual lecturing until nearly the end of his life in 1976, Heidegger's thought has left a major impact on – and in many cases helped found or at least radically reform – a number of areas of philosophy, including phenomenology, hermeneutics, existentialism, ontology, epistemology, the history of philosophy, the philosophy of history, the philosophy of technology, the philosophy of art, the philosophy of language, psychoanalysis and the philosophy of religion.

In the 1920s, Heidegger quickly rose from being Edmund Husserl's assistant to being a collaborator and then rival shaper of the new field of phenomenology, and subsequent generations of phenomenologists (notably such French figures as Maurice Merleau-Ponty, Jean-Paul Sartre and, more recently, Jean-Luc Marion) were influenced as much by Heidegger as they were by Husserl. Although he never accepted Sartre's label, Heidegger's early thought clearly influenced the philosophical and literary movement of existentialism. With his attention to history and the problem of interpretation, Heidegger paved the way for the philosophical hermeneutics of Hans-Georg Gadamer, Paul Ricoeur and Gianni Vattimo. Heidegger's existential analyses of human being were decisive for critical theorists (such as Herbert Marcuse), psychologists and psychoanalysts (such as Medard Boss and Jacques Lacan), and Protestant as well as Catholic theologians (such as Rudolf Bultmann and Karl Rahner). Heidegger's *Destruktion* of the tradition of Western ontology paved the way for Jacques Derrida's "deconstruction" of the "metaphysics of presence", and his account of the epochs of the history of being decisively influenced Michel Foucault's genealogies of "regimes of truth". Heidegger's critique of modern technological society, the questionable role of ethics in his thought, as well as his controversial political engagements and thought, have inspired great discussion and debate (among such figures as Hannah Arendt, Jürgen Habermas, Hans Jonas, Philippe Lacoue-Labarthe, Emmanuel Levinas, Karl Löwith and Jean-Luc Nancy) over the many provocative and thought-worthy issues they raise. Heidegger's writings on poetry and art have become standard reading material, not only for literary and art critics, but also for many poets and artists themselves. In addition to leading Heidegger scholars and continental philosophers (such as Robert Bernasconi, John Caputo, Edward Casey, Françoise Dastur, Richard Dreyfus, Michel Haar, Friedrich-Wilhelm von Herrmann, David Farrell Krell, Luigi Pareyson, Otto Pöggeler, William Richardson, John Sallis, Dennis Schmidt, Reiner Schürmann, Franco Volpi and David Wood, to name just a few, and without mentioning those listed among the contributors to this volume), a wide variety of analytic (or post-analytic), pragmatist, and other North American philosophers (such as Stanley Cavell, Richard Rorty and Charles Taylor) have been significantly influenced by Heidegger's thought, as have many British, Australian, South American and other philosophers around the world. Scholars from India (such as J. L. Mehta) have taken a serious interest in Heidegger's philosophy and, in the Far East, philosophers such as those associated with the Kyoto School in Japan (including Kuki Shūzō and Watsuji Tetsurō, as well as Tanabe Hajime and Nishitani Keiji) have been profoundly affected by their prolonged dialogue with Heidegger and his thought.

This sketch of Heidegger's extraordinary philosophical legacies remains fragmentary (indeed another book would be required to properly introduce the influences of Heidegger's thought), and these legacies continue to grow. As the remaining volumes of his *Collected Edition* (*Gesamtausgabe*) – followed by their translations – steadily become available, more books and articles continue to be published on Heidegger each year than perhaps on any other philosopher. The variety of approaches this scholarship takes ranges from the aggressively polemical to the unquestioningly defensive. There are also, thankfully, many scholars who attempt to steer a course between the bashers and the idolizers to engage in a critical appropriation of and/or a dialogical confrontation with Heidegger's thought. Although it is certainly not my intention to prescribe how the reader should read Heidegger, it is my hope that the present volume will serve to facilitate a genuine understanding of, and thereby an authentic encounter with, his way of thinking.

Notes

1. Theodore Kisiel warns against the abuse of this often cited remark (in which Heidegger apparently rejects the relevance of biography in understanding a philosopher), especially by those who would rather simply ignore the inconvenient aspects and episodes in Heidegger's life. Kisiel argues that ironically the quotation is often taken out of context, given that at the time Heidegger was developing his "hermeneutics of facticity", which stresses "the interplay of the ontic and the ontological" and the "equiprimordiality of the historical with the systematic". Kisiel also points out that Heidegger had begun another course on Aristotle two years earlier (in 1922) by "noting that the 'life and works' of the philosopher are presuppositions for the course" (*GA* 62: 8; Kisiel 1993: 287, 540 n.3).
2. For other biographical highlights see my chronology of Heidegger's life at the back of this book. Safranski (1998) is a well rounded and illuminating philosophical biography. Ott (1993) is an informatively detailed biography that critically examines what Heidegger once (in a letter to Karl Jaspers in 1935) called

"the two great thorns in my flesh – the struggle with the faith of my birth, and the failure of the rectorship [of Freiburg University]" (*ibid.*: 37). Geier (2005) is a concise and very good biography in German. Another excellent source of biographical information available in German is Mehring & Thomä (2003).

3. In trying to steer a middle course between a materialistic and an idealistic understanding of substance, that is, between Thales' "water" or Anaximenes' "air" or Democritus' "atoms" on the one hand, and Plato's "Forms" or "Ideas" on the other, Aristotle makes a distinction between two senses of substance, and wavers between giving priority to one or the other of these. Substance is either a particular something, a "this", or it is the universal characteristic that makes a particular something what it is. According to Heidegger, these two notions of substance in Aristotle – which become the fundamental metaphysical distinction between "thatness" (*Daß-sein*, literally "that-being") or *existentia* (existence) on the one hand, and "whatness" (*Was-sein*, literally "what-being") or *essentia* (essence) on the other – are thought by him as "modes of presencing whose fundamental characteristic is *energeia*", a word that gets translated in the course of the history of metaphysics as *actualitas*, actuality and reality (see *EP* 4–8 = *NII* 402–7). While Heidegger tends to think of this history as a decline from the greatness of the Greek beginning, he also draws attention to the unthought temporal determination of the Greek notion of substance by translating Aristotle's *ousia* as "presence" (*Anwesenheit*). Heidegger claims that what the Greeks experienced, but failed to fully think, was the "presencing" (*Anwesen*) of what presences, that is, the temporality of being as an event of emergence (*physis*) and unconcealment (*alētheia*).

References

Davis, B. W. 2007. *Heidegger and the Will: On the Way to Gelassenheit*. Evanston, IL: Northwestern University Press.

Geier, M. 2005. *Martin Heidegger*. Reinbek bei Hamburg: Rowohlt Verlag.

Kisiel, T. 1993. *The Genesis of Heidegger's "Being and Time"*. Berkeley, CA: University of California Press.

Kuhn, T. S. 1970. *The Structure of Scientific Revolutions*, 2nd enlarged edn. Chicago, IL: University of Chicago Press.

Lovejoy, A. O. 1964. *The Great Chain of Being*. Cambridge, MA: Harvard University Press.

May, R. 1996. *Heidegger's Hidden Sources: East Asian Influences on His Work*, G. Parkes (trans., with essay). New York: Routledge.

Mehring, R. & D. Thomä 2003. "Eine Chronik". In *Heidegger Handbuch: Leben–Werk–Wirkung*, D. Thomä (ed.), 515–39. Stuttgart: Metzler.

Ott, H. 1993. *Martin Heidegger: A Political Life*, A. Blunden (trans.). New York: Basic Books.

Safranski, R. 1998. *Martin Heidegger: Between Good and Evil*, E. Osers (trans.). Cambridge, MA: Harvard University Press.

Further reading

Primary sources

See Heidegger's *Basic Writings*; *Becoming Heidegger: On the Trail of His Early Occasional Writings, 1910–1927*, *Being and Time*; *Country Path Conversations*; *The Heidegger Reader*; *Introduction to Metaphysics*; *Off the Beaten Track*; and *Pathmarks*.

Secondary sources

For introductory and reference works in English see de Beistegui (2005), Dreyfus & Wrathall (2007), Guignon (2006), Inwood (1999), Polt (1999) and Safranski (1998). In German, see D. Thomä (ed.), *Heidegger Handbuch: Leben–Werk–Wirkung* (Stuttgart: Metzler, 2003).

For more advanced studies in English see Bernasconi (1993), Krell (1986), Macann (1996), Pöggeler (1987), Richardson (2003), Sallis (1990, 1993) and Wood (2002).

ONE

Hermeneutics of facticity

Theodore Kisiel

Comprehending factical life in its holistic concreteness: through Dilthey to Heidegger

It was Fichte who first coined the abstract term "facticity" (*Facticität*; later *Faktizität*) for the philosophical tradition. He was thereby not referring to empirical facts or a collection of them, but to the central "fact" of the tradition of modern thought, which takes its starting-point from Descartes' famous regress to the "fact of the I-think", understood as the irreducible limit of reflection behind which one can question no further. It then becomes the ground on which all of modern philosophy takes its stand in order, like Atlas, to move the entire world. The locution of the "fact of the I-think" appears on occasion in Kant's First Critique, which he supplements with another comprehensive fact early in the Second Critique, when he proclaims the moral law, in its correlation with freedom, to be "the sole fact of pure [practical] reason". It might accordingly be called a transcendental fact, although Fichte tended to call it "facticity", especially in his later lecture courses. The posthumous publication of these courses and later works by his theologian son, Immanuel Hermann Fichte, could be considered the most proximate source of the diffusion of the term into the nineteenth-century literature of both philosophy and theology. Nineteenth-century Protestant theology is replete with references to the "facticity" of the events of Christian salvation history, on which the Christian faith takes its original stand. The persistent albeit sporadic use of the term in nineteenth-century writers such as Kierkegaard, Feuerbach, Dilthey and the neo-Kantians is a matter of lexical record (Kisiel 1986–7, 2008).

Dilthey's occasional use of the term is especially influential on Heidegger. In the context of distinguishing between mythical thought and religious experience, the early Dilthey makes the following observation about the world of early humanity:

> [T]his context ... grounded in religious experience ... is likewise conditioned by the way in which reality is given to human beings in those days. *Reality is life* and remains life for them; it does not become an intellectual object by way of knowledge. Therefore, it is in all ways *will, facticity, history*, that is, *living original reality*. Because it is there for the whole living human being and has not yet been subjected to any kind of intellectual analysis and abstraction (hence dilution), it is therefore itself life. ... Life is never exhausted by thought.
> (Dilthey 1988: 161 = 1973: 141, emphasis added, trans. mod.)

And yet life is amenable to thinking, when performed without theoretical intrusion, that is, phenomenologically. In his quest for a critique of historical reason, Dilthey gradually renounces the elevated reason of the detached transcendental ego, "in whose veins flows no real blood" (1973: xviii), and calls instead for a return to the "this-side" of life, to the full facticity of *unhintergehbares* life itself, "behind which [theoretical] thought cannot go", the vital original reality given to human beings to live before they come to think about it, an irreducible ultimate and irrevocable givenness that human beings cannot but live in and are bound to live out. It is the phenomenological return "to the things themselves", in this case, back to the transcendental fact of life itself. Starting from the ineradicable givenness of factic life, the phenomenologist must now enter into this life in order to understand it from out of itself, in its own terms. In his philosophy of historical life, Dilthey's ambition was to develop the "categories" – Heidegger will eventually call them existentials – or basic structures of historical life out of factic life itself, which prior to any thought spontaneously articulates and contextures itself in a manifold of vitally concrete and meaningful basic relations (beginning with I-myself-being-embodied-in-the-world-with-others-among-things) that constitute its immediate lifeworld. In Dilthey's pregnant phrase, "*das Leben selbst legt sich aus*": "life itself lays itself out, interprets itself", generating its own *meaning and senses of direction* in the combined shape and thrust of a *working context and operative continuity of structure* (*Wirkungszusammenhang*) (Kisiel 1993: 134–5).

In fact, human life *is* this self-articulating and therefore fundamentally understandable operative continuity of context. Accordingly, phenomenology as the pre-theoretical proto-science of original experience is a "hermeneutics *of* facticity", whose initial aim is to make explicit the implicit structures into which historical life has already spontaneously articulated itself, "laid itself out", prior to any extraneous thought or alien theoretical intrusion. The young Heidegger thus sharply juxtaposes the historically situated I over against any sort of theoretical I or transcendental ego abstracted in Cartesian fashion from its vital context, thereby denuded of its world, dehistoricized and devitalized (*ibid.*: 45–6; *TDP* 61–6, 74–7, 174 = *GA* 56/57: 73–8, 88–91, 206, 208–9).

This historically situated I will soon be ontologically identified with Da-sein as being-in-the-world (see Chapter 3). The language of life now slides into the language of be-ing. Yet, behind the scenes of Dasein as being-in-the-world, the spontaneous hermeneutics of factic life experience continues to operate as a pre-theoretical primal domain of being. Consider the theme of the understanding-of-being. Human being understands being. But this "understanding-of-being" is at first not conceptual in nature; it is rather the more matter-of-fact understanding of what it means to be that comes from simply living a life. To begin with, we do not know what "being" means conceptually, but we are in fact quite familiar with its sense preconceptually in and through the manifold habitual activity of living. If the term "knowledge" still applies to this understanding of life in its being, it is more the immediate "know-how" or "*savoir faire*" of existence, a knack or feel for what it means to be and how to "go about the business" (*umgehen*) of being that comes from life experience. We already *know how* to live, and this pre-understanding of the ways of being is repeatedly elaborated and cultivated in our various forays into the environing world of things and the communal world of being-with-others, both of which intercalate and come to a head in the most comprehensive of meaningful contexts, the self-world of our very own being-in-the-world.

This repeated cultivation and explication of our pre-understanding of being into habitually reinforced articulated contexts of relational meaning is what Heidegger has called a "hermeneutics *of* facticity", where the "of" is regarded as a double genitive. That is to say, the facticity of life experience, on the basis of a prior understanding, already spontaneously explicates and interprets itself, repeatedly unfolding into the network of meaningful relations that constitutes the fabric of human concerns that we call our historical world. Historically situated existence in its facticity is thoroughly hermeneutical. Accordingly, any overtly phenomenological hermeneutics of facticity, in its expository interpretation of the multifaceted concerns of the human situation, is but an explicit recapitulation of an implicit pan-hermeneutic process already indigenous to historical life. Facticity is through and through hermeneutical (understandable, intelligible, meaningful).

But there is more. Also related to the *hermeneutic situation* of factic life is one of Heidegger's most celebrated "theses", namely, that *Dasein is disclosiveness*, the locus of truth as the unconcealment of be-ing (see Chapter 8). This originary mode of truth is already manifest from the *tacit dimension* of pre-predicative understanding that must be repeatedly explicated out of its precedent latency and concealment, first of all in the persistent exercise of the habit of living, which can then be more overtly explicated by way of deliberative existential and phenomenological exposition. The *hermeneutic situation of factic life itself*, unfolding itself against the background context of the environing world of tool usage and procurement of products, the interpersonal world of social usage and communal custom in being-with-others, and the self-world of striving-to-be and discovering oneself in one's unique being, *is the proximate disclosive arena of originary truth as unconcealment*. Truth is thereby displaced from its traditional locus in judgement and assertion – even seemingly comprehensive assertions such as *Cogito ergo sum* – to the existentially contextualized expository question, especially when it is poised at the doubled frontier of concealment of the human situation in its mystery and its errancy.

The comprehensive disclosive capability of human existence was in fact recognized quite early by the philosophical tradition. Aristotle, for example, observes that "the human soul is, in a way, all beings", that is, it is capable of "coming together with" all being by way of cognitive intellection (*SZ* 14, citing *De anima* 3, 430a14). But for this tradition, which runs from Parmenides to Husserl, the basic mode of knowing is the total transparency of illuminative seeing, intuition, which in temporal terms means a making-present. In the context of a hermeneutics of facticity, by contrast, the basic mode of knowing is interpretive exposition out of a background of understanding that by and large remains tacit, latent, withdrawn and, at most, only appresent, a tangential presence that shades off into the shadows of being's concealment. Discovering beings and disclosing the self and its world take place in a *temporal* "clearing" of unconcealing being that displays an overriding tendency to withdraw into concealment. But this very withdrawal is what draws the enquiring human being to unceasing thought in its questioning pursuit of the *temporal* sense and mystery of being.

Countering ruinance and formally indicating the facticity of life

The facticity of life was first thematized *indicatively and schematically*[1] in the War Emergency Semester of 1919 under the heading of the pre-theoretical "primal something" (*Ur-etwas*) of "life in and for itself" (Kisiel 1993: 21–2, 38, 50–55; *TDP* 186–7, 98 = *GA* 56/57: 219–20, 116). The semesters that follow make factic life the sole and central matter of a phenomenology defined as the pre-theoretical primal science of original experience.

Heidegger's most exhaustive phenomenological treatment of factic life itself occurs in Winter Semester 1921–2, replete with an elaborate system of categories in the spirit of Dilthey that trace the complex motions of life in its relations with the world. The transitive movements of life include to live in, live out of, live for, live against, live with, and so on, something. This "something" that sustains these manifold relations of living is called the "world". The category "world" accordingly names what is lived, what life holds to, the content aimed at by life. Consequently, if life is regarded in its relational sense, the world then characterizes its sense of holdings, its sense of containment. The relational sense of living can be further formally specified as caring. To live is to care. Broadly understood, to live is to care for our privations or needs, for example, "our daily bread". What we care for and about, what caring adheres to, can be defined as meaningfulness. Meaningfulness is a categorial determination of the contextured world. The world and its objects are present in life in the basic relational sense of caring. "An act of caring encounters them, meets them as it goes its way" (*PIA* 68 = *GA* 61: 90). Caring is an experience of objects in their respective mode of encounter, ranging from things and persons to oneself, which respectively occupy the environing world, the shared world and one's own world, the three specific worlds of care. To be an object here is to be met on the path of care and experienced as meaningful. Meaningfulness is to be taken broadly and not restricted to a particular domain of objects, say, objects of "value". Meaningfulness is not experienced as such, but can become explicit in the expository interpretation of one's own life *as factic* (*PIA* 70 = *GA* 61: 93).

The deeper structure of factic life that underlies the *intentional correlation* between us and the world thus proves to be the correlativity of care and meaningfulness. This deep structure might now be properly identified as its facticity, which as an articulated context of meaning is in no way a brute fact closed in on itself but instead a meaningful context open to further development. One such development – Heidegger here calls it the actualization of a tendency inherent in factic life – is for

21

factic life in its caring to enter into the world to the point of becoming taken by it and never managing to return to itself.

Heidegger's first detailed phenomenological account of the ways of decadence – in this semester called "ruinance" (*Ruinanz*) – is presented in an idiosyncratic language and at a level of complexity that will by and large be abandoned in future accounts, as it is in *Being and Time*, where it is described as a "falling" into "inauthenticity" (see Chapter 4). A sampling of just one of the ways of ruinance developed here may suffice. Life's tendency to become totally absorbed in the world can reach the point of abolishing the sense of distance from the world as such. Instead, its sense of distance gets shunted into dispersion, being transported from one meaningful arena to another, now seeking distantiation *within* the meaningful world. The life of care in the shared world is accordingly directed towards rank, success, position, advancement, advantage, superiority (*PIA* 77, 90 = *GA* 61: 103, 121). This care for distantiation and distinction finds ever new gratification in the dispersion, which multiplies itself endlessly. "Life, in its inclination to disperse its relational sense into distantiation, is *hyperbolic*" (*PIA* 78 = *GA* 61: 104). Multiplicity itself becomes a mode of meaningfulness. In its endless quest for variety and novelty, life at times even lapses into the temptation of curiosity, the fascinating "lust of the eyes". In incessantly looking at the world, life looks away from itself. In being drawn into the world, life is in fact in flight from itself. The very multiplicity of possibilities increases the possibilities of mis-taking one's self in ever new worldly ways. One is embarked on a life of interminable mis-takes, a veritable life of errancy. Succumbing to the illusion of infinite possibilities, life sequesters itself off from itself. In so doing, factic life constantly eludes its self and pursues the path of the *elliptical* (*PIA* 81 = *GA* 61: 108), cultivating multiple ways of self-evasion, dissembling and self-deception.

Here, accordingly, a *counter-ruinant* hermeneutics of facticity assumes the role of unmasking dissemblance and disguise, in order to bring factic life back from its lostness in the multiplicity of the world and restore it to itself in its most original self-standing and uniquely unified stance in the facticity of life. The counter-movement to lostness in decadence is the movement of transcendence towards simply finding one's self in the sheer and utter facticity of one's own unique factic situation of simply being-t/here in its full insecurity and radical questionability. It is of the essence of philosophy to be counter-ruinant in its persevering movement towards facticity *pure and simple*. Countering the flight of factic life from itself, it seeks out its own facticity in its fullest temporal and historical concretion, which turns out to be its very own factic self in its unique historical situation, as the unique basis for interpreting its hermeneutic situation. How this is to be achieved calls for a review of the *senses of direction* that underlie the above account of the intentional movements of factic life.

We have already highlighted the containment sense of the world as meaningful context and the relational sense of caring, and stressed the broad formality of these senses interlocked in the most basic of the intentional relationships of facticity. The caring relationship with the world has been mobilized into a multiplicity of forms and manifestations, and thereby brought to concrete actualization. This is its sense of actualization, at this "ruinant" stage by and large improper or "inauthentic". A more proper (*eigentlich*: "authentic") concretion is to be attained by the temporal and historical extension of the actualization sense, its temporalizing sense, which indicates "how the actualization becomes actualization *in and for its [holistically proper] situation*, how it temporally develops, matures, comes to fruition. This temporal ripening is to be interpreted on the basis of the sense of temporalization" (*PIA* 40 = *GA* 61: 53, emphasis added). The factic experiential context now acquires a unique historical thrust in its sense of actualization. This holistic context is to be understood and interpreted not in objective–historical but in actualization–historical terms, as history-in-enactment, as *self*-actualization in one's unique and whole historical context. It is an invitation for the self to-be-historical in and for its own *proper* situation. And it is by way of the temporalizing sense – which in *Being and Time* becomes the "authenticating" unitary movement of originary temporality – that one now "owns up" to one's very own historical situation in its wholeness, thereby itself becoming a proper, historically situated *self*. Pervading the comprehensive temporalizing sense is a sense of the *kairos*, a sense of the timeliness of one's own historical situation coming to its fullness of time, soliciting the *self* to respond with a correspondingly appropriate timeliness in order *to be its time*. Comprehending that situation at once properly and holistically, the temporalizing sense thereby transforms the intentional categories of life into *proper* hermeneutic categories operating in their *properly comprehensive* historical context, categories that are accordingly formally indicative in character, *indicative of one's very own concrete situation in its proper actualization while remaining formal on the level of the holistic life-nexus* (PIA 87 = GA 61: 116). Unified by the properly comprehensive sense of temporalization, the triple-sensed prestruction (the senses of containment, relation and actualization schematized above) of the intentional relation between life and the world now becomes a fully fledged formally indicative concept; and in the end Heidegger considers formally indicative concepts to be the only properly philosophical

23

concepts. The triple-sensed prestruction is itself now translated into the triadic presuppositional structure (of prepossession, preview and preconception) of the *proper* hermeneutic situation, which becomes the concrete site of interpretation out of which life and philosophy will now ripen into full maturity and come to them*selves*.

Since philosophy, radically understood, always starts from the pre-theoretical realm of the facticity of original experience, it does not in fact "pose" or "posit" its presup-positions. For it has already been positioned within its most basic "presupposition", the very facticity of factic life. In Heidegger's early language, its basic *Voraus-setzung* is in fact *Voraus-dasein* (PIA 120–22 = GA 61: 159–61), "pre-existence" in its being-t/here. Rather than a positing, it is more a matter of a radical return to the original facticity of the concrete life-situation in which we already find ourselves positioned, interpretively appropriating it and developing it into *our own unique hermeneutic situation* in which and out of which philosophy is to do its work of expository interroga-tion. Presuppositions of this sort are to be lived, seized as such in order to plunge wholeheartedly into the factically historical dimension of existence (IHS 478 n.4). What is to be brought into view as the basic prepossession of one's own temporally and historically particular her-meneutic situation is the full concretion of factic life itself, which is the sole and comprehensive "object" of philosophical research. And since it is itself a mode of factic life, "philosophical research is itself the explicit *actualization* of a basic movement of factic life and constantly maintains itself within that life" (IHS 158, emphasis added). Philosophy actualizes itself only by way of the radical and concrete questioning that arises from the anxiety over its very own historically particular situation. What is being placed in question is the very facticity of one's own time and generation. Being thus questioned by a historical situation that is uniquely its own, "philosophy is what it can be only as the philosophy of 'its time'" (OHF 14 = GA 63: 18).

It is accordingly incumbent on each time and each generation of philosophers to subject its current hermeneutic situation, which to begin with has been transmitted to it in an already given interpretedness, to a deconstructive regress in order to explicate the hidden motive forces that are operative within that factic interpretation. In the end, phil-osophy's entire history must be subjected to a destructive contestation of its venerable concepts in order to retrieve the original experiences from which they have developed. All this in order to direct the present situation towards a more radical possibility of appropriation of its historical situation. What Heidegger achieves at this stage from the vantage of facticity is a critique of the Greek-Christian tradition of the

24

interpretation of life, especially human life (*IHS* 169–70), somewhat short of the metaphysics of constant presence on the level of being that will quite soon take centre stage and eventually be identified with the Occidental "history of be-ing" (see Chapter 11).[2]

Being thrown and the thrownness of be-ing

Unique to *Being and Time* is its treatment of facticity in close proximity with the sense of the "thrownness" (*Geworfenheit*) of human exist-ence. The interjection of thrownness into *Being and Time* also marks the completion in the radical switch of paradigms from the Husserlian Cogito to the Heideggerian Da-Sein, from an intentionally oriented consciousness to a historically situated ex-sistence, which was percep-tibly imperfectly carried out in the somewhat mixed earlier accounts of the facticity of life.

The sense of thrownness, colloquially put, is the potentially stunning realization that I find myself thrown into a world I did not make and into a life I did not ask for. In this stark and simple revelation of human finitude, one is confronted by the ineluctable radical fact of simply being here, willy-nilly; or, as Heidegger puts it, "the being of Dasein breaks forth as the naked [and pure fact] 'that it is and has to be'" (*SZ* 134). The term "thrownness" aims to convey this existentially radical self-finding of Dasein's purely and simply being-here. "Dasein always 'finds itself' only as a thrown Fact" (*SZ* 328). "The expression 'thrownness' is meant to suggest the *facticity of [Dasein's] being delivered over* [to itself and its having-to-be]" (*SZ* 135). To be sure, Dasein is not a fact in the way that extant things are facts; rather, it is an ex-sisting fact, which continues to be what it always already has been, namely, thrown, carrying this thrownness forward as it throws itself forward, that is, pro-jects itself into its possibilities of being. Taken together as a single trajectory, thrown-projection is a unitary movement that constitutes the finite temporality of Dasein. Like other such Facts, thrownness is *unhintergehbar*: "As existing, Dasein never comes back behind its thrownness" (*SZ* 284). It constitutes one of life's limit situations, that of finding oneself already situated in existence willy-nilly, which, when coupled with the other extreme limit situation, that of death taken as my outermost possibility, the possibility of the impossibility of being-in-the-world, allows us to take over our full finite self in its radical individuality and its wholeness.

But there is more to thrownness than this stark and sheer Fact of simply being here, my being delivered over to the Fact "that I am and have to be". Also belonging to thrownness is the fact that Dasein "has been relegated to a 'world' and exists factically with others" (*SZ* 383). That is to say, we have been thrown not only into sheer being but also into an already contextualized being that we share with others. Thrownness in this context is associated with being born – as life's opposite end from death – into the world (*SZ* 374) and, more specifically, born into a certain heritage that is taken to be a largely historical heritage (*SZ* 383) that might well include elements of family inheritance, such as upbringing, but certainly not biological heredity. This more concrete but still radical thrownness thus refers to the fact that we have been "born", or "thrown", into our particular historical world. "Born" here is somewhat metaphorical in usage, approaching the literal only when it refers to our being born into the historical *community* of a particular *people* and into a particular historical *generation* of that community (*SZ* 384–5). This triad of "sociopolitical" concepts that provides social concretion to the historicality of the human situation also comes from Dilthey (*SZ* 385 n.; Kisiel 2001), who likewise did not understand them biologically but cultivated them in the context of a "history of spirit". As historical beings, we already stand in a tradition handed down to us by and through a progression of generational exchanges of a linguistic community. Factically, we have been preceded and precedented and thereby always already interpreted, and this historical lifeworld of precedence and tradition is the ineluctable point of departure of our own historical existence.

Taking over one's very own historical thrownness accordingly involves taking over one's own heritage (*SZ* 382–4) in the protoaction of proper historicality. In particular, it involves taking over the possibilities of one's heritage that are adjudged to be relevant for one's own current historical situation, as inherited and yet chosen possibilities. The basic historicalizing action of proper historicality takes place in the retracing of the unitary movement of the thrown-projection that is originary temporality; resolutely open for the whole of its unique historical situation, Dasein in the futural forerunning of its own death allows itself to be thrown back into the having-been of its factic "there", where it takes over its own thrownness by transmitting the most pertinent of the inherited possibilities to itself, in order to be there in the timely moment of decision for "its time" (*SZ* 385). Crucial here is the recovery of precedent possibilities that are appropriate for "its time" and its generation. That is why the repetition of a tradition cannot be a rote repetition. The retrieval of precedent possibilities at once involves a re-view and a re-vision of them or, in Heidegger's terms, a countering and a countermanding to the point of a "disavowal of that which in the 'today' is working itself out as the 'past and gone'" (*SZ* 386). The remarkable feature of this process of reinterpretation of precedent possibilities for its time is that our own past now comes to meet us out of the projected future (*SZ* 20), as our proper historical tasks.

Since repetition involves interpretation and reinterpretation in accord with the holistic context of the historical situation into which one is thrown, we have come full circle back to a hermeneutics of facticity, now focusing on the overt disclosive exposition of one's very own situation, the proper site of this more focused, that is, formally indicative (indexical), hermeneutics of facticity. Owning up to the holistic situation as my very own, thereby taking responsibility for it, being responsive to the solicitations and demands exacted by that temporally particular situation, making a precedent possibility latent in my heritage my own by way of repetition and explicitly handing it down to myself: all of these hermeneutic acts of enownment come together in the protoaction (*Urhandlung*) of proper historicality, which resolutely recapitulates the movement of the thrown-projection that is my originary temporality in its ownness and finite wholeness, from future to having-been to the timely moment of decision, where it can be said that "I am my time". Or, to put it in its full finitude and naked thrownness: I am my one-and-only unique and proper lifetime. Historically, this could be called my fate, just as "we are our time" could be the expression of the communal destiny of a particular generation, say, of philosophers.

Resorting to the indexical personal pronouns brings us back to the formally indicative concept, which, as already noted, finds its ultimate actualization only in one's very own temporal situation. The most central of the formal indications calls for this actualization to take place at the level of be-ing itself : "The be-ing *about which* this entity [called Da-sein] is concerned is in each instantiation mine [yours, ours]" (*SZ* 42). Be-ing at its ownmost thus finds its proper expression in the existential declarations of the "personal pronouns, I am, you are, [we are]" (*SZ* 42). Following through on this formal indication by owning up to our most proper be-ing leads us to transform ourselves into the ownmost (*eigenstes*) Da-sein within ourselves, which in turn draws us more or less directly into the event of enownment, propriation, properizing, *das Er-eignis*. For it is in the ownhood and proper-dom of properizing enownment that the I, you and we come together and in each instantiation become them*selves*, in a "selfhood [that] is more originary than any I and you and we" (*CP* 225 = *GA* 65: 320), in short, the unique and proper *selfhood of be-ing* that transcends and comprehends all of the "personal" pronouns. (Put in grammatical terms, the enownment *of* be-ing transforms the indexicals of I, you and we into their more intensive "reflexives", I my*self*, you your*self*, we our*selves*.)

Das Er-eignis, "originary history itself" (*CP* 23 = *GA* 65: 32), is the later Heidegger's most frequently invoked, and deepest, characterization of the Da-sein–Sein relationship (see Chapter 11), which one can surmise to be already taking shape above in the increasingly receptive relationship, to the point of a reversal of initiative, developing between the human being and its thrown situation of be-ing. Dare one say that originarily owned temporality on the level of Dasein, and even more so the event of enownment/propriation on the level of be-ing (see Chapter 5), is now the ultimate facticity, behind which one can go no further? To be sure, not the *fundamentum inconcussum* that Descartes sought but, as temporal, clearly a *fundamentum concussum*, a shakeable foundation, a ground that gives way on to an abyss (*Ab-grund*)?

In a note circa 1929 that belongs among the attempts to complete the fragment that is *Being and Time*, Heidegger remarks:

> *temporality: it is not just a fact, but itself of the essence of the fact: facticity. The fact of facticity* (here the root of the "turn-around" of "ontology" [into a metontology]). Can one ask, "How does time originate?" … Only with time is there a possibility of origination. … But then, what is the meaning of the impossibility of the problem of the origination of time? (*UV* 9, emphasis added)

Concluding unscientific postscript on "formal indication"

The formally indicative dimension of the hermeneutics of facticity has emerged in the above account, first, by way of the senses of direction coming together in the triple-sensed *intentionality* of factic life, which attains its most proper wholeness in a culminating unifying sense of temporalization; and, secondly, in the context of a situated *ex-sistence* finding itself thrown into a historical world and called on to make that historical situation its own by way of an overt disclosive exposition and retrieval of its latent precedent possibilities that are still relevant for its own time and generation, and their projection as our proper historical tasks. The formally indicative dimension, its indexical character, thus finds its proper site in the protoaction of my owning up to my holistic situation in order to come to my proper and whole historically situated self, a protoaction that resolutely recapitulates the thrown-projection that is my originary temporality in its ownness and finite wholeness. Indeed, the entire Division Two of *Being and Time* (*BT*) is devoted to bringing the "ontic–ontological projection of Dasein toward its very own and proper potential-to-be-whole" (*SZ* 313) to fruition in the proper and holistic movement of originary temporality. The lecture courses that follow the publication of *Being and Time* constitute various attempts to sketch out the direction of its never published Division Three (Kisiel 2005). These courses gradually make clear that the formally indicative dimension constitutes a radical revision of the very essence of philosophy. Philosophy is no longer a science, not even the original science of originary experience, but something more originary in its relentless transcending towards the temporal ground of Dasein in order to exist purely out of this disclosive ground. As such, philosophy opens up this possibility of transcendence to factically existing human beings and so points the way and grants them leeway to transcend towards their own temporally particular Dasein, which in each instantiation is mine, yours, ours. In prompting existing individuals to transcend towards this ground, in providing the occasion for this fundamental decision "to let transcendence happen", philosophy is exercising its exhortative function, which Aristotle already designated as the protreptic of philosophy. Philosophy is not a science, but a directive exhortative protreptic.

The course of Winter Semester 1929–30 emphasizes this point from the perspective of Heidegger's very last treatment of formal indication. In contrast to scientific concepts, all philosophical concepts are formally indicative.

> The meaning-content of these concepts does not directly intend or express what they refer to, but only gives an indication, a pointer to the fact that anyone seeking to understand is called upon by this conceptual context to *actualize* a transformation of themselves into the Dasein [within themselves].
>
> (*FCM* 297 = *GA* 29/30: 430, emphasis added, with addendum from *FCM* 296 = *GA* 29/30: 428)

Because such concepts can only convey the call for such a transformation to us without being able to bring about this transformation themselves, they are but *indicative* concepts. They in each instance point to Dasein itself, which in each instantiation is my (your, our) Da-sein, as the locus and potential agent of this transformation. "Because in this indication they in each instance point to a *concretion of the individual Dasein* in man, yet never bring the content of this concretion with them, such concepts are *formally indicative*" (*FCM* 296 = *GA* 29/30: 429). But when concepts are generic and abstract rather than proper to the concrete occasion in terms of which they are to be interpreted, "the interpretation is deprived of all its autochthonous power, since whoever seeks to understand would not then be heeding the directive that resides in every philosophical concept" (*FCM* 298 = GA 29/30: 431). Yet the kind of interpreting that seeks out its very own facticity in each instance is not "some additional, so-called ethical application of what is conceptualized, but ... a prior opening up of the dimension of what is to be comprehended" (*FCM* 296 = GA 29/30: 428–9), namely, the "concretion of [each] individual Dasein", its proper selfhood. The concepts and questions of philosophizing are in a class of their own, in contrast to science. These conceptual questions serve the task of philosophy: not to describe or explain man and his world, *"but to evoke the Dasein in man"* (*FCM* 174 = GA 29/30: 258). Accordingly, philosophy is not a science, but a directive exhortative protreptic, whose concepts are not generic and common, applicable to ALL indiscriminately and uniformly, but rather hermeneutically distributive and proper, applicable to EACH individually in accord with the unique temporal context in which each individual is situated. The same point is made in *Being and Time* in the distinction between "categories" and "existentials" (*SZ* 44–5), between the What-question and the Who-question, between the uniform anyone-self and the proper self of a unique one-time-only lifetime. "ALL men are mortal" is generic and common, stating a neutral scientific fact, while "EACH of us must die our own death" is distributively selective and individuating, singling out each to come to terms with their very own facticity of being-t/here.

These formally indicative, properly philosophical concepts thus only evoke the Da-sein in human being, but do not actually bring it about. There is something penultimate about philosophizing. Its questioning brings us to the very brink of the possibility of Dasein, just short of "restoring to Dasein its *actuality*, that is, its *existence*" (*FCM* 173 = GA 29/30: 257). There is a very fine line between philosophizing and *actualizing* over which the human being cannot merely slip across, but rather must overleap in order to dislodge its Dasein. "Only individual action itself can dislodge us from this brink of possibility into actuality, and this is the moment of decision and of holistic insight [into the concrete situation of action and be-ing]" (*FCM* 173 = GA 29/30: 257). It is the protoaction (*Urhandlung*) of resolute openness to one's own concretely unique situation of be-ing, of letting it be, in each instantiation concretely re-enacted in accord with one's own unique situation and particular "while" of history that authenticates our existence and properizes our philosophizing. It is in such originary action, repeatedly re-enacted from one generation to the next, that ontology finds its ontic founding. Just as Aristotle (and so the metaphysical tradition) founded his *prote philosophia* in *theologia*, so Heidegger now founds his fundamental ontology on "something ontic – the Dasein" (*BPP* 19 = GA 24: 26).

Notes

1. The schematic can be found only in the 1999 edition of *GA* 56/57.
2. It might parenthetically be noted that the concrete factic situation that moti-vates this destructive effort is the current facticity of philosophy itself, coming to fruition as it does in the operative context of the university, which has itself become the intellectual and spiritual locus of generational change (*PIA* 49–58, 122 = *GA* 61: 65–78, 161). And the present generation distinguishes itself from all previous generations by its acute historical consciousness of the past (*PIA* 55 = *GA* 61: 74). The factic historical institution of the university thus already finds itself in a factic life that is through and through historical (*PIA* 57 = *GA* 61: 76). It therefore falls on present generations of philosophers to actualize a thoroughly radical sense of the historical within the staid and venerable tradition of the university.

References

Dilthey, W. 1988. *Introduction to the Human Sciences: An Attempt to Lay a Foun-dation for the Study of Society and History*, R. J. Betanzos (trans.). Detroit, MI: Wayne State University Press. Originally published as *Einleitung in die Geisteswis-senschaften: Versuch einer Grundlegung für das Studium der Gesellschaft und der Geschichte*. Gesammelte Schriften, I, 7th edn (Stuttgart: Teubner, 1973).

Kisiel, T. 1986-7. "Das Entstehen des Begriffsfeldes 'Faktizität' im Frühwerk Heideggers", *Dilthey-Jahrbuch* 4: 91–120.

Kisiel, T. 1993. *The Genesis of Heidegger's Being and Time*. Berkeley, CA: University of California Press.

Kisiel, T. 2001. "Der sozio-logische Komplex der Geschichtlichkeit des Daseins: Volk, Gemeinschaft, Generation". In *Die Jemeinigkeit des Mitseins: Die Daseins-analytik Martin Heideggers und die Kritik der soziologischen Vernunft*, J. Weiss (ed.), 85–103. Konstanz: UVK Verlagsgesellschaft.

Kisiel, T. 2005. "The Demise of Being and Time: 1927–30". In *Heidegger's* Being and Time: *Critical Essays*, R. Polt (ed.), 189–214. Lanham, MD: Rowman & Lit-tlefield.

Kisiel, T. 2008. "On the Genesis of Heidegger's Formally Indicative Hermeneut-ics of Facticity". In *Rethinking Facticity*, F. Raffoul & E. S. Nelson (eds), 41–67. Albany, NY: SUNY Press.

Further reading

Primary sources

The two extant English translations of Heidegger's *Being and Time* by John Mac-quarrie and Edward Robinson in 1962 (*BT*) and Joan Stambaugh in 1996 (*BTS*) both contain the pagination of the 1927 German original *Sein und Zeit* (*SZ*) in the margins. The protoaction of Dasein is formally indicated, especially in Division Two, where the pivotal and summary sections are §§45, 46, 54, 61–6, 69, 74, 83.

The Fundamental Concepts of Metaphysics: World, Finitude, Solitude is the Eng-lish translation by William McNeill and Nicholas Walker of *GA* 29/30, Freiburg course of Winter Semester (WS) 1929–30. See especially §70a, "Formal Indication as a Fundamental Character of Philosophical Concepts", 291–8.

Towards the Definition of Philosophy is the English translation by Ted Sadler of *GA 56/57*, which edits the three early Freiburg lecture courses of 1919. See especially the course of War Emergency Semester 1919, "The Idea of Philosophy and the Problem of World Views", part 2, 53–99, and Appendix II, 183–8.

Phenomenological Interpretations of Aristotle: Initiation into Phenomenological Research is the English translation by Richard Rojcewicz of *GA 61*, the early Freiburg course of Winter Semester (WS) 1921–2. On formal indication, see especially part 2, chapter 2, "Appropriation of the Situation of Understanding", 32–58. On "Factic Life", see especially part 3, 61–115.

See also "Phenomenological Interpretations with Respect to Aristotle: Indication of the Hermeneutical Situation", in *Becoming Heidegger: On the Trail of His Early Occasional Writings, 1910–1927*, T. Kisiel & T. Sheehan (eds), 155–84, 477–80 (Evanston, IL: Northwestern University Press, 2007). This "Natorp-essay" was written in October 1922.

Ontology – The Hermeneutics of Facticity is the English translation by John van Buren of *GA 63*, the early Freibug lecture course of Summer Semester (SS) 1923.

Basic Problems of Phenomenology is the English translation by Albert Hofstadter of *GA 24*, the Marburg lecture course of Summer Semester (SS) 1927.

And see "Unbenutzte Vorarbeiten zur Vorlesung vom Wintersemester 1929/1930: *Die Grundbegriffe der Metaphysik: Welt, Endlichkeit, Einsamkeit*", Heidegger Studies 7 (1991): 5–12.

Secondary sources

See Kisiel (1993: esp. chs 1 and 3) and "The Demise of Being and Time: 1927–1930", in Polt (2005), 189–214; Kisiel & van Buren (1994), esp. ch. 10, "Heidegger (1920–21) on Becoming a Christian: A Conceptual Picture Show", 175–93, which includes examples of formally indicative conceptual schematisms; Raffoul & Nelson (2008), esp. ch. 2, "On the Genesis of Heidegger's Formally Indicative Hermeneutics of Facticity", by T. Kisiel, 41–67; ch. 3, "Factical Life and the Need for Philosophy", by F. Raffoul, 69–85; ch. 4, "The Passion of Facticity", by G. Agamben, 89–112; ch. 7, "Intransitive Facticity? A Question for Heidegger", by R. Visker, 149–91.

TWO

Phenomenology: Heidegger after Husserl and the Greeks

Günter Figal

Translated by Richard Polt

Heidegger's anonymization and universalization of phenomenology

In one of the last texts that Heidegger published, he sketches his "way to phenomenology" and at the same time reflects on the future possibilities for phenomenology:

> The age of phenomenological philosophy seems to be over. It is already taken as something past which is only recorded historically along with other schools of philosophy. But in what is most its own phenomenology is not a school. It is the possibility of thinking, at times changing and only thus persisting, of corresponding to the claim of what is to be thought. If phenomenology is thus experienced and retained, it can disappear as a designation in favor of the matter of thinking whose manifestness remains a mystery. ("My Way to Phenomenology", *TB* 82)

Thus, "in what is most its own", phenomenology does not necessarily have to be realized; it remains what it is, even as a possibility that is only waiting for its realization. But above all, this "ownmost" possibility of phenomenology persists without being bound to a philosophical programme or a philosophical method. As Heidegger characterizes it, it is nothing but the very possibility of thinking. As thinking articulates itself, this possibility takes on various colours – just as, according to Heraclitus, fire takes on the scent of the incense that is mixed with it (fr. B67). Considered in regard to its "ownmost" possibility, phenomenology becomes anonymous. It is the unnamed – and thus usually also the unknown – in all thinking, even if, in the philosophical direction that Heidegger attributes to himself, it has entered, for a limited time, the familiarity of the named.

The anonymity of phenomenology is not a late discovery for Heidegger. In retrospect, it is already apparent as central to his philosophical beginning. He says that in his study of Husserl's *Logical Investigations* – "at first rather led by surmise than guided by founded insight" – he experienced how "what occurs for the phenomenology of the acts of consciousness as the self-manifestation of phenomena is thought more originally by Aristotle and in all Greek thinking and existence". There – and this is already the case for young Heidegger – the matter for philosophical thinking is *alētheia* (see Chapter 8). This is, according to his retrospective explanation, "the unconcealedness of what-is present, its being revealed, its showing itself" (*TB* 79). Thus the anonymous "ownmost" of phenomenology not only constitutes phenomenology's future; it is also already its past and, as such, the past of all philosophy. Because philosophy lives on the basis of its Greek beginning, all philosophy has ultimately been phenomenology, without having been recognized and named as such. The fact that Heidegger still designates his own philosophical beginning as a "way into phenomenology" is not incompatible with this anonymization of phenomenology. True, the access to phenomenology leads one at first into a particular philosophical programme; it familiarizes one with a particular method. Yet in so far as phenomenology is recognized in its essence, it becomes universal and can thus do without its name. In turn, this universalization gives a special weight to a thinking that sets out under the name of phenomenology. With the universalization of phenomenology, its explicit form, the form that carries out this universalization, becomes the truth of all philosophy.

The anonymization and universalization of phenomenology is the fundamental movement of Heideggerian thinking. As such, this movement is his contribution to phenomenology, a contribution no less essential than paradoxical. On the basis of this movement, Heidegger's powerful philosophical work comes to light in a homogeneity that is perhaps surprising, given his relentless alteration and reinterpretation of his own concepts, given his always wakeful readiness for a new beginning. Yet this movement includes even his late turn away from philosophy for the sake of a thinking that wants to articulate "something that it is no longer the matter of philosophy to think" ("The End of Philosophy and the Task of Thinking", *BW* 441). The "end of philosophy" and the "task of thinking" belong together under the point of view of anonymized phenomenology. Philosophy, as Heidegger understands it, lives in the wake of the Greek beginning of the "unconcealment" of phenomena, regardless of whether philosophy is aware of this beginning and whether its concepts are adequate or inadequate to it. And the thinking that goes beyond philosophy in order to think its way into philosophy's "unthought" (*BW* 446) runs up against something that Heidegger, with Goethe, calls a "primal phenomenon" (*BW* 442). Inasmuch as thinking gains access to the "unthought" of philosophy as a primal phenomenon, it is radically different from philosophy and yet, in a nameless way, phenomenological like philosophy. Thus Heidegger's distinctive relation to the philosophical tradition is clarified by the phenomenological character of this thinking.

However, this phenomenological character harbours a tension; it is just as paradoxical as Heidegger's anonymization and universalization of phenomenology, which takes its point of departure from a limited way of questioning, finds phenomenology in all philosophizing and thinking, and yet is capable of finding it only thanks to the limitation of its own way of questioning. Because this kind of questioning remains the point of departure, one must relate the universalization back to it; the thought that all thinking is anonymous phenomenology can illuminate only as much as can the understanding of the phenomena that sustains this thought. And if the thought did not lead to a better understanding of the essence of the phenomena, it would remain dependent on a presupposed phenomenology and would thus fall short of every phenomenological attempt at clarification. Thus the decisive question is what Heidegger's anonymization and universalization of phenomenology contribute to phenomenology.

As we shall see, this contribution is less evident in Heidegger's early thinking than in his later period; as long as Heidegger openly names his thinking phenomenology, his contribution to it remains, in comparison to his later works, fairly conventional. As the years pass, Heidegger's meditations become more concentrated; he turns ever more decisively to the essence of the phenomena themselves, in order to understand the fate of philosophy on the basis of this essence. Yet in his final reflections on the theme, he defines the essence of the phenomena in such a way that this essence is again distinguished from all the philosophical thinking in which it was embedded as a motif. It is the unthought not only for traditional philosophy, but also for Heidegger's own attempt – now seen in a self-critical light – "to ask about a possible task of thinking at the end of philosophy" (*BW* 446). Heidegger emphasizes the question regarding the "matter of thinking" – which is at the same time the matter of anonymized phenomenology – within all thinking, including his own former thought. To be sure, by the same token, the "matter of thinking" is also what has long been "unthought". But once again, this matter has an independent status. The anonymization and universalization of phenomenology are tacitly retracted, so that there can again openly be what this anonymization and universalization tacitly presupposed: phenomenology itself. This is not the solution proposed by Heidegger; but if he makes this solution possible, his contribution to phenomenology leads beyond the domain of his own thinking.

Unconcealing as *alētheia* and *physis*

Heidegger's contribution to phenomenology, and thus also to its anonymization, begins just as Heidegger reports it in his late text: as a critique of Husserl's programme, a critique that aims to see phenomenological experience not as a scientific method, but as a fundamental possibility of human life. Here Aristotle comes into play for Heidegger: the "phenomenology of the acts of consciousness" is traced back to an activity that Aristotle calls *alētheuein* (unconcealing). The essence of human life or "Dasein", as Heidegger will work it out in connection with Aristotle, is uncovering or disclosing. In so far as everything that is, is given in Dasein, it is thinkable in its "unconcealment" only on the basis of Dasein. Under the presupposition that beings show themselves as what they *are* and that, in turn, being consists in self-showing, Heidegger can link his phenomenological adaptation of Aristotle to a revision of Aristotelian ontology. Because every entity shows itself in Dasein, the being of Dasein is the one point of reference in terms of which everything else is understood as something that is. Whatever is uncovered by Dasein and in Dasein announces itself as a phenomenon, and thus announces itself in its being. Ontology, under this presupposition, is possible *"only as phenomenology"*, as *Being and Time* puts it (*SZ* 35).

If we disregard, for the moment, this ontologization of phenomenology – and phenomenologization of ontology – Heidegger's understanding of the phenomenon as we have just sketched it remains quite close to that of Husserl, or, more precisely, to his canonical definition of the phenomenon (see Marion 2002: 68). According to *The Idea of Phenomenology*, "The meaning of the word 'phenomenon' is twofold because of the essential correlation between *appearing* and *that which appears*". Husserl goes on to explain that *phainomenon* properly means "'that which appears,' and yet it is predominantly used for the appearing itself, the subjective phenomenon (if one is allowed to use this expression, which can be misunderstood in a crude psychological sense)" (Husserl 1999: 69, trans. mod.). The definition recurs in the context of Heidegger's thought: a phenomenon is something in so far as it is seen in Dasein in terms of its very appearing, and not as something that appears, something given independently as a fact. The difference from Husserl lies solely in the description of the phenomenal, and in the way in which the phenomenal as such is validated. In Heidegger's sense, what is phenomenal is not the objects of knowledge, but the moments of a world, which can be experienced in their significance; and they are grasped as phenomena not through reflection, but by being withdrawn as really given in Dasein. What is lacking, what denies or withholds itself, shows itself all the more intensely as what is factically given. It is no longer something that appears in fact; rather, it comes into appearance in Dasein.

This is a decisive thought: for Heidegger, an essential moment of the phenomenal is withdrawal. In the "there of absence" (GA 18: 298), something is there in an intensified way. Much the same can be said of something that is brought forth from absence. This too, in Husserl's terms, is not given as "that which appears", but instead is in "appearing". In this sense, according to Being and Time, a phenomenon is "something that proximally and for the most part does *not* show itself at all: it is something that lies *hidden*, in contrast to that which proximally and for the most part does show itself" (SZ 35). The phenomenon is what must be discovered, must be drawn out from concealment. Only this guarantees that it is something that shows itself, and not only something that appears, in the sense of an illusion. A phenomenon is something itself, and not something that looks like something that in truth is something else.

Heidegger remains true to this conviction – that the phenomenality of phenomena is due to the process of discovery – until the early 1930s. When, in the lecture course of Winter Semester 1929–30, Dasein is understood as "world-forming", this is a radicalization of the position of Being and Time. What comes to appear in the course of the "projection" of a world is not only discovered, but is produced (FCM 285; on the concept of world-formation see Figal [2003: 94–110]). To be sure, Heidegger's later clarifications show that here he is thinking not of manufacture but of exhibition: something is exhibited, set out into the realm in which it can be experienced, so that it can thus be experienced in its appearing (GA 43: 219; see also N1 176; Figal 2006b). This radicalization is both problematic and illuminating: it makes it clear that the radicalized thought was not unproblematic even at the start. The radicalization obscures the fundamental trait of phenomena: the fact that phenomena not only are shown or indicated, but show *themselves*. This fact was already marginalized when Heidegger focused on discovery, and in his orientation to production it is lost.

This point may have been a significant factor that led Heidegger to retract his absolutization of production. In doing so, he refers to the beginning of philosophy in Greek thinking, but in a quite different way than he did in the early 1920s. He no longer sees the "first and definitive unfolding" (*IM* 14) of this thinking in the Aristotelian thought of *alētheuein*. Heidegger finds a new fundamental word: the word *physis*.

Even now, *Being and Time*'s identification of phenomenology and ontology stands fast. *Physis*, as Heidegger says in his lecture course of Summer Semester 1935, *Introduction to Metaphysics*, is "the being of beings" (*IM* 19, trans. mod.) because it is "what emerges from itself" or "the unfolding that opens itself up" (*IM* 15). In a third variation of the thought, *physis* is "the coming-into-appearance in such unfolding, and holding itself and persisting in appearance – in short, the emerging-abiding sway" (*IM* 15). In this last formulation, at least, it is clear that Heidegger is thinking of *physis* as the essence of phenomena. It is the appearing in which a thing is something that appears.

Nevertheless, the characterization of appearing as *physis* is still preliminary. Even here, Heidegger's project of finding phenomenology anonymously in Greek thinking is not fulfilled in a completely convincing way. Granted, in one way his characterization ideally fits the understanding of phenomena as what shows itself. Even if self-showing is occasioned by an indicating, it is essential to it that it happens on its own or, one could say, by itself, and it is precisely this originality that is conveyed in the concept of *physis*. The thought of *physis* stands for the objectivity and unconditionality of givenness, which already for Husserl was bound up with the inception of phenomenology.

But in another way, Heidegger's thought is too specific. Something can show itself even if this showing does not occur in *physis*. What shows itself and yet is not a *physei on* must therefore at least be dependent on self-showing in the sense of *physis*. As a phenomenon, it must be understood exclusively on the basis of *physis*, and that is not convincing; it restricts the thought of self-showing too severely.

Heidegger clearly saw this difficulty. He attempted to resolve it in his essay on the beginning of the second book of Aristotle's *Physics* by distinguishing between the "essence" of *physis* and its "concept" ("On the Essence and Concept of *Physis* in Aristotle's *Physics* B, I", in *PM*). According to this distinction, only the "concept" of *physis* ties us to a particular realm of beings, that is, natural beings, whereas the original "essence" of *physis* is supposedly emergence and self-showing without restriction. The restriction, as given with the concept, supposedly can be dispensed with; it comes into play only when one attempts to grasp the happening of *physis* in contrast to production. The restriction was misleadingly attached to *physis* as the fact of emergence.

All the same, we have to ask how the "on its own" that Heidegger wants to grasp with the thought of *physis* could be explained except in terms of the natural or the living (see Figal 2006a: 377–8). Every attempt to define self-showing on the basis of *physis,* or even as *physis* itself, relies on the emergence and growth of the natural. This is not just a model for the "on its own", but its sole realization. Thus the concept of *physis* is not neutral enough to stand for the essence of phenomena. If the essence of *physis* is expressed adequately in its concept, then the reference to this concept is unsuited to the anonymization of phenomenology.

Heidegger draws a conclusion that lies near at hand. He turns back to his early guiding concept of *alētheia,* but no longer understands it, with the *Nicomachean Ethics,* on the basis of *alētheuein.* Instead, he goes back to Parmenides. He reads Parmenides' saying about the self-sameness of thinking and being as a saying about a Selfsame that can be characterized separately and that holds sway in both thinking and being, in so far as it holds them apart from each other and thus holds them together in the "duality" of "disclosure" and "concealment" (*EGT* 87). If this Selfsame is understood as *alētheia* (*EGT* 93), then Heidegger's later position has already fundamentally been reached. *Alētheia* only needs to be explained as the "clearing" in order for the "task of thinking" to be defined in relation to the Greek inception.

The clearing and the task of thinking

Heidegger had already spoken of "clearing" (*Lichtung*) in earlier works. In *Being and Time* the term is used to explain "disclosedness" (*SZ* 133) as well as the kinship of this ontological characteristic of Dasein with the image of the *lumen naturale.* Heidegger also employs the expression in "The Origin of the Work of Art" (see Chapter 9). In fact, we find there that it already has the same meaning that it will come to have in his late texts. He no longer understands "clearing" in terms of light, but rather as "an open place". Beings "stand within and stand out within" this openness, which provides us with a "passage to those beings" (*BW* 178). The clearing is the possibility of phenomena.

It must be admitted that in "The Origin of the Work of Art", Heidegger still gives the term "clearing" a distinctly different accent than it has in his later texts. In the art essay, the clearing is thought as the openness of concealing and unconcealing, and is bound to the "strife" of "world" and "earth". The clearing is thus synonymous with the happening of clearing, in a sense quite consistent with Heidegger's earlier conception: a happening that is now at the same time above all the happening of withdrawal, denial and refusal. The clearing, says Heidegger, "is never a rigid stage with a permanently raised curtain", but instead happens as "concealment" (*BW* 179). Something shows itself inasmuch as it has been drawn out of concealment and indicated. In this way, in the work of art, a world shows itself as the entire context for beings, and beings themselves show themselves too.

But the clearing is considered rather differently in the late text "The End of Philosophy and the Task of Thinking". Here the clearing is called the "place of stillness" that "first grants unconcealment" (*BW* 445), that is, allows the play of concealing and unconcealing. The clearing is the "*free space*" (*BW* 444): what is occupied neither by the present nor by the absent. It is neither beings nor not-beings; it is the interval in which something can show itself and be shown.

As this free space, however, the clearing precedes every unconcealing and concealing. Even light presupposes the clearing, just as it is presupposed "for resonance and echo, for sound and the diminishing of sound" (*BW* 442). The clearing is already there when something is set forth and emerges from what refuses to appear; but the clearing is not a ground (*archē* or *principium*) on the basis of which concealment and unconcealment could be understood. The clearing is no ground but, as Heidegger says with Goethe, a "primal phenomenon" (*Urphänomen*); or, as one would have to say according to Heidegger, a "primal matter" (*Ur-sache*: *BW* 442).

It is especially remarkable, however, that Heidegger takes up this "primal matter" as the matter of a thinking that differentiates itself from all "philosophy". Philosophy as metaphysics is foundational thinking, which the thinking of the clearing renounces. Such thinking finds no purchase in philosophy and thus no beginning. While "at the beginning of philosophy", with Parmenides, the clearing is "named" with the word *alētheia*, "afterward it is not explicitly thought as such by philosophy" (*BW* 446). This remark is extraordinary: here Heidegger implicitly revises the understanding of philosophy that had been in place since the 1922 plan for *Being and Time*, through the *Contributions to Philosophy*, until the lectures of the 1950s. Even in *The Principle of Reason*, Heidegger continues to take his bearings from the concept of *physis*, and so does not fundamentally depart from his views in *Introduction to Metaphysics*.

What Heidegger gives up in his late text is the *myth of the beginning*: his many variations on the history of philosophy as the loss of an originary truth, a loss brought about by tradition (see Chapter 11). This truth, according to the myth, must be retrieved, won back or taken up in an "other beginning". But as it seems now, the history of philosophy is not the tragic history of an involuntary loss, in which what is lost is nevertheless retained and can be brought into view if one goes back to the beginning. Instead, philosophy has always been what it is in the present. But presently, according to Heidegger's diagnosis, it is coming to an end in consequence of its foundational thinking. In his view, one should leave philosophy to this end, which promises relief and liberation for a new possibility. The task of thinking, to which all thinking is now duty bound, is posed only after the end of philosophy.

With this turn away from philosophy in favour of a thinking that is no longer philosophical, because it is no longer foundational, the universalization of phenomenology comes to an end as well. Because at the beginning of philosophy the clearing was not thought, but was at best named by the term *"alētheia"*, the phenomenological interpretation of early thinking can count as an independent possibility. But it is not arbitrary; as an interpretation worthy of the name, it can uncover only what is contained in the texts that have been handed down. However, only it, as an interpretation, uncovers this. In the ancient texts there was nothing intended that was then lost and covered over. The phenomenological element in them comes to light solely through phenomenology.

If this is the case, the phenomenological interpretation can again come forward openly as such. It may – and should – be called phenomenological, instead of lying hidden anonymously in all philosophy and all thinking. Heidegger himself points in this direction when he adopts Goethe's fundamental term "primal phenomenon". This means something that is a phenomenon with particular clarity and distinctness: a phenomenon that shows itself with a special intensity that makes it possible to experience its character as phenomenon. This also implies that it is evidently impossible for primal phenomena to be founded on anything else. They cut off, as it were, any attempt to supply them with a foundation; they cannot be understood on the basis of anything else. Hence primal phenomena, as Goethe says, displace us "into a kind of awe to the point of anxiety" (1991: 792); "we feel our own inadequacy" (*ibid*.: 798). Primal phenomena do not come from anywhere else, and thus they are not "given" either; that would require a giver. At best one can say, with Heidegger: *es gibt sie* ("they are", or literally, "it gives them"; on this expression see *TB* 38–40). But this means that they do not come forth "on their own", like natural things; instead, they appear.

The appearing of primal phenomena may leave the will to foundation speechless; as Goethe says, when faced with such phenomena, "sensible people" prefer to take shelter in "amazement" (1991: 792). But primal phenomena do not have to be accepted speechlessly. They can be interpreted, they can be developed in their structure and moments, and thus they can also be understood as coherent. They can be experienced hermeneutically. In this way, they enliven and cheer us "through the eternal play of experience [Empirie]" (ibid.: 798).

This holds for phenomena that are recognized as such, in general. It holds for primal phenomena only when "experience" is determined by the intensity of the phenomenal. One does justice to primal phenomena only if, in interpreting them, one considers their phenomenality as such. The openness in which they appear, the hermeneutic space that allows them to oppose us as objects and gives us access to them, lies in these phenomena themselves (Figal 2006a: 153–73).

Heidegger's talk of the clearing should probably be understood in this sense. The clearing, then, is not a primal phenomenon, and in fact is not a phenomenon among others, but is the clarity of phenomena, which becomes evident in primal phenomena. It would then be proper to the thinking of the clearing to accept it as such, but not to take it as a separate object. The thought of clearing as such would then belong rather to an "experience" that in turn would be oriented by this thought. The thought would stand at the head of a kind of research and description that, beyond foundational thinking, would stand open to the whole realm of the phenomenal. It would stand at the head of a phenomenology that has come back to itself from anonymity and universality.

References

Figal, G. 2003. *Martin Heidegger zur Einführung*. Hamburg: Junius.

Figal, G. 2006a. *Gegenständlichkeit: Das Hermeneutische und die Philosophie*. Tübingen: Mohr Siebeck.

Figal, G. 2006b. "Machen, was noch nicht da ist. Herstellung als Modell gegen und für die Metaphysik". In *Die Gegenwart des Gegenwär*, M. Drewsen & M. Fischer (eds), 128–37. Freiburg/Munich: Karl Alber.

Goethe, J. W. von 1991. *Maximen und Reflexionen*. In *Sämtliche Werke nach Epochen seines Schaffens*. Münchner Ausgabe, Vol. 17, G.-L. Fink, G. Baumann & J. John (eds). Munich: Carl Hanser.

Husserl, E. 1999. *The Idea of Phenomenology*, L. Hardy (trans.). Dordrecht: Kluwer.

Marion, J.-L. 2002. *Being Given: Toward a Phenomenology of Givenness*, J. L. Kosky (trans.). Stanford, CA: Stanford University Press.

Further reading

Primary sources

See Heidegger's "My Way to Phenomenology", in *On "Time and Being"*; *History of the Concept of Time: Prolegomena*, Preliminary Part; "The End of Philosophy and the Task of Thinking", in *Basic Writings*; *Being and Time*, §7; and *Introduction to Phenomenological Research*, part 1.

Secondary sources

See T. Carman, "The Principle of Phenomenology", in Guignon (2006), 97–119; D. O. Dahlstrom, "Heidegger's Critique of Husserl", in Kisiel & van Buren (1994), 231–44; K. Held, "Heidegger and the Principle of Phenomenology", Macann (1992), vol. 2, 303–25; and Stapleton (1983). See also R. Capobianco, "Heidegger's *die Lichtung*: From 'The Lighting' to 'The Clearing'", *Existentia* 17(5–6) (2007), 321–35.

THREE

Dasein as being-in-the-world

Timothy Stapleton

Heidegger uses the word "Dasein" to refer to what customarily might be called the self or "I"; or, as he more cautiously puts it, to "this entity which each of us is himself" (*BT* 27). But while the denotations of the words "self" and "Dasein" may be the same, the connotations differ radically. When properly understood, "Dasein" captures the unique being of the "I am", one that gets misconstrued by such terms, for example, as "self", "ego", "soul", "subjectivity" or "person". For Heidegger, what constitutes the very "am" of the "I am" is that being is an issue for it: is a question and a matter about which it cares. This entity that I am understands this implicitly. More radically, it *is* this understanding, or the place where this understanding of being occurs. Hence "Dasein" means the self *as* the there (*Da*) of being (*Sein*), the place where an understanding of being erupts into being.

"Being-in-the-world" is Heidegger's descriptive interpretation of the self *as* Dasein. For Heidegger, as we shall come to see, description and interpretation need not be at odds. One sort of interpretation (*Auslegung*), as a laying-out of that which is only tacit, is description. "Being-in-the-world" is intended to capture descriptively various dimensions of what it means for Dasein "to be". But much more needs to be said, in the way of interpretation, about this description.

Dasein and the understanding of being

Being and Time is a work in ontology. It enquires about the meaning of being. Being is always the being (*Sein*) of some entity or being (*Seiendes*);

of trees and tables, *of* human beings and their questions. "Ontic" is the expression Heidegger uses for beings and our way of talking about them, "ontological" for the being of such beings and its language. The ontic and ontological are inseparable. But ontology must always begin with the ontic and move towards the ontological. Moreover, "*Dasein* is ontically distinctive in that it *is* ontological" (*BT* 32). Being ontological here points to that implicit understanding of being that occurs with and in Dasein's existence. But what, more concretely, is this implicit understanding of being?

Let us begin with a simple example. I gaze out of the window and see, against the background of the Masonic Temple's rigid, grey brickwork, the red leaves on the branch of a maple stir in the late afternoon breeze. What I see is a tree, its branches and red leaves. What I apprehend, more precisely, are not just the leaves and the colour red, but the leaves *being* red. I do not say, for instance, "leaves red" or "leaves *and* red", but, rather, "The leaves *are* red", "The clouds *are* gathering", "A man dressed in a plaid kilt *is* walking past". For Heidegger, there is an understanding of being as substance (the being of the leaves) and accident (the being of the redness) that accompanies such simple experiences; that guides and structures them in advance (*a priori*) and makes it possible for what I experience to be what it is. Being as understood in terms of these traditional *categories* is what Heidegger calls "categorial".[1]

One of the first ways Heidegger talks about being is as "what determines entities as entities" (*BT* 25). Being does not "make" beings be in the sense of create or cause them. "To determine" here means something more like opening up a place or space where these entities can show themselves for what they are. Or, as Heidegger sometimes says, being *frees* beings for their being.

Furthermore, this understanding of being *is* itself something. The understanding of being understands its own being as well. While gazing across the garden at the red leaves of the maple, I am at the same time aware that *I am seeing* this. This self-awareness is not something that emerges only when an explicit act of reflection takes place. A pre-thematic self-consciousness is an essential dimension of lived awareness. The crucial question is: what sort of understanding of being accompanies or "determines" this lived self-awareness as the sort of thing that it is? Heidegger claims that all too often the understanding of being that frees objects within the world for their being gets reflected back on the being of the experiencing itself. The "I" gets taken as a substance, although perhaps of some special sort (ego, mind, *res cogitans*, soul), and the "seeing" as an activity of this I-thing.

Ontologically, every idea of a "subject" – unless refined by a previous ontological determination of its basic character – still posits the *subjectum* (*hupokeimenon*) along with it, no matter how vigorous one's ontical protestations against the "soul substance" or "reification of consciousness". (*BT* 72)

Even when subjectivity is understood not as isolated from, but rather as connected essentially and "intentionally" to, the objects of its experience (the position Heidegger associates with traditional phenomenology at that time), nothing changes with respect to the ontology at work. The self or the subject and its acts of awareness are still taken as entities that present themselves to the thematic gaze of reflection, as already there and given so as to be apprehended in such reflection.

Two closely related points should be noted here. First, Heidegger wants to claim that the traditional understanding of being, guided by the notion of substance, is inseparable from the idea of "presence". That which really is, the *ontōs on,* is that which presents itself, and the pre-eminent temporal mode of presentation in which this takes place is in the present. Secondly, there is an intimate connection between this understanding of being and the theoretical attitude itself. When a theoretical orientation is assumed, one stands back and looks, inspects, gets a critical (objective) distance so as to see how things "really are". Whether empiricist (sight and the senses) or rationalist (the eye of the mind, in*sight,* the *eidos* or Idea as that which is illuminated), to be is to be "seeable". Among the guiding ideas in the Western tradition is that the movement from seeming to being, from appearance to reality, requires the assumption of the theoretical attitude. But this move entails positing that understanding of being which is necessary for theory itself.

Heidegger's new, fundamental ontology must combat the considerable weight of both of these prejudices – grounded as they are in language, tradition and a tendency towards such self-concealment that is part of Dasein's own being. The hegemony of the categorial is to be challenged, and Heidegger does so by trying to understand and interpret Dasein's "to be" as being-in-the-world.

An interpretation of being-in-the-world

When Heidegger first introduces the expression "being-in-the-world", he calls attention to several important features. First, although a compound expression, it nonetheless signifies a unitary phenomenon. This unity is an essential one: its different dimensions not so much pieces (like the legs and top of a table) but moments (like the colour and shape of the table top). The hyphenated nature of the expression does nothing but emphasize this elemental unity. Furthermore, Heidegger notes that being-in-the-world is triadic. There is (i) the "in-the-world", (ii) the "being-in", and (iii) the entity or "who" which is as being-in-the-world. Each of these dimensions will be laid out in turn, but with a constant eye kept on their essential interconnectedness.

These analyses (constituting a Dasein analytic) must be understood as an attempt at a "non-categorial" ontology. Heidegger uses the word "*Existenz*" to refer to the unique kind of being that Dasein "is". Rather than categories, the basic ontological concepts to be developed here are accordingly called "*existentiala*", among the most basic of which is being-in-the-world. As an ontological concept, this notion would function in place of, but in a manner not unlike, the concepts of substance and accident in the region of objects or things.

Consider the following diagram.

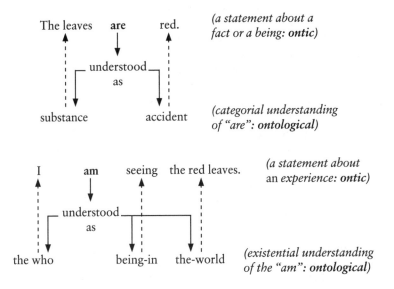

Just as the leaves *being* red is dependent on the categorial understanding of being as substance, "my experiencing of the leaves as red" is dependent on being-in-the-world. This implicit understanding (ontological) accompanies, although necessarily in an implicit manner, the lived experience (ontic) of my seeing the leaves. Both the unity and structure of the experience (in terms of the "I", the act and the object) are determined by the unity and structural integrity of the phenomenon of being-in-the-world. But how? And what, in more detail, is this *existentiale* of being-in-the-world?

The world and its worldhood

The "world" might be considered the referential component of being-in-the-world. It is that towards which Dasein's being moves in its existence. The world should not, however, be understood as the sum total of all objects and possible relationships among them that do or might exist. The world, for Heidegger, belongs to Dasein's being. This expression tries to capture what we mean, for example, when talking about the world of an artist, of a person inhabiting a religious world, or of meeting someone who opened up the world of her family to me. Heidegger describes this as "that *'wherein'* a factical Dasein as such can be said to 'live'" (*BT* 93). Note that the world, then, while a feature of Dasein, is not something subjective, some inner state or idea that stands between the self and the things that are. Living in a familial world is precisely what allows me, for example, to experience those around me as family.

The multiplicity of worlds, however, is not ultimately what Heidegger wants to uncover and describe. He is interested in the phenomenon of the world as such, in the "worldhood of the world": "Worldhood itself may have as its modes whatever structural wholes any special 'worlds' may have at the time; but it embraces in itself the *a priori* character of worldhood in general" (*BT* 93). Are there certain universal and necessary structures that belong to any and all worlds, remembering that "worlds" here means not objects or entities as such but that contextual milieu of meaning towards which Dasein is in its being?

In order to uncover such *a priori* structures, Heidegger turns not towards some special or privileged way of being-in or toward a world, inhabited only at certain moments or times. Instead, what must provide the beginning point for such a "transcendental" analysis is the everyday world in which we continually live, that which is closest to us and out of which other sorts of worlds might emerge: the everyday world of our ordinary surroundings (*Umwelt*). To begin anywhere else would be a mistake for at least two reasons. Were we to choose something like "perception" in the traditional sense of the term and talk about the world of those who see (versus, for example, the world of the blind), or were we to begin with the act of knowing and the world of the theoretician, we would mistake a part for the whole, a particular world and way of being worldly for the world as such. Secondly, such beginning points would covertly import into the analyses an understanding of being as substance or presence-at-hand, and so cover over the genuinely *existential* nature of Dasein's being-in-the-world. Or, as Heidegger is at great pains to remind the reader, "worldhood itself is an *existentiale*" (BT 92).

This everyday world is not one of theoretical contemplation, of trying to describe the way things "look" or to "see" the causal connections between events, but one of practical engagement. Before, and even while, I looked out of the window to describe the leaves of the maple as an object in my field of vision, I was busied with the computer's keyboard, a pencil, papers, books, the clutter of the desktop, a place for my coffee mug, shifting my own body in a less than comfortable chair and so forth. I get up and walk across the room to adjust the blinds, stepping past a filing cabinet and a rocking chair whose frayed wicker back catches the tip of my fingernail. These "things" with which I deal disclose themselves not as objects to be looked at from the outside, nor as entities that might exist "in themselves" were I not *there*. To take them that way requires an extraordinary amount of abstraction and theoretical positioning on my part. That such abstraction from the experience of being engaged in a concernful way with the "gear" or "equipment" (*das Zeug*) of the everyday world comes so easily and "naturally" testifies not to the efficacy of such abstraction, but to the sway of the categorial understanding into which I, as a historically, linguistically and culturally constituted Dasein, so naturally "fall". The phenomenological challenge, one might say, is precisely to arrest this "natural" tendency, one that is grounded in the very being of Dasein.

Uncovering the worldhood of the world entails disclosing those structures that belong to and make possible my engagement with the everyday surrounding world. If I were to describe, for example, the window in my study as encountered in my everyday engagement with it, little heed would be paid to the colour or composition of its frame, to the length, width or weight of the glass. My "experience", rather, is that I am hurriedly closing the window to keep out the rain from an early summer squall. Or, later, I am sliding it open to welcome the now shockingly cool air into a hot and stuffy apartment. What makes possible the window *being* what it is as a window, or as Heidegger puts it at one point, that "from which it acquires its specific Thingly character" (BT 98), are the structures constitutive of the worldhood of the world (along with our understanding of those structures).

These *a priori* structures of worldhood can be sketched out as follows: "with ... in ... in order to ... for the sake of ...". That is, I am engaged *with* the window *in* the act of opening *in order to* let in the cool air *for the sake of* my own comfort. I am busy *with* the remote control *in* pushing what I hope is the right button *in order to* mute the sound *for the sake of* my peace of mind. Heidegger calls this structural totality an "assignment-context" in that the implement encountered is always within a context of assignments: the window, for example, is assigned (or refers to) the work or task (opening, closing, etc.), to the more immediate goal (letting in air), as well as referring to myself and others (my or our comfort) and even to nature at large (the lightness of the window as it slides up or down as a function of the *stuff* of which it is made, along with the window as a way of handling *weather*).

The key idea, however, is that these structures of the worldhood of the world are *a priori* in the sense of being necessary and universal. Imaginatively attempt to eliminate them and the everyday world collapses. Or from the side of the one who is "in" such a world, someone who failed to understand those structures, not theoretically but practically and implicitly, could never encounter a tool or piece of equipment as such. At best, he or she might simply gaze blankly at it. But this would be the empty gaze not of someone who did not understand what it was "for" (the assignment-context), but of someone who did not even understand the idea of things being-for something. These structures are the necessary conditions in the absence of which the world ceases to be.

The universality characterizing these structures is not only that they belong to any and all everyday surrounding worlds (whether I am opening a window, driving a car, moving furniture, etc.). For even when I supposedly go beyond the world of everyday *praxis*, when I come to inhabit the theoretical domains of science, mathematics, logic and so forth, these structures still hold sway. They are not transcended, but only modified. The scientist is still busy *with* a spectroscope *in* the act of observing *in order to* determine the wavelengths of light emitted by a certain compound *for the sake of* our knowing its chemical composition. Even the formal logician is still engaged *with* the logical law of the disjunctive syllogism *in* applying it to a certain line of a proof *in order to* demonstrate the validity of an argument *for the sake of* establishing our certainty of a conclusion. In other words, even when we withhold ourselves from what might be termed our everyday practical engagement with "things" so as just to observe how they are from a theoretical perspective, we do not suspend the functioning of the worldhood of the world. The theoretical world of things that are just present for an observer is a particular modification of, and remains grounded in, the everyday worldhood of the world.

The world, then, is that through which beings are "determined" as beings (tools): that through which they are "freed" for their being. Heidegger wants to identify the world or its worldhood not with being, but rather with being *as* understood in a certain manner. This understanding of being, in contrast to understanding being as presence-at-hand, is described as "readiness-to-hand" (*Zuhandenheit*), an expression that captures the serviceability or usability connotations that belong to the very being of implements. And the tacit *understanding of* readiness-to-hand, the "feel" for these structures that lingers in and holds them open, is what Heidegger calls "circumspection".

Being-in

But in calling attention to circumspection, a second moment of the triadic structure of being-in-the-world comes to the fore: the phenomenon of being-in. Circumspection is a particular *understanding of* being (in contrast to being *as* understood) and as such a mode of being-in. This "understanding of" Heidegger describes as *disclosure*, an opening up of what was closed off or hidden. The act of circumspective concern does not create the structures of worldhood, the assignment context, but rather illuminates or holds them open. Being-in "is itself the clearing", the *Da* of Dasein, and an analysis of this phenomenon of Being-in would entail an explication of "the existential constitution of the 'there'" (*BT* 171).

Being-in, like the world, is an *existentiale*. Accordingly, "in" here cannot mean a kind of objective, spatial relationship as when I might talk about my jacket being in the closet which is in the bedroom, in the apartment I have in Baltimore. Just as the world should not be understood categorially as the totality of objects, "in" must also be given an existential sense. To get the feel for this, Heidegger appeals to the sense of "being-in" as dwelling, residing among or being familiar with. This sense of "in" is what is expressed, for example, when I say that I am *in* to jazz, or that I just cannot get *in* to living in suburbia. One might object that such expressions are metaphorical: that the literal meaning of "in", the primary meaning on which the metaphors draw and expand, is the "in" of objects and objective space. But Heidegger wants to claim precisely the opposite: that the original sense of "in" is the existential one and the "objective" or literal derivative – a modification of meaning that is the result of a shift from practical engagement with gear of the surrounding lifeworld to a theoretical attitude, one that substitutes for the particularities of dwelling and place the homogeneous expanse of Euclidean space.

Understanding (*Verstehen*), as has already been suggested, is one way in which this being-in is realized. But understanding is always

51

complemented and accompanied by another mode of being-in, that of state-of-mind (*Befindlichkeit*). Heidegger describes these two constitutive structures of being-in as "equiprimordial", in the sense that they are equally important and elemental in their capacities to disclose the world. One way of viewing these two modes of being-in might be as existential analogues to what Kant, with reference to the theoretical domain, called the two sources of knowledge: namely, sensibility and understanding. Our capacity to be *affected* by objects, the moment of receptivity in and through which objects are *given*, is what Kant called sensibility. Understanding, in turn, was that faculty through which the objects given in sensibility come to be thought conceptually. Sensibility for Kant testified to the situated nature of our experience: that we do not create the world but always already (time) find ourselves in (space) it.

It is just this notion of "always already being in" that Heidegger highlights with his *existentiale* of state-of-mind. Our being is something to which, as Heidegger says, we are delivered over. There is an elemental "givenness" about my existence. It erupts into the world beyond my control. I did not ask to be born, to be born white and male and of the parents and in the place where I was. This brute *facticity* saturates my Dasein, although not just in the sense of some distant past (see Chapter 1). It is as an ongoing phenomenon continually accompanying my Being-in-the-world. Heidegger describes this feature as a "thrownness" in the sense that I might mean, for example, when speaking about being thrown into a situation that was not of my making. "The expression 'thrownness' is meant to suggest the *facticity of its being delivered over*" (BT 174). Each and every moment of each and every day my being is something to which I have been delivered over as something already there that must be taken up. And it is this phenomenon that is disclosed by state-of-mind in a way that no amount of thought or conceptualization could accomplish. Moods, for Heidegger, are the various concrete ways in which state-of-mind gets worked out. State-of-mind (*Befindlichkeit*), with its resonance in German of how one already *finds* oneself, is our affective capacity to have or *be in* moods. My moods are intimately mine, yet still they happen to me. I *find* myself already in them, whether they be good moods, bad moods or the feel of pallid indifference that might accompany me much of the time. For Heidegger it is the disclosive capacity of moods, as ways in which being-in as state-of-mind is realized, that is crucial. As disclosive, they are ontologically revelatory of an irreducible existential "that-ness", a profound and deep finitude that engulfs and qualifies my being-in all the way down to its very roots.[2]

But such elemental facticity is intertwined with potentiality: "Dasein is Being-possible which has been delivered over it to itself – *thrown possibility* through and through" (*BT* 183). Understanding, the complement of and continually accompanied by state-of-mind, is fundamentally the projection of possibilities. Circumspection, for example, is one way in which understanding uncovers tools for their possible us*ability*, for their service*ability*. This understanding of being as readiness-to-hand frees entities for their involvement and for the array of *possible* ways they can be. The window I engage with is the kind of thing that *can be* closed and opened and a source of needed light and a distraction and an occasion for vulnerability in an urban landscape and an example of a being that *can be* all these things.

When the tacit work of understanding becomes explicit, the network of assignment-relationships opened up through its projection come to be laid out. Such laying-out is what Heidegger calls interpretation (*Auslegung*). Note then that for Heidegger, "interpretation" does not have its usual sense of the imposition of subjective meaning, individual or collective, on things that somehow are already there "in themselves". Understanding is what first makes possible that encounter with beings at all. The very idea of "being in itself" is a function of a certain implicit (and for Heidegger derivative) understanding of being that, when laid out explicitly, comes to be *interpreted* as substance and as pure presence-at-hand. Interpretation does not create but makes explicit this prior "as".

At the same time, Dasein does not just understand the being of the entities it concerns itself with in the world, but it understands itself as well *as* being-in-the-world. If state-of-mind illuminates my intractable facticity and finitude (my always already having been), understanding discloses my potentiality-for-being (my not yet). Dasein is both the point of origin and return in this projective, affective understanding. The understanding of being that arises in Dasein has, as its terminus (the final term in the "with ... in ... in order to ... for the sake of ..." network of assignment references), Dasein itself. In my fumbling with a screwdriver in trying to loosen a frozen fixture in order to stop the tap from leaking, it is "for the sake of" my possible convenience. I understand myself in terms of my possibilities for being, projecting myself towards what I might or could or can be. Note that this need not imply a narrow egocentric interpretation. The same ontological structures could just as well make possible the final referent as "for the sake of" *my* child's ability to sleep peacefully or for conserving *our* water supply. In the latter cases I understand myself *as* being-in a familial or a communal world, but it is my (Dasein's) self-understanding.

The "who" of being-in-the-world

But "who" then is this Dasein? We are now led from the world and its worldhood, through being-in as state-of-mind and understanding, to the third essential moment of the phenomenon of being-in-the-world: to "an approach to the existential question of the 'who' of Dasein" (*BT* 150). The theme taken up here is in many respects an old and well worn one: the topic of personal identity. Previous treatments have been legion. In Descartes, for example, recourse is made to a type of substantive soul, a *res* beneath the *cogitans*. Kant posited a necessary "unity of apperception", an "I think" that must accompany all experience. Husserl sometimes spoke of an "ego-pole" from which the illuminating rays of consciousness emanate. Such accounts, according to Heidegger, presuppose and are nourished by a categorial understanding of being as presence-at-hand.

An existential treatment of the "I-ness of the I" must proceed along a different path. From the outset, in first indicating in a merely formal way the unique kind of being that belongs to Dasein, Heidegger says: "That Being which is an *issue* for this entity in its very Being, is in each case mine .... Because Dasein has *in each case mineness* (*Jemeinigkeit*), one must always use a personal pronoun when one addresses it: 'I am', 'you are'" (*BT* 68). When asked, for example, "who's there?" there's only one answer: "Me". The "who" of Dasein's being-in-the-world, expressed ontically by the term "I", is tinged by an almost ineffably intimate "mineness". "I am" not just *a* person (an instance of a universal or general type), nor even just *this particular* person (as differentiated from all others because of singularities of genetics and life experiences). For this particular person is *me*. Reminiscent of points made in the indirect and pseudonymous writings of Kierkegaard, the *categories* of universal and particular fail to disclose this phenomenon. "Mineness" is an *existentiale*.

Authenticity and inauthenticity are possible modes of being for Dasein because of the "mineness" of my being-in-the-world. These terms, "authentic" (*eigentlich*) and "inauthentic" (*uneigentlich*), contain the German root "*eigen*" (own), and Heidegger says explicitly that he chose them precisely for that reason. I can be my *own* self or not be my *own* self only because this self is mine in the first place. And even when not being my own self, the foundational phenomenon of mineness does not somehow dissolve. Not being my own self is precisely one way, and even the predominant way, in which the phenomenon of mineness is worked out in my everyday being-in-the-world.

For example, it might be fair to say that for the most part my everyday existence is characterized by a deep-seated and powerful habituality:

a habituality that is only all too "natural" and even necessary for ordinary living. My life *carries me* along familiar paths walked by others. It is, of course, still my life. But I enact ways of thinking, feeling and choosing, take up ways of valuing and models of human excellence that, from childhood on, I have learned from others. "The Self of everyday Dasein is the *they*-self" (*BT* 167). Human existence is mimetic and the only way that I can come to myself is by absorbing and inhabiting, both consciously and unconsciously, these ways of others. This in no less true even for those acts of rebellion, non-conformity and gestures of alleged creativity occasioned perhaps by boredom, or the gnawing feeling of not fitting in or of being unfulfilled in the traditional roles that await me. One "habit of being" is exchanged for another that might be a better fit.

But what, then, of authenticity and of the authentic self which is its *own* self? Is such authenticity possible at all? If so, how? And what, first of all, would such a thing even mean? Significant portions of Division Two of *Being and Time* are devoted to an analysis of this theme in terms of anxiety, guilt, conscience, resoluteness, finitude and death, the details of which are far beyond the scope of this chapter. I shall say only enough to shed some light on this phenomenon as it relates directly to the "who" of Dasein as being-in-the-world.

At the end of Heidegger's initial treatment of the "who" or "I" of Dasein in Division One of *Being and Time*, he offers the following synopsis: "*Authentic Being-one's-Self* does not rest upon an exceptional condition of the subject, a condition that has been detached from the 'they'; *it is rather an existentiell modification of the 'they' – of the 'they' as an essential existential*" (*BT* 168). Authenticity is spoken of here as a *modification* of, rather than an escape or detachment from, the inauthentic they-self. And the latter is said to be an *essential* constitutive feature of Dasein's being-in-the-world. The authentic "I" should not, then, be understood as some deep, inner, "real" me: that special part of myself that only I can truly come to know. Nor in terms of a Romantic ideal of a self who, like Rousseau's "noble savage", lives uncontaminated by the ways of culture and civilization. Authentic understanding, authentic being-in-the-world, is predicated on a lucid self-awareness of the truth of Dasein's being, a being that *is* cultural, historical and social. Kant, for example, drew the distinction between heteronomy (determined by the law of others) and autonomy (giving law to oneself). A glimmer of the distinction between the inauthentic and authentic, between the otherness of "the-they" and my own, appears here. But for Kant, human being is constituted by and realized in pure forms of rationality. To be autonomous, for Kant, is to be one's ownmost self as rational. For Heidegger, Dasein has no such pre-given, inherently rational nature. Dasein's essence is its *Existenz*, which is an issue or question for it, characterized by a thrownness and temporal finitude: a being that is "delivered over to itself" and is responsible for what it makes of that. The lucid realization that my "Dasein as being-in-the-world" is "without ground", a truth from which I flee in the habitual "dispersal" into the they-self, provides the possibility for what might be termed an "existential autonomy", in which I take up the burden of, and responsibility for, my existence, as being-with others, where "the-they" that still *is* me neither absorbs nor releases me from the responsibility for my *ownmost* being-in-the-world (see Chapter 4).

Notes

1. The ideas presented above draw heavily on Husserl's distinction between categorial and sensuous intuition as found in Investigation VI of his *Logical Investigations* (Husserl 1970). Heidegger cites these sections of the *Logical Investigations* as having an important influence on his early work.
2. Later in *Being and Time*, Heidegger analyses the mood of anxiety as singularly disclosive of Dasein's being-toward-death, its *mortal* finitude. But all moods, I would suggest, testify to and reveal the *essential* finitude of Dasein's being.

References

Husserl, E. 1970. *Logical Investigations*, J. Findlay (trans.). New York: Humanities Press.

Further reading

Primary sources

See Heidegger's *Being and Time*; *The Essence of Reasons* (see also PM 107–20); *The Basic Problems of Phenomenology*, pt I; *History of the Concept of Time: Prolegomena*; *Kant and the Problem of Metaphysics*, esp. §IV. And see E. Husserl, *Logical Investigations*, J. Findlay (trans.) (New York: Humanities Press, 1970), vol. II, §2, ch. 6.

Secondary sources

See Dreyfus (1992), Gelven (1970: esp. 43–88), and Polt (1999: esp. 23–84).

FOUR

Care and authenticity

Charles E. Scott

Let us begin with a story quoted by Heidegger about "Care":

> Once when "Care" was crossing a river, she saw some clay; she thoughtfully took a piece and began to shape it. While she was thinking about what she had made, Jupiter came by. "Care" asked him to give it spirit, and this he gladly granted. But when she wanted her name to be bestowed upon it, Jupiter forbade this and demanded that it be given his name instead. While "Care" and Jupiter were arguing, Earth (Tellus) arose, and desired that her name be conferred upon the creature, since she had offered it part of her body. They asked Saturn to be the judge. And Saturn gave them the following decision, which seemed to be just: "Since you, Jupiter, have given its spirit, you should receive that spirit at death; and since you, Earth, have given its body, you shall receive its body. But since "Care" first shaped this creature, she shall possess it as long as it lives. And because there is a dispute among you as to its name, let it be called "homo," for it is made out of humus (earth). (*BTS* 184, trans. mod.)

Heidegger includes this story in *Being and Time* in order to show that awareness of the definitive role of Care in human being is ingrained and pre-theoretical in our historical lineage. He is saying in effect that the language of this book might be difficult in its effort to forge a new interpretation of human being, but the basic awareness that guides it was articulated long before philosophy began. This ancient story shows that people's common way of being bears an intrinsic sense of

MARTIN HEIDEGGER: KEY CONCEPTS

– a fundamental attunement to – the necessity of both careful responsibility for our lives and world and the inevitability, in living, of loss and misfortune. According to the sense of the story, the form of human being is one of Care; human being is shaped by Care. If Heidegger is to give his own, philosophical account of human being in accord with this ancient and definitive sense, he must, on his own terms, describe the structure of Care that defines human, worldly life.[1]

A second and equally important part of this story is found in the crucial function of Saturn, the God of time. Only by his mediation do the otherwise fractious elements of Spirit, Earth and Care come together and allow Care's figure to appear as human. Whereas Care is the origin and meaning of human life in the world, time constitutes the origin and meaning of the unified structure where Care takes place. People have to care because worldly life is always coming to pass; nothing escapes the impact of time. Time rules the appearance and passage of human being. I shall return to this thought.

Heidegger's words and concepts articulate a philosophical interpretation of human being. The characters of the story, on the other hand, signify a basic experience of human life without the aid of philosophy. Awareness of this experience, as Heidegger understands it, is part of a deep and usually unconscious Western heritage that constitutes our world of meaning; it is an experience of the origin and destiny of human life. One of Heidegger's goals in *Being and Time* is to show the ways the meaning of Care and the rule of Time have been covered over and forgotten in patterns of ordinary living as well as in our most sophisticated manners of thought. Although this covering over might appear initially as insignificant, he finds it to be one of the most destructive aspects of our cultural tradition, destructive not only of the quality of individual lives but also of the capacity of societies to create the conditions for human thriving.

Everydayness and the question of the meaning of being

The ways we care and what we care for govern our lives to a considerable degree. The energy in our dedications measures the intensity of our lives, and what we commit ourselves to gives our lives their direction and character. Usually people appear to concern themselves with what most others around them show concern for: the details of ordinary life and the values that indicate normalcy and acceptability in a given environment. Heidegger calls this kind of normalcy "everydayness". There is a type of anonymity in it, one typified by our ordinary usage of "they", as in, "They say you should exercise to stay healthy". Or the anonymous "one": "One simply does not wear white shoes with a black tuxedo". "Anonymous" here describes actions and attitudes that lack an individual's singular authorship: one does not even decide to be one of the ones; one already is one when one cares to look.

If I relate to myself as one is expected to do, if I see myself the way others see me, if I go along to get along, I make choices as though I were not my own life. I intend what they intend for me. We talk as one does. The ordinary chitchat of group-talk is one example of what Heidegger calls inauthentic existence. We all know what we mean, and we stay on the surface of things. The way I live is as though time were merely a measure of parts of duration and caring meant no more than looking after things the way one is supposed to. Heidegger calls this modality of living, when everydayness defines our existence, inauthenticity.

It is hard not to be inauthentic. Everydayness does not go away. We are social beings who require common identities, systems of signs and routine practices. People, Heidegger says, always find themselves thrown in a world and so "thrown" into the situations of a given culture as well as into the inevitabilities of being human. We cannot avoid such "thrownness". Unsituated and non-historical meaning and signification do not happen. Human spirit does not occur flesh-free. The syntheses of body and reflective consciousness are never outside time. We find ourselves occurring with answers and meanings that were generated and mutated over time and under all manner of circumstances. "Thrownness" means in part that alertness, rationality and other aspects of living always happen in the midst of realities, truths, unresolved ambiguity, complex entanglements and the strange, given requirements of being alive.

The story of Care indicates we can understand intuitively that we have to plan ahead and take care of things in order to survive, that we can feel as if our spirits do not belong to the earth, and that bodies will pass away and turn into *humus*. In Heidegger's interpretation in *Being and Time* this intuitive understanding means that intrinsic in human being is a preverbal and pre-rational sense that being – the very occurrence of life – is in question: as creatures of Care we are continuously passing away and beginning again as we care for our lives and, in its earthly time, human being provides no permanent answers to the question of why it is happening at all. The *question* of the meaning of being forms the *meaning* of *Being and Time*: the meaning of the book is found in a question that is not susceptible to a definitive answer on the basis of the occurrence of life. In the question of being's continuing to be, lives open out in a world without guarantees for continuation and without any sustaining presence to define whatever is yet to happen.

The question of being arises concurrently with the happening of human being. It is a question *of* being as it happens: being brings with it no guarantees that it will continue to be. Before we consider the ways people can live authentically with the question of being, however, we need to note some of Heidegger's helpful distinctions.

Ontic and ontological: human beings and Dasein

"Ontic" refers to the way something specifically exists (*BTS* 11–12). It refers to beings. As we saw in Chapter 1, beings in their facticity have significance in the ways they come to light and exist in particular circumstances. The story of Care, for example, is ontic in the sense that it, as a particular myth, speaks of life by a narrative that tells the deeds of specific, divine characters. It does not formulate a conceptual account of being, of the way human life inevitably appears. The story, rather, tells about the natural make-up and destiny of humans by saying which mythological figures formed them. It is not concerned with the general structures of Dasein (see Chapter 3) or with a methodology for making carefully conceptual and holistic claims about being.

"Ontological", on the other hand, refers to language and concepts about the ways beings inevitably occur. It refers directly to being as the ground of beings. *Being and Time,* as composing a fundamental ontology (*BTS* 11–14), is a philosophically disciplined account of the way being happens regardless of the circumstances, and when Heidegger speaks of being he addresses the necessities of our lives. Being implicates every aspect of human living, and a proper account of being will describe the structural inevitabilities of our existence. "Care" on his terms, for example, means the *inevitability* of concern, uncertainty, insecurity, projecting ahead and maintaining all aspects of our human engagements, as well as the desirability of responsibility and dedication. This inevitability for human being indicates the ontological character of the term, Care, as distinct from instances of concern, solicitude and organization. Philosophers can recognize these latter, ontic events as attesting to Care when they develop a method and language that can make evident the appearance of the ontological dimensions in particular occurrences. Our emphasis falls on the inseparability of ontic and ontological dimensions in human existence: ontic occurrences always have an ontological dimension, and ontological structures appear only in ontic happenings.

"Dasein" names for Heidegger the ontological dimension of human being, and *Being and Time* is a fundamental ontology in the sense that it provides an account of the way human beings must occur. Instead of giving an account of universal structures of human subjectivity, as many post-Kantian philosophers did in order to speak of human nature, Heidegger gives a description of the way Dasein happens. "Being-in-the-world" is a synonym for Dasein and names the way all people happen as interconnections with existing beings. We are beings who are constituted by worldly relations. When we speak of ontological inevitabilities and possibilities in this context we are speaking of Dasein, of the *happening* of perceptive worldly events. We can call specific individuals who live in their particular ways human beings. We will call their unified and occurring ontological structures Dasein. Human beings can live in ways more or less attuned to the inescapable ground of their existence, more or less ensnared by their environments, more or less in sync with the way they are ontologically.

Mortal temporality

According to the story of Care, Saturn, the God of time, is the decisive factor in adjudicating between and unifying the incompatible elements of Earth, Care and Jupiter (Spirit). Saturn rules humans' "temporal sojourn in the world" (*BTS* 185). Heidegger too addresses the unifying importance of Time but in an ontological account of it. Although the ontological structure of Care describes the meaning of human being in its constant neediness, it does not give unity to the occurrences of Dasein or account for the simultaneity of ontic and ontological circumstances in the midst of which people always find themselves. The welter of ontic circumstantial determinations into which we find ourselves thrown includes such things as physical and cultural inherit-ance and social and familial conditions. We are formed by all manner of worldly relations, and even our ability to recognize and deal with them is constituted by historical, cultural and social relations. We also find our existence defined by multiple unchosen ontological structures that determine the way our lives occur and make them fundamentally questionable instead of giving them timeless meaning and importance. Further, existence is torn by the simultaneous occurrence of the divisive difference between ontic and ontological determinations. As we saw, both universal structures and non-universal relativities constitute all human, worldly events and give vastly different types of meaning. In the midst of ontic answers to ultimate questions and everyday certainties, the lack of permanent certainty meant by Care always requires us constantly to plan and organize with concern. No answers or establishments eliminate the destabilizing force of Care. A gulf of difference ambiguously connects the specificities and universalities of existence. A present and always continuing identity does not rule this connection. Rather, the question of the meaning of being pervades Dasein while the many significances, purposes and plans for living motivate people to do much of what they do without question and as though being were guaranteed forever. And poor Care, in its powerful insufficiency, is not able even to give unity to the very being it defines.

Dasein's unity is found in the structure of finite time. The key to temporal unity, far from a pre-temporal and established basis for true human identity and action, is the phenomenon that Heidegger calls being-toward-the end or being-toward-death (*BTS* 231). Care defines the need of being human: the need to cope with circumstances and to project ahead of itself by planning, proposing, expecting and other future-oriented attitudes and actions. Care projects people now into the future by virtue of the inability of any present to continue as it is without end. Further, "the question of the meaning being" names the absence of final answers in the occurrence of life. There is no indication why being is, why we are shaped by Care, or that being will continue to be. "Being-toward-the-end" names the temporal mortality of being in all of its aspects, and Heidegger's description of it leads us directly to the issue of authenticity.

"With death", Heidegger wrote, "Da-sein stands before itself in its ownmost potentiality-of-being" (*BTS* 232).[2] The ability to die is both an ontological characteristic and something that each individual must go through; it is one's "ownmost" potentiality. Heidegger continues: "In this possibility, Da-sein is concerned about its being-in-the-world absolutely" (*ibid.*). Death gets my very specific attention because with it my being in the world comes to an end. Indeed, one's own inevitable "possibility of no-longer-being-able-to-be-there" (*ibid.*) brings starkly together individuals and their ontological inevitability: having to die shows most clearly the unity of finite time in the calamitous intimacy of existential requirement and personal singularity. The question of being reaches a singular disclosure, and the tear between ontic and ontological finds its destiny. Nothing is resolved in this disclosure. We find, rather, dissolution required by mortality's governance of temporality. Always coming to the end defines our capacity to be, our "ownmost potentiality for being" (*ibid.*).

In the immediacy of this ability not to be, Da-sein "is *completely* thrown back" upon itself (*ibid.*). The ontic and ontological dimensions together show a strange summons. I cannot avoid my own mortality no matter how successfully I forget it. I may refuse to own it and act inauthentically as though "they" die when I die. But according to Heidegger's account, I, not one, not they, must live my ending. This observation does not mean that people die in total isolation. The person who is able to die is very much a being-with-others (*BTS* §26), and this ontological capacity to cease is a structural part of being-in-the-world-with-others. The point is, rather, that being able not to be composes a possibility for individuals singularly to own – decisively to choose to be – their existence in its ontological necessities. An individual consciously opens up to the ontological immediacy of his or her being as though unlocking everyday closure to it. If people do not evade their ability to die and affirmatively relate to it in the ways they connect with the world and themselves, their lives can accord with the necessities of their being. They can live authentically and their own lives will show, as distinct from cover over, the way people fundamentally are.

Heidegger emphasizes that always coming to the end defines life. It defines life's incompleteness at any given moment, its potentiality, its power yet to be. The *absence* of perfectly completed life means possibility and futurity as long as being is happening.

Authenticity and resoluteness

When Heidegger speaks of people making their ability not to be their own, he does not have in mind being morbid or preoccupied with one's death (*BTS* 241). He means being attuned with one's Dasein, that is, attuned to the temporal structure of the way human beings have to be. Rather than living as though they were fulfilling the manifest destiny of some pre-established goals for all mankind, people foresee the world in terms of incomplete possibility. They care for people and things with the anticipation that lives will continue to be incomplete, marked by possibility and always in need of care. An opposite to such attunement is found in attitudes that treat people and things as no more than present realities, as though they were completed in some way or as though lives and spiritual identity were fully formed. Heidegger intends a way of living in which the ontological meaning of Dasein is apparent in an individual's life such that the incomplete and never fully grasped potentiality for being is apparent in the ways people live.

An authentic way of existing is one that requires individuals to take responsibility for their attitudes and actions. They individualize themselves as distinct from yielding the authority for their lives to others. Far from a rugged individualism that sanctions preference and idiosyncrasy for their own sake and the fantasy of self-sufficiency, Heidegger has in mind the singularity of a person's being alert to his or her own connection with the inevitabilities of existence throughout the world. The formal generality of the ontological structure becomes specifically and concretely one's own in the ways a person understands and connects with other living creatures. The way people appropriate Dasein as they interact in the world determines who each of them is in his or her singularity. Our "who", our singular selves, are constituted as world-relations. They do not become atomic entities by virtue of their decisive affirmation of their being. Indeed, their being is being-in-the-world, and authenticity is first, last and always intrinsically social, cultural and historical. But authentic individuals, as Heidegger interprets them, live in the everyday world and all of their entanglements with a quiet distance, with a clear and open sense of the priority of finite possibility and need over static reality. They are alert to their unsubstitutable liability to the dynamic and enabling mortality of being-in-the-world. They are dedicated to letting its unsettling futurity shine through their interactions.

Authenticity is grounded in Dasein as distinct from a particular society's practices. Authenticity could take place in all cultures and on the part of extremely different people. Dasein "calls" or "summons" individuals out of their everyday oblivion and to one's "own-most potentiality-of-being-a-self" whatever their circumstances (BTS 249). Heidegger names this summons the call of conscience, perhaps a misleading phrase, but one that names Dasein's insistent inclination to its own way of occurring in the midst of people's ordinary concerns and distractions (BTS 251ff.). As we forget our ontological inheritance in our everyday inauthentic existence, Dasein "calls" us back to the basics of our being.

The call of conscience happens as a mood in Dasein, an immediate and indelible feeling of disjunction and homelessness in the world. In the midst of everyday familiarity and identity there occurs a subtle, quiet, speechless mood of something lacking, of profound instability, of Angst. Heidegger describes this mood as "the most elemental disclosure of thrown Da-sein" (BTS 255). The very givenness of unavoidable thrownness in the world as mortally temporal is unsettling in the thick of our normal senses of meaning and significance. We usually know a wide variety of things we can count on. Dasein, on the other hand, manifests a lack of completed reality in the occurrence of present things. The concreteness of existence is eerily misleading. A sense that it could have been otherwise, that it has a weird ability to be otherwise or to cease being altogether, such a sense persistently pervades the mortal occurrence of ontic being in the world. This ontological sense might not be exactly the embodiment of Jupiter's gift of spirit to "Homo", but it does constitute an affective disclosure of Dasein's unceasing temporal difference from present real things. *Angst* is something like a haunted spirit that seems to whisper, as though to itself, "better take care ... it's coming to pass ... you come from nowhere ... where are you headed ... who are you?"

The call constitutes a kind of self-understanding on Dasein's part. In the mood of *Angst* Dasein occurs as immediate awareness of its own indefinite possibility and Care. It summons itself to care for itself by heeding its own feeling of mortal temporality. By paying attention to the ontological mood, people have a sense of their own difference from the absorptions of the day. They know that they transcend their circumstances in their ability yet to be. *Angst* communicates to people their transcendence of present reality, their thing-like roles, and the sum total of objectification and calculation. We experience this transcendence, ironically, not in a transcendental identity but in our always being indebted to the future (*BTS* 258ff.).[3]

We have seen that any living present of being-in-the-world lacks completion: it is not yet finished; it is characterized by mere possibility, by futurity. Consequently, Dasein and human beings are never something merely and objectively present. *Being* mortal, they are *not* fully there. They are present and yet to be at the same time. In that sense they are indebted to the future. Dasein is thus the ground for its own lack. How might people take responsibility for being this way? That is a major issue when we consider authenticity.

Authenticity is clearly not a matter of growing into an ideal identity. It means rather deciding to remain affirmatively alert to what no one can change: Dasein's mortal character of Care and the consequent impossibility of complete grasp of anything. In the force of such a decision people want to experience consciously their and others' basic *Angst* and incompleteness. They want their own attitudes and sensibilities to remain attuned to the way they fundamentally are and to attest to their "belonging to the being of Dasein" (*BTS* 266). Authentic people renounce overwhelming instrumentalism, and they practise a certain reticence and careful respect before other beings: they let beings show themselves in their own events. Authenticity means that people check their impulses to control and define their worlds by invasive actions. The differences of others thus often interrupt unconsidered inclinations to do what we are supposed to do under the banner of normal morality. Our ideals and values often change as we appropriate the many differences among people and affirm their freedom and search for meaning.

"Resoluteness" names a major aspect of authentic ways of being in the world (*BTS* 272ff.). We see that authentic people determine themselves with Dasein in mind. They care for the ontological difference that gives all living events transcendence of their objective values and identities. The strange and wonderful intangibility of people and things consists in part in their potentiality for being and their ability not to be. Authentic people are concerned to make their environments friendly to this intangibility and to the wonder of being when there is no clear reason for it at all. A body of intentions like these constitutes what Heidegger calls resoluteness: authentic people are resolved – strongly dedicated and open – to an affirmative attunement in their daily lives to the non-objectifiable intangibility of all events. The Care of Dasein meets itself in authentic lives in the world.

This resoluteness is "anticipatory" (*BTS* 279ff.). When people are attuned affirmatively to their being, they understand that their ungraspable eventuation means the strange freedom of always coming to the end of presence. In anticipatory resoluteness people make their daily decisions in clear understanding of Dasein's open and deathly occurrence. They *own* being-toward-death in those decisions and in the ways they carry out their projects and plans. A deep personal change occurs in such anticipatory resoluteness. Although the forces of everyday life continue, the everyday, normal self is qualified and enriched by a dimension of selfhood developed in decisive attentiveness to its ontological difference from the ontic aspects of existence. This dimension in being a self is ready for its inevitable *Angst* and uncertainty as well as for the inevitability of everyday occupations. It develops an understanding of beings in their anxious struggle to be and, I believe, on Heidegger's terms, an inclination to compassion that such alertness can breed. In Heidegger's words: "The resoluteness toward itself first brings Da-sein to the possibility of letting the others who are with it 'be' their ownmost potentiality-of-being, and also discloses that potentiality in concern which leaps ahead and frees" (*BTS* 274). Formally stated, authentic people care for the Care of others.

"Anticipatory resoluteness" thus names for Heidegger authentic, ontic appropriation of the meaning of existence (Care) and of the meaning of Care (mortal temporality). In it, people's ontic and ontological aspects find an area where they are complementary: people care for the meaning of being-in-the-world, and they do so by owning the mortality of their temporal being as they interact with others. In anticipatory resoluteness people individuate themselves according to the inevitabilities of their being, and their lives compose a genuine disclosure of the way being-in-the-world takes place.

You might have noticed that in Heidegger's account of authenticity the question of the meaning of being trumps questions of social justice, and the interruptions of everyday values trump issues of normative ethics. How can we hope, Heidegger asks in effect, to address practical issues wisely if we are oblivious to the meaning of being alive? The question of the meaning of being is neither a religious nor a theoretical question for Heidegger. It names the unresolvable uncertainty of finite being. Ignoring that question – leaping in and taking over by means of fully confident moral and political schemes and ideologies – leads to a perpetuation of inauthentic lives in which our goods and bads constitute oppressive refusals of our own being and continual violation of the way humans happen in the intangibility of their time.

The tragedy of using lives primarily for instrumental ends and according to hierarchical categories, the spiritual costs of ingrained banality and heedless certainty, the enormous dangers inherent in careless use of natural resources, the flight from life's inevitabilities in some destructive systems of belief, and the dangers that come with increasing technological sophistication and control are examples of areas where authenticity as Heidegger thinks of it could have direct bearing on people's assessments and responses. They might also be examples of developments that would not have grown as they did were authenticity a leading cultural and social component. *Being and Time* does not provide specific answers or values for addressing these crucial problems. But it does suggest a beginning for a way of thinking and living that intends a different direction of existence in comparison to the ones that spawned the kinds of crises that affect all of our lives today.

Notes

1. I shall capitalize Care when I refer to it as an ontological structure or as the figure in the story. I shall use the lower case when I refer to care as an attitude or verb. I shall also use the capitalized Time when I refer to it as an ontological structure.
2. *BTS* uses the word Da-sein instead of Dasein. Unless I quote directly from that text, I shall use Dasein.
3. Heidegger speaks of being guilty regarding the future. His native German uses the same word, *Schuld*, for "debt" and "guilt", and it can also mean "sin". One of his goals was to show that Dasein, and not divine presence, accounts for a human sense of basic insufficiency. That intention is not clearly expressed in English when "guilt" and "debt" are aligned in *Being and Time*. I shall use "debt" and "lack" in this context and avoid the misleading use of "guilt".

Further reading

Primary sources
See Heidegger's *Being and Time*, part I, chapter VI; part II, chapters I–IV.

Secondary sources
See Bernasconi (1993); Davis (2007); Krell (1986: esp. "Mortality, Interpretation, and the Poetical Life"); Polt (1999: esp. "Being and Time, Division II and Beyond"); Scott (1990); and Zimmerman (1986).

FIVE

Being and time

Richard Polt

At first – before this "first" was generated or the "after" was wanted – time was not, but was at rest with itself in what *is*, and itself kept quiet in what *is*. But there was a busy, active nature, wanting to rule itself and be its own, choosing to seek more than the present, that moved itself, and time moved too; and always moving on to the "next" and the "later" and to what is not the same but one after another, we turned our journey into a long stretch and fabricated time as an image of eternity. For there was an unquiet power of soul that always wanted to transfer what it saw there into something else, that was unwilling for the whole to be present to it all at once.   (Plotinus, *Enneads* 3.7.11)

The human being is a creature of distance! And only by way of the real primordial distance that the human in his transcendence establishes toward all beings does the true nearness to things begin to grow in him.   (Heidegger, *MFL* 221)

Plotinus and Heidegger – one of the greatest Platonists and a philosopher who viewed Platonism as a colossal dead end – have this in common: for them, time is not simply an aspect of change, or a subjective framework for perceiving change. Time is rooted in our very essence, in our concern with our own being. For us, our existence is at issue: we are faced with the task of making someone of ourselves, of deciding who and how to be. But this means that there is a gap between our given being and our possible being, between facticity and futurity. The future – not simply as a set of events that have not yet been realized, but as the need to come to grips with our own existence – generates time and, along with it, generates our interpretations of the world and all that is in it.

The contrast lies here: Plotinus, harking back to the roots of Greek thought in Parmenides and anticipating much of the later Western tradition, sees the primal event, the event that distances the present from the future, as a fall. Full presence, full being, would not be torn asunder; it would be a self-contained plenitude without distance. Against this tradition, Heidegger asks why we understand being as presence in the first place, and proposes in *Being and Time* that this understanding is made possible by our own temporality. Our extension into future, past and present is more primordial than our encounters with present entities. When we take presence as the definitive sense of being, we lose sight of its roots in time, and inevitably misunderstand ourselves; this absorption in the present, not the loss of eternity, is the true fall. Heidegger thus seeks his founding insights not in a putative moment of full presence, but in the recognition of our deep temporality.

Time as the horizon for being

The publication of Wilhelm Dilthey and Count Yorck's letters on historicity was the occasion for Heidegger to compose what was to serve as the first draft of *Being and Time*, a 1924 text titled *The Concept of Time* (*GA* 64).[1] Here Heidegger puts it bluntly: "*Each Dasein is itself 'time'*" (*GA* 64: 57); "Dasein is history" (*GA* 64: 86). Time and history are neither obstacles to our fulfilment nor simply arenas in which we happen to act, but are the heart of our own being. To be human is to be temporal and historical; conversely, time and history can be understood only with reference to ourselves.

In conjunction with Heidegger's hermeneutics of facticity (see Chapter 1), these thoughts on temporality point to a new ontology of the *human* way of being. But humans also use time as a general ontological guideline, a way of understanding *all* entities (time serves as an ontological criterion when we distinguish being and becoming, or timeless and temporal realms; *SZ* 18). Heidegger's temporal interpretation of human being thus demands a new approach to the question of being in general, as well as a critique of how time and being have traditionally been understood.

Being and Time develops these thoughts with the aim of showing that time is the "horizon" for any understanding of being (*SZ* 1, 17, 235): our temporality makes it possible for being to mean something to us. Were we not temporal, we could not distinguish entities from nonentities; beings could not make a difference to us, or strike us as significant. We could not "be there" at all: there would be no Dasein, and thus no one to whom being could be given.

Division One lays the groundwork for the thesis that time is the horizon for being by means of a phenomenology of everyday being-in-the-world (see Chapter 3). We find ourselves "thrown" into a given situation (*SZ* §29); we also "project" possibilities in terms of which we understand ourselves and other beings (*SZ* §31). Dasein is "*thrown possibility* through and through" (*SZ* 144): both projection and thrownness are at work whenever we are absorbed in a present state of affairs. This analysis culminates in a conception of Dasein's being as "care", which is given an implicitly temporal definition: "ahead-of-itself-being-already-in-(the-world) as being-amidst (entities encountered within-the-world)" (*SZ* 192, trans. mod.).

Division Two deepens this interpretation of Dasein and brings out temporality more explicitly by considering phenomena that interrupt and transcend everydayness. In facing my own death, I recognize that all my possibilities are shadowed by my possible non-existence (Division Two, ch. I). In facing my primordial guilt, I recognize that I am responsible for choosing my own defining possibility and that I have to do so on the basis of what I already am (ch. II). In "anticipatory resoluteness", I respond authentically to death and guilt; this authentic response yields insight into the primordial temporality of Dasein (ch. III) and enables us to reinterpret everydayness in terms of this temporality (ch. IV). In the dramatic climax of *Being and Time*, Heidegger points to "historicality" as the deep temporality of being with others in a group that shares a heritage and is working out a communal destiny (ch. V). Finally, he argues that the ordinary conception of linear clock time arises from everyday falling (ch. VI).

Let us look more closely at the three dimensions of Dasein's "primordial temporality": future, past and present.

Futurity essentially involves our concern with who we are: Dasein is "*being out toward* what it is not yet, but can be" (*GA* 64, 46). Thus we always understand ourselves and our surroundings in terms of a possible way for us to be (*SZ* 43, 86). Facing up to death allows us to recognize this futurity as a "coming in which Dasein, in its ownmost potentiality-for-being, comes towards itself" (*SZ* 325). What Heidegger means by "death" and whether his emphasis on it is appropriate have long been subjects of controversy. It is helpful to remember that "death" does not mean "demise", or the termination of human life (*SZ* 247). Heideggerian "death" is really *mortality*: a possibility rather than an actual event. Death is "the possible no-longer-there" (*GA* 64: 52), or the possibility of the impossibility of being-there any more (*SZ* 250). If this possibility is actualized, we cease to exist, and nothing can have meaning for us. But as long as we are existing, the possibility of death stands before us, urging us to choose to exist authentically, to decide on one possible way of being-in-the-world at the expense of others that we must forego (*SZ* 285). The phenomenon of "being-towards-death" thus reveals possibility as such, in a sense that cannot be reduced to present actuality.

Pastness, or having-been, is also essential to us: Dasein "*is* its past, whether explicitly or not" (*SZ* 20). Whether we take our facticity for granted or appropriate it creatively, we are situated in a milieu into which we have been "thrown". We experience this thrownness as mood, which plays an essential role in disclosing the world (*SZ* §29). Pastness also collaborates with futurity: "Only in so far as Dasein *is* as an 'I-am-as-having been,' can Dasein come towards itself futurally in such a way that it comes *back*. ... The character of 'having been' arises, in a certain way, from the future" (*SZ* 326). Choosing a possible way to be requires making something of what one already finds oneself to be: one has to take up one's own past as an unavoidable burden and inheritance. In this way, the past provides possibilities for the future: Dasein "has already got itself into definite possibilities" (*SZ* 144) or "abandoned itself" to them (*SZ* 270); resoluteness discloses these possibilities as such (*SZ* 298) by "repeating" or retrieving them (*SZ* 339, 385): appropriating them as guiding interpretations of existence.

This authentic, futural retrieval of the past is "precisely proper becoming-present" (*GA* 64: 94): it "discloses the current Situation of the 'there'" (*SZ* 326) and achieves a "moment of vision" (*SZ* 328, 338). Presence, then, is at its fullest not when time is suspended or when we live only in the "now" (as if such things were possible), but when we draw most authentically on the future and past dimensions of our being. Heidegger thus denies presence its traditional ontological priority, and insists that the present becomes available to us only through the interplay of future and past (*SZ* 350–51). The traditional focus on presence is not simply an intellectual error, but is due to "falling", or Dasein's tendency to get absorbed inauthentically in the present (*SZ* 328).

Heidegger emphasizes several traits of primordial temporality (*SZ* 329–30). First, it is *ecstatic*: the future, past and present are ways in which we "stand out" into possibilities, facticity and the current situation. Time does not consist of pointlike instants, but stretches into three dimensions. Secondly, the primary temporal ecstasis is the *future*: the present and past are awakened as such by Dasein's need to pursue

72

some *possible* way of existing (as Plotinus puts it, the soul wants to "rule itself "). Time is also *finite*, in that the future is always limited by the possibility of death; this is not to deny that the universe will outlast me, but futurity itself is disclosed to me only because I am faced with mutually exclusive possibilities, all of which are exposed to the possibility of my own extinction.

These traits of temporality may not be apparent in everydayness, and when we conceive of time using everyday common sense, we do so in very different terms: we picture time as a line whose intervals can be measured by a clock, and we assign priority to the present instant. This ordinary conception of time is impoverished; even aside from the aspects of temporality that are disclosed only in authenticity, a phenomenological inspection of everyday temporality shows that the ordinary conception omits several crucial features. Everyday time is *public* and *worldly*: we share our time with others with whom we share our world (*SZ* 411–12). Furthermore, everyday time is *datable* and *significant*. It is not an empty, formal structure, but is tied to particular events and purposes; time is always time *for* this or that (*SZ* 407, 414). The phenomenon of the *right* time – the appropriate moment – is primary. Of course, there can also be wrong times and so-called "senseless" events, but these are the exceptions that prove the rule: we understand them in terms of appropriateness. Thus, although we may correctly lay out a timeline for certain purposes, this quantitative, neutral succession is founded on meaningful time, and not the other way round; significance trumps sequence.

Our everyday unawareness of primordial temporality and our tendency to reduce all time to clock time must stem from a certain inauthenticity in everyday temporality itself. The authentic future, past and present consist in anticipation (authentically facing death), repetition (retrieving past possibilities), and the moment of vision (see Chapter 4); their inauthentic, everyday counterparts are awaiting, forgetting (one's own thrownness), and making present (*SZ* 336–9). Because it is mired in these relatively oblivious modes of temporality, everydayness is insensitive to the genuinely unique; nothing seems to happen for the first or last time (*GA* 64: 75–6; *SZ* 370–71). In contrast, primordial time plunges us into "the unique this-once-ness [*Diesmaligkeit*] of [our] being-*there*" (*GA* 64: 82). The urgency of our own existence is diluted in everydayness, and we tend to notice only the changes occurring in the entities we encounter, changes that lend themselves to measurement in terms of linear clock time. Such measurement is legitimate within its limits, but primordial time is phenomenologically prior: were it not for the ecstatic time of Dasein, we could not encounter other entities to begin with, much less measure their changes (*SZ* 333). In order to reconnect to this primordial temporality, we cannot just sharpen our concepts; we must seize on our own existence authentically. I cannot simply ask, "What is time?"; I must ask myself, "*Am* I time?" (*GA* 64: 83).

The unfinished and never published Division Three of Part One of *Being and Time* was supposed to pass beyond this account of Dasein's temporality in order to support the main thesis of the work. Heidegger planned to show how our temporality (*Zeitlichkeit*) functions as the horizon for being, such that being itself is characterized by "Temporality" (*Temporalität*) (*SZ* 19). Although this project was not completed, we can find the rudiments of it in several texts. According to §69c of *Being and Time*, the three "ecstases" of time disclose three "horizonal schemata" in terms of which we can understand the modes of being. Thanks to the horizonal schema of "the for-the-sake-of-itself", we understand possibilities (*SZ* 365; see also *MFL* 208). Thanks to the horizonal schema of "what has been", we understand facticity (*SZ* 365). Thanks to the horizonal schema that Heidegger dubs *praesens*, we understand presence-at-hand and readiness-to-hand (*BPP* 305–7). The question, then, is how these various modes of being cohere and can be brought together under a single concept (*SZ* 333).

One might try to resist Heidegger's subordination of natural, linear time to the temporality of Dasein: was there not a time before Dasein? In 1935 he replies: "strictly speaking, we cannot say there was a time when there were no human beings. At every *time*, there were and are and will be human beings, because time temporalizes itself only as long as there are human beings" (*IM* 88–9). He makes much the same claim some three decades later: "Strictly speaking, we cannot say what happened before the human being existed. Neither can we say that the Alps existed, nor can we say that they did not" (*ZS* 55–6). These passages are very similar to the claims in *Being and Time* that truth and being are dependent on Dasein (*SZ* 212, 226–7). Heidegger's point is not the triviality that there would be no one to say or know anything about beings if no one existed. Nor is he espousing absolute idealism: the view that it is false or meaningless to claim that there are entities in themselves, independent of us. Instead, this claim is both meaningful and correct, but its meaning and truth always presuppose the fundamental significance and disclosure that belong to Dasein's temporal existence. That is, factually correct statements about pre-human nature depend on the human temporality that allows these statements to be intelligible. This means that such statements can never explain human temporality itself; our time can never be reduced to empirical facts.

We could thus speak with William Blattner of "Heidegger's temporal idealism". Realism and idealism may be superficial categories, yet idealism has the advantage of recognizing that being cannot be reduced to beings, "but is already that which is 'transcendental' for every entity" (*SZ* 207). Similarly, Dasein's temporality is transcendental for every event within time. Tracing our temporality back to a set of facts in serial, objective time would be a reductive "myth" (see *SZ* 6). There can be no empirical account of the origin of Dasein's time, because Dasein's time is what makes all accounts possible. As Heidegger puts it in 1927, "[Dasein's] *time is earlier than any possible earlier* of whatever sort, because it is the basic condition for an earlier as such" (*BPP* 325).

The inception of time and the event of being

Although Heidegger never countenanced naturalistic explanations of human time, he became dissatisfied with the transcendental standpoint of *Being and Time* shortly after its publication, and embarked on a philosophical transformation that can be summed up in the slogan: "from the understanding of being to the happening of being" (*GA* 40: 219). The new phase of his thought that comes into full swing in the 1930s understands being itself as happening historically, and recognizes Dasein's facticity as a way in which we ourselves are claimed by the happening of being and participate in its unfolding destiny (see Chapter 11). Ecstatic time is no longer simply primordial, and natural time is not simply derivative; we are indebted to nature, but are raised above it at founding moments that generate ecstatic, meaningful time.

As we have seen, *Being and Time* stands in the transcendental tradition inaugurated by Kant: just as Kant enquires into the structures of subjectivity as the conditions of the possibility of experience, Heidegger enquires into the temporality of Dasein as the condition of the possibility of understanding being and beings. But the transcendental approach threatens to obscure Dasein's profound historicity and facticity; it tends to create the impression that Dasein stands above all other beings and functions as a framework that sets a fixed horizon for what being can mean. In his lecture course of Winter Semester 1929–30, Heidegger thus calls the whole notion of a temporal horizon into question. "What does it mean to say that time is a horizon? ... we do not have the slightest intimation of the abysses of the essence of time" (*FCM* 146).

If Dasein is not something like a transcendental subject hovering above other beings, then Dasein is part of what there is: it is an entity amid entities, even though it is extraordinary because it has some understanding of being. The project of interpreting this condition is described under the rubric of "metontology" in *The Metaphysical Foundations of Logic*: "the entity 'man' understands being … the possibility that being is there in the understanding presupposes the factical existence of Dasein, and this in turn presupposes the factual presence at hand of nature" (*MFL* 156–7, trans. mod.). We thus need a way to think about the thrownness of our thinking: the indebtedness of our understanding of being to an ontic ground from which it emerges. Heidegger now tries to grasp this dual character of Dasein, doing justice not only to our projection of a meaningful "world", but also to our dependence on an "earth" on which our world is grounded, an earth that we can never fully comprehend (see "The Origin of the Work of Art" [1935], in *BW*).

Heidegger's new perspective makes it legitimate to ask: how does Dasein's time – the ecstatic temporality that grants us access to other entities – first emerge? "The primal fact … is that there is anything like temporality at all. The entrance into world by beings is primal history pure and simple" (*MFL* 209). Can we enquire into this primal fact, and investigate how historical time begins? "Can one ask, 'How does time arise?'" Heidegger increasingly believes that one can, but he cannot give the Platonist answer: "through the deformation and restriction of eternity" (*UV* 9). Nor can he try to answer the question in physical or biological terms; this empirical, naturalistic approach would simply disregard the whole problematic of being while naively presupposing some ontology. Dasein's temporality is not to be reduced to scientific findings about nature, since science itself depends on this temporality. "Primal history" must emerge from nature as *earth*, which is deeper and more mysterious than the nature discovered by science.

In order to reflect appropriately on the origin of time, Heidegger begins to think in terms of a mysterious founding event from which meaningful time and being erupt. This event is, to put it paradoxically, the time when time begins. "Ever since time arose and was brought to stand, since then we *are* historical" ("Hölderlin and the Essence of Poetry", in *EHP* 57). This origin of time is an "inception" (*Anfang*) rather than a mere "beginning" (*Beginn*). According to the 1941 text *Über den Anfang*:

> "beginning" … means a distinctive position and phase in the course of a process. But … here the word "inception" is supposed to name the essence of be-ing [*Seyn*].… To start inceptively [*Anfangen*] is to seize oneself and raise oneself up in the appropriating event itself, the event as which the clearing essentially happens.   (*GA* 70: 9–10)

Only in an inception does a clearing open against concealment; in inception, the difference between being and non-being takes place. With the obsolete spelling *Seyn*, Heidegger here indicates this event of inception, rather than a particular sense of what it is to be; all such senses are generated in the inception. Our mission is to participate creatively in this event that is the source of truth, worldhood, history and Dasein itself. In this event, a qualitatively new kind of time, meaningful time, comes to be in a way that cannot be reduced to the natural sequence that precedes it: "Why is this sudden moment of 'world history' essentially and abyssally other than all the 'millions of years' of worldless processes? Because this suddenness lights up the uniqueness of be-ing ... The 'moment' is the origin of 'time' itself" (*GA* 66: 113–14). An inception emerges from the earth and founds a new, ecstatic temporality that spreads open a world.

Heidegger often thinks of inception as a poetic event (see Chapter 14). "Poetry is the fundamental happening of be-ing as such. It founds be-ing and must found it" (*GA* 39: 257). Poetry happens at the times when time itself happens most intensely: the moments that Heidegger, following Hölderlin, calls "the peaks of time" (*GA* 39: 52, 56). These poetic peaks are the origin of ecstatic, primordial time:

> In this holding-sway-forward of what has been into the future, which, pointing back, opens what was already preparing itself earlier as such, there holds sway the coming-towards and the still-essentially-happening (future and past) at once: originary time. ... This originary time transports our Dasein into the future and past, or better, brings it about that our being as such is a transported being – if it is authentic, that is. ... In such time, time "comes to be" ...   (*GA* 39: 109)

This passage recalls *Being and Time*'s description of the ecstatic interplay of future, past and present. But while the language of *Being and Time* can suggest that ecstatic temporality is a fixed structure, Heidegger now presents time as gushing forth at great historical moments that establish a way of existing for a people or an age.

Poets are not the only founders; in the mid 1930s Heidegger typically speaks of the triumvirate of poet, thinker and statesman. "Founding" is, among other things, a political concept, and it is not a coincidence that Heidegger is thinking about the founding of time during a period of revolution and political "inception". What is at stake, as he says in 1934, is "a transformation of our entire being in its relation to the power of time ... this transformation depends on ... how we temporalize time itself. ... [We] *ourselves are time*" (*GA* 38: 120).

The *Contributions to Philosophy* (1936–8; hereafter *Contributions*) give the inception of time and being the name *Ereignis*, which normally means "event" but also echoes the word *eigen* (own, proper). The appropriating event is "the event of the grounding of the there" (*GA* 65: 183). In this event, Dasein comes into its own because it comes to belong to the happening of being (see Chapter 10). At this moment, we are seized or appropriated by an inception. We can then properly "be there", and things can gain their proper places and significance. Entities become interpretable, accessible, explicable; but the original appropriating event cannot itself be explained as if it were just an entity. It eludes our search for grounds; it is an abyss.

We could also think of *Ereignis* as the event in which the human being becomes, as Heidegger put it in *The Metaphysical Foundations of Logic*, "a creature of distance". *Being and Time* already insisted that the fact that our own being is an issue for us is essential to temporality and to our understanding of being. But how does our being *come to be* an issue for us? We must first be separated from our own being, so that it becomes something towards which we can adopt, or fail to adopt, a stance. We are indebted, then, to a strange event, the event of estrangement itself: a disquieting event in which we are distanced from ourselves, so that we are then faced with the *task* of being ourselves. As the domain of selfhood unfolds, so does the "there": the space in which we can encounter and interpret beings (*GA* 65: 320).

The appropriating event would take place at a "site of the moment" where "time-space" would emerge. Heidegger's tentative description of time-space (*GA* 65: §242) is best read not as a transcendental account of the "formal concepts" of time and space in general (*GA* 65: 261), but as an attempt to speak of a unique moment that would initiate (or perhaps re-initiate) meaningful time and space. The *Contributions* describe time-space as an "abyssal ground" that opens a domain of unconcealment, yet denies this domain any absolute foundation. Time-space implicates us in the unfolding of Western history as Heidegger understands it: it ties us back to "the first inception" of the revelation of being among the Greeks, readies us for "the other inception" that may bring a new destiny of being, and ties us to the present as the site where the current "abandonment" of being must be endured.

As this last thought suggests, for Heidegger in this period, being is not constantly given; "be-ing is at times" (*das Seyn ist zuzeiten*; *GA* 70: 15). How often do these times come? Has such a time ever fully taken place? The answers are elusive. "When and how long being 'is' cannot be asked" (*GA* 69: 145).

Receiving the gift of time and being

In the last phase of his thought, beginning around 1940, Heidegger de-emphasizes the quasi-political moment of inceptive founding, and instead concentrates on cultivating gratitude for time, truth and being as dispensations from *Ereignis* itself. As we can see in the *Zollikon Seminars* of the 1950s and 1960s, where Heidegger introduces a group of psychiatrists to phenomenology, he remains loyal to *Being and Time*'s analysis of everyday temporality: it is datable, ecstatic, public and significant. But he now seeks authentic temporality neither through deathbound resoluteness nor in powerful moments of inception, but in *Gelassenheit* – a non-wilful "releasement" that can admit us into unconcealment, allowing us to receive the gift of being (see Chapter 12).

The late lecture "Time and Being" (1962) is an introduction to *Ereignis* as that which gives both being and time. Being appears to be governed by time, because being seems tantamount to presence, which is a temporal determination. Time, in turn, appears to be governed by being, because time seems to be constantly present (*TB* 3). Yet neither time nor being is an entity; we can say only that they are given. How are they given, then? Being is given as an anonymous donation, so to speak: it is "sent" by a hidden source (*TB* 8). Time is given as the "time-space" (*TB* 14) or "nearness" (*TB* 15) that opens in the extending of future, past and present. In the giving of being and time we can discern "a dedication [*Zueignen*], a delivering over [*Übereignen*] into what is their own [*ihr Eigenes*]" (*TB* 19). The fitting word, then, for the source that gives us being and time and unites them is *Ereignis*. *Ereignis* withdraws or conceals itself, so it includes its own "expropriation"; yet it also appropriates us, bringing us into our own. Because *Ereignis* intimately constitutes us, we cannot objectify it in propositions (*TB* 23).

Heidegger's reflections in this lecture are highly abstract and preliminary. It would seem, though, that he has backed away from thinking of *Ereignis* as the time when time begins. In contrast to the *Contributions*, which frequently describe *Ereignis* as an inceptive or inaugural happening (e.g. *GA* 65: 57, 183, 247), several post-war essays insist that it is not a happening at all (*IDS* 36; *OWL* 127). Heidegger warns us that "time itself is nothing temporal" (*TB* 14) and that we should not misconstrue appropriation – again, "something which is not temporal" – as an event within time (*TB* 20, 47). Heidegger has apparently returned to a quasi-transcendental standpoint. The usual sense of the word *Ereignis* (event) seems to have disappeared: *Ereignis* is no longer a historical inception from which truth and being erupt, but appears to be a timeless ground (see Polt 2005).

We can conclude with a few historical comparisons. Heidegger stands in a tradition that links time with the soul; like Augustine, for example, he highlights our ecstatic extension into the three dimensions of time, an extension that Augustine identifies with the mental acts of expectation, recollection and attention (*Confessions* 11.27–8). Husserl's phenomenology of "internal time consciousness" also follows this line of thought; here Husserl applies his discriminative genius to temporal experiences such as "protention" and "retention" (see Husserl 1991).

Heidegger insists that there is more at stake in time than the observation of passing events: our very self is ineluctably temporal, because it is in time that we discover or create who we are and where we stand. Augustine comes close to this insight through his concern with the temporality of sin and redemption (see *PRL* 127–84), but his Christian Platonism orients him towards the eternal and leads him to see time itself as fallen. As for Husserl, his paradigmatic example of temporal experience is listening to a series of tones: a case of disengaged observation that may not shed light on temporal phenomena that grip us personally, such as guilt or fate. Heidegger, who edited a volume of Husserl's lectures on time, never explicitly criticizes his mentor's approach, but he must have seen it as derivative and limited; the temporality of observation presupposes the deeper temporality of Dasein's being-in-the-world.

In the name of retrieving this temporality, Heidegger deconstructs traditional ontology. This deconstruction can help us untangle certain conundrums about time and being. For example, philosophers have often asked whether time itself exists: it seems to consist of what is no longer, what is not yet, and what is only for an infinitesimal instant (Aristotle, *Physics* 4.10; Augustine, *Confessions* 11.14). Heidegger's approach allows us to "show on the basis of 'time' that this kind of question cannot be asked anymore" (*GA* 64: 61 n.). When we ask whether time "exists" or "is", we presuppose some understanding of being – and almost inevitably, we understand presence as the primary or central sense of being (*GA* 64: 101; *SZ* 25–6). But if *Being and Time* is right, our access to presence is itself made possible by time. Time, then, cannot be subordinated to presence; time itself makes presence meaningful.

Heidegger's temporal deconstruction of traditional ontology is not a demolition; it brings out the limited validity of the tradition. An ontology of presence has its legitimate scope as "an ontology of the world in which every Dasein is" (*GA* 64: 103): that is, it illuminates the present-at-hand entities within this world. What it cannot illuminate is Dasein's own temporality and historicity.

Heidegger leaves us with no final solutions, but with fresh concepts and new questions. Among many, we can mention the problem of how to conceive of God once traditional notions of time and being have been exposed to the Heideggerian critiques. Platonism is a powerful factor in traditional theology, and monotheists may find it almost impossible to understand their religion except in relation to a timeless presence. Heidegger's thought suggests the perhaps refreshing, perhaps troubling, alternative of thinking of a god as an event: "passing by" may be precisely how the gods are present (*GA 39*: 111). It may be that our deepest destiny does not return us to a divine eternity, but awakens us to the opening of a divine distance: a distance that is also a divine nearness.

Note

1. A short lecture based on this text, by the same name, is also included in this volume of the *Collected Edition* and is available in English (*CT*).

References

Aristotle 1969. *Physics*, H. G. Apostle (trans.). Bloomington, IN: Indiana University Press.

Augustine 1961. *Confessions*, R. S. Pine-Coffin (trans.). Baltimore, MD: Penguin.

Husserl, E. 1991. *On the Phenomenology of the Consciousness of Internal Time (1893–1917)*, J. B. Brough (trans.). Dordrecht: Kluwer.

Plotinus 1966. *Enneads*, with English trans. by A. H. Armstrong. Cambridge, MA: Harvard University Press.

Polt, R. 2005. "Ereignis". In *A Companion to Heidegger*, H. L. Dreyfus & M. Wrathall (eds), 375–91. Oxford: Blackwell.

Further reading

Primary sources

See Heidegger's *The Basic Problems of Phenomenology*; *Being and Time*, Division Two; "The Concept of Time", in *Becoming Heidegger: On the Trail of His Early Occasional Writings, 1910–1927*; "Time and Being", in *On Time and Being*; and *Zollikon Seminars: Protocols – Conversations – Letters*, esp. 33–67.

Secondary sources

See Blattner (1999); Dastur (1998); Polt (2005: esp. chs 2, 9, 11); Polt (2006: esp. 72–87 on *Ereignis* as event and 180–92 on time-space); and Wood (2001: pt III).

SIX

The turn

Thomas Sheehan

The term *die Kehre* – "the turn" – has an over-determined and complex history in Heidegger's work and has led to major misunderstandings of his project. As Heidegger clearly says in *Contributions to Philosophy* (*GA 65 = CP*), the turn is simply the bond between *Dasein* and *Sein*. Therefore, the turn in its basic and proper sense is the central topic of Heidegger's thought. It is not, as many think, the 1930s shift in Heidegger's approach to his central topic. The *Kehre* in its basic and proper sense never "took place", least of all in Heidegger's thinking.[1]

I shall distinguish three meanings of "the turn": (i) the basic and proper sense – the bond between *Dasein* and *Sein*; (ii) the 1930s shift in how Heidegger treated that bond; and (iii) the act of resolve as a transformation in one's relation to that bond.

Because the turn is Heidegger's central topic, explaining it entails reviewing the core of Heidegger's thought. This chapter will attempt to do that within a new key, one that translates Heidegger's technical terms out of an ontological and into a phenomenological register. That re-translation is the necessary prologue to understanding what the *Kehre* is and is not.

Some conventions: in referring to "the turn" (not "the turning"!) in this chapter, I shall favour the German word *Kehre*, which Heidegger interprets as the "reciprocity" (*Gegenschwung*) of *Dasein*'s need of *Sein* and *Sein*'s need of *Dasein*. The Latin *reci-proci-tas* means literally "back-and-forth-ness", which is how Heidegger understands the tension or "oscillation" (*Erzittern*) between *Dasein*'s thrownness into and its sustaining of *Sein*.[2] Also I shall sometimes use the technical term "world" as the name for *Sein*.[3] As regards the structure of *Being and Time*, I shall use the formula "*BT* I.1–2" to abbreviate Part One, Divisions 1 and 2; and "*BT* I.3" to abbreviate the unpublished Part One, Division 3, "Time and Being". Finally, I use "man" and "human being" as gender-neutral and as the most formal of indications of what Heidegger means by *Dasein*.[4]

Re-reading Heidegger

Aron Gurwitsch correctly noted that the one and only issue of philosophy – including Heidegger's philosophy – is the question of meaning (*Sinn*) (Gurwitsch 1947: 652). But on the other hand Heidegger's key terms "being itself" and "the being of beings" come from a *pre*-phenomenological metaphysics of objective realism, and to that degree are an obstacle to understanding his project in general and the *Kehre* in particular. If one chooses (unwisely, in my view) to continue using those pre-phenomenological terms, one should be clear that Heidegger himself understood *Sein* phenomenologically, that is, within a reduction from *being* to *meaning*, both (a) as giving meaning to the meaningful (= *das Sein des Seienden*) and (b) as the meaning-giving *source* of the meaning of the meaningful (= *das Ereignis*).

When Heidegger speaks of *das Seiende* ("beings"), he is referring to things not as just existing-out-there (*existens*) but rather in so far as they make sense within human concerns and thus are meaningful and significant (*bedeutsam, verständlich, sinnhaft*). Even what is "just out there" (*das Vorhandene*) is meaningful as, for example, "what happens to be of no practical interest at the moment". In short, *das Seiende* is "the meaningful", and *das Sein* gives it meaning. To adapt Woody Allen's phrase: meaning is just another way of spelling being.[5]

In his first course after the First World War, Heidegger made the point by asking his students what it is they directly encounter in lived experience. Is it beings? things? objects? values? No, he insisted. What one encounters is

> *the meaningful* [das Bedeutsame] – that is what is primary, that is what is immediately in your face without any mental detour through a conceptual grasp of the thing. When you live in the world of first-hand experience, everything comes at you loaded with meaning, all over the place and all the time. Everything appears in a meaningful context, and that context *gives the thing its meaning*.   (GA 55/57: 73.1–5 = *TDF* 61.24–8)[6]

83

To underline the point Heidegger frequently refers to this phenomenological "being of beings" as *das Anwesen des Anwesenden*: the meaningful presence of whatever is meaningful. Likewise he glosses the Greek *on* and *ousia* as *paron* and *parousia*, that is, not mere "beings" and their "beingness" but meaningful things and their meaningfulness.

Let us then revisit Aristotle's famous sentence about the meanings of the word "being": "The term 'being' has many meanings, but all of them point analogically toward one thing, one single nature" (*Metaphysics* IV 2, 1003a33–4). Read in a phenomenological key, that says:

The word "meaningful" has many senses, but all of them point analogically toward a unified "meaning itself" [*Sein selbst* as *Ereignis*] that is the source of all meaning.

Before applying all of this to the *Kehre*, and in order to emphasize that Heidegger's work is anchored in a framework of *meaning*, I translate some of his terminology out of the usual ontological register into a phenomenological one (see Table 1).

The following may suffice for now:

1. All the terms in the chart have the character of what Aristotle calls *to proteron tēi physei* and *to ti ēn einai*, that is, that which, in any given situation, is always-already (*a priori*) operative. The terms in section II name the *a priori* process of meaning-giving. This process has no chronological date: it does not occur only occasionally but is always-already operative. It is the basic structural factum that is *a priori* at work in conjunction with human being.[7]
2. The terms in section II refer to the *meaning-giving source* of the meaningfulness of things. However, this source is not some hypostasis separate from and lying behind the meaning of the meaningful. Rather, the genitive in such phrases as *Wesen/Lichtung/Wahrheit/ Da des Seins* indicates a pleonasm: *Sein selbst is* its *Wesen/Lichtung/ Wahrheit/Da*. That is, *Seyn* (*das Wesen des Seins*) is the *a priori* condition whereby things get their meanings. And such meaning-giving never happens apart from human being.
3. Readers who are uncomfortable with the translations in the chart can simply substitute – without any damage to the argument – the traditional Heideggerian code words for the terms I use here, namely, be-ing / beyng, being itself, being, beingness, and beings; the swaying/destining/essencing/presencing/clearing/truth of being, along with enowning, enquivering, cleavage and the like.

Table 1.

I	*Sinn, Bedeutung*	sense, meaningfulness, meaning
	Sinn haben	something makes sense
	Verstehen	to make sense of something
	Seiendes	the meaningful, whatever makes sense
	Seiendheit des Seienden	the meaning of a meaningful thing
	Ereignis	the meaning-giving source of the meaning of a meaningful thing
II	*Sein selbst*	
	Seyn	
	Es gibt Sein	
	Welt	the *a priori* process of meaning-giving in and with human being
	Wesen des Seins	
	Wahrheit des Seins	
	Lichtung des Seins	
	Schickung des Seins	
III	*das Da des Seins*	"where" meaning-giving is *a priori* operative
	Dasein	man as sustaining/holding open the *a priori* process of meaning-giving
	Entwerfen	projectively sustaining/holding open the *a priori* process of meaning-giving
	geworfen	thrown into sustaining/holding open the *a priori* process of meaning-giving
	Ereignis	the appropriation of man to sustaining the *a priori* process of meaning-giving
	Kehre	the turn: the reciprocal bond of man and meaning

What the *Kehre* is and is not

The basic question motivating all of Heidegger's work is quite simply "How does meaning occur at all?" (= the question about the *Sinn/ Wahrheit/Wesen des Seins*). This basic question is focused on the meaning-giving source that enables (*läßt sein*) the meaning of things. Notice the crucial distinction between Heidegger's lead-in question about the meaning of the meaningful (*die Seiendheit des Seienden*), and his basic question about the meaning-giving *source* of the meaning of the meaningful (*Grundfrage*: *das Ereignis*).[8]

1. *The meaningfulness of the meaningful* refers to the simple but astonishing fact that things are meaningful at all. Heidegger called this "the wonder of all wonders: that things *make sense*" (PM 234.18).[9] This lead-in issue is the traditional one about *on hēi on* or *ens qua ens*, but now understood in a phenomenological mode: "What is the most basic structure of the things we encounter?", to which Heidegger answers, "Things as such are meaningful: they make sense".

2. *The meaning-giving source* of the meaning of the meaningful – also called "meaning itself" or "meaning as such" – refers to the *a priori* process whereby anything meaningful has its meaning. The early Heidegger analysed this source-of-meaning as the bond of "being-in" and "world". This is the man–meaning bond that he originally called being-in-the-world (*In-der-Welt-sein*) and later on called *Lichtung-sein* (GA 69: 101.12). This man–meaning phenomenon will eventually be named *Ereignis*, the appropriating of man to the task of sustaining meaning-giving (GA 65: 261.25–6 = CP 184.27–9; see also Chapter 10).

To put this in schematic form, Heidegger's *basic* question was about the *source* of his lead-in issue.

The *Grundfrage* concerns the meaning-giving source:

The

Anwesen-lassen	*letting*-come-about
Es gibt	*a priori* givenness
Schickung/Geschick	giving/givenness
Seyn	coming-to-pass
Wahrheit	disclosure
Welt	world

of

the meaning of the meaningful
die Bedeutung des Bedeutsamen
das Anwesen des Anwesenden
das Sein des Seienden

Regardless of the terms given here, the phrase "meaning-giving source" is merely heuristic at this point. It names an unknown "X" that motivates and guides the basic question while remaining as yet undetermined. But whatever it might turn out to be, the meaning-giving source is operative only in and with human being. In 1955 Heidegger insisted that just as the process of meaning-giving constitutes man, so too man co-constitutes the process of meaning-giving.

> We always say *too little* of "meaning [*Sein*] itself" when in saying "meaning", we leave out its presence *in and with* human being and thereby fail to recognize that human being itself co-constitutes [*mitausmacht*] "meaning". We also always say *too little* of human being if, in saying "meaning" …, we posit human being for itself and only then bring what has been so posited into a relation with "meaning".   (GA 9: 407.22–8 = PM 308.3–9)[10]

At the beginning I remarked that "*Kehre*" is an over-determined word in Heidegger's work. It is now time to explain what that means. Richard Rorty was fond of saying, "When your argument hits a wall, make some distinctions." And distinctions indeed must be made because, in keeping with Aristotelian *pros hen* analogy, Heidegger used the word *Kehre* in many distinct senses, all of them related to one basic, proper sense. Just as there is the analogy of being, or meaning, so likewise there is the analogy of *Kehre*.

What I have said about the *Kehre* up to this point – that it is the reciprocal bond of *Dasein–Sein* – is based on Heidegger's *Contributions to Philosophy*, written in 1936–8. That is, I have been dealing exclusively with the basic and proper sense of *Kehre*: the reciprocity or tension between man's being *required for* and man's *holding open* the fundamental factum of meaning-giving. Throughout his career, however, Heidegger used the term *Kehre* in at least two other senses that are analogically related to but not identical with the basic sense. To keep things distinct, I shall use "*Kehre*-1" to designate the basic *Kehre* discussed in *Contributions*, and shall designate the other meanings of *Kehre* by subsequent numbers.

Kehre-1: the fundamental and proper sense of the term

In 1969 Heidegger stated simply and directly what the central topic of all his thinking was.

> The basic idea of my thinking is precisely that meaning [*Sein*], i.e. the process of meaning-giving [*die Offenbarkeit des Seins*],

requires human being; and conversely that human being is human in so far as it stands in [i.e. sustains] the process of meaning-giving.   (*GA* 16: 704.1–5 = *MHC* 82.30–33)

In short, Heidegger's central topic is the man–meaning bond as allowing things their meaning. Throughout his later work Heidegger will use two key terms to name that bond. Human being, he writes, is (i) required (*gebraucht*) (ii) to belong to (*zugehören*, i.e. to sustain) the world (*GA* 65: 251.24–5 = *CP* 177.30–31).[11] These two terms – *Brauch* and *Zugehören* – parallel the early Heidegger's terms "thrownness" (*Geworfenheit*) and "projectively holding open" (*Entwurf*) (*GA* 65: 261.1–3 = *CP* 186.7–10).[12]

Man is by nature hermeneutical, ever in need of meaning and ever making meaning possible (cf. *GA* 21: 151.4–5).[13] Meaning is man's life-breath. Take it away, obliterate its source, and there is no human being left. Correlatively, in order to operate at all, meaning requires human being as its grounding "where". Without *Sein* there is no *Dasein*. Without *Dasein* there is no *Sein*. Man must be *claimed* for, or *appropriated* to, or *thrown* into, sustaining the *a priori* process of meaning-giving. And as claimed/appropriated/thrown, man is required to *projectively hold open* meaning-giving. The tension of those two *is* the fundamental factum, the *Kehre* in its basic and proper sense. Heidegger writes:

> Appropriation has its innermost occurrence and its widest reach in the turn. The turn that is *a priori* operative in appropriation is the hidden ground of all other subordinate turns, circles, and circularities, which themselves are obscure in their provenance, remain unquestioned, and are easily taken in themselves as the "ultimate".   (*GA* 65: 264.1–3 = *CP* 186.7–9)

In *Being and Time* the analysis of the meaning-giving reciprocity was to be treated in two steps, respectively in *BT* I.1–2 and in *BT* I.3.

Figure 1 (opposite) shows, within the oval, the two ways in which human being is *a priori* related to world: (a) "actively", by projectively holding open, sustaining, and grounding the meaning-giving world; and (b) "passively", in so far as man is claimed by or thrown into sustaining the world. Everything within the oval is the fundamental structural factum. Outside the oval are the places where and the modes in which Heidegger planned to analyse that factum.

Outside the oval: From the beginning Heidegger had already programmed into his work a *reversal of direction* (*Umkehrung*) between I.1–2 and I.3. *Being and Time* would emphasize *Dasein* (= *BT* I.1–2). Only

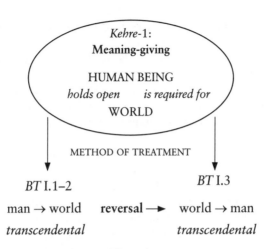

Figure 1.

then would it reverse direction and emphasize *Sein* (= *BT* I.3). The first step would show how human being projectively holds the world open. The second step (the reversal) would show how the meaning-giving world *requires* human being, such that man is *thrown* into the meaning-giving process. Both steps were to be worked out in a transcendental–horizonal framework in which human being is understood as projecting the horizon (opening the arena) of meaning-giving.

Heidegger made a first stab at *BT* I.3 in his 1927 course "Basic Problems of Phenomenology", where he continued to use the transcendental–horizonal approach of *BT* I.1–2. However, the effort made little progress, and at that point Heidegger's plan to work out *BT* I.3 within a transcendental framework collapsed.

Kehre-2: the *seinsgeschichtlich* approach

Shortly after publishing *Being and Time* Heidegger began shifting his method for treating the second step in his programme, the reversal of direction. Instead of a consistent *transcendental* approach in both steps, Heidegger adopted what he called a *seinsgeschichtlich* approach to *BT* I.3. This shift in treatment constitutes *Kehre*-2, of which William J. Richardson's *Heidegger: Through Phenomenology to Thought* (2003) is the authoritative treatment. As Heidegger writes in "Letter on Humanism" (1947), *BT* I.3 was foreseen as the place "where the whole project gets reversed [*sich umkehrt*] as regards the 'what' and the 'how' both of thinking and of what is thought-worthy" (*GA* 9: 328.2 with n.a = *PM* 250.1 with n.a).[14]

The reversal that Heidegger is talking about is the already planned reversal of direction *from* man → world *to* world → man. However, that second step, "Time and Being", "was held back because my thinking failed to adequately express this reversal and did not succeed with the [transcendental] language of metaphysics" (*GA* 9: 327.32–328.4 = *PM* 249.37–250.4).

In the mid 1930s, as a result of the inability of transcendental thinking to express the reversal of direction programmed for *BT* I.3, Heidegger changed his way of treating the second step of the process from a transcendental–horizonal to a *seinsgeschichtlich* approach centred on how man is required for meaning-giving to be operative at all. In Figure 2, note that *Kehre*-2 stands outside the oval: it is merely a way of treating *Kehre*-1 and is not at all identical with the basic and proper sense of the turn.[15] Note as well the shift from a transcendental to a *seinsgeschichtlich* approach, which constitutes *Kehre*-2.

Usually mistranslated as "being-historical", the term *seinsgeschichtlich* has nothing to do with history and everything to do with *Es gibt Sein* (*GA* 46: 94.11–14). We may translate that latter phrase as: "Meaning-giving is a priori operative wherever there is human being" – which means that the *Schickung/Geschick des Seins* (the "sending" or "giving" of meaning) is the same as the meaning-giving bond of man–meaning. The presupposition of the *seinsgeschichtlich* approach is that meaning

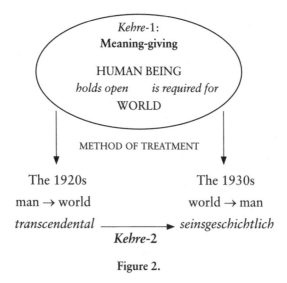

Figure 2.

is always-already given with human being itself rather than through some projective activity on the part of this or that person. Moreover, the emphasis now is less on man projectively *holding open* the world and more on man's *being required* to hold open the world. On this *seinsgeschichtlich* basis the later Heidegger could bring the work of *BT* I.3 to fruition outside the limitations of transcendental method.

There are two texts that, taken together, clarify the new *seinsgeschichtlich* approach: first, a note in *Being and Time,* and secondly, the 1930 essay "On the Essence of Truth".

As regards the first text, in a crucial marginal note that he added to *Being and Time* §9 ("The Outline of the Treatise"), Heidegger spells out the formal stages in the progression of *Kehre*-2. The numbers here are mine.

1. The transcendental difference.
2. Overcoming the horizon as such.
3. The turn around into the source.
4. Meaning from out of this source.[16]

This note outlines the four steps that go to make up *Kehre*-2.

Number 1 refers to the transcendental framework of *Being and Time* and of Heidegger's courses and shorter works up to the autumn of 1930. The transcendental difference is an early name for the "ontological difference" and is the distinction between the meaning-giving world sustained by human being *and* whatever shows up within that world.

Number 2 refers to *Kehre*-2, the shift from the transcendental to the *seinsgeschichtlich* approach for working out "Time and Being".[17] Note that this step entails overcoming the horizon *as such* – that is, in so far as it is taken *as* a transcendental horizon – while leaving that field intact for further *seinsgeschichtlich* investigation. In other words, the gains of *BT* I.1–2 – the temporal holding-open of world – remain in place, but the sequel (*BT* I.3) ceases to use a transcendental–horizonal approach.

Number 3 refers to the *seinsgeschichtlich* working out of *BT* I.3 (= *Kehre*-2) and specifically the turn of the analysis to a focus on the abiding source of meaning-giving while, in the process (and as already planned), reversing the approach *from* man → meaning *to* meaning → man.

Number 4 refers to the outcome of the analysis: an understanding and acceptance of the fact that all meaning derives from the finite meaning-giving source, which soon will be called *Ereignis*, the *a priori* "appropriation" of man for sustaining meaning-giving.

To conclude, from this marginal note it is clear that Heidegger's central topic, *Kehre*-1, remains unchanged even while the method for treating it shifts from transcendental to *seinsgeschichtlich* (*GA* 9: 328.7–8 with n.c = *PM* 250.7–8 with n.c).

As regards the second text, Heidegger says that his 1930 essay "On the Essence of Truth" already offered "a certain insight into the thinking of the *Kehre* from 'Being and Time' to 'Time and Being'" (*GA* 9: 4–8 = *PM* 250.4–7).[18] Heidegger is referring here to *Kehre*-2, the shift to a *seinsgeschichtlich* approach. The question now is where and how *Kehre*-2 fits into the 1930 essay and what the shift in the "thoughtworthy" consists in.

"On the Essence of Truth" demonstrates two things:

1. Truth as correspondence is made possible by human freedom, which is man's *a priori* relatedness to the meaningful (= sections 1–5 of "On the Essence of Truth").
2. Human being is bound up with *two newly formulated* dimensions of the *hiddenness* of the meaning-giving source (= sections 6–7 of the essay):
   (a) the source as intrinsically concealed (*Verbergung* as the "mystery");
   (b) the source as overlooked and forgotten (*Irre*).

With some effort one can recognize that point 1 is cognate with *BT* I.1–2, namely, human being as sustaining the meaning-giving world, man as *alētheia* and *Zeitlichkeit*. But in 2(a) Heidegger adds a *new* dimension to *BT* I.3 by showing that the source of all meaning is intrinsically "concealed" (i.e. unknowable in the strict sense of the term) if only because in order to know what meaning-giving is, we would have to presuppose that very meaning-giving itself. At best we can only experience *that* the source is, without knowing *what is responsible* for it. We can sense our fate (facticity) as thrownness into finite and mortal meaning-giving and then either embrace it in an act of resolve (authenticity) or flee from our essential involvement in it (inauthenticity) (see Chapters 1 and 4). Moreover, as 2(b) argues, this concealed source of meaning is for the most part overlooked *because* it is intrinsically concealed.

According to Heidegger, between §5 and §6 of the essay – that is, between points 1 and 2 – there occurs "the leap into the *Kehre* that is a priori operative in appropriation" (*GA* 9: 193 n.a = *PM* 148 n.a).[19] This simple phrase is actually quite complex. What Heidegger refers to as "the leap" corresponds to number 2 in the marginal note to *Being and Time*: the "leap" is *Kehre*-2. (He calls it a "leap" because he considers it impossible to make a smooth and simple transition from a transcendental to a *seinsgeschichtlich* approach.) However, the leap of *Kehre*-2 lands one in *Kehre*-1 along with the *seinsgeschichtlich* way of treating it. Thus "the leap into the *Kehre* that is a priori operative in appropriation" means overcoming the transcendental–horizonal approach of *BT* I.1–2 and starting afresh with the *seinsgeschichtlich* ("meaning-is-already-given") approach of *BT* I.3. And with that fresh start, and with his new recognition of the twofold hiddenness of the source, Heidegger says he finally arrived at the site from out of which he experienced and wrote *Being and Time*, namely, (i) the intrinsic hiddenness of the source of meaning and (ii) the overlooking and forgetting of that hiddenness (*GA* 9: 328.9–11 = *PM* 250.8–10).[20]

Heidegger summarizes the ultimate intent of "On the Essence of Truth" in a chiasmic thesis: *Die Wahrheit des Wesens ist das Wesen der Wahrheit* (*GA* 9: 201.3–19 = *PM* 153.27–154.2).[21] To translate that sentence as "The truth of essence is the essence of truth" is to say nothing. Properly interpreted, the sentence says: "The process of meaning-giving" (*die Wahrheit des Wesens*) is "the source of truth-as-correspondence" (*das Wesen der Wahrheit*).

Unfortunately Heidegger's less than precise language has contributed to the confusion between the *Kehre*-1 of *Contributions to Philosophy* and the *Kehre*-2 of "On the Essence of Truth" and "Letter on Humanism". Heidegger finally came to distinguish clearly between the two only in his letter to William J. Richardson (April 1962) when he denominated *Kehre*-2 as a "shift" (*Wendung*) in his approach to the central topic, as contrasted with *Kehre*-1, which is operative in the very content (*Sachverhalt*) of the central topic (*PMH* xvii.25 [*Wendung*]; xix.6–7 [*Sachverhalt*]).[22]

A final note on *Kehre*-2: does a sentence like "Meaning-giving *claims* or *calls* man" risk anthropomorphizing the meaning-giving process? Yes, it does. Given Heidegger's penchant for using anthropomorphic metaphors to express his central topic, there is always the danger of hypostasizing meaning-giving into a Super-Power endowed with agency, a cosmic Something that "does things" to human beings, such as "drawing" them into meaning-giving. For example, the later Heidegger will use the term *Ereignis* for the man–meaning bond. That technical term refers to the fact of meaning-giving in so far as it "requires" human being (*brauchen*) to belong to (*zugehören*) and sustain that fundamental fact. However, *Ereignis* is said to "appropriate and own" (*ereignen*) man as *Sein*'s own "property" (*Eigentum*), while in turn making possible man's proper authenticity (*Eigentlichkeit*). Do all these metaphors mean that *Ereignis* is a Super-Something with power to act on human beings?

If such a monstrosity is to be avoided at all costs, what then about the later Heidegger's apparent quasi-hypostasization of *Sein*?

Richardson answers that question with exquisite *délicatesse*: "Only truly great philosophers should be indulged for their obscurity".[23]

Kehre-3: the transformation of human beings

A final use of the word *Kehre* – we shall call it *Kehre*-3 – refers to the existentiell transformation (*Verwandlung*) of human beings and their worlds of meaning by way of an insight into *Kehre*-1 and a corresponding act of resolve. Heidegger himself points to this usage in his letter to Richardson. Arguing that *Kehre*-3 was at work in his thought as early as 1937–8 when he was in the process of carrying out *Kehre*-2, Heidegger quotes his own words from a lecture course he taught that winter:

> Over and over again we have to insist: What is at stake in the question of truth ... is a transformation in human being itself. ... Man comes into question here in the deepest, broadest, and genuinely fundamental perspective: human being in relation to *Seyn* – i.e. in *Kehre*-2: *Seyn* and its truth in relation to human being. The determination of the essence of truth is accompanied by a necessary transformation of man. The two are the same.[24]

The existentiell–personal transformation that is *Kehre*-3 had actually been at issue as early as *Being and Time*, the motto of which was, in effect, "Become what you already are" (*GA* 2: 194.3 = *BT* 186.4).[25] Heidegger understands that sentence as an exhortation coming from one's own nature to *become* that very nature by way of a personal conversion from living inauthentically to becoming what and how one essentially is. *Being and Time* is ultimately meant as a phenomenological protreptic to coming back to and taking over the facticity that defines human being.[26] It is an exhortation to personally assume one's hermeneutical mortality, one's making sense of things while always living at the point of death.[27] Only in such a radically first-person act of conversion is authentic meaning-giving at work.

If, in *Being and Time*, *Kehre*-3 was the radical transformation from self-alienation to liberation, in a later lecture entitled "Die Kehre" (1949) Heidegger steps back and takes a global view of the possibility of such a transformation in today's Westernized world.[28]

Recall that *Being and Time* defined man as concernful and temporal being-in-the-world, thrown into sustaining meaning-giving. A world is

a specific formation of meaning, a particular *Geschick des Seins* (givenness of meaning) that is always-already operative in and with human
being. To review:

1. Each world, as a meaning-giving field, requires a corresponding
   way of "being-in-it", more precisely, a way of man's being appropriated to sustaining that world. We may call the specific way of
   "being in" and "living" a world the existential ethos of that world.
   Sustaining a world existentially and living its ethos existentielly
   makes us "complicit" in that world's mode of giving meaning to
   things.
2. The meaning-giving bond of man–meaning is intrinsically "hidden",
   that is, unknowable in the strict sense (see above), even though we
   are able to sense our attunement to that particular formation of
   meaning (*GA* 46: 221.14–6).
3. Even though we are *a priori* appropriated to sustaining the worlds
   we live in, for the most part we overlook and forget the very man–
   meaning bond – the appropriation – that constitutes them. Early
   on, Heidegger called this condition "fallenness" and in the 1930s
   he called it "errance" (*Irre*).

In his 1949 lecture, Heidegger focuses on three issues: (i) how sense
is made in the present formation of meaning; (ii) the danger that the
present formation of meaning poses to the man–meaning bond; and
(iii) the possibility of liberation from that danger by the "conversion"
mentioned above.

The Construct

Heidegger sees today's Westernized man as locked into a global paradigm of meaning that he calls *Ge-stell*, which I translate as the "Construct" (see also Chapter 13). (*Gestell* is derived from Meister Eckhart's
neologism *Gestellnis*, which translates the Latin *forma* and ultimately
the Greek *morphē*, namely, that as which something is construed.[29])
This growing global ethos, dominated as it is by techno-think (*Technik*), is characterized by a compulsion to construe everything as a mere
resource to be exploited for consumption, whether that be nature ("raw
material") or human beings ("human resources").

The paradox of the Construct is that in so far as human beings are
appropriated to sustaining that specific formation of meaning, they
ineluctably are complicit in and collaborate with the exploitation of
themselves as well as of nature and each other. And yet all of this – the

95

Construct, its ethos of exploitation, the techno-think that is its way of disclosure, and our essential complicity with all of that – is itself a *Geschick des Seins*, a gift of meaning that, like every other *Geschick*, overlooks and forgets appropriation, the hidden meaning-giving source of all meaning.

The Danger

In the Construct, as in any other paradigm of meaning, the appropriation of human being that sustains the ethos of exploitation is "hidden" for the reasons given earlier. And as in any other *Geschick des Seins*, that hiddenness is generally overlooked. However, what is specific to the Construct's form of appropriation is a *third* level of hiddenness. The lock that the Construct has on us owing to our complicity in its ethos of techno-think and exploitation effectively *obscures the fact that we overlook our appropriation to it*. The Construct traps us in a vicious circle that blinds us to *any* mode of appropriation and therefore occludes what Heidegger calls "the mystery of human being" (*GA* 9: 195.23 = *PM* 149.28), namely, human facticity as thrownness into sustaining the intrinsically hidden factum. And human being, as appropriated to sustaining the Construct, colludes in blocking any awareness of its exploitative appropriation, or of any other possible appropriation for that matter.

To summarize in the reverse order: in the current paradigm of meaning there is, then, a threefold hiding of *Kehre*-1. The Construct (i) effectively obliterates (ii) one's overlooking and forgetting (iii) of the naturally hidden appropriation of oneself to sustaining any formation of meaning. The result is that today we are trapped in a prison of self-alienation.

A possible liberation from the Danger

Heidegger argues that although the Construct effectively blots out all traces of the true nature of man, it nonetheless harbours the possibility of a radical transformation of the Construct into another, non-exploitative paradigm (*GA* 79: 69.24–5 = *QCT* 39.3–4). Every *Geschick des Seins* holds the possibility of such a change in so far as the hidden and indomitable source of meaning (the *Es gibt Sein*) remains an inexhaustible treasure of yet further meaning-giving.[30] Heidegger's hope is that at least a few souls will experience what he calls a "brief glimpse into the mystery from out of errance" (*GA* 9: 198.21–2 = *PM* 151.36) – a flash of insight into the source of all meaning – and thus, by an act of resolve, will step through and beyond the Construct.[31]

Paradoxically he finds the possibility of liberation *within the very danger* posed by the Construct. Yes, the Construct *is* the Danger in so far as it imposes a virtually complete blackout of appropriation in any form. And yes, the result is a pervasive feeling of deep boredom, of profound alienation from the grip that meaning itself has on human being. Heidegger's hope, however, is that this stifling atmosphere of alienation from one's own nature will eventually lead to a personal epiphany in which one finally recognizes the danger *as* the danger it is and thereby awakens to one's true nature. *Being and Time* couched such an epiphany in the language of a decisive *Augenblick*, a sudden insight into oneself as mortally bonded to meaning-giving. In the 1949 essay, the epiphany is discussed analogously in terms of a *Blitz/Blick*, a lightning-flash of insight (Heraclitus, fr. 64: *keraunos*) that can lead to the transformation of oneself and of the current world of meaning.[32]

We see, then, (i) that the intrinsic hiddenness of appropriation facilitates (and to that degree is responsible for) the overlooking of appropriation; (ii) that the *gift* of the current formation of meaning (which occludes its own source) is an ethos of disclosure that understands everything as an exploitable resource; and (iii) that all this adds up to the immense Danger of utter self-alienation. However, (iv) once the alienating power of that Danger is seen for what it is, the current self-endangering of the man–meaning bond can be transformed, at least for a few individuals, into a non-alienating world of meaning. Heidegger poses this possibility in Hölderlin's words:

Where the danger expands, that which frees us
Also grows   ("Patmos", 3–4)

In the moment of insight, described as an epiphantic "lightning bolt", an elite few who are now exploited and alienated might raise anew, within *themselves* and not merely in formal philosophy, the question that goes to the core of human being: how does meaning occur at all? At that point one might say with Heraclitus (fr. 119), *ēthos anthrōpōi daimōn*: to live authentically is to live the mystery of the thrown sustaining of meaning.

Notes

1. Citations in this chapter refer to texts by page and line, separated by a period. All translations are my own (see the glossary at the end of this chapter), but I shall refer the reader to the corresponding pages in existing English translations with an "=". The present text corrects my earlier account (Sheehan 2000).

2. *Gegenschwung, Gegenschwingen, Erschwingen*: GA 65: 251.24, 261.25–6, 262.2–4, 263.19–20 = CP 177.30, 184.28–9 and 36–7, 185.38–9. (That last text shows that the gods are various formations/*Geschicke* of meaning.) On reci-proci-ty: GA 65: 381.26–7 = CP 266.25. For *Erzittern*, GA 65: 262.9 = CP 185.3, *et passim*. Definitely *not* "enquivering".

3. Compare GA 9: 332.3–4, "Die Lichtung selber aber ist das Sein" with GA 9: 326.15–6, "Die Lichtung des Seins, und nur sie, ist 'Welt'" = PM 253.1 and 248.36–7 respectively.

4. GA 10: 128.13–14 = PR 86.20. Both "man" and "human being" translate the Greek *anthrōpos* understood as *Dasein:* human being in its *a priori* structure. On formal indication, see Dahlstrom (2001: 242–52).

5. See Allen's comments on his film *Matchpoint*, Cannes, 12 May 2005, in Ebert (2005: 852).

6. When Heidegger says that "the world worlds" (*die Welt weltet*), he means that the world allows for the meaning of whatever is found within the world.

7. GA 65: 261.22–3 = CP 184.25–6: "Die Wahrheit des Seins und so dieses selbst west nur, wo and wann Da-sein"; GA 65: 263.28–9 = CP 186.3–4: "Das *Seyn* und die Wesung seiner Wahrheit ist des Menschen, sofern er inständlich wird als Da-sein"; GA 65: 264.1 = CP 186.3: "Das Sein 'ist' des Menschen".

8. Meaning as such (*Anwesen als solches*) always entails meaning-*giving* (Anwesen-*lassen*: GA 14: 45.29–30 = TB 37.5, where it is misprinted), just as in medieval philosophy, having *esse* always entails giving *esse*: "Omne ens actu natum est agere aliquid actu existens" (It is the nature of every being-in-act to effect something [else] existing in act) (Thomas Aquinas, *Summa contra gentes*, II, 6, no. 4). At GA 9: 369 = PM 280, note "d" equates *Sein, Wahrheit, Welt, Sein*, *Ereignis* and *Sichankündigen des Seins*. GA 9: 201.30–2 = PM 154.12–4 equates *Sinn, Entwurfbereich, Offenheit* and *Wahrheit* as the meaning-giving source of the meaning of the meaningful. On "the last god" as *die Wahrheit des Seyns*, see GA 65: 35.2 = CP 25.16.

9. In Heidegger-code: "daß Seiendes *ist*": GA 9: 307.23–4 = PM 234.18. See also GA 52: 64.24–5.

10. See also GA 9: 412.1–3 = PM 311.21–3). Also see GA 8: 85.13–9 = WCT 79.19–22. Thus, whenever I use "man" or "human being", I intend them as completed by the word *Sein* – as in "man–meaning".

11. With "sustain" I translate Heidegger's (i) *Entwurf als Offenhalten*, "projection as holding open/sustaining", (ii) *ausstehen* as at GA 9: 332.19 = PM 253.14, and in the sense of *ausstehend* at GA 65: 35.6–7 = CP 25.20.

12. *Geworfenheit* and *Entwurf* become *gebraucht* and *wahren der Augenblicksstätte*, respectively. Regarding thrownness as being-appropriated: "die Er-eignung, das Geworfenwerden": GA 65: 34.9 = CP 24.32–3; "geworfener ... er-eignet": GA 65: 239.5 = CP 169.12. Heidegger sometimes refers to the interface of thrownness and holding-open as "kehrig", that is, reciprocal: for example, GA 65: 261.29 = CP 184.32; GA 65: 265.26 = CP 187.21.

13. "Weil Dasein in seinem Sein selbst bedeutend ist, lebt es in Bedeutungen und kann sich als diese aussprechen".

14. The change in *thinking* refers to abandoning the transcendental approach. The change in *what is thought-worthy* refers not just to the shift from BT I.1–2 to BT I.3, but more specifically to the world's "claiming" man to sustain meaning-giving. The basic thought-worthy matter for Heidegger is always the factum of meaning-giving: GA 79: 70.28–9 = QCT 40.11–12.

15. It is important to distinguish between (i) the reversal in the direction of the analysis, namely *from* man → world *to* world → man, which was programmed into *BT* from the start and which was initially intended to proceed within a transcendental framework, and (ii) the shift from a transcendental to a *seinsgeschichtlich* framework. Only the latter is *Kehre-2*.

16. "Die transzendenzhafte Differenz./Die Überwindung des Horizonts als solchen./ Die Umkehr in die Herkunft./Das Anwesen aus dieser Herkunft" (*GA* 2: 53 n.a = *BTS* 35.33–5). For a variant story of the transition to the later work, see *GA* 65: §132 = *CP* §132. Heidegger first uses the term "ontological difference" in his 1929 essay "Vom Wesen des Grundes". In this marginal note he uses the (presumably pre-1929) term "transcendental difference" in place of "ontological difference". Regarding "transzendenzhaft" as "ontologisch", see Müller (1949: 73–4).

17. See *GA* 65: 250.14–17 = *CP* 176.33–6: "Deshalb bedurfte es der Bemühung … die Wahrheit des Seyns aus dessen *eigenem* Wesen zu fassen (Ereignis)".

18. "… gibt einen gewissen Einblick in das Denken der Kehre[-2] von 'Sein und Zeit' zu 'Zeit und Sein'".

19. "Zwischen 5. und 6. der Sprung in die (im Ereignis wesende) Kehre".

20. "In ihr [= *Kehre-2*] gelangt das versuchte Denken erst in die Ortschaft der Dimension, aus der 'Sein und Zeit' erfahren ist, und zwar erfahren in der Grunderfahrung des Seinsvergessenheit" (*GA* 9: 328.9–11).

21. Although Heidegger presents the thesis in the reverse order to the above, he insists that the subject of the sentence is *die Wahrheit des Wesens*.

22. Also in *GA* 11: 149.21–2 and 149.34–5, respectively.

23. My thanks to my colleague Professor Richard Capobianco for the report of this *bon mot*.

24. The text first appeared in *PMH* xxi.7ff. It has since been published in *GA* 45: 214.15–27 = *BQP* 181.5–15.

25. "… werde, was du bist!" The phrase stems from Pindar's *Pythian Odes*, II.72: *genoi' hoios essi mathōn*.

26. Coming back to and taking over: *GA* 2: 194.3; 431.13, 21–2, 34; 506.21–2; 524.2 = *BT* 186.4; 373.16, 21–2; 374.7; 434.34–5; 448.34.

27. Human being makes sense of things *because* it is mortal. Making sense means "taking X *as* …", that is, synthesizing "over" (i.e. both despite and because of) separation (*diairesis*). The ultimate separation "over which" we synthesize (i.e. make sense) is our own death. I translate *Sein-zum-Tode* as "being at the point of death".

28. Note that in 1952 Heidegger calls *Kehre-3* a *Wende*, "a turn today against the raging of the technological world" (*MLS* 281.17–18 = *LW* 228.14–15).

29. *GA* 81: 286.6–10. See *GA* 9: 276.6 = *PM* 211.5. "Construct" is derived from the Latin *construere*, to pile up and arrange.

30. See *GA* 65: 241.17–8 = *CP* 170.34–5: *die Verweigerung* = *die erste höchste Schenkung des Seyns*; and *GA* 65: 246.17–9 = *CP* 174.6–8: *das Sichentziehende* as *höchste Schenkung*.

31. "A few": *GA* 65: §5 = *CP* §5. Also "Das stille Einverständnis Weniger", *MLS* 208.9–10 = *LW* 163.9.

32. Note that, in the lightning flash of insight, what shows itself/comes to pass is *world*: *GA* 79: 73.13 and 74.25 = *QCT* 43.22 and 45.13–6.

Glossary of translations and paraphrases

Anwesen meaning-giving; *traditionally*: presence
Anwesendes the meaningful; *traditionally*: present beings
Da des Seins "where" [the meaning-process occurs]; *traditionally*: the t/here of being
Dasein human being; man [in a gender-undifferentiated sense]; the "where" [meaning occurs]; *traditionally*: being-there; being-t/here
entwerfen to sustain or hold open [meaning-giving]; *traditionally*: to project, project open
Ereignis appropriation; *traditionally*: the event of appropriation
Es gibt Sein meaning-giving occurs with human being; *traditionally*: it gives Being, there is Being
Gegenschwung reciprocity; *traditionally*: counter-resonance
Geschick a formation of meaning-giving; *traditionally*: a destiny of being
Ge-stell Construct; *traditionally*: enframing
In-der-Welt-sein being *a priori* in meaning; *traditionally*: being-in-the-world
ist [something] makes sense; *traditionally*: [something] is
Kehre the turn; *traditionally*: the turning
Kehre-1 the man–meaning bond
Kehre-2 the reversal of direction [from man to meaning]
Kehre-3 the transformation of man [from fallenness and inauthenticity to authenticity]
kehrig reciprocal; *traditionally*: turning (adj.)
Lichtung the process of meaning-giving; *traditionally*: the clearing
Offenbarkeit des Seins the process of meaning-giving; *traditionally*: the openness/revealedness of being
offenhalten to sustain/hold open the meaning-giving process
Seiendes the meaningful; *traditionally*: beings
Seiendheit meaningfulness; *traditionally*: beingness
Sein meaning-giving; *traditionally*: being
Technik techno-think; *traditionally*: technicity, technology
Umkehr reversal [of direction]; cf. *Wende/Wendung*
verstehen to make sense of; *traditionally*: to understand
Wahrheit the process of meaning-giving; *traditionally*: truth
Welt meaning-giving context, world; *traditionally*: world
Die Welt weltet the meaning-giving context gives meaning; *traditionally*: the world worlds
Wende/Wendung shift [of direction]; cf. *Umkehr* and *Kehre-2*
Wesen the occurrence of meaning-giving; *traditionally* essence, essencing; essential sway

References

Dahlstrom, D. O. 2001. *Heidegger's Concept of Truth*. Cambridge: Cambridge University Press.

Ebert, R. 2005. *Roger Ebert's Movie Yearbook, 2006*. Riverside, NJ: Andrews McMeel Publishing.

Gurwitsch, A. 1947. "Review of Gaston Berger, *Le cogito dans la philosophie de Husserl*". *Philosophy and Phenomenological Research* 7(4) (June): 649–54.

Müller, M. 1949. *Existenzphilosophie im geistigen Leben der Gegenwart*. Heidelberg: F. H. Kerle.

Richardson, W. J. 2003. *Heidegger: Through Phenomenology to Thought*, 4th edn. New York: Fordham University Press.

Sheehan, T. 2000. "*Kehre* and *Ereignis*". In *A Companion to Heidegger's Introduction to Metaphysics*, R. Polt & G. Fried (eds), 3–16, 263–74. New Haven, CT: Yale University Press.

Further reading

Primary sources

See Heidegger's "The Turning", in *The Question Concerning Technology and Other Essays*, 36–49; "On the Essence of Truth", in *Pathmarks*, 136–54; and "Letter on Humanism", in *Pathmarks*, 239–76.

Secondary sources

See Richardson (2003). See also J. Grondin, *Le tournant dans la pensée de Martin Heidegger* (Paris: Presses Universitaires de France, 1987) and F.-W. von Herrmann, *Wege ins Ereignis: Zu Heideggers Beiträge zur Philosophie* (Frankfurt: Vittorio Klostermann, 1994).

SEVEN

Heidegger, National Socialism and the German People

Charles Bambach

To raise the question of Heidegger and National Socialism, and to raise it precisely *as* a question rather than as an already foregone conclusion, is to enter into one of the darkest and most fiercely debated topics within Heidegger's thinking. Not only is this a question about philosophy and politics, of the Platonic guardian and his relation to the leadership of the polis; it is also – if not primarily – an ethical question about the support of one of Europe's greatest philosophers for perhaps the most terrible and violent regime in her history. There are so many dimensions to this question – of Heidegger's personal involvement as rector and academic leader (*Führer*) of Freiburg University from 1933 to 1934, of his fall from power and his claims of being persecuted in the Reich, of his post-war interrogation by the Freiburg University de-Nazification committee, of his public silence on the National Socialist years and the Holocaust, and his famous defence in the *Spiegel* interview of 1966. There is also the testimony of his contemporaries, including his students (Karl Löwith, Hermann Mörchen, Rainer Marten and Herbert Marcuse), his colleagues (Karl Jaspers), his friends/family (Elisabeth Blochmann, Elfride Heidegger, Heinrich Petzet) as well as the vast secondary literature that, after the publication of works by Victor Farias (1989), Hugo Ott (1993), Jacques Derrida (1989), and Philippe Lacoue-Labarthe (1990), spawned the notorious *l'affaire Heidegger*, whose echoes still resound in current discussions of the philosopher.

To genuinely think the question of Heidegger and National Socialism, however, means to attend to its *philosophical* meaning rather than to its merely factical relation to issues such as party politics, personal ambition, ideological affinity or rhetorical excess (all of which no doubt constitute a telling chapter in the story of Heidegger and politics). The twelve years of National Socialist rule in Germany (1933–45) coincide with some of the most important years of Heidegger's thinking: the years of his so-called "turning", when he writes *Contributions to Philosophy*, develops his notion of the history of being and another beginning, and delivers important lectures on Hölderlin, Nietzsche and the Presocratics.

In what follows I should like to approach the question of Heidegger's embrace of National Socialism by reflecting on its ontological significance in terms of the ontical commitments that Heidegger made. In order to do this we shall need to consider not only Heidegger's "official" involvement with National Socialism in the period of his rectorship (1933–4), but also the reasons for his break with the institutions of the Reich and how that break shapes the direction of his later thought.

The Rectorial Address of 1933

In late April of 1933, just three months after Hitler's rise to power, Heidegger is elected as rector of the University of Freiburg and on 1 May he officially joins the National Socialist German Workers' Party (NSDAP). In his Rectorial Address of 27 May 1933, "The Self-Assertion of the German University", he issues a call to the German *Volk* to become who they are in and through a renewal of their resolve "to stand firm in the face of German fate in its extreme distress" (*SU* 30 = R 10). In the heady atmosphere of the National Socialist revolution of 1933, Heidegger comes to believe that he has the unique opportunity to shape the National Socialist movement in an originary philosophical way, to become the Führer of the German university, which he sees as the catalyst for revolutionary change. The Rectorial Address announces a bold mission for the German *Volk* whose sense of itself can come, Heidegger believes, only through the philosophical direction of a spiritual (*geistiger*) *Führer*. If at this time the intellectual leadership of the Nazi movement was still up for grabs (with other prominent Nazi professors such as Ernst Krieck, Alfred Baeumler and Hans Heyse vying for ascendancy), Heidegger's address announces his own philosophical brand of National Socialism rather than merely affirming Hitler's political takeover.[1] Heidegger's enemies (both in 1933–4 and after the war) interpreted his decision to join the NSDAP as opportunistic and megalomaniacal, and one can certainly find such motives at work in his essays and addresses from this period. But it would be both cynical and simplistic to maintain that this was his primary motivation.

Heidegger genuinely put his faith in the possibilities afforded by the National Socialist revolution, which he viewed as only the precursor and precondition for a second ontological revolution that would bring the German *Volk* (People) to its proper historical mission as the saving force in the history of the West.[2]

This eschatological vision of German destiny grew out of Heidegger's own profound disenchantment with the course of German politics following Germany's crushing defeat in the Great War and the humiliation inflicted on it by the Treaty of Versailles. Drawn to Hitler by his bold affirmation of the renewal of the German *Volk*, Heidegger understood his own task as rector as parallel to Hitler's. In his very first lecture course as rector in Summer Semester (hereafter SS) 1933, Heidegger declared:

> Of the greatness of the historical moment through which the German *Volk* is now passing, this is what academic youth knows. The German *Volk* as a whole comes to itself; that is, it finds its leadership. In this leadership the *Volk* (which has come to itself) creates the state. The *Volk*, which forms itself in the state and establishes its permanence and continuity through it, grows up into a nation. The nation takes upon itself the fate of its *Volk*. Such a *Volk* attains its spiritual commission among peoples and creates its own history ... *All essential leadership lives from the power of a great and fundamentally concealed vocation.* This is first and last the *spiritual commission of the Volk* that reserves for itself the fate of a nation. What matters is to awaken the *knowledge of this commission* and to root it in the heart and will of a *Volk* and the individuals in it ... This knowledge concerning the *spiritual–political commission* of the German *Volk* is a knowledge about its future. (GA 36/37: 3–4)

Heidegger goes on to claim that by asking the question about its commission, vocation and destiny, the German *Volk* enters into the genuine realm of philosophy, since philosophy is nothing other than "essential" questioning (which he understands in turn as a questioning concerning the essence of being). But such questioning does not take place on its own; it requires a fundamental decision by the *Volk*, a resoluteness to become authentically what it is. In this sense Heidegger understands the *Volk* not as a fixed historical essence, but as a possibility of historical becoming that sets for itself a task (here National Socialism can be literally thought of as a move-ment). In §74 of *Being and Time* Heidegger links this form of anticipatory resoluteness to the possibility of retrieving the past, not as something merely gone or outdated, but as the choice for authentically retrieving "the possibility of existence that has-been-there (*dagewesen*)" (*SZ* 386). In other words, to speak the language of fundamental ontology, the historicity of the *Volk* – its futural fate retrieved from the possibility of its having-been – lies in its resolute decision to make itself "free for the struggle to come" by handing itself over to the "there" (*da*) of the moment (*Augenblick*). In this resolute openness to the authentic temporality of its fate, the *Volk* understands itself in terms of a communally shared destiny rather than as an assemblage of individuated egos or a collective "subject". In this new self-understanding Heidegger finds the basis for his political commitment to National Socialism. Yet what the *Volk* requires to grasp the authentic meaning of its historicity is the leadership of a truly great poet, philosopher and/or statesman (*GA* 39: 51; *EM* 47). In their struggle (*Kampf*) to disclose the concealed meaning and direction of the *Volk*'s destiny, these leaders expose both themselves and their countrymen to the danger and distress of "the incessant questioning struggle concerning the essence and being of entities" (*GA* 36/37: 12). The Rectorial Address presents itself as an ontological call for the hardness (*Härte*) of will required to initiate such questioning so that a space can be opened up for "the most constant and hardest self-reflection" (*SU* 29 = *R* 9, trans. mod.).

"The Self-Assertion of the German University" takes up this task of questioning by thinking the political revolution of National Socialism as the first step in transforming the historical legacy of Germany's defeat in the Great War into a national awakening to the *Volk*'s authentic destiny.[3] Drawing on his earlier phenomenological engagement with St Paul's epistles (*GA* 60: 98–105, 114, 149–50), which focused on the early Christian experience of resolute wakefulness to the *kairos* moment of "the coming of the Lord" (*parousia*), Heidegger envisages the *Volk*'s awakening as an attunement to the *kairos* moment of revolutionary possibility. In this sense, the euphoric self-renewal brought on by Hitler's coming to power can be understood as the preparation for instituting a transition to an "other" beginning: not only for the German *Volk* but through them for the history of the West. The site for this national awakening (*Aufbruch*) was to be the university, but not the middle-class definition of the university as a place to choose a career or to gain an "education". On the contrary, Heidegger contends, the genuine essence of the university lies in science (*Wissenschaft*). Science in its present form, however, offers a mere semblance of what it originally meant for the early Greeks; hence Heidegger calls for a radical rethinking of the essence of science in terms of its original roots in the ancient Greek practice of *philosophia*, which Plato (*Theaetetus* 155d) and Aristotle

(*Metaphysics* 982b) both conceive as "wonderment" (*thaumazein*) rather than as mere evident or self-certain knowledge. *Thaumazein*, or what Heidegger termed "the initial wondering perseverance in the face of what is", constitutes the root, the beginning and the *archē* of genuine science (*SU* 33 = *R* 13, trans. mod.). Yet within the contemporary university, philosophy has become merely another technical discipline, a discipline unaware of its original relation to the other disciplines and to its own proper essence. What is required in Heidegger's estimation is a rethinking of "the essence of truth": not as "adequation" or the correspondence between a judging subject and a perceived object, but as a *movement* of Heraclitean oppositions, a mutually implicating interplay between harmony and conflict, concord and discord, consonance and dissonance. On Heidegger's reading, truth is *polemos* or *Aus-einander-setzung*, a setting out (*setzen*) and apart from (*aus*) one another (*einander*) that involves *Kampf*, struggle and conflict. To grasp the logic of this *Kampf* between the coming to presence and rescinding of truth demands "being completely exposed to (*Ausgesetzheit*), and at the mercy of, what is concealed and uncertain", of being attuned to the originary Greek experience of truth as *alētheia* – the primordial play in phenomena between concealment (*lēthē*) and unconcealment (*a-lēthēs*) (*SU* 33 = *R* 13; see also Chapter 8). If the German *Volk* is to come into its authentic destiny of sheltering *alētheia*, if it is to attain a "primordially attuned knowing resoluteness toward the essence of being", Heidegger claims, it must pursue its originary kinship with "the *Volk* of the Greeks whose ancestral stock and language have the same origin as we do" (*GA* 36/37: 6). As Heidegger put it in the Rectorial Address:

> All science remains bound to the beginning of philosophy and draws from it the strength of its essence, provided that it still remains equal to this beginning … The beginning still *is*. It does not lie *behind* us as something long past, but it stands *before* us … The beginning has invaded our future; it stands there as the distant injunction (*Verfügung*) to us to recover its greatness.
>
> Only if we resolutely submit to this distant injunction to win back the greatness of the beginning, only then will science become the innermost necessity of our existence. Otherwise, science will remain something in which we become involved purely by chance or will remain a calm, pleasurable activity, an activity free of danger, which promotes the mere advancement of learning. If, however, we submit to the distant injunction of the beginning, then science must become the fundamental happening of our spiritual existence as a *Volk*.   (*SU* 32–33 = *R* 12–13, trans. mod.)

In this pro-vocative call to his fellow Germans to heed their vocation as the only *Volk* capable of recovering the originary power of the first Greek beginning, Heidegger clearly emphasizes the necessity of submission, sacrifice and self-renunciation, even as he interprets all of this as a necessary part of wilful self-assertion. What the university demands of us all, Heidegger proclaims, is

> the originary, common will to its essence (*Wesen*) ... which is the will to science as the will to the historical–spiritual commission of the German *Volk* as a *Volk* that knows itself in its state. Science and German fate must *above all* come to their essential will to power. (*SU* 30 = *R* 10, trans. mod.)

This unflagging commitment to a Nietzschean form of self-assertive will-to-power marks Heidegger's Rectorial Address in the most striking way (see Chapter 12). And it is this "massive voluntarism" (as Derrida terms it) that has emerged as one of the defining characteristics of Heidegger's early commitment to National Socialism in the name of the "*Volk*", "spirit (*Geist*)" and "will": three terms whose meaning will profoundly change as Heidegger becomes ever more disenchanted with "official" National Socialism (Derrida 1989: 37; Davis 2007: 65–99). The Rectorial Address's commitment to a quasi-Platonic educational state grounded in work-, military- and knowledge-service depends on the communal resolve to *will* the futural happening of the *Volk* and to find in this will the strength and energy to fashion a community of teachers and workers, soldiers and students, all bound to their mission of preparing an/other beginning by "standing-firm" in the storm of European nihilism.

The Rectorial Address has rightly been criticized for its unmistakable affinities to National Socialism – its rejection of liberal academic freedom, its embrace of the principle of *Gleichschaltung* (the levelling of German society), its commitment to the *Führerprinzip* (leader-principle), its affinity with "the blood and soil" rhetoric of hard-core Nazi ideologues – but in December 1945, in response to questions from the de-Nazification commission in Freiburg, Heidegger defended his actions as rector and maintained that they sought "to oppose the advance of unsuited persons and the threatening supremacy of the party apparatus and party doctrine" (*MHNS* 17 = *R* 24). In this sense, Heidegger claimed, the Rectorial Address constituted a form of "spiritual resistance (*geistiger Widerstand*)" to National Socialism and in his official letters and report to the Freiburg commission he maintained that his Nietzsche lectures, delivered from 1936 to 1944, were conceived as nothing less than a "confrontation (*Auseinandersetzung*) with National Socialism" (*MHNS* 42–51). From the beginning Heidegger framed this defence of his National Socialist ties by separating the "political" and the "philosophical" aspects of this question. In his famous *Spiegel* interview of 1966, for example, he grants that the political events of 1933 were hardly unknown to him, yet he maintains that at the time he was more of an observer than a participant: "I certainly followed the course of political events between January and March of 1933 and occasionally talked about them with younger colleagues as well. However, my work was concerned with a more extensive interpretation of pre-Socratic thinking" (*MHNS* 42 = *GA* 16: 653).

Despite Heidegger's contentions, however, it is difficult to separate his National Socialist politics from his philosophy since they were so profoundly joined in his work. Heidegger himself was convinced that originary philosophy could only be done in dialogue with politics, something that has to be understood here not as the institutional, legal, military or socioeconomic aspects of statecraft or legislative–executive decision-making, but as the historical–ontological site within which Dasein struggles to find its place and its own sense of being rooted: in a community (*Gemeinschaft*), a *Volk*, a tradition and a history. Hence, Heidegger could write so passionately about his commitment to the earth, the homeland, the native ground and the "inner belonging of [his] own work to the Black Forest and its people that comes from a centuries-long and irreplaceable rootedness [*Bodenständigkeit*] in the Alemannic–Swabian soil" (*GA* 13: 10–11). This is what Heidegger means in the Rectorial Address when he writes of "the power that comes from preserving at the most profound level the forces that are rooted in the soil and blood of the *Volk*" (*SU* 33–34 = *R* 14, trans. mod.). The earth in this sense is not a natural region demarcated by the boundaries of settlement nor a mere geographical or political enclosure measured by the science of cartography; rather, "earth" for Heidegger becomes what the ancient Greeks termed "*chthōn*", the place where humans dwell and form a homeland.[4]

During his time as rector Heidegger committed himself in an institutional way to bringing about the sweeping changes necessary for the "total transformation of German Dasein" (*GA* 16: 192). The vision put forward in the Rectorial Address was of a *Volk* reawakened to the forgotten Greek disposition of wonder, awe and *thaumazein*, of a German community so attuned to the Heraclitean play of concealment/unconcealment that it would reject the careerist and technocratic application of learning that dominated the contemporary university with its educational calculus of measurement, management and computation. But the failure of the rectorate – this "thorn in my flesh" as Heidegger described it – would crush his ambitious hopes to take upon himself the institutional leadership of this "German awakening" (*HJB* 157). Instead, in his Freiburg lectures Heidegger would ever more powerfully embrace his own idiosyncratic form of National Socialism, a "private National Socialism" as the National Socialist Minister of Culture and Education, Otto Wacker, termed it, one that "circumvented the perspectives of the [official] party program" (*GA* 16: 381).

Heidegger, the Holocaust and charges of anti-Semitism

In one set of his Freiburg lectures from SS 1935, "Introduction to Metaphysics", Heidegger offered a forceful critique of the contemporary ideological position of National Socialism, which he saw as trapped in a cultural form of subjectivist worldview- and value-philosophy. "What is peddled about nowadays as the philosophy of National Socialism", he declared, "has not the least to do with the inner truth and greatness of this movement" (*EM* 152). But what genuinely constitutes "the inner truth and greatness" of National Socialism? In his 1953 revision of these lectures Heidegger claims that it has to do with "the encounter between global technology and modern humanity".[5] This nexus between National Socialism and global technology would provide the question-frame within which Heidegger would think through his political ties into the post-war era. Even in his 1949 Bremen lectures he goes so far as to circumscribe the atrocities of the Holocaust within his pervasive analysis of "*das Gestell*": the enframing structure of modern technology that manifests beings solely as available resources on constant standing reserve to be calculated, consumed and stockpiled for instrumental purposes (see Chapter 13). There he writes:

> Agriculture is now motorized food industry, the same thing in its essence as the manufacturing of corpses in the gas chambers and extermination camps, the same thing as the blockading and starving of countries, the same thing as the manufacturing of hydrogen bombs. (*GA* 79: 27)

And yet, as prescient as Heidegger's critique of modern technology proved to be, it remained "scandalously inadequate" as a way of addressing the torture and systematic extermination of Jews by the Nazi regime (Lacoue-Labarthe 1990: 34).

One of Heidegger's former students, Herbert Marcuse, wrote to him in 1947 expressing his shock that Heidegger could defend "the world historical guilt of the Nazi system" by equating "the torture, the maiming, and the annihilation of millions of people with the forcible relocation" of East Germans at the end of the war (*HC* 164). Nonetheless, Heidegger did offer a "defence" of Nazi Germany's position and, aside from a few private letters/conversations, he remained silent on the Shoah, never acknowledging his complicity in the National Socialist *Gestell* of terror. As for charges of anti-Semitism, Heidegger's defenders can console themselves by noting that there is no systematic doctrine of biological racism within his writings, something that cannot be said of his National Socialist colleagues in philosophy, Alfred Baeumler, Ernst Krieck and Hans Heyse (see Sluga 1993). And yet in both his official and private correspondence one can find troublesome expressions about the "Judaification of the German spirit", and warnings as early as 1916 that "the Judaification of our culture and universities is frightening to be sure and I believe the German race (*Rasse*) should summon as much inner strength as it can to reach its peak".[6] No matter how we try to contextualize or qualify these kinds of statements, or dismiss his collusion with Hitler's regime as an early "error" on his part – "the greatest stupidity in my life" Heidegger is reported to have said (Petzet 1993: 37) – we are left with troubling questions about Heidegger's place in the history of Nazi Germany and in the history of philosophy. And while doubts remain about Heidegger's "culpability" in the atrocities of the Nazi terror, it is hard to deny that his post-war cover-up of his National Socialist ties and his failure to clearly address the horrors of Auschwitz stand out as egregiously inadequate responses to the question of philosophical responsibility. Yet what of Heidegger's writings from the post-rectorate period (1934–45), those composed after his official withdrawal from public life in the National Socialist regime? How do they appear under the scrutiny of later reflection?

Heidegger's "private" National Socialism: Hölderlin, the Greeks and the other beginning

After Heidegger resigned as rector in April 1934, he retreated to his philosophical routine of writing and teaching as he abandoned his ambition to become the philosophical leader of the National Socialist movement. In the Winter Semester (hereafter WS) 1934–5 he delivered his first set of lectures on *Hölderlin's Hymnen "Germanien" und "Der Rhein"*, which, like the SS 1934 lectures on *Logik*, continued

Heidegger's focus on the *Volk* and on the question: "Who are we?" (*GA* 38: 34–64; *GA* 39: 48–59). In no uncertain terms Heidegger declares: "the Fatherland [is] the historical beyng of a *Volk*" (*GA* 39: 120). But now Heidegger seeks to offer a subtle critique of the "more dubious and noisy patriotism" spouted in official Nazi propaganda. Instead, he claims that "this historical beyng of the *Volk*, the Fatherland, is cloaked in mystery forever in keeping with its essence" (*ibid*.). What the *Volk* "is" remains recalcitrant to the ideologue's grasp; only in be-coming, only as a move-ment that accepts its futural mission to come to itself via a retrieve of the first Greek beginning, can the *Volk* hope to shelter its "essence". More than ever before, Heidegger will rethink this "essence" in terms of a new Hölderlinian myth of temporality. "The hour of our history has struck", Heidegger proclaims (*GA* 39: 294). By SS 1942 in *Hölderlin's Hymn "The Ister"* (*HHI = GA* 53) Heidegger will have renounced the aggressive, self-assertive nationalism of his early National Socialist years to embrace a more originary form of *völkisch* nationalism: a politics of the *archē* that he founds in/as language, history and autochthony. Each of these three spheres becomes the site for the homecoming of the German *Volk*. In its poetic confrontation with the first Greek beginning, the *Volk* of Hölderlin's invocation takes upon itself the call of/from beyng to fulfil its ontological destiny as those called on to prepare the transition to an "other" beginning.

In this turn away from the ambitions of the Rectorial Address Heidegger no longer conceives of the hoped-for revolution as imminent; on the contrary, after 1937 he slowly loses his faith in "official" National Socialism and instead embraces an Alemannic *Volksreligion* of *Heimat*, hearth and Hölderlin that defers the political revolution in favour of a poetic form of national renewal. Here Heidegger turns to Hölderlin's notion of "the festival" and of festal time as that which founds anew the time of the *Volk*-community. "'The festival' is itself the ground and essence of history", Heidegger declares; and, in turn, "to think the essence of history means to think the West in its essence from out of its relation to the first beginning, i.e., to the Greek world and to Greece" (*GA* 52: 68). The festival announces "the appropriative event" (*Ereignis*) that conciliates gods and humans in kairological time, a time of celebration, benefaction and consecration that is more originary than the calendrical time of planning, policy and the political. It is this festal time that Hölderlin had already uncovered in Sophocles' tragedies that Heidegger seeks to retrieve for an originary German politics of "authentic history" (*GA* 52: 77).

On this basis Heidegger will rethink his earlier notion of time as the historicity (*Geschichtlichkeit*) of Dasein in terms of a new reading of the destiny (*Geschick*) of be-ing as *Ereignis* (see Chapter 10). This shift *within* Heidegger's thinking – from the fate of Dasein to the destiny of the *Volk* by way of a Hölderlinian reflection on the essential homelessness of human being – will provide a pathway into the larger question of a "turning" (*Kehre*) of/within the history of being. This new being-historical mode of thinking will ultimately lead Heidegger to abandon the National Socialist politics of the *Volk* for a poetic–ontological interpretation of an *a*political *Volksreligion* that draws its inspiration from the archaic Greek experience of the polis as "the essence of being and of truth" (*GA* 54: 132). In his Parmenides lectures of WS 1942/43 (delivered during the bitter German defeat at Stalingrad that proved to be the turning point of the war) he will abjure the very language and conceptuality of politics, writing: "The essence of the Greek polis is grounded in the essence of *alētheia* ... The polis is neither city nor state ... It is the abode of the essence of historical man that discloses and conceals beings as such" (*GA* 54: 132–7). As the pole around which all beings turn, the polis becomes the place of settlement, where "the historical dwelling (*Aufenthalt*) of Greek humanity" takes place. In this abode, Dasein abides the conflictual play of concealment and revelation that defines the nature of truth. In this sense the polis serves as the site where Dasein inhabits the habitudes of its native and indigenous habitat in such a way that it comes to confront its essential homelessness as its sole and proper "home".

In his SS 1942 lectures *Hölderlin's Hymn "The Ister"*, Heidegger takes up again this Sophoclean–Hölderlinian theme of "coming to be at home in not being at home" and claims it as "the highest thing that the poet must poetize" (*GA* 53: 147–51). As he deconstructs the meaning of the "political" back to its ontological ground in the polis as the site for the possibility for "poetic dwelling" (*GA* 53: 137–9, 171–3), Heidegger comes to think of dwelling as bound up with the question of our *ēthos/Aufenthalt*. In these habitual haunts of our habitat and settlements – habits that come to be un-settling, uncanny and *unheimlich* precisely because they engage the fundamental homelessness of human being – Heidegger finds the measure for the possibility of poetic dwelling. This possibility of finding a proper historical dwelling place for the German *Volk* will preoccupy Heidegger long after the collapse of National Socialism. His late work will thoughtfully take up this question of "dwelling", abiding in the "abode", "becoming homely" and embracing a people's "destiny": topics that Heidegger will think in dialogue with Sophoclean tragedy and Presocratic philosophy. As Heidegger becomes ever more convinced that the Nazis' form of National Socialism is but another instance of the same machination, unbridled subjectivism, and drive for dominion over the earth as in modern Cartesian metaphysics, he turns to the archaic Greeks for a different ideal of German homecoming.

What becomes fundamental to this turn is the way Heidegger sets the Presocratic experience of *alētheia* into an engaged confrontation with Sophocles' insight into the essential homelessness/uncanniness (*Unheimlichkeit*) of the human being. Here Heidegger comes to embrace the tragic dimension of human being and its Oedipal legacy of *hybris/Vermessenheit* that transforms Heraclitean *logos* into a calculative–instrumental form of measurement (*Messen*) that can be deployed in the service of machination and control. It is only by experiencing this ontological legacy of homelessness, this deep and ineradicable sense of our own *Unheimlichkeit*, Heidegger claims, that the German *Volk* can hope to find again their home in being. By experiencing the question of truth's conflictual essence between hiddenness and unhiddenness as a question about the conflctual essence within human being itself, between its homelessness and its primordial yearning for its lost home within being, Heidegger comes to think Sophoclean uncanninesss as the nature of tragedy itself (*GA 54*: 134). In this persistent questioning of the riddles and enigmas of Greek tragedy Heidegger grapples with what he considers to be the most difficult and urgent questions facing the *Volk*, questions that traditionally get posed under rubrics such as "ethics" and "justice". Rejecting the standard ways of interpreting the Greek notions of *dikē* and *ēthos* as "justice" and "ethics", Heidegger treats them, rather, as primordial ways of attuning ourselves to a non-human measure for dwelling poetically on the earth. In experiencing the earth as our proper abode (*ēthos/Aufenthalt*) and understanding the human being as only one part of an overarching balance of forces within the fourfold of being (see Chapter 15), as part of the jointure (*Fug*) of joinings (*Fügungen*) that join together in the ad*just*ment (*dikē*) of being, there emerges for him the possibility of poetic dwelling that Hölderlin held out as the destiny of the Germans (*EGT* 40–47 = *HW* 326–33; *PM* 270–76 = *WM* 187–94; *PLT* 211–27 = *GA 7*: 189–208).

This kind of thinking about *ēthos*, *dikē* and ontological homelessness constitutes for Heidegger "the sole summons that calls mortals into their dwelling" (*GA 7*: 164). It is in this primordial thinking of *alētheia* as bound up with the homelessness of modern humanity that Heidegger experiences "German Dasein in its originary bond with the Greeks" (*MLS* 186). And while there still persist troubling traces of a human, all too human, German exceptionalism in Heidegger's writings after 1942, we can also find there formal indications that can be read as a devastating critique of historical National Socialism and its reign of

terror. Heidegger's work will never be free of the legitimate moral out-
rage that attends its reception and interpretation. His personal failings
were staggering and his unwillingness to honestly address his mistakes
constituted insularity at best and prideful arrogance at worst. And yet
his later writings put forward a challenge to any simple moral calculus
that could account for the barbarities of National Socialism, even his
own "private" strain. To read Heidegger's work on tragedy against
the tragedy of his own contorted involvement in German politics is to
confront the enigma that is Heidegger's legacy. For to think the question of the tragic means nothing less than to confront the irresolvable
paradox of exemplary greatness and tragic blindness that marks the
texts of Heidegger's beloved Sophocles. This thinking of the tragic
as what involves abiding the irreconcilability of inward contradiction
might even help us, once again, to more thoughtfully address the question of "Martin Heidegger and National Socialism".

Notes

1. Sluga (1993) provides the background for the Rectorial Address.
2. See especially Heidegger's letter to Elisabeth Blochmann, *HBB* 60.
3. "The Great War must be spiritually conquered by us in such a way that it
   becomes an inner law of our Dasein" (*GA* 16: 283).
4. For the ancient Greek interpretation of the earth in its profound relation to
   dwelling and the gods, see Sophocles, *Antigone* v.368ff. and *Oedipus Tyrannus*,
   vv. 736, 939.
5. For a discussion about the controversial status of this "addition", see Gregory
   Fried and Richard Polt's "Introduction" to *IM*.
6. For some examples of Heidegger's callous remarks about Jews, see *MLS* 51,
   112, 116.

References

Davis, B. W. 2007. *Heidegger and the Will: On the Way to Gelassenheit*. Evanston,
   IL: Northwestern University Press.
Derrida, J. 1989. *Of Spirit: Heidegger and the Question*, G. Bennington & R. Bowlby
   (trans.). Chicago, IL: University of Chicago Press.
Farias, V. 1989. *Heidegger and National Socialism*. Philadelphia, PA: Temple Uni-
   versity Press.
Lacoue-Labarthe, P. 1990. *Heidegger, Art and Politics: The Fiction of the Political*,
   C. Turner (trans.). Oxford: Blackwell.
Ott, H. 1993. *Martin Heidegger: A Political Life*, A. Blunden (trans.). New York:
   Basic Books.
Petzet, H. 1993. *Encounters and Dialogues with Martin Heidegger, 1929–1976*, P.
   Emad & K. Maly (trans.). Chicago, IL: University of Chicago Press.

Sluga, H. 1993. *Heidegger's Crisis: Philosophy and Politics in Nazi Germany*. Cambridge, MA: Harvard University Press.

Further reading

Primary sources
See Heidegger's *Die Selbstbehauptung der deutschen Universität; Gesamtausgabe 16: Reden und andere Zeugnisse eines Lebensweges; Gesamtausgabe 36/37: Sein und Wahrheit; Heidegger Jahrbuch IV: Heidegger und National Sozialismus*, esp. "Dokumentationsteil"; and *Martin Heidegger/Elisabeth Blochmann Briefwechsel* (all in German).

Neske & Kettering (1990) includes "The Rectorate 1933/34: Facts and Thoughts" as well as various primary and secondary texts relevant to Heidegger's political thought. Wolin (1993) includes "The Self-Assertion of the German University" as well as various primary and secondary texts relevant to Heidegger's political thought.

Secondary sources
See Bambach (2003); de Beistegui (1998); R. Bernasconi, "Heidegger's Alleged Challenge to the Nazi Concept of Race", in Faulconer & Wrathall (2008), 50–67; Fried (2000); Rockmore (1992); and Zimmerman (1990). See also M. Gillespie, "Martin Heidegger's Aristotelian National Socialism", *Political Theory* 28(2) (2000), 140–66; and T. Kisiel, "The Essential Flaw in Heidegger's 'Private National Socialism", in *Philosophie und Zeitgeist im National Sozialismus*, M. Heinz (ed.), 291–311 (Würzburg: Königshausen & Neumann, 2006).

EIGHT

Truth as *alētheia* and the clearing of beyng

Daniel O. Dahlstrom

The Greek word *alētheia* is typically translated as "truth". Once this translation is in place, interpretations of *alētheia* trade on the meanings primarily associated with "truth". The traditionally dominant meaning in this regard is correctness (the correctness of a thought or assertion) and, in fact, as early as Homer, a cognate of correctness, *homoiōsis*, served as a synonym for *alētheia*. Thus the correctness (*orthotes*) of a thought or assertion tends to be understood in terms of its agreement or correspondence (*homoiōsis*) with a state of affairs. Nevertheless, Heidegger takes exception to the interpretation of *alētheia* as correctness or correspondence alone, regarding it as a derivative notion of truth. This sort of interpretation overlooks the fact that *alētheia* has a much richer significance that notions of correctness presuppose. *Alētheia* in that more basic sense signifies the "unhiddenness" (*Unverborgenheit*) of what is asserted. For example, "The tree is sprouting" is true, that is, correct, only if the tree shows sprouts. Since what is hidden is hidden *from* someone, truth as the unhiddenness of "things" also entails their actual or potential presence *to* someone, someone with an understanding of them. The unhiddenness signified by *alētheia* is accordingly irreducible to either subjects or objects. Not surprisingly, so taken were certain Greek thinkers with this sheer manifestness or presence of things that they identified it as a principal way of saying of something that it exists.

While a remarkable achievement, the appreciation of truth as unhiddenness is, Heidegger insists, far from the end of the story. For, as its privative nature suggests, "un-hiddenness" (*a-lētheia*) supposes a hiddenness. That hiddenness is not traceable simply to either the obstruction of some entities by others or the shortsightedness of some observers. Nor is it merely the absence in the past out of which the presence of what is present emerges (like the tree before and after sprouting). Also hidden is what it means for each respective entity as well as entities as a whole to be at all – not least when being is equated with the manifestness or presence of things. Heidegger accordingly argues that the essence of truth is neither the correctness of assertions nor the unhiddenness of beings, but the truth of beyng, that is, the interplay of that hiddenness and unhiddenness (or, equivalently, absencing and presencing, the strife between earth and world). Truth in this most fundamental sense – the truth of beyng – is the hidden "openness" in the midst of beings that grounds their unhiddenness and, thereby, the correctness of assertions and thoughts about them (CP 239–46, 249–50 = GA 65: 342–51, 357).

Although Heidegger investigates truth as *alētheia* throughout his career, the investigations typically move through the three steps just noted: the *correctness* of thoughts and assertions, the *unhiddenness* of beings and the *clearing* for beyng's self-concealment. He investigates these three conceptions with the understanding that, historically, truth in some sense defines human existence and human beings define themselves by the way they conceive truth. He accordingly emphasizes the enormity of the human transformation at the beginning of Western thinking, initiated by the Greek understanding of *alētheia* as the unhiddenness of beings. He also projects the need for a new beginning, a transformation that corresponds to the "truth of beyng", the clearing presupposed by truth as *alētheia* (unhiddenness). This chapter traces the general steps in Heidegger's investigation with an eye to exposing the human transformations that, in his eyes, the interpretations of truth as *alētheia* in the first beginning and in a new beginning respectively entail.

Correctness, unhiddenness of beings and the clearing of beyng

In ordinary discourse, we typically use the adjective "true" to designate a property of some thing or some thought or assertion. These usages are related. For example, we say that someone is a true friend because she corresponds to our idea of what a friend should be; we say an assertion is true ("'She's a friend' is true") because it corresponds to the state of affairs of which it is asserted. Truth, on this view, is the correctnesss of that correspondence. Beginning with Plato and Aristotle, Heidegger claims, this general conception of truth has been regnant in philosophy as well. As one piece of evidence, he cites Aquinas's definition of truth as "the correspondence of the thing and how it is understood" (*adaequatio rei et intellectus*), while noting that modern thinkers tend to focus on the correspondence of what is understood *to* the thing (*adaequatio intellectus ad rem*). Equating what is understood with what can be *asserted or judged* of the thing, modern thinkers largely take their bearings from the logical prejudice that the assertion or judgement, silent or spoken, is the site of truth and truth itself is the correctness of the assertion.[1]

Yet the correspondence theory of truth is beset with some basic problems. Correspondence is not identity or even likeness. Assertions are not pictures that can be compared for their accuracy with something pictured. The term "correspondence" would appear to be highly figurative at best, tacitly drawing on uses of a family of words (e.g. "agreement", "similarity") that tenuously lend it significance. Moreover, any truthful account of truth as correct correspondence seems either to beg the question of what "truth" means or to suppose as its warrant some further correspondence that must be similarly warranted in turn, and so on *ad infinitum*.[2]

Nevertheless, we distinguish true (correct) assertions from false ones and Heidegger has an explanation for this capacity. An assertion, he submits, correctly corresponds to a thing when it manages to represent what presents itself and, indeed, represent it "as it is". The ordinary notion of truth as correct correspondence, far from being the last word on the subject, draws on, even "presupposes" a process of presenting or "uncovering" things as they are. The relevant thought or assertion can be said to correspond correctly to something because it forms part of a way of behaving towards the thing in question, that lets it present itself such as it is in itself. Not everything that we think or say is of this sort; indeed, we may speak of things' origins ("that's from China") or their utility ("that'll be a big help to us"). But we also think and speak of things precisely in terms of how they present themselves. For this attentiveness to things as such to take place or, in other words, for us to be bound by such standards of correctness, we have to be free for what can open itself up in our midst (*SZ* 218, 224; *PM* 140–41, 143–4; *BW* 177–8). Allowing things to present themselves-as-they-are is an openness to them, precisely in so far as they are said to be. But this openness amounts to nothing if things do not also open themselves up to us. The Greeks, Heidegger stresses, already experienced this openness as the unhiddenness (*Unverborgenheit*) of things and, indeed, grounded the conception of truth as correctness on this notion of unhiddenness (even when it was not really obvious to them that they were doing so). For the Greeks this "unhiddenness is a determination of *entities themselves* and not somehow – like correctness – a character of *an assertion about* them" (*BQP* 106 = *GA* 45: 121, trans. mod.). Indeed, our ordinary notion of truth as correctness "stands and falls" with truth as the unhiddenness of entities (*BW* 177; see *BQP* 85–91, 112ff. = *GA* 45: 96–103, 129ff.). As noted earlier, Heidegger submits that this experience of truth as unhiddenness is captured by the Greek word usually rendered as "truth", namely, *alētheia*. In this word, the first letter *a* serves as a privative prefix for *lētheia*, a term that derives from a family of expressions, such as *lēthē* (forgetfulness) and *lanthanein* (remaining hidden) (*SZ* 219; *EGT* 104 = *VA* 251; *CP* 237–8 = *GA* 65: 339).[3]

In his 1937–8 lectures Heidegger expands the account of the openness presupposed by truth as correctness to include, in addition to the openness (unhiddenness) of things to us and our openness (freedom) towards them, the openness of the realm "between the thing and the human being" as well as the openness of one person (*Mensch*) to another. Thus he refers to a fourfold yet unitary openness that underlies and enables the idea of truth as correctness. "Correctness of representing anything is only possible if, in each case, it can establish itself in this openness as what carries it and spans over it. The openness is the ground and soil and play-space of correctness" (*BQP* 19 = *GA* 45: 20, trans. mod.).[4] But that openness is more than the unhiddenness of things or even that unhiddenness together with the freedom of being-here (*Dasein*). It is the "enowning event" that makes possible that un-hiddenness and the freedom of being-here precisely by sustaining the hiddenness or self-concealing of things.[5]

Exploiting a familiar trope throughout his writings, Heidegger refers to this openness as a *clearing* (*Lichtung*) and "the truth of beyng" (given that the being of beings is equated with their unhiddenness). The straightforward significance of *Lichtung* in German is, like "clearing" in English, an open space in a forest, for example a glade. For Heidegger's purposes, it is particularly relevant that the open region of a clearing allows for light but also supposes the density and darkness of the surrounding forest and that it signals human handiwork (*ausgeholzte Stelle im Wald*, "cleared land in the woods"). In *Being and Time* Heidegger alludes to the significance of "clearing" in connection with uses of "light" (*Licht*) and cognate metaphors, for example "illuminate" (*erleuchten*) and Descartes' *lumen naturale* (natural light). Given the grounding role that the metaphor of light plays in Plato's thinking, these allusions suggest modes of retrieving the original experiences at work in the very beginnings of Western thinking. At the same time, however, already in *Being and Time* Heidegger distinguishes these senses of "light" from the clearing constitutive of them and making them possible (*SZ* 133, 350–51). In later writings, Heidegger is even more explicit about this relationship between the grounding sense of the "clearing" and the derivative metaphors of "light" in regard to the question of truth. As Heidegger puts it in one of his last works, "Light can stream into the clearing, into its openness, and let brightness play with darkness in it. But light never first creates the clearing. Rather light presupposes it ....The clearing is the open region for everything that becomes present and absent" (BW 442).

The metaphor of a clearing would be misleading if it were taken for something already in place and static, unmoved either by the encroaching forest or by our arrival. The clearing, as Heidegger understands the openness grounding other senses of truth, is not like that any more than an actual clearing is. Instead, the clearing is the event, the time-space that enables things to come into the open, precisely by keeping the hiddenness itself hidden. The clearing (or, as Heidegger at times also puts it, the clearing in contention with concealment) is the end of Heidegger's analysis of truth, as the un-grounded ground – or, in other words, the grounding abyss (Ab-grund) – of the other levels of truth (BW 178, 186–7, 441–6; CP 230–31, 243–50 = GA 65: 329–30, 348–57; M 279–80 = GA 66: 314).

This gloss on the significance that Heidegger attaches to the clearing helps explain why he also speaks of the "truth of beyng" to characterize the openness underlying the other senses of truth. Whereas "being" (Sein) signifies the sense in which particular beings (Seiendes) are understood to be, "beyng" (Seyn) refers to the event (Ereignis) in which that signification and understanding historically take hold – even if only to be forgotten or treated with indifference. The historical determination of an understanding of the being of beings arises out of the dynamic event of beyng taking hold of being-here (Da-sein), unfolding (wesend) but concealing itself in the process. Heidegger accordingly observes that truth in the primordial and essential sense is the truth of beyng and the truth of beyng is not the clearing simply but the clearing for the self-concealing of beyng – although it remains an open question, Heidegger tellingly adds, whether we will succeed in owning up to it (CP 182ff., 192, 239–40, 243–4, 327–8 = GA 65: 259ff., 273, 342–3, 348–9, 465–6).

Truth's freedom

The clearing, the most basic sense of truth entailed by conceiving truth as alētheia, includes, as noted, an openness on our part, namely, an openness to what can open itself up in our midst. Inasmuch as truth as correctness presupposes our being-free for the self-presentation on the part of beings, freedom in the sense designated is essential to truth (*PM* 142). Freedom, understood as letting entities be, consummates (*vollzieht*) what Heidegger deems the original Greek intimation of truth as *alētheia*, the unhidden character of entities (*PM* 146).

By construing human freedom as essential to truth, Heidegger opens himself up to the objection that he violates the traditional, "metaphysical" sense of truth's objectivity, where truth is conceived as one of the conditions of knowledge ("suitably justified true belief"), and not vice versa (*PM* 143). What Heidegger understands by freedom in this connection is, of course, by no means equivalent to knowledge; nevertheless, introducing freedom as a constitutive condition of truth exposes his account to an analogous objection. If the truth depends on human freedom, how can its vital role as an objective, unbiased constraint on knowledge and action be sustained?

Heidegger responds to this objection by noting that the freedom in question is anything but caprice or even something at a human being's disposal. Instead, in advance of any sense of "negative" and "positive" senses of freedom (being unencumbered and empowered), a freedom for the truth consists in an active engagement with beings precisely with a view to letting them present themselves as they are. Opening oneself up in this way to the unhidden character of things is a matter not of losing oneself in them, but of "stepping back in the face of them [the entities] so that they can reveal themselves in what and how they are and the correspondence that presents them can take the correct measure [*Richtmaß*] from that" (*PM* 144). The freedom that is essential to truth is, in other words, a matter of letting beings be and opening ourselves to them in all their manifestness. This exposedness to beings' unhiddenness both defines our existence (*ek-sistieren*) and co-constitutes the dynamic clearing described above (*PM* 143–4).

Yet the foregoing account, while accurate in some respects, is misleading to the extent that it suggests (a) that the clearing is essentially that unhiddenness, (b) that beings and human beings are somehow already in the clearing and (c) that we accordingly know (possess the truth of) who we are as human beings. The clearing makes possible that unhiddenness of things (truth as *alētheia*) because it is a clearing for beyng's self-concealing. Moreover, as itself a hidden, grounding event, this truth of beyng is not a transcendental feature of human subjects, the ahistorical condition of the possibility of the unhiddenness of beings and the correctness of assertions. Indeed, this event is by no means foregone and we are not by ourselves in a position to make it happen (although there is reason to think that it can happen and that we can prepare for it). For similar reasons, it remains an open question whether we are truly here (*da*). To be sure, there can be no openness to the being of beings without a projection, on our part, of their being. In this sense, the truth of beyng supposes our being-here (*Da-sein*) as the very disclosiveness of being. But this projection is suitable only to the extent that it corresponds to beyng itself or, in other words, to the extent that it is brought into its own by beyng itself. As Heidegger puts it in the 1930s, this reciprocal movement of beyng (*Seyn*) and being-here (*Da-sein*) – the former needing the latter, the latter belonging to the former – is the "turning" (*Kehre*) in beyng that constitutes it as an "event" or, more precisely, the "enowning" (*Ereignis*) of being-here by beyng (see Chapters 6 and 10). But our being-here in this way, cor-responding to beyng, requires our transformation from preservers of the unhiddenness of beings to guardians of the openness for beyng's self-concealment (*CP* 177, 184, 286–7 = *GA* 65: 251, 261, 407; *BQP* 163–4 = *GA* 45: 189–90).

Truth's errancy and mystery

While derivative, the conception of truth as correctness is the starting-point for enquiry into truth as *alētheia*.[6] Its relevance lies, among other things, in the centrality of bivalence, the possibility of correctness or incorrectness. When someone describes an unusual or surprising event ("the glacier is melting") and someone who has not seen it expresses scepticism, she may feel the need to say "No, it's true". These words are not simply an iteration; they assert that the opposite state of affairs does not obtain and, indeed, that its not-obtaining (like what does obtain) is not based simply on its being asserted. Without the possibility of the opposite, the adjective "true" is superfluous. "Only because truth and untruth are *in essence not* indifferent to one another, but instead belong together, can in general a true sentence enter into pointed opposition to the corresponding untrue sentence" (*PM* 146).

The truth of beyng grounds this bivalence, just as it grounds truth as *alētheia*. We have already noted how the possibility of correct assertions depends on both our openness to entities and their openness to us. But neither of these conditions need be met or, better, fully met; nor, for that matter, can they be. That is to say, truth entails untruth across sub-jective and objective dimensions. We may intentionally try to dissemble or we may innocently overlook some things or aspects in the course of presenting others; this errancy on our part – caught up in untruth as fundamentally as truth (*SZ* 222–3) – goes hand in hand with our freedom. But, even more fundamentally, things also present themselves to us in puzzling and misleading ways that give rise to illusions and error (*BW* 179). We noted earlier how, according to Heidegger, being-free-for the way entities are, while constitutive of truth's essence, is not a matter of anyone's arbitrary whim. But if truth is not simply a prerogative of a human stance towards things, nor is un-truth (*PM* 146–7).

Moreover, just as truth is not primarily an assertion, so untruth cannot be traced invariably to an incorrect judgement alone. Indeed, in so far as we understand the openness of entities to us and, correlatively, our being-free-for that openness as essential to truth, then the very opposite of truth in this sense, a hiddenness, is essential to truth. While not to be confused with falsity, this hiddenness, like falsity, is essential to truth as *alētheia*, since the unhiddenness of things, as noted earlier, supposes the clearing, as both the openness in the midst of beings and the enowning event in which being conceals itself.

The hiddenness or absence (*lēthē*) entailed by experiencing truth as *alētheia* is the hiddenness not simply of this or that particular entity but entities as a whole. "The hiddenness of entities as a whole, the genuine non-truth, is older than every manifestness of this or that entity" (*PM* 148). But hidden as well is the fact of this hiddenness itself. Heidegger refers to the fact that this hiddenness itself is hidden as the mystery (*Geheimnis*). This mystery pervades our being-here (*Da-sein*) and our being-here preserves this mystery. This mystery is not simply what is enigmatic, unexplained or questionable within the domain of what is manifest and accessible. As long as such enigmas are construed as merely way-stations on the way to what is or can make them accessible, that is, as long as "the hiddenness of entities as a whole" is indulged merely as a limit that occasionally announces itself, "the hiding as the basic happening has sunk in forgetfulness" (*PM* 149).

Truth's transformations

The basic sense of freedom that consists in letting entities be, bringing them into the open and being open for them, is foundational for all behaviour. But this freedom has come to be "resolutely" oriented to the presence of things, having "closed itself off" from any hiddenness or absence (*PM* 149). That very freedom at work in the original Greek conception of truth as the unhiddenness of things facilitates forgetfulness not only of the mystery (the underlying "truth of beyng") but even of the unhiddenness itself (as the being of beings). At times Heidegger identifies Plato's Cave Allegory – the yoking (*sugon*) of *alētheia* to the manifest way things look in the light, that is, the *look* or *idea* of them – as the "key place" for this devolution from unhiddenness to correctness (*homoiōsis*).⁷ As a result, that freedom itself disappears in this forgetfulness, exemplified by our proneness to become absorbed in what is at any moment apparent, accessible and manipulable.

Heidegger's interpretation of truth as *alētheia* is, in his terms, thoroughly historical (see Chapter 11), requiring an understanding of ourselves as something that began with the groundbreaking, Greek experience of truth. The aim of interpreting truth as *alētheia* is to make another beginning, based on appreciation of the limits of that understanding. But for this reason Heidegger recognizes that he must explain the unquestioned status that truth as unhiddenness largely enjoyed among the Greeks (*BQP* 114–15, 119–20 = *GA* 45: 132, 138). The explanation lies, he submits, in the fundamental mood principally motivating Greek thinking, namely, the astonishment (*thaumazein*) at something quite ordinary, indeed, the most ordinary aspect of things: the fact that they are and that they are what they are. Thanks to this wonder, that most ordinary aspect of things becomes the most extraordinary, the wonder at beings in so far as they exist (*on hēi on*) or, equivalently, are manifest and unhidden. "The basic mood of *thaumazein* necessitates the pure recognition of the extraordinariness of the ordinary" (*BQP* 147 = *GA* 45: 171, trans. mod.). This wonder at "the being of beings" (*Sein des Seienden*) first sets them in the midst of beings as such (i.e. as unhidden) and, in the process, attunes human beings to truth and inaugurates Western thinking. This thinking is so taken by the unhiddenness of things and so committed to attending to things in so far as they are unhidden that it finds nothing in that unhiddenness (*alētheia*) to question.⁸ The human transformation initiated by Plato and Aristotle consists in corresponding to the prevailing unhiddenness of things (their *physis*), actively cultivating and sustaining as much, in a mode of knowing that the Greeks called *technē* (see Chapter 13).⁹

This "technical" way with things, necessitated by wonder, provides fertile soil for distorting *alētheia* as unhiddenness into mere correctness. The more the recognition of the entities in their unhiddenness develops into *technē*, the more unavoidable it becomes that the looks of entities (the "ideas") alone provide the measure of them and require constant correspondence with those "looks". The original essence of *alētheia* is ineluctably lost and, with it, the fundamental mood necessitating it. Beings become objects, truth becomes the correctness of representing them, and astonishment at the sheer existence (unhiddenness) of things gives way to indifference to being as simply the most commonplace of commonplaces. Along the way, a desire to become increasingly familiar with ever more things and to become facile in reckoning and computing with them gradually takes hold (*BQP* 155–6, 158 =*GA* 45: 180–81, 184; *M* 91–2, 154–5 =*GA* 66: 109–10, 177).

The conception of truth as correctness is, Heidegger contends, no more a question today than the conception of *alētheia* as unhiddenness was for most Greeks. The seemingly self-evidential character of conceiving truth in terms of correctness alone reinforces and is reinforced by an indifference to the question of what it means to be at all, an indifference that Heidegger famously dubs "the forgottenness of being". With this forgottenness, he maintains, "the truth of beyng is denied entities. The entities *are* and yet remain abandoned by beyng and left over to themselves in order thus to become only the object of machination" (*BQP* 159 =*GA* 45: 185, trans. mod.). Heidegger suggests that the nihilism of denying entities and human beings "the truth of beyng" might be "the concealed ground of a still concealed, fundamental mood that would compel [*nötigte*] us to a different necessity, [that] of a *different* primordial questioning and beginning" (*BQP* 160 =*GA* 45: 186, trans. mod.). (Indeed, he implies that this necessity has been shaping his entire deliberation on the question of truth; *BQP* 161 =*GA* 45: 187.) That fundamental mood would involve, among other things, a kind of restraint (*Verhaltenheit*) in which questioning turns to what deserves to be questioned above all else, the hiddenness of beyng, and does so "for the sake of the beyng of beings as a whole" (*CP* 12 =*GA* 65: 16, trans. mod.). Heidegger's characterization of this restraint is complex and multifaceted.[10] However, in conclusion we can perhaps allude to its significance by recalling the observation, cited earlier, that beyng (*Seyn*) and being-here (*Da-sein*) – the former needing the latter, the latter belonging to the former – are in a constant interplay (*kehriges Verhältnis*), a process of presencing-and-absencing that Heidegger characterizes as the "enowning event" (*Ereignis*). Restraint attunes us to this enownment and, in the process, demands that we begin to think anew, thinking "from out of this enownment", as it were, steadfastly and decisively yet humbly about the truth of the beyng of beings: as the enowning event that grounds their unhiddenness to us and our openness to them. Although we are no longer preservers of the astonishing unhiddenness of beings (as the Greeks putatively were), restraint transforms us into vigilant guardians of the clearing for the self-concealing of beyng (*CP* 177, 184, 286–7 =*GA* 65: 251, 261, 407; *BQP* 163 =*GA* 45: 189–90).

MARTIN HEIDEGGER: KEY CONCEPTS

Notes

1. See *SZ* 214, 226; *PM* 137–8 =*VWW* 177–8; *ETP* 1–2 =*GA* 34: 2; *BQP* 9, 14–18, 22–3 =*GA* 45: 8–9, 15–18, 23–4.

2. For many contemporaries this is a false dilemma, generated by failing to recognize the equivalence of ascription of truth to a proposition ("*p*" is true) and the (disquoted) proposition itself (*p*) as in Tarski's formulation "'*p*' is true if and only if *p*". On this disquotational, deflationist approach, see Quine (1992: 79–82).

3. Paul Friedländer criticizes the notion that with Plato the meaning of *alētheia* degenerates – epochally – from unhiddenness to correctness (1969: 221–9). While Heidegger acknowledges the Greeks' acquaintance with both senses, he contends that the sense of unhiddenness is largely taken for granted and accordingly tacit and unquestioned by them (*BQP* 95, 174ff. =*GA* 45: 108, 204ff.). Yet he does later concede that it was misleading to name *alētheia* in the sense of the clearing "truth" (*BW* 446–7 =*ZSD* 77).

4. Ernst Tugendhat famously charges that construing disclosedness as more basic than correctness forfeits the traditional, critical function of setting truth set off from falsity (1970: 331–62). But Heidegger insists that since truth as correctness is derivative and since the primordial truth is a projection (*Entwurf*), correctness does not apply to it (*CP* 229 =*GA* 65: 327).

5. The foregoing account is drawn from "On the Essence of Truth" (*PM* 136–54), drafted between 1930 and 1943. In *Being and Time* Heidegger also identifies a truth more fundamental than correctness. After characterizing the *uncovering* of entities and Dasein's *disclosure* of being (its own and others') as respectively ontic and ontological levels of the understanding constitutive of its being-in-the-world, Heidegger concludes that Dasein's disclosedness (or "clearing") is "the most primordial phenomenon of the truth" and "the ontological condition of the possibility that assertions can be true or false" (*SZ* 226; see *SZ* 132–3, 147, 170, 220, 350–51). In *Being and Time* talk of the unhiddenness of entities is couched in the manner of their being uncovered; in "On the Essence of Truth", Heidegger emphasizes how entities open themselves up to us. In the 1929 essay "On the Essence of Ground", the account is even more streamlined: propositional truth (correctness) is grounded in ontic truth – the "manifestness of entities" – and ontic truth is grounded in ontological truth – the "unveiledness of being" (including Dasein's foregoing understanding of an entity's being) (*PM* 103–4). By the mid 1930s Heidegger speaks of the clearing as a process of *Da-sein's* being enowned (*er-eignet*) by *Seyn*; hence the translation of *Ereignis* here as the "enowning event".

6. By challenging the equation of truth with correctness, Heidegger also hopes to expose its alliance with certain conceptions of being. Underlying the medieval version of this correspondence (*adaequatio*) is the divinely created character of things (*res*) and understanding (*intellectus*): a structure surviving in post-medieval notions that everything can be made subject to planning by a self-legislating world-reason (*PM* 138–9).

7. *PM* 155–82, esp. 173, 176–7; *ETP* 17–81 =*GA* 34: 21–112; *BQP* 155–6 =*GA* 45: 180–81; *CP* 232–5 =*GA* 65: 331–5; *M* 91–2 =*GA* 66: 109–10. Repeatedly revising his interpretations of Plato and Aristotle, Heidegger occasionally traces modern logical prejudices (truth exclusively as correctness) to them, joint saboteurs of the "early Greek construal of truth" as unhiddenness (*BQP* 15,

126

89ff., 97–8 =*GA* 45: 15, 101ff., 111). But the story also runs back to Presocratic thinkers (notably, Heraclitus) who did appreciate the hiddenness supposed by truth as *alētheia*.
8. *BQP* 144–51, 158 =*GA* 45: 167–74, 184. Plato, *Theaetetus* 155d2ff; Aristotle, *Metaphysics* 982b11ff; Heidegger contrasts *thaumazein* (*Er-staunen*) with other phenomena (*Sichwundern, Verwunderung, Bewunderung, Staunen, Bestaunen*) that, instead of construing the ordinary as extraordinary, focus on something extraordinary relative to the ordinary; see *BQP* 136–7, 142ff., 149–50 =*GA* 45: 157–8, 163ff., 173–4.
9. *BQP* 153ff. =*GA* 45: 178ff. As the knowing and basic behaviour in which the preservation of what is astonishing – the beingness of beings – is preserved, *technē* is something wholly other than *physis* that belongs most essentially to it.
10. Heidegger characterizes *Verhaltenheit* in numerous ways, for example *holding back* from any pretension to ground the truth of beyng in beings or being, *holding out* creatively in that grounding truth as itself an abyss (*Ab-grund*), and *holding on to (controlling) itself* as it leaps ahead into the event of the conflict of earth and world, the interplay of presences and absences, and *Seyn* and *Dasein* (*BQP* 4 =*GA* 45: 2; *CP* 10–17, 23–5, 261–2, 277 =*GA* 65: 14–23, 33–6, 375, 395–6).

References

Friedländer, P. 1969. *Plato*, 2nd rev. edn. Princeton, NJ: Princeton University Press.
Quine, W. V. O. 1992. *Pursuit of Truth*, rev. edn. Cambridge, MA: Harvard University Press.
Tugendhat, E. 1970. *Der Wahrheitsbegriff bei Husserl und Heidegger*. Berlin: de Gruyter.

Further reading

Primary sources
See Heidegger's *Basic Writings*, esp. "The Origin of the Work of Art",139–212; *Being and Time*, §44; *Contributions to Philosophy (From Enowning)*, pt V; *Mindfulness*, pt V; and *Pathmarks*, esp. "On the Essence of Truth", 136–54, and "Plato's Doctrine of Truth", 155–82.

Secondary sources
See Dahlstrom (2001), Sallis (1995b) and M. Wrathall, "Unconcealment", in Dreyfus & Wrathall (2007), 337–357. See also J. Hersey, *The Question of Ground and the Truth of Being: Heidegger's WS 1931/2 Lecture Course*, dissertation, Catholic University of America (2007); and K. Maly, "From Truth to *Alētheia* to Opening and Rapture", *Heidegger Studies* 6 (1990), 27–42.

NINE

The work of art

Jonathan Dronsfield

Overcoming aesthetics

Heidegger's writings on art carry out what he sees as the task of providing "a new content for the word 'art' and for what it intends to name" (*IM* 140). From the mid 1930s to the end of the 1950s Heidegger's work is shaped by a persistent engagement with art. Prior to this he writes nothing substantive on art, and barely mentions art in any publication or lecture. But the 1930s sees major works featuring sections dedicated to art, aesthetics and poetic language, to which lecture courses in 1936 (on Nietzsche), and in 1934, 1941 and 1942 (on Hölderlin), are also devoted, as are numerous essays throughout the 1940s and 1950s. "The Origin of the Work of Art", begun in 1935 but not published in full until 1960 – in other words, it spans the whole of the period in question – is Heidegger's most sustained treatment of art, and it is that text that this chapter focuses on. "The Origin of the Work of Art" comprises three lectures, an Epilogue and an Addendum. It is important to note that the essay appeared in two distinct forms and at two separate times: as lectures before the war[1] and in print after the war.[2] Between the first oral version of 1935 and the first full published version of 1960 the text undergoes constant revision and clarification, and has significant sections added.[3] The Epilogue is "in part, written later" than the lectures. The Addendum is made in 1956, and "explains some of the leading words". The full print version retains "the changing use of language" over the duration of this time.[4] The very last line appeals to the "quandary" of an author "having to speak in the language most opportune for each of the various stations on his way" (*BW* 212). It remains open whether this essay is to be seen as but one station, or as the span of the way.

Why must the word "art" be given a new content? Because art has been reduced to "a routine cultural phenomenon" (*BW* 203), "a sector of cultural activity" (*QCT* 34); because philosophical aesthetics has reduced art to the display of the beautiful, where the beautiful, as an object of taste, is the merely enjoyable, where art is just one among many things to be experienced. Enjoyment and experience of art will never be able to discern whether the object enjoyed or experienced is essentially art or the product of an illusion or a machination (*CP* 356).[5] But does what Heidegger calls for as art in "The Origin of the Work of Art" need or warrant the name "art"? In *Contributions to Philosophy*, written over the early years of "The Origin of the Work of Art", 1936–8, but not published until 1989, in a section devoted to "'Metaphysics' and the Origin of the Work of Art", Heidegger puts forward the following claim: "a moment of history that *lacks art* can be more historical and more creative than times of a widespread art business" (*CP* 355). With this notion of lack of art (*Kunstlösigkeit*) Heidegger is disavowing not genuine art, but rather the derivative popular conception of art that links it with "culture" and "aesthetics", a conception that goes right back to the end of Greek art. It is only after the end of the great period of Greek art – "that brief but magnificent time" (*QCT* 34), a moment co-extensive with the end of Greek philosophy – that aesthetics begins, according to Heidegger (*N1* 80).

What Heidegger is after is an understanding of art as something akin to Greek art (if we can still call it art): the opening up of the being of beings (*IM* 140), "a single, manifold revealing", "a revealing that brings forth truth into ... appearing", what the Greeks called *technē* (*QCT* 34; see Chapter 13). And for this fundamental orientation to be won back for art, aesthetics must be *overcome*. And to accomplish this entails taking on the way in which metaphysics conceives beings as objectively representable, since this is exactly what finds expression in aesthetics as "the ground for what is heretofore the ownmost of Western art and its works" (*CP* 354). Part of what frames "The Origin of the Work of Art" is Hegel's judgement – Hegel's *Aesthetics* is "the most comprehensive reflection on the essence of art that the West possesses", for Heidegger, precisely because it stems from metaphysics (*BW* 204) – that in its highest vocation, namely the way in which truth obtains existence for itself, art "is and remains for us a thing of the past" (Hegel 1975: 11). In "The Origin of the Work of Art" at least, Heidegger will contend otherwise, arguing that art is still needed as an essential and necessary way in which truth happens, one that is decisive for human being's historical existence.

In seeking to retrieve this new content for what is named "art", Heidegger claims to be laying out not a definition of what is "ownmost" to the work of art, for that too would be metaphysical, and too metaphysically philosophical, but the conditions for a *decision* about what is ownmost to art (*M* 28), for putting the truth of being to a decision (*CP* 355). Thus, while "The Origin of the Work of Art" provides no answers to the question of what art is, and instead gives what Heidegger calls "directives" (*Weisungen*; *BW* 211) for continued questioning about it, at the same time Heidegger sets out the task of overcoming aesthetics in such a way as to require of us a decision as to how we stand with respect to art. Moreover, for Heidegger art is a way of questioning, and the refusal to give answers to the question of what art is indicates not just how Heidegger understands philosophy, as the unfolding of the question of being, but the importance he attaches to art's questioning in this unfolding. The insistence on questioning, on the work of art as questioning, on an answer only having force if rooted in and not detached from questioning, and on the task of the thinker on art to question in terms of the work (*BW* 194–5), all of which is commensurate with thinking being as a *question*, emerges explicitly towards the end of the lecture, and most especially in what is added to it. This is the sense in which, for Heidegger, we need to see art as a riddle, an enigma (*Rätsel*; *BW* 204), and it goes some way to explaining why at the outset Heidegger sets out how and why the movement of questioning about art must be circular, for only through a circular movement of questioning will the question of the origin of the work of art be held open (*BW* 144; *OWAF* 331–2; compare "What is decisive is not to get out of the circle but to come into it in the right way", *BT* 195). Origin is not to be understood as the beginning of a causal process leading to some *thing*, in the form of an object, for example, or an answer. Thus art *is*, for Heidegger, not because there are works of art; on the contrary, there are works of art because art is, because art happens. Heidegger understands art to be an origin, and of what and how it is the origin is the question.

Art as truth

Heidegger's questioning of the work of art begins with its thingly character. He identifies three definitions of thingness – "as bearer of traits, as the unity of a manifold of sensations, as formed matter" (*BW* 156) – and finds all three wanting, because they define the thing in terms of subjective experience, of immediate, lived experience. And perhaps, says Heidegger, "lived experience is the element in which art dies" (*BW* 204). But it is the last of the three definitions that interests Heidegger: the thing as formed matter, the definition of which derives its dominance from accounting for the thingly character of products of human making: equipment, purposeful and useful things, things at once familiar and yet intermediate between a mere thing and a work. Heidegger refutes the definition of an artwork in these terms, because it does not do justice to the work character of the work of art. It is at this point that he introduces an example, a "pictorial representation" of "a common sort of equipment – a pair of peasant shoes" painted by van Gogh (*BW* 158). And in Heidegger's description of those shoes, the painting "speaks". It speaks in such a way as to displace us to somewhere other than where we usually are. That place Heidegger names truth (*BW* 161).[6] In this work of art the truth of the shoes has set itself to work. It is not that the truth has been set to work; it is that truth sets itself to work in the painting, where truth is both the subject and the object (*BW* 202). "Art is the setting-itself-into-work of truth" (*BW* 165, trans. mod.), a double genitive in which the truth of the shoes and the world in which they are used appears for the first time.

At the same time the artwork opens up in its own way; it is self-subsistent. Indeed, the creative process is destructive: "almost like a passageway", which allows the work to emerge, but in which the artist is destroyed (*BW* 166) or sacrificed (*M* 28). Thus not only is the artwork for Heidegger not an object of taste, but it is not the product of a genius subject either. Moreover, the artist is not in control of the work. But by self-subsistent Heidegger does not mean to imply that artworks are autonomous, or "works in themselves" (*M* 28). When we view a sculpture in a museum or a painting in a gallery we are looking at art that has in an important way passed into the realm of tradition and conservation through objectification. What Heidegger calls the "art industry" deals only with artworks as objects; indeed, it objectifies them, at the expense of their "work-being". Heidegger asks, "Where does a work belong?" The question is itself revealing of how Heidegger understands art. Heidegger answers, "The work belongs, as work, uniquely within the realm that is opened up by itself. For the work-being of the work occurs essentially and only in such opening up" (*BW* 167). The implication that this happens once only, in the "original" siting of the work, is borne out by Heidegger's choice of example to illustrate the point: the Greek temple. To enquire into the truth of the work and become more familiar with what the question of truth involves, it is necessary "to make visible *once more* [erneut *sichtbar zu machen*] the happening of truth in the work" (*BW* 167, emphasis added). In other words, making visible now, now that the temple has passed, is an operation of language and of philosophy, and not something that can simply be viewed in the work.

The work of art makes visible what is otherwise invisible – the world: in the case of the temple the radiance of the light of day, the invisible space of air, the appearing of things, and the ground on which and in which humans base their dwelling. The work of the temple is to open up a world of beings such as to show things in their emergence. It is not that the world comes first, to which the temple is then added; it is that a world of beings first emerges as what it is, *and* that humans' way of seeing that world is first given to them in the setting up of the temple: "The temple, in its standing there, first gives to things their look and to men their outlook on themselves" (*BW* 168). This is the basis on which Heidegger can say that artworks are essentially historical: they found the very means by which humans can perceive and thus decide about the world. Artworks are where the "world worlds" in the sense that they allow the world to be seen again but for the first time. But this view remains open only in so far as the work remains a work, that is, only in so far as the artwork keeps open for decision what it shows to emerge. A decision "bases itself on something not mastered, something concealed, confusing; else it would never be a decision" (*BW* 180). The world of beings opened for decision by the work is more fully in being than is the decided perceptible world we ordinarily inhabit. The work holds open the world by liberating what Heidegger calls the free space of its open region (*BW* 170). This is the first of two features of the work-being of the work.

The second is the materiality of the work. Here Heidegger introduces an important distinction that touches on a question structuring much art theory of the latter half of the twentieth century. The material of made things, tools, pieces of equipment, is used up in the fabrication of them; it disappears into the form, it is subjugated to usefulness. Such things are more useful the more their materiality is subsumed by usefulness. But the materials out of which an artwork is made are not used up in this way. On the contrary, they come forth for the first time, made visible in the open region of the world the work sets up. Art, then, can be opposed to technical–scientific objectification on the basis of the way in which its materiality exceeds and escapes calculation and mastery (*BW* 172). This materiality Heidegger calls "earth". Thus the work of the temple is not just to show things in their emergence, but to illuminate that in and on which they emerge, to set the world thus opened back again on earth. Earth is brought forth, it is unconcealed, but that does not mean that it is penetrable. We may analyse it, we may try to grasp it, but it will forever withdraw from us. We will not see earth for what it properly is unless we accept it as that which is essentially self-secluding and undisclosable. It is through the ways in which the materials of an artwork are arranged that the earth's self-secluding nature is unfolded. It is the excess of its materiality that denies us the possibility of ever fully mastering the work in our interpretations of it.

The play of concealment–unconcealment

What is the relation of world to earth, the two essential components comprising the work-being of the artwork? It is a happening, a movement, where each attains to its essence through its resistance to the other – world and earth are opponents belonging together intimately – hence it is a relation of strife (*Streit*; BW 174). The world unconceals earth's self-seclusion; earth tends to draw the world into its concealing. The world makes visible what is otherwise invisible; the earth is materiality that can never be explained or accounted for in terms of what can be shown. The movement between the two is one of concealing–unconcealing and showing–withdrawal, and what happens in the movement is a drawing apart and a holding apart, such that what Heidegger calls a clearing (*Lichtung*; BW 178) is won. But this open region must be established, taken into possession and attain constancy, and it can only do this, says Heidegger, through the presence of a being. Here we find an opening to one of the reasons why Heidegger has very little to say about abstract artworks (and it bears too on the question of the privileging of the linguistic over the visual in Heidegger's work, to be addressed below): if the open region is always in need of a being or beings for its establishing and maintenance, then this would appear to privilege figuration, where the figure would enact the play of concealment–unconcealment in its *de*-figuration. Indeed, the fact that art that is "objectless" and "non-representational" (*gegendstandlose*) can be shown in museums testifies to modern art's historical appropriateness, and has more to do with metaphysics than would be implied by what Heidegger contends is its self-conception – "productions no longer able to be works ... something for which the suitable word is lacking" (*PR* 34) – because such exhibitions prove that objectless works are no less objectifiable, by the culture industry, by aesthetics, than are representational ones.[7]

The clearing is where we encounter those beings we are not, and are granted access to the being that we are. Any being we encounter in a work of art always at the same time withholds itself in a concealment. Any being that is concealed is at the same time brought into the open in its concealment. Thus truth, unconcealment, is also concealment (indeed, a double concealment, since beings can both refuse themselves and present themselves as other than what they are). Truth, then, cannot be a matter of correspondence or correctness, of representation or representational content (see Chapter 8). Truth happens when the counterplay of world and earth is unconcealed, always in a particular way, that is, with the presencing of a being, through an unconcealment that is at the same time a concealment. (Another way truth happens is with the thinker's questioning; hence Heidegger's insistence that the questionableness of beings is not something negative but that which is most questionworthy about them, and the question a way of keeping open the play of concealment–unconcealment of what is questioned.)[8]

At the same time that a being is brought forth into the open and a world revealed thereby, a rift (Riss) is formed between earth and world, which sets itself back into earth in the form of the materiality of the work: "the gravity of stone, the mute hardness of wood, the dark glow of colors" (BW 188). The materiality forces itself into the open region as self-secluding, and intensely resists the openness of the world. It is through the resistance of the earth that the strife with world is fixed in place in the form of a figure (Gestalt; BW 189). The figure is the particular way in which the material of the artwork is arranged – through placing (Stellen) and enframing (Ge-stell, from which the sense of montage [Montage] is excluded; BW 209) – such as to structure and shape the strife and rift between world and earth, and beings and materiality, where materiality is not used up but on the contrary is "set free" to be "nothing but itself". The production of a piece of equipment is completed when the matter is formed according to use and subsumed by that use. Not so a work of art, for which the process of creation sets matter free to participate in the happening of truth. Truth needs matter, what Heidegger calls earth. Truth happens in being composed ("indem sie gedichtet wird"; BW 197). Such is the essential way in which truth is related to creation. Its createdness is part of the work and stands out from it each time in a particular way. It is creation in the sense that what is brought forth each time as the arrangement, framing and fixing in place of the strife between earth and world "never was before and will never come to be again" (BW 187), and "can never be proved or derived from what went before" (BW 200).

The createdness of a work is its "that it is", and that it is is just what is unusual about it. Its "that it is" is projected ahead of it in the manner of a thrust. The unusualness of its being a work, its extraordinariness, is thrust into the openness of the everyday and the ordinary, opening up another space into which we viewers are displaced, an openness in which our ordinary and usual ways of being in the world are restrained, allowing the work to set up and reveal the otherness of the world. In this way Heidegger tries to account for the self-subsistence of the work, in opposition to the way in which aesthetics situates the artwork in a subject–object relation, on the one hand making of it an object of lived experience or the stimulator of such experience,[9] and on the other making of experience something private and the possession of a subject. Instead, Heidegger sees art as the grounding of being for and with one another (*BW* 193). Those who let the work be in this way and are able to stand in its truth and in the openness of beings thus revealed, including the beings that they themselves are, Heidegger calls "preservers" (*Bewahrenden*). The responsiveness of preservers is equated with resoluteness (*Ent-schlossenheit*) as it is set out in *Being and Time*. Preservers are as much part of a work's createdness as its creator. Art is a creative preserving of truth. Here we arrive at what it is that the work of art is the origin of: "If art is the origin of work, this means that art lets those who essentially belong together at work, the creator and the preserver, originate, each in his own essence" (*BW* 196). Art *lets* this happen: as an origin (*Ursprung*) art is a leap (*Sprung*; *BW* 202; see also *CP* 354), a primal leap bringing things into being from out of its source in the rift.

A historical people to come?

A work needs preservers, but may not immediately find them. Indeed, Heidegger suggests that a work is all the more tied to preservers "when it is still only waiting for them" (*BW* 192). Art throws truth towards "coming preservers" (*BW* 200). Coming preservers are a historical group of human beings. This theme, of what we might call a "people to come", is taken up in *Contributions to Philosophy*, and it brings us to a controversial aspect of Heidegger's conception of the work of art: its relation to history, more specifically to a historical people – and indeed, the people of a nation. In his "Athens lecture" from 1967 Heidegger remarks about modern art that it "no longer originates from the formative borders of a world of the people and nation" (*HK* 15; see Chapter 7), as if this were a failing.

That the happening of truth in the work is a matter of composition forms the basis of another contentious aspect of Heidegger's account. Heidegger argues that all art is in essence poetic (*BW* 197–8). And while he states that poesy in the narrow sense is but one mode of poetic composition in the wider sense, he goes on to aver "the linguistic work, poetry in the narrower sense" as privileged, because "language preserves the original essence of poetry" (*BW* 198–9). Heidegger's contention here is that language brings beings into the open for *the first time*, by naming them, and that all other creation, building and plastic creation, happens only in the openness of this naming. Thus naming means bringing beings both to word and to appearance (see Chapter 14). And this naming has to be seen from both sides, as it were: that of creation, and that of preserving. On the other hand, language is not restricted by Heidegger to the sayable, for it includes the unsayable: poetic language as a projective announcement of beings in their unconcealment prepares the sayable, and at the same time "brings the unsayable as such into the world" (*BW* 199).[10]

And this is the moment at which both controversial aspects of the account conjoin. Bearing in mind what was said earlier, that art is a founding in that it gives humans not just what they see but the way they see, Heidegger wants to say that poetry is a founding in a threefold sense: bestowing, grounding and beginning, to each of which there corresponds a preserving. The saying of poetry bears "the concepts of an historical people's essence, that is, of its belonging to world history" (*BW* 199), and these are *pre*formed: but not by what we have already, but by what is bestowed by breaking through what is already at hand. The unsayable is the *already* cast, but in the form of that which is hidden from humans, enclosed in the earth, and which must be drawn forth and set upon the ground. The unsayable is the "withheld determination of historical Dasein itself" (*BW* 200), a determination that prepares for another beginning. This other beginning for Heidegger is the founding of art when it instigates the strife of truth. But it happens when it is demanded by beings as a whole: "art attains to its historical essence as foundation" when beings demand a grounding in openness (*BW* 201) – as happens, and for the first time for humans, in Greece. Thus what was the thrust of the work of art is now the thrust of humans' beginning history again, humans' displacement into their being a people, the people that they already are or at least were always endowed to be, but which we have never yet seen, at least in the form of a work of art.

Notes

1. The first version of the lecture was presented in November 1935 at the Society for the Study of Art in Freiburg/Breisgau. Two further presentations followed, culminating in a three-part series of lectures at the Freie Deutsche Hochstift in Frankfurt/Main at the end of 1936.
2. The essay was published for the first time in 1950, in *Holzwege*. It appeared in revised form, to include the Addendum, as *Der Ursprung des Kunstwerkes*, for Reclam in 1960, the text of which reappears as *Holzwege*, volume 5 of the

Gesamtausgabe. The Reclam version also forms the basis of the English translations in *Poetry, Language, Thought* and (with minor changes) the revised edition of *Basic Writings*. The last version of the essay, again revised (for instance to include notes from Heidegger's own copies of the Reclam printing and the third [1957] edition of *Holzwege* [Bernasconi 1993: 243 n.3]), is the 1960 Reclam edition of *Holzwege*, which appears independently of the *Gesamtausgabe*.

3. The very first elaboration of the essay appeared in print only in 1989, and was never presented publicly. According to the editor and executor Hermann Heidegger, the manuscript was "kept in a slipcase, together with the lectures on the same topic". See "Prefatory Remarks" (*OWAF* 329).

4. See explanatory note by Heidegger (*PLT* xxiii–xxv). Heidegger's later language is undoubtedly indebted to his encounter with the poetry of Hölderlin, lines of which end the lecture; but is it an example of "substituting *Denken und Dichtung* for science" as is argued by Lacoue-Labarthe, and what relation might that have to what Heidegger calls (in 1945) the overcoming (*Verwindung*) of nihilism through the hymning of what is German ("im dichtenden Denken und Singen des Deutschen") (*RFT* 29; Lacoue-Labarthe 1990: 55)? See Bernasconi (1993) and Taminiaux (1993) for detailed accounts of the differences and political significances of tone, emphasis, example and language across the various versions of the essay. Petzet argues that the lectures "were not allowed to be published" at the time of their composition because they "deviated too much from … official ideology of art" (Petzet 1993: 134).

5. Photography and, especially, cinema seem to be the arts Heidegger reserves most scorn for in this respect; both "have their norm in the ownmost of the metaphysically completed 'art' as the organization of the all-producing and all-constituting makability of comportments, fashion, gestures and 'live-experience' of 'actual' 'lived-experiences'" (*M* 24), to which Heidegger adds "sentimentality" in his lectures on Hölderlin's *Der Ister*. See also: "Modern human beings nowhere have an originary 'lived experience' of artworks anymore… but only of the machine and its destructive essence" (*HHI* 114).

6. But as Meyer Schapiro points out in his 1968 critique, Heidegger nowhere tells us exactly which of the many paintings of shoes by van Gogh he is referring to, "as if the different versions are interchangeable, all disclosing the same truth". Schapiro contends that the painting is of the artist's own shoes, not those of a peasant, and that Heidegger is guilty of the very thing he was seeking to avoid: the projection of a subjectivist interpretation onto the painting (Schapiro 1994). And Jacques Derrida in turn shows how neither Heidegger nor Schapiro can find warrant within the painting to claim that the shoes "belong" at all; indeed, that they are even a pair. Rather, Derrida argues that both Heidegger and Schapiro have to presuppose that the shoes are a pair as a condition of making them available for a subject, in two senses: a subject who can stand in them, whom they would identify as the subject of the painting, and a subject able to put before himself the painting as an object. In this both Heidegger and Schapiro transform the essential uselessness of the painting into something bearing use value, serving them in their desire to appropriate the picture for their own ends, indeed normal usage and normative ends, at the expense of its being a work of art. Against which Derrida suggests that the painting of the shoes was made in order that the shoes, as painted, remain there, in the painting: something they can do only if the painting itself manifests a remainder, an excess (Derrida 1987). Compare Heidegger's questions in his only other text referencing van Gogh's

painting of the shoes: "What is in being here? The canvas? The brushstrokes? The patches of color?" (*IM* 38).

7. In the late 1950s Heidegger was particularly taken by the paintings of Paul Klee. Such was the impact of seeing Klee's work (and reading his texts) that in 1959, according to Petzet and Pöggeler, both of whom were in conversation with Heidegger at that time, Heidegger considered, indeed *tried* according to Pöggeler, writing a second part to "The Origin of the Work of Art" (Pöggeler 1994: 121; Petzet 1993: 146). For excerpts from Heidegger's notes on Klee (which are not generally available to the public), see Seubold (1993). For an account of Heidegger's engagement with the work of other modern painters during this period, in particular Becker-Modersohn, van Gogh, Cézanne, Picasso and Braque, see Petzet (1993: ch. 6, 133–58).

8. Heidegger gives a further example of how truth happens in this way: the act that founds a political state (*BW* 187).

9. In this respect, Nietzsche's concept of art as "the greatest stimulant of life" (Nietzsche 1968: 426) is the culmination of metaphysics as machination, because as a stimulant it must of necessity be nurtured (*HHI* 88; *M* 27). Heidegger takes the remark to be Nietzsche's "*major statement on art*" (*N1* 76).

10. For Heidegger's account of openness, now named "the region" (*die Gegnet*; *AS*: 6) in modern graphic art – which, in dealing with space, in "controlling" it, is confirmed in its modern character – see his 1969 essay, carved on a lithographer's stone for the sculptor Chillida (Petzet 1993: 158), "Art and Space".

References

Bernasconi, R. 1993. *Heidegger in Question: The Art of Existing*. Atlantic Highlands, NJ: Humanities Press.

Derrida, J. 1987. "Restitutions of the Truth in Pointing". In his *The Truth In Painting*, I. McLeod (trans.), 255–382. Chicago, IL: University of Chicago Press.

Hegel, G. W. F. [1835–8] 1975. *Hegel's Aesthetics: Lectures on Fine Art*, vol. 1, T. M. Knox (trans.). Oxford: Clarendon Press.

Lacoue-Labarthe, P. 1990. *Heidegger, Art and Politics*, C. Turner (trans.). Oxford: Blackwell.

Nietzsche, F. [1882–8] 1968. *The Will to Power*, W. Kaufman & R. J. Hollingdale (trans.). New York: Vintage Books.

Petzet, H. W. 1993. *Encounters & Dialogues with Martin Heidegger 1929–1976*, P. Emad & K. Maly (trans.). Chicago, IL: University of Chicago Press.

Pöggeler, O. 1994. "Heidegger on Art". In *Martin Heidegger: Politics, Art, and Technology*, K. Harries & C. Jamme (eds), 106–24. New York: Holmes & Meier.

Schapiro, M. [1968] 1994. "The Still Life as a Personal Object – A Note on Heidegger and van Gogh". In his *Theory and Philosophy of Art: Style, Artist, and Society*, 135–42. New York: George Braziller.

Seubold, G. 1993. "Heideggers nachgelassene Klee-Notizen". *Heidegger Studies* 9: 5–12.

Taminiaux, J. 1993. "The Origin of 'The Origin of the Work of Art'". In his *Poetics, Speculation, and Judgement: The Shadow of the Work of Art from Kant to Phenomenology*, M. Gendre (trans.), 153–69. Albany, NY: SUNY Press.

Further reading

Primary sources

See Heidegger's "Art and Space"; "The Origin of the Work of Art", A. Hofstadter (trans.), in *Basic Writings*; *Poetry, Language, Thought*; and "Of the Origin of the Work of Art (first elaboration)".

Secondary sources

See R. Bernasconi's "The Greatness of the Work of Art", in Bernasconi (1993), 99–116; and Lacoue-Labarthe (1990). See also O. Pöggeler, "Heidegger on Art", in *Martin Heidegger: Politics, Art, and Technology*, K. Harries & C. Jamme (eds), 106–24 (New York: Holmes & Meier, 1994); and J. Taminiaux, "The Origin of 'The Origin of the Work of Art'", in his *Poetics, Speculation, and Judgement: The Shadow of the Work of Art from Kant to Phenomenology*, M. Gendre (trans.), 153–69 (Albany, NY: SUNY Press, 1993).

TEN

Ereignis: the event of appropriation

Daniela Vallega-Neu

Ereignis becomes a – if not, indeed, *the* – fundamental concept in Heidegger's philosophy in the 1930s. Heidegger works out the thought of *Ereignis* between 1936 and 1938 in what is often called his second major work (after *Being and Time*), namely *Beiträge zur Philosophie (Vom Ereignis)*.[1] From this time on, *Ereignis* comes to name how being occurs in its truth. Despite the centrality of the concept of *Ereignis* for Heidegger, the writings in which he actually develops this concept were not meant for "the public ear"; they were texts written without didactic considerations in an attempt at an originary (poietic) language, a language one may call "experimental" or "esoteric" (in the literal sense) and that is certainly strange with respect to common discourses in philosophy. Following Heidegger's wishes, these texts started appearing as volumes of Heidegger's *Gesamtausgabe* (*Collected Edition*) only in 1989, the year that *Beiträge zur Philosophie (Vom Ereignis)* was published.[2]

Since *Beiträge zur Philosophie* (*Contributions to Philosophy*; hereafter *Contributions*) is the work in which Heidegger for the first time lays out his thought of *Ereignis*, we shall need to consider especially this work and how *Ereignis* is thought in it. In fact, the fundamental articulation of *Ereignis* in this work gives access to the entire corpus of Heidegger's work, up to his last writings. But since in his last period Heidegger's thinking undergoes another shift (although a less radical one than the one designated as his "turn"), it makes sense to give the articulation of *Ereignis* in this last period some special consideration as well.

Ereignis in German usually means "event", but, as in many other instances, Heidegger likes to play with a wider semantic field that opens up once we hear the word more literally by breaking it up into its two semantic components *er-* and *-eignis*. The prefix *er-* carries the sense of a beginning motion or of an achievement, whereas *-eignis* refers to the word *eigen*, which in German usually means "own", but which is also at play in a word that is familiar to us from Heidegger's *Being and Time*, namely *eigentlich*, in English "proper" or "authentic". This has led scholars to translate *Ereignis* not only as "event" but also with the neologism "enowning", or as "appropriation", or as "the event of appropriation".

Before proceeding to present Heidegger's thought of *Ereignis* in *Contributions*, it may be useful to note that the word *Ereignis* appears as a main concept (although not exactly in the sense that it will have for Heidegger after 1936) in a lecture course Heidegger gave at the very end of the First World War, that is, even before he wrote *Being and Time* (which was published in 1927). In this lecture course of 1919, Heidegger already begins elaborating a difference between a scientific–theoretical approach to things, and a – more genuine – pre-theoretical approach to things. He points out that in a scientific–theoretical approach to things the peculiar involvement of the one who questions and deals with things is lost. We posit a subject and an object and describe their relation in terms of a *Vorgang*, an objective occurrence. This is, however, not the way things occur if we pay close attention to the way we experience our surroundings (*Umwelterlebnis*).[3] In the latter case, we find that there is neither a subject nor an object, yet at the same time we find ourselves involved with whatever we encounter. Our peculiar involvement when experiencing our surroundings is what Heidegger calls, in this early lecture, *Ereignis*, in contrast to objectively described occurrences (*Vorgang*). Just as in his later work, *Contributions*, in this lecture course from fifteen years earlier, Heidegger hyphenates the word and draws attention to the root meaning "own" in it. He writes:

> *Er-leben* ["lived experience"] does not pass by me, like a thing that I would posit as object; rather I *er-eigne* ["en-own" or "appropriate"] it to myself and it *er-eignet sich* [this would commonly be translated as "it happens"; if we attempted to render the literal sense, we may render it as "appropriates itself", or it "en-owns itself"] according to its essence. And if, looking at it, I understand lived experience in that way, then I understand it not as process [*Vor-gang*], as thing, object, but rather as something totally new, as *Ereignis*. (*TDF* 63 = *GA* 56/57: 75, trans. mod.)

This lecture course from 1919 foreshadows themes that Heidegger will elaborate in *Being and Time* (1927), although in the latter he uses neither the word *Vorgang* nor the word *Ereignis* in his analysis of our (pre-theoretical) being-in-the-world.[4] He also avoids the words *Leben* (life) and *Erleben* (lived experience) because of his critique of a sub-jectively based "life-philosophy". When he again picks up the concept *Ereignis* as he begins planning *Contributions* in 1932,[5] it no longer refers merely to the way we experience our surrounding world. By this time, Heidegger's thinking and conceptual articulation of the question of being will have undergone several changes. These shifts take place during the course of his attempt to think the event of being as such beyond subjectivism and scientific–theoretical objectivism, while at the same time articulating in increasingly original ways the peculiar manner in which we humans find ourselves originarily in our being and within being as such.

Ereignis and the turning in *Ereignis*

In order to understand the fundamental concept of *Ereignis*, we need to understand especially one aspect of the turn[6] in Heidegger's thought in the early 1930s, namely the abandonment of the transcendental–horizonal approach to the question of being in the attempt to speak more inceptually, more originally, *from within* an authentic experience of being.

In the project of *Being and Time*, being as such is questioned by means of the transcendence of the being of the questioner, namely Dasein. Dasein – our being or existence, we in how we are in the world – always already transcends (steps beyond) our own particular being such that in our being-in-the-world the being of other beings and thus being as such is also disclosed. After the publication of the first two divisions of part one of *Being and Time*, Heidegger realized that this approach still invites readers to think in a representational manner: we are tempted to think that there is an entity (Dasein) that transcends into the open horizon of being (and world), a horizon we also tend to represent to ourselves in a quasi-objectifying way. The task, then, for Heidegger, becomes not to think and speak *towards* the open horizon of being, but from *out of* it. In §132 of *Contributions*, he writes: "What counts is not to step beyond (transcendence) but to leap over this difference [between beings and being] and with it over *transcendence* and to question in an inceptive way from out of beyng and truth" (*GA* 65: 250–51).[7]

This is possible only if thinking attempts to stay attuned to an authentic mode of being in which the thinker finds himself/herself displaced (Heidegger speaks of a "leap") from both everyday and theoretical modes of being and thrown into the (abyssal) openness of being as such. This openness is what Heidegger calls the *truth* of beyng. (In *Being and Time* this is thought as the temporal horizon into which Dasein always already transcends.) The truth of beyng needs to be sustained in order to occur as truth, and this is why thinking needs to *be* (-sein) there (da-) in that openness. It is then that thinking may find itself *ereignet*, "appropriated", by beyng and beyng in its truth can be experienced and thought as *Ereignis*, as appropriating event. In other words, the notion of *Ereignis* arises out of an experience of being in which Dasein finds itself thrown into the openness of being and appropriated in its being.

To explain this further (yet still in a preliminary way): out of the experience of being thrown into the abyssal openness of being we experience a disclosing event in which we also first find our own being; we experience our being as *er-eignet* (en-owned) or "appropriated" in that event. This appropriation does not occur simply passively but requires a response from the one who will first through this response find herself coming to "herself" in this event.

This is why Heidegger says that the disclosure (truth) of beyng needs *Da-sein* as the site of its occurrence and *Da-sein* is appropriated by this disclosure. Heidegger speaks in this context of the *Kehre im Ereignis*, the *turn in the appropriating event*.[8] The truth (disclosure) of beyng occurs only through *Da-sein* (and thus human being – *not* human being*s*), and *Da-sein* – in turn – occurs only through the truth of beyng.[9] The responsiveness of the one who finds himself thrown into and appropriated in the disclosure of beyng is what constitutes the *-sein* of the *Da-*, the *-being* of the *there*[10] (the disclosure of truth), and thus Da-*sein*, *being*-there, that is, being in the disclosure of truth.

Ereignis, Ent-eignis and the historicality of being

Part of the difficulty of this thought of *Ereignis* is that we cannot wilfully subject ourselves to the experience of being as appropriating event, and, without at least some sense of this experience what Heidegger attempts to think and say can simply sound hollow and absurd. However, Heidegger believes that there is a fundamental attunement latent in our epoch that makes it possible for at least a few of us to find themselves exposed to that abyssal openness of beyng out of which we may experience beyng occurring as *Ereignis*. In *Being and Time* it was the fundamental attunement of anxiety that was shown to displace us from our familiar dealings with things such that our being emerged authentically in its finitude, that is, in its being towards death. In *Contributions*, the basic disposition that transposes us into the disclosing event of the truth of beyng is both manifold and also historical (in the sense of *geschichtlich*); it is the disposition of an epoch rather than that of an individual human being.

Heidegger names the basic dispositions that in their unity displace us into the abyssal openness of beyng: "shock" (*Erschrecken*), "restraint" (*Verhaltenheit*) and "diffidence" (*Scheu*). Shock entails the experience of the abandonment of beings by being in the domination of machination (*Machenschaft*) and adventure (*Erlebnis*; often translated as "lived experience") such that beings are reduced to mere variables for calculation and to means for adventures. As a consequence, even the need for questioning being does not arise. In order to find the question of being again, the abandonment by being and forgottenness of being first need to be experienced as a plight. What thinking then realizes, attuned by shock, is that in our epoch being does not occur as an appropriating event but rather as a refusal (*Verweigerung* or *Versagung*).[11] Thus beyng, at first, is experienced as withdrawal, that is, not as appropriation but as ex-propriation, as *Ent-eignis*. Heidegger writes: "In this epoch 'beings' are … expropriated by beyng [*des Seyns enteignet*]" (*GA* 65: 120). Thus the truth of beyng, disclosed in shock, reveals itself as lacking ground such that truth has the character of an abyssal opening. Heidegger believes that this abyssal truth needs to be sustained if beyng is to find a site (*Da-sein*) and if the possibility of the appropriating event (*Ereignis*) is to be preserved. The sustaining of the abyssal opening of beyng as withdrawal is made possible by the dispositions of restraint and diffidence that dispose Dasein together with shock.

Ent-eignis, expropriation in the sense indicated above, thus has a "negative" connotation: it indicates that in our epoch *Er-eignis* does not (yet) occur and the truth of beyng remains concealed. This implies what Heidegger calls, in *Being and Time*, the fallenness of Dasein. It also refers to what, in his essay "The Essence of Truth", he calls untruth in the sense of errancy (*Irre*; *BW* 132–3). But Heidegger speaks of *Ent-eignis* also in a "positive" sense, namely in terms of the originary concealment that belongs to the truth of beyng even when it holds sway as *Er-eignis*.[12] Although Heidegger does not use the term *Ent-eignis* in that sense in *Contributions*, he does so in his later essay of 1962, "Time and Being", where he speaks of "*die Enteignis*": "Expropriation [*Ent-eignis*] belongs to Appropriation as such. By this expropriation, appropriation does not abandon itself – rather, it preserves what is proper to it [*sein Eigentum*]" (*TB* 22–3 = *ZSD* 23). Even if, as Heidegger still seems to hope when he writes *Contributions*, another beginning of history were to be granted to humanity such that beings were no longer abandoned by beyng and the truth of beyng were to hold sway as *Ereignis*, beyng would not simply "give itself completely" and be "fully present", but there would remain an essential concealment, a reserve that belongs to the holding sway of the truth of beyng. This essential reserve bears within it essential possibilities of beyng, possibilities of epochal "beginnings", and therefore needs to be preserved in its concealedness.

Contributions is, in Heidegger's understanding, a work of transition that first attempts to prepare the site, namely Da-sein, that would allow for the truth of beyng to hold sway as *Ereignis*. That moment (*Augenblick*) would be the moment of the grounding of another beginning of history. In that moment, beings would not be expropriated by beyng but instead would shelter the truth of beyng. In terms of this historical occurrence, then, *Ereignis* remains an event of which one can have only a presentiment. (*Ahnung*, presentiment, is another basic disposition of the thinking of *Ereignis*; see GA 65: §§5, 6, 128.) This presentiment arises in being displaced in shock into the disclosure of beyng as withdrawal, as well as in meditating on what Heidegger calls the first beginning of Western thinking. In the first beginning, the truth of beyng is experienced – disclosed in wonder – as coming to presence (*Anwesenheit*) such that the concealed dimension of being withdraws "behind" what comes to presence in this coming to presence. Eventually the coming to presence itself is not experienced any more and being is thought just in reference to presented things. Being then becomes the most general, empty concept, instead of being experienced as a temporal event through which beings come into presence: being withdraws and is forgotten and beings remain abandoned by being.

The presentiment of the truth of beyng as event (a presentiment that arises once thinking, attuned by shock, experiences the abandonment of being) does not simply place *Ereignis* in a distant future; Heidegger understands the basic disposition of presentiment to arise out of *Ereignis*: "Man has a presentiment of beyng … because beyng appropriates him to itself [*das Seyn er-eignet ihn sich*]" (GA 65: 245). There are, Heidegger suggests, a few untimely poets and thinkers who already find themselves appropriated, although *Ereignis* does not yet hold sway such that it determines the way beyng discloses itself in an epochal way. Heidegger calls these few *die Zukünftigen*, the ones to come.

We may, then, distinguish three ways of speaking of *Ereignis*:

1. *Ereignis* names a historical occurrence that is the *Augenblick*, the moment that would mark the other beginning of history. In this moment beings are no longer abandoned by beyng and the truth

of beyng holds sway as appropriating event. To *Ereignis* in this sense also belongs *die Enteignis* as the originary withdrawal and concealment out of which all appropriation occurs. *Ereignis* in this sense does not yet hold sway and first needs to be prepared through the grounding of *Da-sein*.

2. *Ereignis* in the first sense is a "possibility" that already calls out to a few poets and thinkers. Heidegger's own attempt to articulate *Ereignis* – by listening to the words especially of the poet Hölderlin – is an attempt to speak out of such a preliminary and transitional presentiment of it. Those who find themselves responding to this more originary call of beyng no longer live in the oblivion of beyng that holds sway in machination and adventure (which is rooted in the withdrawal of the truth of beyng), but rather experience the withdrawal of beyng as such.

3. *Ereignis* holds sway as *Ent-eignis*, that is, as the withdrawal of beyng and the abandonment of beings by being in the present era of machination and adventure. *Ent-eignis* (expropriation) is a form of *Ereignis*, although a "negative" one. Whereas *Ereignis* is analogous to the authenticity (*Eigentlichkeit*) of resolutely facing up to one's own mortality, *Ent-eignis* is analogous to the inauthenticity (*Uneigentlichkeit*) of fleeing from the possibility of one's own death (see Chapter 4). It is crucial to see that expropriation is a form of appropriation in order to understand how, for Heidegger, the era of machination – later he speaks of technology in terms of the *Ge-stell* or "framework" (see Chapter 13) – bears in itself the possibility of a turning to the event of appropriation in a more originary sense.

The full expanse of *Ereignis*: Da-sein, gods and humans, world and earth, beings

Up to this point, this chapter has focused on introducing the notion of *Ereignis* by paying particular attention to the relation between the truth of beyng, being-there (*Da-sein*) and humans. However, *Ereignis* has other essential dimensions, namely those of the gods, world, earth and beings. Being-there is not simply the turning point between the truth of beyng and humans such that we may picture to ourselves some "beyng" that relates to humans through being-there. If we wanted to look for some element "counter-posed" to humans in the appropriating event, we would have to find it in the gods. In §191 of *Contributions*, Heidegger writes: "Being-there is the *in-between* between humans (as the ones grounding history) and gods (in their history)" (*GA* 65: 311). Our being is appropriated in relation to the gods such that we are assigned (*Zueignung*) to the gods and the gods are consigned (*Übereignung*) to us.

In §267 of *Contributions*, Heidegger speaks of the gods as the ones who need beyng (which means that Heidegger does not think the gods as supreme beings).[13] That need resonates in the need that humans experience when, attuned by shock and restraint, they realize the abandonment of beings by beyng and the forgottenness of beyng in our epoch. For Heidegger, this abandonment and forgottenness, the withdrawal of being, goes along with what the poet Hölderlin speaks of as the flight of the gods. Accordingly, if *Ereignis* is to occur historically such that a new beginning of history is founded, the gods are required; more specifically, what Heidegger calls "the passing of the last god" [*Vorbeigang des letzten Gottes*] is required. Just as *Ereignis* holds itself in reserve even when it occurs historically, the gods (and the last god) also keep themselves in a hidden dimension. Heidegger thinks that for the appropriating event to occur, we need to attend to that hidden dimension; and if we find ourselves appropriated in the event, if in shock, restraint and diffidence we endure the abyssal opening of beyng, then we find ourselves "assigned" (*zugeeignet*) to that hidden dimension. Thus gods and humans emerge in *Ereignis* both in their separation (*Geschiedenheit*) as well as in their assigned/appropriated encounter.

It is *within* this encounter, that is, in the in-between of being-there opened up in the deciding encounter between gods and humans, that the strife of world and earth and the relation to beings are situated in the thought of *Contributions*.[14] Once being-there is appropriated, the truth of beyng finds a locale (namely being-there, *Da-sein*). With this locale is disclosed the "strife of world and earth" that Heidegger developed more in detail in the essay "The Origin of the Work if Art" (*BW* 143–212; see Chapter 9). The strife of world and earth is related to what Heidegger calls the "sheltering" (*Bergung*) of the truth of beyng into beings (especially words, but also works and deeds). The truth of beyng occurs as *Ereignis* only when it is sheltered into beings, which implies for Heidegger above all a sheltering into words.[15] (Otherwise beings remain *ent-eignet*, "expropriated" by beyng, as discussed above.) That is why the passing of the last god (which would mark the grounding of the other beginning of history) occurs at the same time as the sheltering of truth in beings. In this grounding of the truth of beyng in being-there, beyng and beings are transformed into their simultaneity (*GA* 65: 14).

But this simultaneity does not abolish all difference (it should be kept in mind that difference does not mean separation) between beyng and

147

beings. According to what Heidegger thinks during the time he is writing *Contributions*, the strife of earth and world functions as a kind of medium between the truth of beyng and beings. He says that the truth of beyng cannot be "directly" sheltered in beings but first needs to be transformed into the strife of world and earth (*GA* 65: 391).

Ereignis in Heidegger's later thought

What follow are some brief indications of how and where the notion of *Ereignis* appears and also undergoes some changes in Heidegger's later thought.

Ereignis *as the mirror-play of the fourfold* (enteignende Vereignung)
The account of the relations between "gods and humans" and "world and earth" in *Contributions* foreshadows his later thinking of the "fourfold" (*Geviert*) of divinities and humans, sky and earth (see Chapter 15). The essays "The Thing" from 1950 (*PLT* 161–84 = *VA* 157–80) and "Building Dwelling Thinking" from 1951 (*BW* 347–63 = *VA* 139–56), in which Heidegger exposes the fourfold are – viewed from the horizon of *Contributions* – essays in which Heidegger thinks ahead into modes of sheltering wherein beyng and beings are transformed into their simultaneity. In these essays, two of the four terms of the fourfold change slightly with respect to *Contributions:* In *Contributions*, Heidegger speaks of the "strife of world and earth"; in the later writings, the relation between sky and earth, together with the relation between mortals and divinities, is said to constitute the "worlding" (*Welten*) of the world. What changes is also a certain "foundational" relation that Heidegger maintains in *Contributions* when he says that the strife of world and earth occurs *within* the deciding encounter of gods and humans. When speaking of the fourfold in the essay "The Thing", Heidegger says that *Ereignis* occurs through the appropriating mirror-play of the fourfold such that "each of the four mirrors in its own way the presence of the other. Each therewith reflects itself in its own way into is own, within the unity of the four" (*PLT* 177 = *VA* 172, trans. mod.). In this context, Heidegger uses the term *Vereignung*: "The mirroring appropriates [*ereignet*] – by clearing each of the four – their own essence into the simple appropriation [*Vereignung*] to each other" (*PLT* 177 = *VA* 172, trans. mod.). The prefix "ver" has (in this context) the sense of an achievement; we may thus literally translate *Vereignung* as "achieving appropriation". The essay "The Thing" also

contains a different use of the term *"enteignen"* (expropriate) than in *Contributions*. When speaking of the fourfold, Heidegger plays with a different (more positive) meaning of the prefix *ent-*; now he stresses the sense of "letting go" or "letting free" that the term contains (whereas in *Contributions* he emphasized the sense of privation). He writes: "Each is expropriated, within their mutual appropriation [*Vereignung*], into its own being [*zu seinem Eigenen enteignet*]". Heidegger sums up: "This expropriative appropriating [*dieses enteignende Ereignen*] is the mirror-play of the fourfold" (*PLT* 177 = *VA* 172).[16]

Ge-stell *as a preliminary form of* Ereignis

In a seminar on Heidegger's lecture "Time and Being" (1962), Heidegger mentions, as I have noted, a number of texts that constitute different "ways into *Ereignis*" (*TB* 36 = *ZSD* 38–9), among which is included the above-mentioned essay "The Thing". Accordingly, we may say that Heidegger's meditations on the mirror-play of the fourfold are one way into the event of appropriation. Another one is his meditations on *Ge-stell*, translated as "framework" or "enframing" (see *QCT* and Chapter 13). *Ge-stell* names for Heidegger the relation between humans and beyng in our epoch, an epoch marked by a "technological" relation to things. Through the notion of *Ge-stell*, Heidegger reflects further on what in *Contributions* he speaks of in terms of machination, calculation and adventure. An experience of the truth of beyng as appropriating event first requires that we experience and acknowledge the abandonment of beings by beyng and the occurrence of appropriation in terms of an expropriation (withdrawal). This requires a meditation on the essence of technology and the way it determines our relation to things. It is by turning towards machination (not by turning away from it) that we may experience and think the truth of beyng as *Ereignis*. After *Contributions* Heidegger continues to hold on to that necessity and also pushes this thought a little further such that he increasingly understands the way beyng occurs in the epoch of technology as a preliminary form of *Ereignis* (and not just as the end of the way in which *Ereignis* occurs as expropriation in the first beginning, that is, in the epochs of metaphysics). In *Identity and Difference* (1957, i.e. twenty years after he wrote *Contributions*) Heidegger writes that we need to pay attention to the claim that speaks in the essence of technology:

> Our whole being [*Dasein*] everywhere finds itself challenged
> – sometimes playfully, sometimes urgently, sometimes rushed,
> sometimes pushed – to devote itself to planning and calculating

everything. … The name for the gathering of this challenge which places man and being towards each other [*einander zu-stellt*] in such a way that they challenge each other is "the framework" [*das Ge-stell*].   (*IDS* 34–5 = *ID* 22–3, trans. mod.)

The belonging together of man and beyng through this mutual challenging reveals "that and how man is appropriated over [*vereignet*] to being, and being is appropriated [*zugeeignet*] to human being" (*IDS* 36 = *ID* 24). Thus, realizing how we are challenged into the planning and calculating of everything reveals a certain (that is, expropriative) manner of how our relation to beyng occurs through the event of appropriation. This is why Heidegger speaks of *Ge-stell* as a "preliminary form" of *Ereignis* also in the seminar on "Time and Being" (1962) (*ZSD* 57 = *TB* 53).

Ereignis *as* Er-äugnis
Shortly after the above quoted passage from *Identity and Difference*, Heidegger points out an etymology of *Ereignis* that traces it back to *Er-äugnis* (*Auge* means "eye"), which relates to "*er-äugen*, meaning to catch sight of something, to call something through the gaze, to appropriate [*an-eignen*]".[17] Although Heidegger does not explicitly make the connection in *Identity and Difference*, one can easily relate *Er-äugnis* to *Augenblick*, which is the "moment" (literally translated: "glance of the eye") in which the truth of beyng holds sway as appropriating event.[18]

Ereignis *and* Geschick *(the sending of history)*
The moment of the grounding of the truth of beyng in *Da-sein* marks, according to *Contributions*, the moment of the beginning of the other beginning of history. In *Contributions* it remains somewhat ambiguous whether *Ereignis* only names how beyng occurs initially, in the moment of decision of the other beginning, or whether Heidegger thinks of the possibility of a whole epoch in which appropriation occurs more fully than in metaphysics and humans find a renewed originary relation to the divine, to earth, to sky, and to beings disclosed within a historical world.[19]

It is only later, in "Time and Being" (1962), that Heidegger makes a clearer differentiation between *Ereignis* and the history of being in its epochal forms.[20] Here, Heidegger thinks of *Ereignis* in terms of the sending of epochs. He calls the history of being that is sent *Geschick*.

Geschick can be translated as "destiny" and is related to the word *schicken*, "to send". He writes:

> In the sending of the destiny of being, in the extending of time, there becomes manifest a dedication [*Zueignen*], a delivering over [*Übereignen*] into what is their own [*Eigenes*], namely of being as presence and of time as the realm of the open. What determines both, time and being, in their own, that is, in their belonging together, we shall call: *Ereignis*, the event of appropriation.
> (*TB* 19 = *ZSD* 20, trans. mod.)

The event of appropriation is nothing "behind" being and time but rather names their appropriation, the event of their coming into their own and in relation to each other.

Heidegger points out that the appropriat*ing* (*Ereignen*) conceals itself as "it gives" time and "it gives" being, that is to say, the giving withdraws "behind" or "underneath" what is given. In the German sentence, *Es gibt Zeit* (which would usually be translated as "there is time" but which literally means "it gives time"), the *es* has a similar function as in the sentence "it rains". There is no thing that rains. Similarly, there is no thing that gives time or gives being. Appropriation occurs as the giving, but in such a way that as "it" gives, "it" conceals itself. As the sending of time and being, the event of appropriation is not itself a form of being but rather determines the history (or histories) of being: "This, however, what is sending as appropriation, is itself unhistorical [*ungeschichtlich*], or more precisely without destiny" (*TB* 41 = *ZSD* 44, trans. mod.). Accordingly, for a thinking that turns into the event of appropriation as a sending that withdraws or conceals itself (here is where Heidegger speaks of *die Enteignis* or expropriation in the more original sense), "the history of being as what is to be thought is at an end" (*TB* 41 = *ZSD* 44, trans. mod.). Heidegger discusses these thoughts again in one of the seminars held in Le Thor in 1969. Once again the differentiation between *Ereignis* (the translators here translate it as "enowning") and the history of being is drawn: "There is no destinal epoch of enowning. Sending is from enowning [*Das Schicken ist aus dem Ereignen*]" (*FS* 61). Heidegger also specifies that "in enowning, the history of being has not so much reached its end, as that it now appears *as* history of being".

We may summarize, then, that in his later thought Heidegger understood *Ereignis* to be the event of appropriation out of which epochs of being occur.[21] These epochs of being are fundamental ways in which being occurs and humans relate to this occurrence (for instance, by being challenged to calculate and plan everything as in our current epoch of technology). The event of appropriation itself remains concealed in the way being discloses in each period. When thinking enters the event of appropriation, these epochs appear as such and can be thought as such; at the same time, thinking finds itself appropriated by this "untimely" event called *Ereignis*.

Notes

1. See Heidegger's indication of this in *TB* 43 = *ZSD* 46. The full title of the currently available English translation of *Beiträge zur Philosophy (Vom Ereignis)* (*GA* 65) is *Contributions to Philosophy (From Enowning)* (*CP*). A new translation, by Richard Rojcewicz and Daniela Vallega-Neu, is forthcoming with Indiana University Press.

2. *Beiträge zur Philosophy* is followed by *Besinnung* (written 1938–9, published as *GA* 66 in 1997), *Die Geschichte des Seyns* (written 1938–40, published as *GA* 69 in 1998), *Über den Anfang* (written in 1941, published as *GA* 70 in 2005), and works that remain to be published: *Das Ereignis* (written in 1941–2, forthcoming as *GA* 71), *Die Stege des Anfangs* (written in 1944, forthcoming as *GA* 72), and *Zum Ereignis-Denken* (forthcoming as *GA* 73). Only a few texts (lectures) published during Heidegger's lifetime explicitly deal with *Ereignis*. In *On Time and Being* (*TB* 36) Heidegger names the "Letter on Humanism", four lectures given in 1949 ("The Thing", "The Enframing", "The Danger" and "The Turning"; in *GA* 79), "The Question Concerning Technology", and "Identity and Difference" (*IDS*). We should add to these texts the lecture and seminar on "Time and Being" (in *TB*) as well as "Four Seminars" (*FS*).

3. Here Heidegger uses the word *erleben* in a positive sense. Much later, in *Contributions*, Heidegger uses "*Erlebnis*" to designate a mode of lived experiencing that is oblivious to a more originary sense of being.

4. Friedrich Wilhelm von Herrmann (1994: 5–26) outlines Heidegger's path from the early lecture course of 1919 to the elaboration of the thought of *Ereignis* in *Wege ins Ereignis*.

5. Although Heidegger began writing *Contributions* in 1936, according to von Herrmann (1994: 1), the plan for the work was there already in spring 1932.

6. See Chapter 6. See also Vallega-Neu (2003: pt 1). A further discussion of Heidegger's way to *Ereignis* can be found in Pöggeler (1998: 4–36).

7. All translations of passages from *Contributions* are my own. For the context of the passages, see *CP*, which provides the German pagination of *GA* 65. Note that "beyng" renders Heidegger's archaic way of writing *Sein* (being) as *Seyn*. With the "y" Heidegger intends to indicate that being should be understood in terms of an occurrence and not as a being or entity of some kind that we may represent.

8. This is what Heidegger addresses in the "Letter on Humanism" as the more original meaning of *Kehre* (*BW* 231–2 = *GA* 9: 328).

9. See *GA* 65: 311. Note that *Da-sein* (written with a hyphen) becomes in *Contributions* the site of disclosure for both the truth of beyng and our own being, which means that the notion of *Da-sein* is further displaced from its subjective connotations.

10. "Da" in German means both "here" and "there".
11. See *Contributions*, the part or "fugue" titled *Anklang* (translated as "Resonating", or "Echo"), §50, and following sections (*GA* 65: 107ff.).
12. Heidegger also develops this sense of truth in "The Essence of Truth" (*BW* 130–31).
13. "*Appropriation [die Er-eignung]*, that in the plight out of which the gods need beyng, beyng necessitates being-there in order to ground its own truth, such that it lets hold sway the in-between – the appropriation [*Er-eignung*] of *Dasein* through the gods and the assignment [*Zueignung*] of the gods to themselves" (*GA* 65: 470). On the question of god/s in Heidegger's thought, see Chapters 16 and 17.
14. See §190 of *Contributions* (*GA* 65: 310), where Heidegger even diagrams this relation.
15. See "The Origin of the Work of Art", where Heidegger speaks of poetry in a larger sense as encompassing all creation and preserving of a work (*BW* 199). For the relation between language and *Ereignis*, see Vallega-Neu (2002) and Dastur (1993).
16. For the relation between *Ereignis* as the mirror-play of the fourfold and Heidegger's thought of *Gelassenheit*, see Davis (2007: 231–8).
17. *ID* 24; this passage is missing in the English translation. Heidegger speaks briefly of *Er-äugnis* also in an essay of 1959 titled "Der Weg zur Sprache" ("The Way to Language") in *Unterwegs zur Sprache* (*BW* 417 = *GA* 12: 246).
18. See McNeill (1999: esp. 217).
19. See in this context §45 of *Contributions*, where Heidegger suggests that the grounding of the truth of beyng may finally determine a people.
20. Heidegger's meditations, especially in *Über den Anfang* (*GA* 70), one of the texts following *Contributions*, pave the way towards that differentiation.
21. These epochs are usually equated with the epochs of Western thought, namely the Greeks, the Middle Ages, modern thought and the current epoch of technology. But all these epochs belong to metaphysics, and metaphysics may be seen as one large epoch in relation to which Heidegger thinks the possibility of another beginning of history. (On Heidegger's conception of the history of being, see Chapter 11.)

References

Dastur, F. 1993. "Language and *Ereignis*". In *Reading Heidegger: Commemorations*, J. Sallis (ed.), 355–69. Bloomington, IN: Indiana University Press.
Davis, B. W. 2007. *Heidegger and the Will: On the Way to Gelassenheit*. Evanston, IL: Northwestern University Press.
Herrmann, F. W. von 1994. *Wege ins Ereignis*. Frankfurt: Vittorio Klostermann.
McNeill, W. 1999. *The Glance of the Eye: Heidegger, Aristotle, and the Ends of Theory*. Albany, NY: SUNY Press.
Pöggeler, O. 1998. *The Paths of Heidegger's Life and Thought*, J. Bailiff (trans.). Amherst, New York: Humanity Books.
Vallega-Neu, D. 2002. "Poetic Saying". In *Companion to Heidegger's "Contributions to Philosophy"*, C. E. Scott, S. Schoenbohm, D. Vallega-Neu & A. Vallega (eds), 66–80. Bloomington, IN: Indiana University Press.

Vallega-Neu, D. 2003. *Heidegger's "Contributions to Philosophy": An Introduction.* Bloomington, IN: Indiana University Press.

Further reading

Primary sources
See Heidegger's *Identity and Difference*; *On Time and Being*; "Letter on Humanism", in *Basic Writings*, 217–65; *Contributions to Philosophy (From Enowning)*; "The Thing", in *Poetry, Language, Thought*, 161–84.

Secondary sources
See R. Polt, "Ereignis", in Dreyfus & Wrathall (2007), 375–91; Scott *et al.* (2002); and Vallega-Neu (2003). See also O. Pöggeler, "Being as Appropriation", *Philosophy Today* **19**(2) (1975), 152–78.

ELEVEN

The history of being

Peter Warnek

From history to *Ereignis*

The unfolding of the fullness of being in its transformations looks
at first like a history of being. But being has no history in the way
a city or a people has a history. What is historical about the history of being is to be determined clearly and solely through the
way being happens, which means … from out of the way there
is/it gives being [*Es Sein gibt*].   (*TB* 8 = *ZSD* 7–8, trans. mod.)

The short lecture "Time and Being", in which this dense passage is
found, contains Heidegger's final attempt to address in a sustained and
explicit manner a central topic of his thinking.[1] Yet in this passage we
find him questioning precisely the *historical* character of the history of
being. On the face of it, this is indeed an odd question: what are we to
make of a history that is *not* historical in the way that all other histories
are considered historical? In its unique way of being historical, the history of being remains unlike every other history and breaks somehow
with the entire class of histories.

Heidegger is clear. If we want to achieve what he calls here a *determination* of the uniquely historical character of the history of being, we
must attend to the way in which being happens in its utter singularity;
and this means, he says, as a giving or a sending, or even as a "destiny".[2] How are these statements to be understood? Strictly speaking,
we cannot say that being *is*, since such a formulation only reverts to the
language of being itself. To say that being *is* only assumes in advance
what must not be taken for granted, and thus only passes by what still

needs to be thought. Heidegger asks instead that we think the way in which "it gives" being. Here he exploits the sense of a German idiom that is without exception rendered in English as "there is", but can also be heard, if one attends to its literal sense, to speak of a giving.[3]

Admittedly, this literal sense of the idiom for the most part receives no consideration. But if we follow Heidegger and consider being in this way, it becomes possible to distinguish three important moments: (i) being as a gift, namely, as given; (ii) that which gives what is given; and (iii) the giving itself. And if we then proceed to ask *what* gives being, at first we are at a loss as to how to approach such a question without already turning what gives being into something present, in other words, into something that once again takes being for granted. In this impasse, however, we become aware of the need for a "step back" from a metaphysical tradition that has long been preoccupied with being only as something given, and we are turned towards the question of the event of the giving itself.

Near the end of this lecture Heidegger offers a word for such a giving: *Ereignis*. This word may be translated for now as "event of appropriation" or as "enowning", as long as such translations are taken with enough indeterminacy to let the matter show itself in a way appropriate to it (*TB* 20 = *ZSD* 21; see also Chapter 10). At first there is no need to posit in advance any definitions. What is important is to find a way to experience appropriation appropriately. At the same time, it is not insignificant that in the attempt to experience appropriation appropriately we already find ourselves caught up in the language of appropriation. Yet if we are to experience the uniquely historical character of being, Heidegger is clear that the way leads to *Ereignis*. "[T]he singular task of this lecture consists in gaining a glimpse of being itself as *Ereignis*" (*TB* 21 = *ZSD* 22, trans. mod.). *Ereignis* is not offered as another name for being, another attempt to say what being is. Rather, in the encounter with being as *Ereignis* what emerges is the "belonging together of being and time" (*TB* 19 = *ZSD* 20).

Preparing historical transformation: reception and destruction

That the task of achieving a determination of the historical character of being would call for a transformation or an estranging of our ordinary sense of history and time should come as no surprise, especially if we consider that in the foreword to the same lecture Heidegger emphasizes that we should expect great difficulties in understanding him. We are warned from the very beginning that a thoughtful encounter with the lecture demands somehow placing in abeyance our prevailing expectations with regard to how we might receive what he has to say. This difficulty that concerns the *reception* of Heidegger does not have to do primarily with the conceptual complexities of his thinking, nor does it simply concern his notorious habit of exploiting and twisting ordinary words, but is rather first of all connected to the task introduced above: namely, the difficulty of determining the history of being solely from the way being happens as a giving or destiny. Yet Heidegger's warning also implies that such expectations carry a certain inevitability, however inappropriate they may be to the matter at hand. The implication is that we are caught up in these expectations, and they cannot simply be dispensed with, or ejected by edict. This fact alone should give us pause.

If addressing the history of being is a possibility at odds with customary expectations, then such a task cannot be isolated from the way in which it *already* finds itself situated in a time and place. Our ability to be receptive to Heidegger's thinking, in other words, is already framed or conditioned by a metaphysical lineage that we have inherited but not chosen. This means that before history and being can be taken up as questions in an explicit way, the very posing of these questions finds itself claimed by history, or caught within history. What does such a situation, as historical, have to do with the history of being as it would twist free from ordinary history?

The situated character of the lecture, as it owns up to operating within certain ineluctable hermeneutic prejudices, is presented initially as an obstacle or as a hindrance to our understanding, in so far as we are asked to prepare ourselves to move beyond the limits it would otherwise impose. In attempting to overturn or dismantle our historical prejudices, the lecture thus seeks to enact what Heidegger designates as a destruction or, perhaps better, a *de-structuring* of the metaphysical tradition, but in doing so it seeks to direct us to something entirely unanticipated and unheard of. The transformation into the estranging sense of the history of being thus calls for a destruction that would reveal how history ordinarily taken covers over and obscures being as a giving, sending or destiny. "Only the dismantling of the coverings – this means the destructuring – offers to thinking a provisional glimpse into what then reveals itself as the destiny of being" (*TB* 9 = *ZSD* 9, trans. mod.).

We should note, however, that this strange sense of destiny or history does not emerge from a place that is simply external to our situation, no more than the shared horizons of understanding can be viewed simply as limits, or mere deficiencies. If the operative limits of our understanding can be surpassed or broken apart, this occurs first of all by accepting them as they unavoidably impose themselves upon the hermeneutic situation and grant a starting-point to the lecture. As limits they can be grasped as positive and enabling because they are already related to the possible appearance of something else, something other.

The task of achieving a determination of *Ereignis* as it reveals the history of being can be said, then, to be one of dismantling or breaking down the limits of philosophy as metaphysics in order to make available what is harboured within such limits. The history of being thus lies concealed within a history that already claims us. While on the one hand the appearance of the history of being breaks with what first began as the history of metaphysics, on the other hand this first beginning also already belongs to an *other* beginning as it remains concealed in the first beginning.[4] Metaphysics is thus a history caught in the "oblivion" or forgetting of being.

Thinking the history of being exposes this oblivion or concealment as a certain failure, but not in order to remove the concealment. In the protocol to the seminar that followed the lecture "Time and Being", it is made clear that the heretofore forgetting of being is not to be overcome or negated. The forgetting is not to be surpassed by a recovery of something forgotten; "the previous non-thinking is not a neglect, but is to be thought as something that follows from the self-concealing of being" (*TB* 29–30 = *ZSD* 31–2, trans. mod.). What is at stake here is thus the un-concealing of an ineluctable concealment. And the history of being emerges only when we become attentive to the oblivion as such, when we begin to think in the oblivion and attend to it thoughtfully. At the same time, it becomes clear that thinking in this way does not attempt to offer merely another account of history. In attempting the de-structuring that would open up the granting of being itself, or being as *Ereignis*, by exposing the oblivion, such thinking also prepares itself for an actual historical transformation. This transformation entails nothing less than the *ending* of philosophy in an exhaustion of the metaphysical project that has sought to say what being is. The task of thinking thus emerges in the ending of philosophy. But our relation to this possible transformation remains merely preparatory; it is not to be regarded as new founding (*TB* 60 = *ZSD* 66). Strictly speaking, one may not undertake to "produce" the transformation, because any attempt at enacting such a *poiēsis* must already rely on an interpretation of being that once again reverts to the legacy of metaphysics. Production becomes possible in the anticipation of what is to be produced and thus such anticipation is always first of all grounded in the being of what is to be produced (*TB* 45–6 = *ZSD* 49).

Yet in the same foreword to the lecture we are told that while the task of thinking remains provisional and preliminary, it also cannot be circumvented or bypassed. The encounter with what is strange asserts itself unavoidably, with a kind of necessity. Heidegger asks in this context that we attempt to follow what he says not as a series of propositions that contain or present a content. Instead, he asks that we follow the lecture as a series of what he calls *indications*: we are to look for what shows itself through a kind of pointing.[5] What is at issue here cannot be presented directly but calls for a possible response or participation on our part. The text does not stand simply as a container of meaning, but solicits our response, and is to be decided in our receptivity (*TB* 26 = *ZSD* 27–8). It thus cannot be assumed that Heidegger has a philosophy (*TB* 48 = *ZSD* 51). As attentive readers, we cannot bypass a responsibility as participants or interlocutors in the matter Heidegger seeks to address.

Another history: from the being of beings to being as such

What, then, is the strange necessity opened up in venturing to think the history of being? If the being of beings has always been understood as the essence of beings that is always present, and if such presence has been thought thereby to precede and transcend the coming to be and passing away of beings, what business does anyone have speaking of its *history*? What could be more out of place than to speak of the history of what is ever present as it is? How, then, is being as such actually given?

The only answer that philosophy – and this, according to Heidegger, has always meant metaphysics (*TB* 55–6 = *ZSD* 61) – has been able to offer to this last question is that being is given in so far as beings *are*. This is to say, along with Heidegger, that being has been thought since the Greek beginning as the being of beings, or as the ground of beings. While on the one hand beings in their transiency must be grounded in some sense of being, on the other hand being itself is thought to refer only to the ongoing presence of what is.

This *difference* between being and beings, as a mutual implication or intimacy between transiency and presence, is always presupposed when being is taken as presence. At the same time, such presence itself – what it is and how it might be said – has since the Greek beginning never ceased to be a question. Philosophy has never been in a position to do away with this question of "ontological difference". The simple fact that being continues to assert itself as a question, that it is always encountered in this way – even if in the mode of denial, when, for example, in positivism or when it is claimed to be the "emptiest of all empty concepts" (*TB* 6 = *ZSD* 6) – already means that it is also *not* simply given.

It remains an intractable matter that philosophy cannot relinquish or bypass, but as such it also continues nonetheless to withhold itself from us. Being continues to elude us, to *retreat* in the mode of asserting itself. This experience of the *withdrawal* of being, as it continues to claim human thinking ineluctably, offers a decisive starting-point for gaining a determination of what is said with *Ereignis*: to the appropriation of being there always belongs an inevitable expropriation, an erasure in the granting of being.

Moreover, that metaphysics takes being as the *presence* of beings over and against beings as they emerge and dissolve in time means also that a determination of time unknowingly sustains ontological difference. Every metaphysics of presence already operates within a given understanding of time, one that privileges presence, and takes the past as the no longer present and the future as the not yet present. But to think the presence of being in its withdrawal, to attend to the expropriation that belongs to the sending, calls for a reconfiguring of time itself, in which presence emerges as only *one* mode of time among others. This reconfiguring of time Heidegger calls "true time", in which there is an "extending of time" beyond presence and the opening up of the *presencing* of beings (*TB* 10–17 = *ZSD* 10–18; see also Chapter 5).

Still, we must exercise extreme caution in claiming that a history can be found in the experience of such a withdrawal or withholding. As I have already pointed out, Heidegger warns us in the passage with which I began against confusing the history of being with our ordinary ways of thinking history. It is evident that Heidegger is not at all interested in the history of a concept or idea. There is no doubt that, viewed as a practice, thinking the history of being is carried out through a reading of texts, but the history of being, as Heidegger attempts to think it, must not be mistaken for some kind of *doxography* that would chronicle the various things philosophers have claimed or asked about being. It should not in any way be confused with a mere history of philosophy that would be developed and determined through the lineage of the question of being as it begins with the Greeks and has been inherited from them. Heidegger asks us to avoid representing the history of being as a lineage of interpretation or as a sequence of events (*WCT* 164 = *WhD* 103).

If the history of being is not a history in any recognizable way, it might be helpful to consider briefly how history is ordinarily conceived. Historical thinking looks into the historical grounds of beings and so exposes their contingency. To speak of history, to raise the question of the history of something, is to assume a time when that something did not yet exist, just as it is already to assume, at least implicitly, the

160

possibility of its no longer being. To write a history of sexual practices, or to enquire into the history of a sovereign state, to offer two examples, is already to delimit in some way the unquestioned legitimacy these historical beings otherwise enjoy. By recounting and anticipating the origination and ending of things, historical thinking thus assumes that events have context, and that in order to be understood they must be taken as situations framed by conditions that surpass the events themselves. While the conception of causality operative in history undoubtedly differs from that of physics, the beings under historical investigation are nonetheless grasped only in so far as they fall within the influence and determination of such heterogeneous conditions. In its own way the principle of reason holds sway in historical thinking no less than in logic and other forms of research.

When history erupts with unexpected revolutions, when it interrupts itself with the emergence of something unheard of, previously unthinkable and unanticipated, this does not at all derail the convictions of historical research and historiological thinking. These events only compel such thinking to reinterpret and to reconfigure the narratives and grounding principles that had dominated beforehand. Historiology, in fact, cannot abide the incoherence of a pure interruption, and must categorically refuse the appearance of something like an unconditioned causality. Yet who can deny that the movement of history has nevertheless always been defined precisely by such strange moments of impossibility, by turning points that mark, as Hannah Arendt might say, the birth of the new? From this perspective, it remains true that we are always travelling headlong towards something unimaginable, towards what we never saw coming as a possibility, and that this horizon of impossibility defines the future. We know that we are now the past for *this* future, and such a future past will be left unthought by us, *will have been* unthought. Yet the predictive claims of historical understanding continue to persist because they permit and even demand endless reinterpretations within such transformative upheavals. We witness again and again how even the most fanatical forms of eschatology permit endless postponements and revisions. The predictive claims of historiology will never be abandoned because our familiarity with the world we live in today presupposes and relies on such an understanding of what is possible, a trust in our everyday convictions. No doubt this familiarity with the world, the trust we have in the ground we walk on, is itself a function of being historically situated, but history also makes us aware of the contingency of every situation.

Historical thinking thus has an undeniably subversive consequence: it exposes how all human institutions are able to stake out a claim to absolute authority only through a terrible pretence that seeks to deny their historical character. The inevitable contingency of all things historical, the realization that everything in history appears only as a part of an endless chain of passing conditioned conditions, is often countered by the appeal to a natural or divine order. One might be willing to concede that human values have their genesis in time while also insisting that the true ground of such values transcends these merely historical beginnings. The right of a political cause, for example, does not have to wait for popular confirmation, no more than the veracity of a geometric demonstration depends on an act of intuition by the geometer, no more than the regularity of the earth's gravitational force on the objects on its surface depends on the insights of a Newton or a Galileo.

We thus see that history, or more precisely "historiology" (*Historie*) as a domain of research, operates within a pre-given sense of being, a determination of *what* it is that it investigates. Being as the ground of beings is always already operative in every historical determination, even if the study of history does not actually investigate or question the being of things in this sense. Whereas historiology implicitly assumes a fixed transcendental or metaphysical sense of the being of historical events, every determination of history according to a destiny or destination must remain provisional and subject to revision based on the transformations of history itself. The grounding of history in an implicit sense of being thus only masks an abyss that is the movement of history itself. Heidegger is drawing a crucial distinction here between two German words, both of which generally get translated into English as "history":[6] *Historie* (historiology as an objectification of the ontic events of history) and *Geschichte* (history as the "sending" or *Geshick* that first determines the ontological meaning of those events). Whereas *Historie* remains implicitly determined by being, *Geschichte* is to be thought as the disclosure of being itself. The former still implicitly relies on a transhistorical ground, whereas the latter opens up being in its historical transformations.

Epochal sendings as destiny

How, then, can being itself, or being as such, be historical? Thinking the history and happening of being as a giving, or as *Ereignis*, is a matter of thinking an origination or an event in such a way that the iteration of being itself – as the being of beings or as the ground of beings – is not already taken for granted.[7] Yet the passage cited at the beginning of this chapter does tell us that we are concerned with an unfolding and that this unfolding does look at first *like* a history because it involves an abundance of transformations. Heidegger is referring here to the history of Western thinking as a *lineage* of attempts to name being as presence. Arguably, Heidegger's entire philosophical career is devoted to elaborating and carefully questioning this lineage. In the texts published along with "Time and Being" and within the lecture itself, we find several passages that chronicle these metaphysical determinations that have prevailed. The names offered include, among others, the Greek *hen* of Parmenides, the Platonic/Aristotelian *logos*, Aristotle's *energeia* and medieval *actualitas*, the monad of Leibniz, Kant's transcendental making possible of objectivity, Hegel's dialectical mediation of absolute spirit, Marx's historical process of production and Nietzsche's will to power.[8] Given that such lists refer in compressed form to the entire scope of Western thinking, it is not possible to overstate the simplification that is enacted through the mere rehearsing of these names.

But the history of being does not show itself immediately in such a history of the naming of being. This is why Heidegger says that the transformations only look at first *like* a history of being. The history of being does not show itself at all in the unfolding of these transformations, unless one attends to the withdrawal of being as it becomes manifest in the transformations, which is to say, unless one sees what remains hidden in the giving or sending of being. Only in a destructuring do the transformations as such make evident an oblivion of being that is not said in the names themselves, and thus point to the *Ereignis* character of being as a sending that withdraws. The sending and the withdrawal do not occur as two distinct moments.[9] What appears in the history of metaphysics, then, is an absence. It is in this precise sense that Heidegger speaks of the "epochs" of the history of being: each of the epochs is established through a totalizing name for the ground of what is. Yet what is decisive is that every such name also obliterates or obscures a remainder or an abyss and, precisely as the totalizing and grounding name that it presumes to be, it *must* leave this remainder or abyss unthought. This necessity is precisely what is meant by the destiny of the being.[10] The word "epoch" in this context does not refer, then, only to an era in which a certain name for being holds sway; rather, if one hears the original Greek sense of *epoche*, the epochs of being refer also to a withholding that holds sway throughout the history of metaphysics.[11]

The epochal transformations of the history of being show that in each attempt to name being, to say what it is as the ground of beings, being itself undergoes an erasure or falls into oblivion. In other words, being *as such* remains unthought *within* the epochs, in so far as what defines an epoch is its singular way of taking being for granted as presence, as something already given, as the being of beings. The different names for being – precisely in their difference – all have in common, then, this distinctive trait, namely, that they enact a covering over of the retreat in the becoming manifest of being as ground. As a history, then, it can be said that being shows itself as ground only by hiding itself as a groundless sending from nowhere.

Heidegger thus says that the epochs *overlap* – which is to say, that they have an affinity and are connected – but also, again attending to the literal expression, that they *cover over* or obscure each other in a difference that determines all of them precisely as a sending withdrawal. There is an untranslatability that prevails *between* the epochal groundings, a moment that eludes each of them in their totalizing claim and yet reveals that they belong together in such an excessive strangeness. Thus, the destiny in question here is not first of all a lineage, in the sense that it can be determined according to a logic. It is not a sequence of events determinable in the opposition between necessity and chance. The epochs do not "belong together" except in the step back into the destined withdrawal, in which what becomes evident is the belonging together of the strange as strange.

Yet we see that when Heidegger speaks of the destiny of being, it is also the case that he finds, in the withdrawal that prevails throughout the epochal sendings, a kind of trajectory towards a greater oblivion: "what is appropriate shows itself in the belonging together of the epochs. The epochs overlap each other in their sequence so that the original sending of being as presence is more and more covered over in different ways" (*TB* 9 = *ZSD* 9, trans. mod.). And precisely because our age is determined by the ultimate oblivion of being, as the age of technology, in which all beings are at the disposal of the wilful subject and determined according to the mere "framing" or positing by this subjective will (see Chapters 12 and 13), our age is uniquely positioned to experience the sending as withdrawal, as a groundless grounding. This is why Heidegger says that the encounter with being as *Ereignis* is now *necessary*, not according to a logic of history, but according to the destined withdrawal of being in which every possible necessity and logic of history collapses. The history of metaphysics, in other words, since its beginnings with the Greeks, has led to a culmination or an exhaustion of the possibilities for naming being. The *ending* of metaphysics and philosophy – from its beginning with the Greeks, and as it first culminates in Hegel's systematic logic, but also as it attains a more thorough exhaustion in Nietzsche's inversion of Platonism – appears precisely in the ultimate epoch of metaphysics. The groundless withdrawal of being announces itself most explicitly in the most totalizing project.

Our interpretation of history no less than that of being is still connected to this Greek legacy.[12] The engagement with metaphysics that is enabled through destructuring the history of being is both necessary and at the same time only the transition to another thinking. The lecture thus ends with the remarkable statement that the overcoming of metaphysics itself must be abandoned and left to itself (*TB* 24 = *ZSD* 25). From the perspective of the step back, the only thing necessary is that every historical necessity and logic has been exhausted. All that can be said is that the history of metaphysics *reveals* a destiny in which the oblivion of being finds itself increasingly *covered over*. The history of being is thus the destiny of the West only if one thinks destiny as the necessity of withdrawal and withdrawal as expropriation.

Yet Heidegger also suggests at times that thinking the history of being becomes a necessity because without such a thinking we have no chance of gaining a perspective on our situation today.

> What counts here is to say something about the attempt to think being without regard to its way of being grounded in beings. The attempt to think being without beings becomes necessary, because otherwise, it seems to me, no possibility prevails for actually bringing into view what today *is* encompassing the earth, to say nothing of a satisfactory determination of the human relation to what for a long time has been called "being". (*TB* 2 = *ZSD* 2, trans. mod.)

But this claim, namely, that thinking the history of being can have a privileged bearing on our historical moment, must at first be held apart from the unique difficulties connected with thinking the happening of being as such.

Hence, in addition to the distinction between historiology and history, we must conclude that there are also two distinct senses of history that assert themselves in Heidegger's thinking; and, even if they are not entirely separable, it is imperative to maintain an awareness of the difference between these. On the one hand, it often seems that Heidegger is not only making a descriptive claim about our historical situation as it is delimited by the oblivion of being in an age of technology, but also making prescriptive and even predictive claims about our response to this situation. On the other hand, however, the withdrawal of being cannot be put to work in this way, and must not be mistaken for some kind of predictive logic. As Heidegger would be the first to remind us, the history of being can only be thought by way of meditative recollection (*besinnliches Andenken*), and it is inevitably distorted when it is subjected to any kind of pragmatic planning or calculative control. Failing to maintain this distinction can only have disastrous consequences for understanding Heidegger's thinking of the history of being. We are otherwise likely to take the history of being as an attempted mythology of Western thinking, and thereby to import particular cultural and historiological prejudices into what Heidegger wants to think as the abyssal event of being itself. The danger persists, in other words, that we will reason simply *from* our understanding of our situation *to* the history of being, rather than understanding ourselves – which means also the horizons of our understanding and the limits of our powers of reason – as situated within a clearing of the historical destining of being. Admittedly, Heidegger himself may not have always succeeded in making clear this distinction between the happening of being and a mythos or grand narrative of the West.[13]

Notes

1. A summary of the development of "the history of being" in Heidegger's thinking would have to consider at the very least the discussion of "historicity" as it emerges towards the end of *Being and Time* (in which the disclosure of being is said to be historical) as well as the prolonged engagement with the history of metaphysics throughout the 1920s and 1930s, especially as it is dealt with in *Introduction to Metaphysics* and in *Contributions to Philosophy*, as this leads to his first thorough elaboration of the thought of the history of being in the second volume of Heidegger's *Nietzsche* (N4 200–250 = NII 335–98; and also NII 399–490). For a translation of these latter texts, see EP.
2. It is important to note the verbal affinity between "sending" (*Schicken*) and "destiny" (*Geschick* or *Geschicklichkeit*), which is lost in the English translation.
3. The verb in the German idiom, "es gibt...", is *geben*, which means "to give". The idiom appears in German in situations where in English one says "there is ...", for example when one says "there is water in the well" or "there are criminals in the government". In the protocol to the seminar following the lecture "Time and Being", Heidegger clarifies how the giving spoken of in "es gibt" opens up a host of relations and, in particular, tells us that this suggests an availability to humans for a possible appropriation. The "it" in question here and the sense of the "giving", of course, still need elaboration, no less than the sense of appropriation. See *TB* 38–40 = ZSD 41–3.
4. *Contributions to Philosophy* offers an extended treatment of this relation between the first and other beginning.
5. For this reason, the protocol of the seminar that followed the lecture speaks of the lecture as an "experiment" that entails certain risks. "The lecture's risk lies in the fact that it speaks in propositional statements about something essentially incommensurable with this kind of saying" (*TB* 25 = ZSD 27).
6. Note that the English word "history" ambiguously refers to both the events of history and the study of those events.
7. This is the precise difficulty Heidegger confronts in his attempt to think being

THE HISTORY OF BEING

"itself" or "as such". "To think being itself appropriately requires us to relinquish being as the ground of beings in favor of the giving which prevails concealed in unconcealment, that is in favor of the It gives" (*TB* 6 = *ZSD* 5–6, trans. mod.).

8. This list could be expanded. Even Heidegger's own lists are not exhaustive. See *TB* 56 = *ZSD* 62; *TB* 7 = *ZSD* 7; and *TB* 9 = *ZSD* 9.

9. In *The Principle of Reason* Heidegger writes: "In the destiny of being the history of being is not thought from the point of view of a happening that can be discerned through a movement and process. Rather the essence of the history of being is determined from out of the destiny of being, from out of being as destiny, from out of that which sends itself to us insofar as it withdraws itself from us. Both the self-sending and the self-withdrawing are one and the same, not twofold … Talk of the sending of being is not an answer but rather a question, among others the question concerning the essence of history, inasmuch as we think history as being and think essence from out of being. Initially the historical character of being is most bewildering …" (*PR* 62 = *SG* 109, trans. mod.).

10. "The history of Western thinking for its part must then give pointers which, if we were to follow them, would grant us a bit of a glimpse, even if still obscure, into what is here called the history of being. The history of being is the destiny of being, that sends itself to us insofar as it withdraws its essence" (*PR* 61 = *SG* 108, trans. mod.).

11. "The history of being means the destiny of being; in such sendings both the sending as well as that which sends withhold themselves in the announcement of themselves. To withhold oneself in Greek is *epoche*. Hence the talk of the epochs of the destining of being …" (*TB* 9 = *ZSD* 9, trans. mod.).

12. "What was thought and poetized in the beginnings of Greek antiquity is today still present, so present that its essence, still closed to itself, confronts us everywhere and comes upon us, there most of all where we suppose such a thing least of all, namely in the domination of modern technology, which is thoroughly foreign to antiquity but nonetheless still has in antiquity its essential origin. In order to experience this presence of history, we have to free ourselves from the still prevailing historical representation of history. The historical representation takes history as an object, within which a happening transpires that at the same time passes away in its transiency" (*QCT* 158 = *VA* 43–4, trans. mod.).

13. See Heidegger's clarification of the above extract in the Protocol (*TB* 32–3 = *ZSD* 35). In the Protocol it is made clear that the history of being must be removed from every "anthropological concern".

Further reading

Primary sources

See Heidegger's *Being and Time* (trans. Stambaugh), pts V and VI; *The End of Philosophy*; *Introduction to Metaphysics*; *Nietzsche: Vol. IV, Nihilism*; *The Principle of Reason*; and *What is Called Thinking?*

Secondary sources

See de Beistegui (2003); Bernasconi (1985); Ruin (1994); and Schürmann (1987).

TWELVE

Will and *Gelassenheit*

Bret W. Davis

The transition out of willing into *Gelassenheit* is what seems to me to be the genuine difficulty.   (*GA* 77: 109; see *DT* 61 = *G* 33)

Introduction: *Gelassenheit* as authentic non-willing

Gelassenheit, generally translated as "releasement", is a key word of Heidegger's later thought. Indeed, it names nothing less than the fundamental attunement (*Grundstimmung*) with which he says human beings are to authentically relate to other beings and to being itself. It contrasts with the fundamental attunement – or rather dis-attunement – of the will.[1] In modern times, human being is essentially will-ful; the will, according to Heidegger, is the historical determination of the essence of modern humanity. In fact he claims that, in the epochs of modernity, the being of beings as such is revealed – albeit in the form of extreme self-concealment and even abandonment – as "will to power" and ultimately as the technological "will to will".

By way of thoughtfully meditating on this historical determination of being and human being as will, Heidegger looks forward to, and attempts to prepare for, a turn in the history of being and a corresponding turn in the essence of humanity. It is crucial to bear in mind that this turn from will to *Gelassenheit* would *not* involve a mere reversal within what Heidegger calls "the domain of the will", a turnabout, for instance, from will-ful assertion to passive submission. Rather, Heidegger's thought calls for a twisting free of this entire domain of the will and a leap into a region of non-willing letting-be that is otherwise than both will-ful activity and will-less passivity. Moreover, this turn from the domain of the will to a region of non-willing is not just another historical transformation, for it involves a radical "step back", a returning (*Rückkehr*) to enter into (*Einkehr*) a more originary relation to being and to beings. Paradoxically, Heidegger thinks, it is in the nihilistic abyss of our will-ful abandonment that we might undergo this conversion and first truly awaken to our most proper way of being.

One can see, then, how central this turn from the will to *Gelassenheit* is for the later Heidegger. But how did he come upon this problem of will and possibility of non-willing in the course of his path of thought? What does he mean by "will"? How would the transition out of its domain take place? And what, finally, is meant by non-willing and *Gelassenheit*? These are the questions that I shall attempt to address in this chapter. Let me begin here with some introductory comments on the term *Gelassenheit*.

Gelassenheit is generally translated into English as "releasement". However, it should be kept in mind that it is a quite common German word that conveys a sense of "calm composure". In colloquial language, "*sei gelassen*" means something like "remain calm" or even "stay cool"; a *gelassener Typ* is, we might say, a "laid-back guy". More originally, and more pertinent in the present context, *Gelassenheit* refers to the state of mind attained by way of a profound existential or religious experience of letting go, being let, and letting be. As the nominal form of the perfect participle of *lassen* (to let), *Gelassenheit* has a long history in German thought (Ritter 2006: vol. 3, 220–24). It was coined in the thirteenth century by Meister Eckhart (Eckehart 1963: 91), and subsequently used by a number of mystics, theologians and philosophers. Heidegger too adopts the word *Gelassenheit* from the German mystical tradition, and yet he explicitly distances his use of the concept from a certain theological understanding.

In the context of Christianity, *Gelassenheit* is generally thought to entail a releasement from – a renunciation or abandonment (*Ablassen*) of – self-will, which enables a releasement over to – a deferral or leaving matters up to (*Überlassen*) – the Will of God. Heidegger certainly draws on this tradition. And yet, while he acknowledges that "many good things can be learned" from Eckhart, Heidegger clearly seeks to distinguish his notion of releasement from one that would lead merely to a deferential obedience to a divine Will (*GA* 77: 109; *DT* 62 = G 33–4).[2] Such a conversion would remain squarely within the domain of the will rather than evincing a twisting free of this domain as such.

In order to understand why Heidegger is satisfied with neither humanistic (transcendental) nor theistic (transcendent) voluntarism, we need to understand the radical critique of the will that lies at the heart of his later thought. According to his history of being (see Chapter 11), the being of beings in the epochs of modernity is will. In accordance with this historical delimitation of being, not only are modern human beings essentially will-ful, but the Absolute itself is understood as Will.[3] In anticipation of a turn to an "other inception" in the history of being, Heidegger speaks of *Gelassenheit* as a *releasement from* thinking as kind of willing, indeed from all modes of being as willing, and a *releasement into* a non-willing manner of being-in-the-world. But in order to understand the nature of Heidegger's *Gelassenheit* and why it is central to his later thought, we need to first understand how, along the way of his own path of thought, he himself turned initially to and then subsequently away from the will.

Heidegger's turns to and from the will

Heidegger's abiding concern is with the question of being. More specifically, it is with the question of the *relation* between being and human being, that is, the relation between being (*Sein*) and the being-there (*Dasein*) of human existence (see Introduction and Chapter 6). The often remarked "turn" in his thought-path in the 1930s can be understood as a shift in orientation within this relation, namely, from a focus on Dasein's temporal projections of the meaning of its being to an emphasis on the event of the truth of being (or "beyng") as determined though its historical "sendings".[4] Less remarked on but no less remarkable, Heidegger's thought-path also underwent a "second turn" around 1940, a turn *from* a tendency to think the relation between being and human being in terms of will, and a turn *to* a sustained attempt to think this relation in terms of a non-willing letting-be (*Sein-lassen*) and releasement (*Gelassenheit*).

In *Being and Time* (1927), Heidegger stressed the role of human Dasein in resolutely projecting the meaning of its being. Although humans are always "thrown" into given situations, they do not simply passively receive a meaningful world, or, when they do, they are inauthentically letting others (*das Man*) decide for them (SZ 193, 239). Faced with her own mortality, in "resoluteness" a human being must "choose" for herself her life-project, her "for-the-sake-of-which" (*Umwillen*) (see e.g. SZ 12, 84, 298), a choice that then gives teleological structure and meaning to the "equipment" she finds "ready-to-hand" in her "environment" (see SZ §§14–18). While the role of the will in *Being and Time* is largely implicit – and indeed extremely ambivalent,

in so far as the anticipation of one's own death and the "call of conscience" are occasions for the interruption of the will as much as they
are for its resolute reassertion – in texts from 1928 and 1929 Heidegger
explicitly claims that this world-forming decision is carried out by a
kind of finite yet transcendental will. "World … is primarily defined by
the for-the-sake-of-which. … But a for-the-sake-of-which, a purposive-
ness [*Umwillen*], is only possible where there is a will [*Willen*]" (*MFL*
185 = GA 26: 238). This "will" is not an act *in* the world, but rather
a prior determination of the very significance *of* the world, that is to
say, this transcendental or "ontological" will opens up and establishes
the context of meaningfully related entities within which any specific
"ontic" act can take place (*PM* 126 = GA 9: 163).

In 1930, in an interpretive appropriation of Kant's practical philosophy of autonomy (that is, of "giving the law to oneself"), Heidegger
roots the question of being in the question of freedom, and he defines
freedom as a finite yet "pure willing", that is, as a concrete will that
"actually wills willing and nothing else besides" (*EHF* 193 = GA 31:
285). Ironically, this willing that wills only its own willing in some ways
prefigures "the will to will" that Heidegger later sees as the nihilistic
abandonment of being into its modern determination as will, which he
then says "was incipient in Kant's concept of practical reason as pure
will" (*EP* 101 = VA 85). Indeed, such a voluntaristic determination
of the meaningful context of the world contrasts, not only generally
with the later Heidegger's concern with listening to and waiting upon
being, but also sharply and specifically with his later understanding of
freedom in terms of a "letting beings be" (*PM* 144 = GA 9: 188) that is
"*originally* not connected with the will" (*BW* 330 = VA 28).

The most disturbing form of Heidegger's middle-period philosophy of will appears during his brief but deeply troubling alliance with
National Socialism (see Chapter 7). At that time he developed a political
form of voluntarism, in which it is not the individual will but rather the
will of the *Volk* that must be resolutely enacted. Near the close of his
Rectorial Address of 1933, Heidegger proclaimed:

> Whether such a thing [as the collapse of the "moribund pseudo-
> civilization" of the West] occurs or does not occur, this depends
> solely on whether we as a historico-spiritual *Volk* will ourselves
> …. But it is our will that our *Volk* fulfill its historical mission. …
> We will ourselves.   (*SU* 38 = R 19; also see GA 38: 57)

Surely the darkest moments of Heidegger's embrace of the will are
found in his political speeches during this period, when he claims that

171

"we are only following the towering willing of our *Führer*" (*HC* 60 = *GA* 16: 236), since: "There is only the one will to the full Dasein of the state. … The *Führer* has awakened this will in the entire *Volk* and has welded it into a single resolve [*Entschluß*]" (*HC* 49 = *GA* 16: 189). In subsequent years, Heidegger comes not only to deride Hitler in private as "the robber and criminal of the century" (Vietta 1989: 47), but also to criticize explicitly the idea that the will-ful egoism of the individual subject can and should be overcome by way of "inserting the I into the We". Through this, Heidegger comes to recognize, will-ful "subjectivity only gains in power" (*QCT* 152 = *GA* 5: 111).

It was a few years after his entanglement with Nazism that Heidegger began to radically turn away from the will. In his close reading of Schelling in 1936 (*ST* = *SA*) he reflected on the evil depths of egoistic self-will, and in *Contributions to Philosophy* (1936–8) what he calls "the most proper will" is neither that of the individual ego nor that of the *Volk* that wills itself, but rather that of those who think ahead into Dasein and who exercise restraint (*Verhaltenheit*) in order to open themselves to the appropriating event of beyng (*CP* 11 = *GA* 65: 15). Heidegger's turn from the will takes place most clearly and decisively, however, over the course of his decade-long (1936–46) interpretation of and confrontation with Nietzsche's philosophy of the "will to power".[5]

While at first linking the notion of will that he found celebrated by Nietzsche with his own notion of "resoluteness" (*N1* 48 = *NI* 59), Heidegger's interpretation of Nietzsche's philosophy of the will to power became increasingly critical, until finally he writes: "For Nietzsche, will to power is the ultimate *factum* to which we come. What seems certain to Nietzsche is questionable to us" (*N4* 73 = *NII* 114). What Heidegger finds questionable is not the fact that being is determined as will to power *in the historical epoch of modernity*, but rather that this is the only possible or the most appropriate determination of being. He asks: "But the will to power itself – where does it originate…?" Heidegger's answer is that in the epoch of modernity "being radiates its own essence as will to power" (*N4* 181 = *NII* 239). When being reveals itself as will, however, it does this only by concealing its most proper essence of letting-be. Being shows itself as will only in an extreme "epoch" (from the Greek *epechein*, meaning to keep in or hold back) of being's withdrawal into self-concealment and hence abandonment of beings to nihilism (see *N4* 201ff., 239 = *NII* 338ff., 383).

The later Heidegger thus does not deny the historical determination of being and human being as will. But he does come to see this modern voluntarism as epochally problematic, indeed as the crux of what is amiss with the entire Western tradition and its descent into nihilism. "If being is 'will' ... The essence of modern metaphysics can be presented by means of the complete unfolding of this hypothetical statement" (*GA* 67: 159). With Nietzsche's utterance, "Life is will to power" (see Nietzsche 1967: §§1067, 685, 693; 2006: 271, 330), Western metaphysics is said to complete itself (*N3* 18–19 = *NI* 492). This completion is the end of a decline from the Greek beginning or "inception" (*Anfang*), an inception that is itself ambivalent, in so far as it both enabled a profound apprehension of being and yet also set the Western tradition on a metaphysical path of descent that culminates in nihilistic voluntarism and technological machination. Heidegger's later thought is dedicated to preparing for an "other inception" of the history of being, and this entails not just carrying out a personal conversion but participating in a "being-historical" turn from the metaphysics of will to a thinking of non-willing or *Gelassenheit*.

Heidegger's mature critique of the will

For the later Heidegger, the will is deeply problematic. Indeed, he even suggests at one point that "in general the will itself is what is evil" (*GA* 77: 208). But what exactly does Heidegger mean by "will"? In his writings on Nietzsche, Heidegger comes to define the will as follows: willing as a "commanding" is "the fundamental attunement of one's being superior" to others (*N3* 152 = *NI* 641). "To will is to will-to-be-master" (*QCT* 77 = *GA* 5: 234). In willing, one reaches out beyond oneself so as to increase the territory under one's command; willing is, in short, "being-master-out-beyond-oneself [*Über-sich-hinaus-Herrsein*]" (*N1* 63 = *NI* 76). Willing thus involves a dynamic movement of going out beyond oneself and conquering. I suggest that this can be understood as a circling movement of *ecstatic-incorporation*, in the sense that, in willing, one exceeds oneself only to bring this excess back into oneself. One stands outside oneself, but the aim of this *ekstasis* of willing is always to incorporate the other back into one's own domain. The will's movement of self-overcoming is always in the name of an expansion of the subject, an increase in its territory, its power.

The will to power is thus not a blind striving or a mere will to live; it is rather a will to increase as well as preserve the power of the subject (*QCT* 80 = *GA* 5: 237). Indeed, we could say that the subject of will itself gets constituted through this dynamic process of preservation and enhancement of power. "With the word 'will' I do not in fact mean a faculty of the soul, but rather that wherein the essence of the soul, mind, reason, love, and life is based according to a unanimous yet hardly thought through doctrine of occidental thinkers" (GA 77: 78). The fundamental (dis)attunement of the will underlies all these determinations and modes of subjectivity.

The will is thus not just one faculty alongside others, such as thinking, for thinking itself, "conceived of in the traditional manner as representing, is a willing" (GA 77: 106; DT 58 = G 29). From Leibniz's conjunction of *perceptio* and *appetitus* through German idealism's linkage of will and reason (GA 77: 53; VA 110 = NII 222–3; N3 222 = NII 299), thinking and knowing have been determined as willing, and this means first of all as subjective representation. Representation is a matter of willing in so far as it "inspects everything encountering it from out of itself and in reference to itself" (N3 219 = NII 295). In representational thinking, one first strives to go out beyond things to delimit a horizon – a transcendental schema – through which and only through which things must show themselves as objects for subjects (GA 77: 98).

Yet the will of metaphysical representation and even the will to power do not yet, according to Heidegger, completely unveil the essence of the will. The will is fully unleashed as the technological "will to will". "The basic form of appearance in which the will to will arranges and calculates itself in the unhistorical element of the world of completed metaphysics can be strictly called 'technology'" (EP 93 = VA 76). Technology, Heidegger says, is a way of revealing things or, rather, a way of not letting them be revealed as "things" with their own integrity, or even any longer as "objects" (Gegenstände) standing over against representing subjects. In the technological worldview all beings are reduced to mere "standing-reserve" (Bestand), that is, to material and energy resources for the preservation and enhancement of the cybernetic system of the Ge-stell (see Chapter 13), the enframing of the world for no other purpose than an endless will to more of the same, more power, more will.

Through technology, nature is reduced to a resource from which energy is unlocked, transformed, stored up, distributed and switched about, ever at the beck and call of human will. Ultimately even human beings are threatened with reduction to "human resources". In fact, says Heidegger, "self-assertive humans" were all along, "whether or not they know and will it as individuals, … the functionaries of technology" (PLT 113 = GA 5: 271, trans. mod.). The will, by which humans assert themselves over all that is, first by representationally objectifying the world and ultimately by reducing things to standing-reserve for their projects of mastery, does not originate in humans themselves. At one point Heidegger goes so far as to say: "The opinion arises that the human will is the origin of the will to will, while in fact humans are willed by the will to will without experiencing the essence of this willing" (*EP* 101 = *VA* 85, trans. mod.).

And yet, Heidegger says elsewhere,

> precisely because humans are challenged more originally than are the energies of nature, i.e., into the process of ordering, *they are never transformed into mere standing-reserve*. Since humans drive technology forward, they *take part* in ordering as a way of revealing. (*QCT* 323 = *VA* 22, emphasis added)

Humans can never be wholly reduced to cogs in the wheel of the technological will to will. Heidegger suggests that the core of our essence radically precedes and exceeds the will (*PLT* 113–14 = *GA* 5: 293–4). That core is *Gelassenheit*, a non-willing fundamental attunement to and correspondence with being (*GA* 77: 145–6; *DT* 82–3 = *G* 61). The existence of this core also means that we are co-responsible for the fate of the world, in so far as we are called on to correspond to being, to engage in the determination of its historical sendings, and to take part in a historical turn to a way of being otherwise than the will (*QCT* 39 = *GA* 79: 70).

Twisting free of the domain of the will

What would it mean to turn away from the will, and by what means would this take place? It would seem that there can be no will-ful answer to the problem of the will, any more than there can be a technological answer to the problem of technology. The "will to overcome", Heidegger tells us, is emblematic of the problem of nihilism, and thus cannot be its solution (see *N4* 243 = *NII* 389). But how else can we undertake or undergo a transition out of the will? We need to disaccustom ourselves from the contradictory *will* to reach *Gelassenheit*, and yet this disaccustoming itself seems to require *Gelassenheit*. Evidently we need to somehow anticipate or "think out toward" that to which we are in transition in order to undertake/undergo the transition itself (see *GA* 77: 68, 108).

Yet how do we even thoughtfully anticipate non-willing; what would human "activity" be like if it were radically otherwise than willing? "Perhaps", Heidegger says at one point, "we come to know what non-willing is only once we have reached it" (*GA* 77: 76). But how might we begin to approach this realization? We at least know what non-willing is other than: the will. More fully thought, genuine non-willing would be otherwise than the entire "domain of the will". After all, as Heidegger points out, even the expression "non-willing" (*Nicht-Wollen*) could be used to name a variety of comportments, and most of these remain squarely within the domain of the will. Most forms of negating and refusing willing are mere variations of the "will" (*GA* 77: 76–8). Since resignation and passivity signify a mere lack or deference of willing, they too would succeed only in manifesting privative modes within what Heidegger calls "the domain of the will". And since mere opposition remains a slave to that which it opposes, and in so far as "revolutions" merely overturn something within a domain without altering the domain as such (see *GA* 77: 51; *GA* 54: 77), non-willing cannot be attained by a mere will-ful rebellion against willing.

Nevertheless, in order to "twist free" of the domain of the will, Heidegger does acknowledge that there is an indispensable role to be played by going *through* a paradoxical "willing non-willing" (*GA* 77: 51–2, 58–67). To that extent, Heidegger's own notion of "non-willing" is itself explicitly and unavoidably ambiguous. He writes:

> Non-willing still signifies, on the one hand, a willing, in that a No prevails in it, even if it is in the sense of a No that directs itself at willing itself and renounces it. Non-willing in this sense means: to will-fully renounce willing. And then, on the other hand, the expression non-willing also means: that which does not at all pertain to the will. (*GA* 77: 106; see *DT* 59 = *G* 30)

Heidegger goes on to suggest that a transitional "willing non-willing" should be understood as a renunciation of willing that prepares for letting oneself into an engagement in the essence of thinking, which is not a willing. In an analogous manner, he speaks of a movement through an initial to an authentic sense of *Gelassenheit*:

> *Gelassenheit*, as releasing oneself from transcendental representing, is in fact a refraining from the willing of a horizon. This refraining also no longer comes from a willing, unless a trace of willing is required to occasion the letting-oneself-into a belonging to the open-region – a trace which, however, vanishes in the letting-oneself-into and is completely extinguished in authentic releasement. (*GA* 77: 142–3; see *DT* 79–80 = *G* 57)

Heidegger thus tells us that "being-released" (*Los-Gelassensein*) from the will is only the first moment of *Gelassenheit*, and not its most proper sense (*GA* 77: 121). While non-willing as a radical negation of the (domain of the) will would enable this initial sense of *Gelassenheit* as being-released-from, the authentic sense of *Gelassenheit*, which we would be released-into, would correspond to the second and more radical sense of non-willing as "what remains absolutely outside any kind of will" (*DT* 59 = G 30).

The correspondence of *Seinlassen* and *Gelassenheit*

How then does Heidegger characterize authentic non-willing or *Gelassenheit*? In a sense, all of his later texts – all of his meditations on building, dwelling, thinking, poetizing and so on – can be read as attempts to think non-willing(ly).

In *Country Path Conversations* (1944–5; CPC = GA 77), a key text for the topic of this chapter that I have been frequently citing, Heidegger identifies *Gelassenheit* with an authentic kind of "waiting" (GA 77: 115–17, 120–25, 216–21, 225–34). Rather than will-fully positing a transcendental schema that anthropocentrically determines how beings can show themselves, we are to engage in an attentive waiting upon the "open-region" that surrounds our limited horizons of perception and intelligibility and lets them be in the first place. The resolute openness of this "waiting upon" is contrasted with an "expecting" that represents – or will-fully projects – in advance what it then passively awaits. On the one hand, in contrast to a passive resignation that would abandon the search for knowledge, authentic thinking as *Gelassenheit* and waiting involves a courageous and mindful "surmising" (*Vermuten*) that enables a "coming-into-nearness to the far" (GA 77: 116, 148). On the other hand, in contrast to the aggressive interrogation that characterizes technology and the natural sciences, such thinking as attentive waiting that surmises would neither predetermine nor demand the full disclosure – the unbounded unconcealment – of that upon which it waits. Rather, *Gelassenheit* as attentive waiting is a thoughtful remembrance, a restrained comportment, an indwelling forbearance, which steadfastly stays within being (beyng) as the open-region or "abiding expanse" that requires our thoughtful participation for the appropriating events of its clearings of truth (GA 77: 147–8; see also Chapters 8 and 10).

In the "topology of beyng" (FS 41 = GA 15: 335) of Heidegger's later thought, it is the open-region of being (beyng) that "enregions" humans and "bethings" things (GA 77: 139–40), bringing us back to where we essentially belong. Released (*losgelassen*) from will-ful representation and released over to (*überlassen*) a resting in the open-region, authentic

Gelassenheit receives from the open-region its movement towards it (*GA* 77: 117, 122). But this relation should not be understood simply in terms of the "activity" of being as the open-region and the "passivity" of human being, in so far as these terms are rooted in the domain of the will. Heidegger clearly states that "*Gelassenheit* lies ... outside the distinction between activity and passivity ... because it does not belong to the domain of the will" (*GA* 77: 109; see *DT* 61 = *G* 33). He denies that it is a matter of "impotently letting things slide and drift along". *Gelassenheit* is rather a kind of "higher activity", namely that of "resolute openness" (*Ent-schlossenheit*) understood as a "self-opening for the open" (*GA* 77: 143–5; see *DT* 81 = *G* 59) and as a patiently enduring "standing within" it. This "indwelling [*Inständigkeit*] in releasement to the open-region" is said to be nothing less than "the genuine essence of the spontaneity of thinking" (*GA* 77: 145; see *DT* 82 = *G* 60).

Thus, when Heidegger says that in our destitute times "we are to do nothing but wait", he also says that this is "not simply a matter of waiting until something occurs to humans". Waiting as *Gelassenheit* is the essence of genuine thinking, and such thinking "is not inactivity but is itself the action which stands in dialogue with the world mission" (*OG* 110 = *GA* 16: 676). The play of the sending of being calls on humans to "play along" (*PR* 113 = *SG* 188). When "language speaks" (*die Sprache spricht*), it does not ask humans to just shut up and listen, but rather beckons them to "cor-respond" (*ent-sprechen*) so that through this "corresponsive saying" thinking is able to "bring to language ever and again [an] advent of being" (*PM* 275 = *GA* 9: 363).

Moreover, Heidegger tells us that the "activities" of being as the open-region "can hardly be spoken of as will" (*GA* 77: 143). Being as the open-region "enregions" humans in a manner that requires (*braucht*) them in order to open up a world that lets beings truly be (see *GA* 77: 147). Heidegger attempts to step back from the dualistic subject–object grammar, which would determine the relation between being and humans in terms of activity and passivity. He thinks being (beyng) as a middle-voiced appropriating event of giving and requiring (*Es gibt* as *Es brauchet*); being requires human Dasein as the site of the gift of its arrival and withdrawal (*WCT* 189 = *WhD* 116).

Near the end of his career Heidegger stated, "the deepest meaning of being is *letting* [Lassen]" (*FS* 59 = *GA* 15: 363). In *Gelassenheit*, human being properly corresponds to, and participates in, this *Seinlassen* of being itself.

Gelassenheit toward things … and other humans

Gelassenheit names not only our authentic relation to being, but also our proper comportment to beings, to entities. When Heidegger speaks of "releasement toward things" (*Gelassenheit zu den Dingen*), on the one hand he is concerned with preserving the human essence and its relation to being from a tendency to "fall" into the ruination of "running around amidst beings" (*Umtrieben an das Seiende*) that characterizes the everyday life of the anonymous they-self (*das Man*) (*PM* 92 = *GA* 9: 116). There are clearly echoes of Eckhart's "detachment" when Heidegger writes:

> We can use technical devices, and yet with proper use also keep ourselves free of them, that we may let go of them at any time … as something which does not affect our inner and real core. … I would name this comportment toward technology, which expresses "yes" and at the same time "no", with an old word, releasement toward things. (*DT* 54 = *G* 23)

Yet Heidegger is also concerned with taking care of things by sparing and "properly using" them. Letting things be is not simply a matter of passively leaving them alone or abandoning them. We should note that in German *lassen* is used as a modal auxiliary not only in the sense of passively *letting* something happen or *allowing* someone to do something, but also in the sense of *having* something done (for example, having one's car repaired). Moreover, *sicheinlassen auf etwas*, literally "to let oneself into something", means "to get involved or to engage oneself in something". Hence, while *Seinlassen* (letting-be) may be used in common speech to mean "to leave alone or stop doing", Heidegger's *Sein-lassen* entails rather a *Sicheinlassen auf* in the sense of a non-willing engagement that attentively lets beings be themselves. He writes in this regard:

> Ordinarily we speak of letting be … in the negative sense of leaving something alone, of renouncing it, of indifference and even neglect. … However, the phrase required now – to let beings be – does not refer to neglect and indifference but rather the opposite. To let be is to engage oneself with beings [*Sein-lassen ist das Sicheinlassen auf das Seiende*]. (*PM* 144 = *GA* 9: 188)

Heidegger goes on to say that this engaged letting-be is not, to be sure, a will-ful or calculative manipulation of beings. The difficulty, once

179

again, is how to twist free of the very domain of the will (passivity as well as activity) into a region of non-willing, where we are both open to the mystery of being (its withdrawal into concealment) and engaged in participating in its events of unconcealment. Such events would open a world wherein things can show themselves in meaningful ways without being wholly reduced to objects of subjective representation or stand-ing-reserve for technological manipulation. As beings of releasement, we are called on in this manner to assist in letting other beings be.

Let me end by raising a question for those who wish to think not only with, but also after, Heidegger. Presumably, *Gelassenheit* also names our proper comportment to one another. This would undoubtedly involve attentively letting others be, rather than either passively neglecting or actively "leaping in" and taking over their existential concerns (*SZ* 122). Unfortunately, the later Heidegger had precious little to say about ethics, other than to say that the thinking of being could itself perhaps be thought of as "originary ethics" (*PM* 271 = *GA* 9: 356). After his errant involvement in the Nazi politics of communal self-assertion, he also had precious little to say about politics. Bringing *Gelassenheit* into the interpersonal dimension of ethics and politics thus requires us to think further down the road after Heidegger, beyond not only his vol-untaristic *Volk*-politics of the early 1930s, but also beyond his lingering suspicions of democracy. Of course, today's democratic societies are not without their fundamental problems, and these problems are certainly not unrelated to Heidegger's critique of the technological machinations of the will to will. But what might a "democracy to come" (Derrida) look like were it to be infused with an interpersonal attunement of *Gelassenheit*? Presumably, such a politics of non-willing would take the form of a democracy based on mutually attentive conversation rather than intersubjective litigation, a dialogical sharing of voices rather than procedural compromises between will-fully antagonistic subjectivities. But could such a political attunement be established? How could it, after all, be regulated, much less enforced? Perhaps, rather, we must continuously find ways to resolutely yet gently infuse the safety-net proceduralism of liberal democracy with a fundamental attunement of *Gelassenheit* through meditative thinking and practice, responsive education and responsible social critique, and the cultivation of forums for open-minded conversation between individuals and groups. A fully engaged *Gelassenheit* would in these ways be always on the way to carefully letting other humans, among other beings, be.

Notes

1. The aim of this chapter is to introduce and concisely explicate this topic of will and *Gelassenheit* in Heidegger's thought. For a detailed and critical study, see Davis (2007).
2. In fact, Eckhart's *Gelassenheit* and its relation to the Will of God (or the "God of Will") is far more complex than Heidegger's passing critique implies. See Schürmann (1978), Caputo (1990) and Davis (2007: ch. 5). For Heidegger's complex and evolving relation to Christianity and his ideas of divinity, see Chapters 16 and 17.
3. Prior to Schopenhauer and Nietzsche, it is Schelling who first explicitly announces that "willing is primal being". See Schelling (1987: 231); *ST* 170 = *SA* 207; *GA* 49: 84.
4. For Thomas Sheehan's meticulous account of "the turn", which stresses that the term *Kehre* in Heidegger's thought most properly refers to the reciprocity between being and human being (*Sein* and Dasein), see Chapter 6. On the multiple senses of the turn or turning in the context of Heidegger's thought, see also Davis (2007: 61–5).
5. Also noteworthy are Heidegger's extensive notes on Ernst Jünger from the 1930s and after, in which he critically reflects on what is viewed as the contemporary legacy of Nietzsche's metaphysics of the will to power in the technological reduction of humans to "workers" (see *GA* 90).

References

Caputo, J. D. 1990. *The Mystical Element in Heidegger's Thought*, reprinted with corrections. New York: Fordham University Press.

Davis, B. W. 2007. *Heidegger and the Will: On the Way to Gelassenheit*. Evanston, IL: Northwestern University Press.

Eckehart, M. 1963. *Deutsche Predigten und Traktate*, J. Quint (ed. & trans.). Munich: Carl Hanser.

Nietzsche, F. 1967. *The Will to Power*, W. Kaufmann & R. J. Hollingdale (trans.). New York: Vintage Books.

Nietzsche, F. 2006. *The Nietzsche Reader*, K. A. Pearson & D. Large (eds). Malden, MA: Blackwell.

Ritter, J. (ed.) 2006. *Historisches Wörterbuch der Philosophie*. Basel/Stuttgart: Schwabe.

Schelling, F. W. J. 1987. "Philosophical Investigations into the Essence of Human Freedom and Related Matters", P. Hayden-Roy (trans.). In *Philosophy of German Idealism*, E. Behler (ed.), 217–84. New York: Continuum.

Schürmann, R. 1978. *Meister Eckhart: Mystic and Philosopher*. Bloomington, IN: Indiana University Press.

Vietta, S. 1989. *Heideggers Kritik am Nationalsozialismus und an der Technik*. Tübingen: Niemeyer.

Further reading

Primary sources

See Heidegger's *Country Path Conversations*; *Discourse on Thinking*; *The Question Concerning Technology*; *Schelling's Treatise on the Essence of Human Freedom*; *Nietzsche: Volumes I and II* (San Francisco: Harper & Row, 1991); and *Nietzsche: Volumes III and IV* (San Francisco: Harper & Row, 1991).

Secondary sources

See Caputo (1990); Davis (2007); A. Mitchell, "Praxis and *Gelassenheit*: The 'Practice' of the Limit", in Raffoul & Pettigrew (2002), 317–38; and Schürmann (1987: 245–50). See also R. Ohashi, *Ekstase und Gelassenheit: Zu Schelling und Heidegger* (Munich: Wilhelm Fink, 1975).

THIRTEEN

Ge-stell: enframing as the essence of technology

Hans Ruin

Along with his greetings to the tenth annual meeting of the Heidegger Circle in the United States in 1976, Heidegger sent a short piece of writing, one of the very last by his hand. In it he raised again a question that by then had become perhaps the most persistent concern of the last decades of his life, namely the question of *technology*. By this he meant the need to understand and critically reflect on the sense and significance of the increased technologization of the world in modernity. He writes there that a world stamped by technology is also a world characterized by a forgetfulness of being, and he urges the participants to ponder its significance and effects (in Sallis 1978: 1). The most important concept in this context, and that by means of which he sought to capture the essential character of this momentous transformation, was that of *Gestell*, normally translated as "enframing". Its common lexical meaning in German is "frame" or "rack". But as a philosophical term it is a neologism, and Heidegger often hyphenates it as *Ge-stell* to indicate that it draws its meaning from a series of related concepts built around the root verb *stellen* (to place or put), such as *herstellen* (to produce) and *vorstellen* (to represent). It is also related to the word *Gestalt*, meaning figure or configuration. In his 1953 lecture, "The Question Concerning Technology", one of the most widely read and discussed essays from his post-war period, he writes: "We now name the challenging claim that gathers man with a view to ordering the self-revealing as standing-reserve: *Ge-stell* [enframing]" (*BW* 324 = *VA* 23).

In order to understand this enigmatic statement, and in order to grasp the meaning and significance of the notion of *Ge-stell* in Heidegger's thinking as a whole, we need to consider it not only in the context of his thinking on technology, but also in the context of his understanding of the meaning of being and its historical transformations. The goal here is to recall this context through a summary of some of the most important texts and passages that lead up to the forging of this new concept. In the course of this analysis it will become clear that the theme designated by *Ge-stell* is not something entirely new, which emerges only in the post-war writings. On the contrary, it is important to see how and to what extent it is in fact rooted in his very earliest phenomenological attempts to elucidate the meaning of being and human existence, in particular as this is first articulated in his critical elucidations of the philosophy of Aristotle.

Technology and art: critique and retrieval of Greek *technē*

A key text in this context, and one to which Heidegger would always return, is the sixth book of Aristotle's *Nicomachean Ethics*. This is a good starting-point, as it is also the most detailed attempt by a Greek writer to define the sense of *technē* in contrast to other human capacities. Aristotle here defines *technē*, the Latin translation of which is *ars*, as one of the five principal intellectual capacities or virtues. It is an intellectual capacity that has to do with making or creating (*poiēsis*) something new in accordance with a reflexive rational capacity. As such it also has to do with truth and falsity. Indeed, at the very outset of the sixth book of the *Nicomachean Ethics* Aristotle writes that there are "five ways in which the soul achieves truth, namely through art (*technē*), scientific knowledge, prudence, wisdom, and intelligence" (1139b). Among the many works and passages in Greek philosophical writings that Heidegger explores in his critical appraisal of Western metaphysics, this line holds a singular importance. It contains the kernel not only of what he will later claim to be the "Greek conception of technology", but also of the genuine ontological meaning of the phenomenon of technology as such, as well as of the phenomenon of truth. We shall come back to this again towards the end of our discussion, as it surfaces in a key passage in the essay on technology.

Heidegger's most intense interpretative confrontation with the writings of Aristotle takes place during the formative years of the early 1920s. From this period we have the famous text submitted to Paul Natorp in 1922, the so-called "Natorp Report" or, as its full title reads, "Phenomenological Interpretations with Respect to Aristotle: Indication of the Hermeneutical Situation" (*IHS*). This text contains not only the outline of his own basic philosophical orientation, as this is

184

systematized in *Being and Time* some years later, but also the first deci-sive formulations for understanding his thinking on technology, and the anticipation of the concept of *Ge-stell*. For here Heidegger asks how the being of life, of human existence, is grasped in Greek thinking. He stresses the importance of attending to how it is that the vocabulary of early Greek metaphysics is forged, and to the guiding models and motives for its ontology.

How are we to critically understand what Aristotle means by sub-stance, *ousia*? In designating the most fundamental nature of being by this term, Aristotle has been guided, Heidegger argues, by an understanding of being as something fabricated, in *poiēsis*, and thus as something placed at hand, as something that has been produced (*Hergestelltsein*). The German word is important here, for it marks the first in a long sequence of concepts forged around the root verb *stellen*. In Greek metaphysics being is thought, in its general essence, as something produced and grasped in language through its *eidos*, its visible form. And this way of making being appear, stand forth and thus be true, Heidegger continues, is the way of *technē*. So the technological understanding of being is in fact what we could call the basic Greek model of understanding being, the one according to which Greek meta-physics built its fundamental conceptual structure. Only by becoming critically aware of what we could thus call a certain technical bias in the very construction of metaphysical language can we also engage in an exploration directed towards other, complementary and supposedly also more fundamental senses of being. Metaphysics understands and thus conceptually constructs being according to a model of production. This conclusion is not simply a descriptive hypothesis that concerns the first emergence of a metaphysical conceptuality; it also holds a critical potential. For in questioning the validity of the original conceptual con-figuration, a space for critical reflection on the inherited understanding and meaning of being is also opened up.

When Heidegger publishes *Being and Time* five years later, the core of its argument is the critique of a substantialist metaphysics that understands being in terms of presence-at-hand (*Vorhandenheit*). The connection to the earlier analysis of the "technical" roots of meta-physics is not, however, obvious at first glance. For in *Being and Time*, the explicit theme of technology and *technē* hardly appears at all. In *Being and Time* the critique of substance ontology takes as its starting-point not the Greek "technical" sense of being, but rather the modern, Cartesian construction of the meaning of being as pure extension in space (see *BT* §§19–21). This understanding of being presupposes a distanced perspective that contemplates nature simply as a calculable material extension, as is shown in the famous example of Descartes' meditation on a piece of wax as an extended thing removed from its context of use.

In order to deconstruct this understanding of thinghood as present-at-hand objectivity, Heidegger takes a step that is somewhat surprising in view of his earlier analysis of Greek metaphysics. For in searching for a different conceptual avenue for thinking the being of reality he turns instead to the Greek word for things, *pragmata*, which etymologically signifies "that with which we are concerned" in praxis. These entities are not meaningless spatial extensions, but always contextually mean-ingful things embedded in a whole surrounding world of concerns. Their mode of being is, as he says, "readiness-to-hand" (*Zuhanden-heit*). Their meaningfulness presupposes precisely that they are not objectified, but rather lived with in a pre-reflective referential context. From this perspective it is also possible for him to develop his analysis of "world" as something more than simply a constellation of material bodies. The primary phenomenon of world is a meaning-context, into which we are always already thrown. The objectified world of calculable entities as represented in natural science is in fact a secondary phenom-enon that grows out of the more original lived world as its theoretically mediated modification. What makes this analysis rather confusing from the perspective of the earlier critique of substance metaphysics is that here it is not the Greek instrumental and technical understanding of being that explains an original forgetfulness but, on the contrary, it is the artefact, the tool or equipment, in the form of the Greek *pragmata*, that is brought forth as a critical lever against the distanced and objectifying Cartesian understanding of nature in modernity. This is what permits Heidegger to speak of readiness-to-hand as a more original manifesta-tion of being than presence-at-hand.

From one perspective the ontology developed in *Being and Time* could thus be described as an ontology of the artefact and the tool, since the being of readiness-to-hand is argued to be more fundamen-tal than the secondary and theoretically mediated presence-at-hand. Heidegger even argues in *Being and Time* that the original manifesta-tion of nature is also a readiness-to-hand, since nature first appears as a meaningful-something in relation to the overall concern of human Dasein. And in *Being and Time* this destructive retrieval of a more origi-nal source of manifestation on the model of equipment or artefact is not criticized, but rather presented as a positive finding. Even though the reason behind this analysis was clearly to reflect critically on the form of objectification of nature that emerges with modern science and its metaphysics, still the implications of it become problematic, not least for Heidegger himself. For if nature is understood on the model of equipment or readiness-to-hand, then the phenomenological analysis would seem to reinstall precisely that subjectivist and anthropocentric determination of the world that it also sought to transcend. If we read *Being and Time* from this angle, we can understand why Heidegger subsequently distances himself from its analyses.

An important text in this regard is the essay "On the Origin of the Work of Art" (*BW* 143–212) from 1935–6, which marks a further step in the genealogy of the technical in Heidegger's thought. In conjunction with his attempt to develop a phenomenological analysis of the artwork (see Chapter 9), he also expands his earlier critique of substance ontology. He states that the being of the artwork cannot be grasped on the model of objective entities as present-at-hand. But, and this is the noteworthy step, nor can it be understood according to the model of the tool as something ready-to-hand. Furthermore, nature too cannot in the end be understood according to either of these models. For natural being is characterized rather by an elusive auto-emergence (*eigenwuchsig*). When we turn to the artwork we find that it is different from *all three* of these types of being. The artwork is a very special way of bringing together and letting the being of nature appear, which does not consume it as raw material for the purpose of its own projects, but rather allows it to come to presence for its own sake. It is in this sense that the artwork is a "happening of truth". In clear contrast to the analysis in *Being and Time*, the mode of equipmentality is what lies here in the way of grasping the genuine phenomenon of nature; the latter can be discerned only through the event of the artwork. The work of art, as a work of truth, is what reveals the deeper meaning of nature that is concealed as long as nature is interpreted only through the traditional – technically inspired – matrix of matter and form. In this way the artwork essay marks a new step in Heidegger's thinking, a step that raises to a whole new level the role and significance of art and the poetical. However, it thereby also leads to a more complex picture concerning the genuine meaning of Greek *technē*. For, as Heidegger himself also notes, the Greek word for art (German *Kunst*) is also *technē*, and the artist is a *technites*. So, from the point of view of the artwork essay, there is indeed a positive legacy of the Greek understanding of *technē*, not as a production of the ready-to-hand instruments of our immediate life concerns, but rather as a poetic bringing forth of something into its presence.

While *technē* in the sense of art is given an increasingly important role in Heidegger's continued critical assessment of the Western metaphysical tradition and its substantialist understanding of being, *technē* in the modern sense of technology becomes a theme of increased critical concern from around the same time. If we take the liberty of generalizing, Heidegger's development from around the time of the artwork essay (1935–6) could in fact be described precisely in terms of these two divergent meanings of *technē*. On the one hand, *technē* in the sense of the fabricated artefact functions from the inception of metaphysics as the matrix for thinking being as a disconnected entity, a metaphysical thinking that comes to the fore definitively in modernity, where the truth or event of being is covered over and domesticated in a representational and objectifying understanding. On the other hand, *technē* as art emerges as a unique avenue towards thinking the event of truth in a way that does not objectify being but rather permits it to prevail in its own essence, that is, in its dual nature as at once presence and absence. As we shall see later, the essay on technology contrasts these themes in a most explicit manner.

From the worker and the world picture to the *Ge-stell*

The more "negative" side of the technical, and Heidegger's emergence as a critical thinker of modern technology, is not something that belongs only to his post-war period, as was often believed to be the case. The decisive confrontation with technology is of an earlier date, and more or less simultaneous with the composition of the artwork essay. For this was also the time when he read and initiated his critical dialogue with the thought of the contemporary writer Ernst Jünger. In 1932 Jünger published a much read and discussed dystopian essay entitled *Der Arbeiter* (*The Worker*). In this text, Jünger ventures to think modernity in the wake of Nietzsche's analysis of nihilism as the loss of a transcendent source of meaning. Jünger, who was a decorated war hero from the First World War with profound personal experience of the new technological warfare, here sees the emergence of a new type or configuration (*Gestalt*) of human being, "the worker". Human being as the worker has entered into a symbiotic relation with the machine and with technology in the form of labourer or soldier, and is thus a completed manifestation of a will to power. Jünger's book is an attempt to articulate a distanced and objective analysis of a transformation in human being's relation to nature, mediated through technology. He describes what he sees as the essence of modernity, where a technologically mediated will to power has made it its task to shape the world according to its own vision and for its own purpose.

The material from Heidegger's early and intense preoccupation with the writings of Jünger was made available only recently, which is why the full significance of the latter's analysis for Heidegger's own thinking on technology and the *Gestell* has not been fully recognized. In the relevant volume from his *Collected Edition* (*Gesamtausgabe*), Heidegger writes that with the character or figure – the *Gestalt* – of the worker, the subjectivity of man reaches its completion as a domination or mastery of the earth (*GA* 90: 40). And in the very notion of *Gestalt*, which for Jünger served as a kind of optics or eidetics by means of which he sought to capture the essence of the historical present, Heidegger traces an inheritance from the Platonic *idea* as that which visualizes being in a fixed figure or essence. It is in these both sympathetic and critical reflections on Jünger's thought of the worker and its *Gestalt* that the thought of *Ge-stell* is first conceived, even though the word itself appears only later. In a *Festschrift* for Jünger, published in 1955, Heidegger contributed a piece entitled "Over 'the Line'", which was later republished under the title "On the Question of Being". In this text he picks up his earlier analysis of *The Worker* and Jünger's understanding of the *Gestalt*, stating explicitly that the essence of the *Gestalt* should be understood as emanating from what he himself in the meantime had thought as *Ge-stell* (*PM* 303 = *GA* 9: 401).

The most important published text from the pre-war period for the development of Heidegger's thought of the *Ge-stell* is, however, "The Age of the World Picture", a lecture presented in 1938 in the context of a conference on the contemporary image of the world, *Weltbild*, and later published in the collection *Holzwege* (*OBP* 57–85 = *GA* 5: 75–113; also in *QCT* 75–113). This lecture starts by stating a position around which he will circle for the rest of his life: namely, that what is today in need of thoughtful meditation (*Besinnung*) is science and machine technology. He then develops his basic argument that machine technology is not a consequence of science; rather, both science and machine technology are rooted in a more fundamental sense of technology, which he equates with modern metaphysics. In this metaphysical constellation, being is understood as something represented (*vorgestellt*) and visualized so as to be made available for manipulation and domination by a subjective will (see Chapter 12). Even art and the humanities tend to be drawn into the orbit of the metaphysical constellation of technology. Art becomes a source of aesthetic pleasure and the humanities are organized according to the same pattern of production of results as the natural sciences. The researcher, Heidegger writes, becomes a technician who works by means of experiments to produce results that can be measured in terms of their effects for the academic establishment.

This whole development and transformation in the way being comes to presence is traced back to the inception of modern philosophy, the

Cartesian conception of certitude, in which human being emerges as a subject that projects the world before it as an object, represented and explained. Thus the very question posed by the conference, concerning the emergence of the "modern world picture", becomes in itself a symptom for how the world appears in modernity, namely as precisely a picture or image, a projection of representational vision. In this new constellation, humans lose contact with that which cannot be calculated; it withdraws into the shadows, and the world appears as a scene of loss of meaning and transcendence.

A critical awareness of this condition may easily lead to romantic escapism, an urge to reach back into the past or into tradition. But Heidegger's remedy to this situation is not to escape it, but rather to confront it as such, to develop an experience of technological modernity as "destiny", that is, as a "sending" (*Schicksal, Schickung*) of being within which we stand. This destiny as sending is not to be knelt down before, but rather confronted philosophically through a new mode of questioning, and also of listening, through a "poetic questioning" and a "thoughtful meditation" (*Besinnung*). The task of such a reflection is also to recall human beings to their own finitude, and to the finitude of the way the world presents itself in this totalizing view. If we read Heideggger's critique of Cartesianism, modernity and technology simply as an attempt to distance himself from this whole constellation, his thinking easily takes on the appearance of a nostalgic attempt to escape the present, a somewhat arcane and pathetic critique that can easily be countered by recalling the many remarkable benefits for humankind that have come from this modernity, in terms of both political liberties and improved material living conditions. But what he is pointing towards is rather a non-evaluative or extra-moral perspective in which we can begin to sense how both the enormous benefits and the huge calamities of modernity emerge as two sides of the same underlying movement, that is to say, as the tragedy of modernity.

At the end of the published version of "The Age of the World Picture", Heidegger added a series of a notes, one of which explains "representation" (*Vorstellung*) as "a placing [*stellen*] something out from oneself, and thereby securing it [*sicherstellen*]" (*OBP* 82 = *GA* 5: 108, trans. mod.). Being is thus no longer that which is present, but instead obtains the meaning of that which is placed before a subject as an object or *Gegenstand*. With this analysis, the foundation for his later thinking on technology in terms of the *Ge-stell* is essentially in place, even though the actual concept or philosopheme is still not forged as such. This takes place only in a text that he composes ten years later, in 1949, which bears the title "Das Ge-stell", a text to which we now turn.

Ge-stell as a move beyond mastery and will

After the war, during the years when Heidegger was not permitted to teach at the university, he was invited to give lectures in various places. In a cultural club in Bremen he gave four such talks in 1949 under the general title "Insight Into That Which Is", the second of which was called "Das Ge-stell" (in GA 79). This is the first version of the text that was later to become "The Question Concerning Technology". Here he builds on the analysis in "The Age of the World Picture", developing the semantics of *stellen* in a depiction of nature and humans as placed before an exploiting demand. Here we can see how he finally gathers the various modes of *Stellen* (placing, setting), of which he has spoken in previous texts – *Vorstellen* (representing), *Herstellen* (producing), *Bestellen* (ordering), *Ausstellen* (exposing), and *Verstellen* (displacing, distorting) – now forging them in the new concept of *Ge-stell*. The prefix has a peculiar resonance here. The German "Ge-" can imply a "gathering together", such as in a *Gebirge*, a mountain range. In *Ge-stell* the various modes of *stellen* are gathered to depict the way the world manifests itself in an age of technological willing. *Ge-stell* designates the essence of technology (*Technik*), an essence that comes to the fore with the rise of the modern natural sciences at the end of the sixteenth century. But it is important for his analysis that, unlike the standard view, technology is seen not as the outcome of experimental science, but the other way round: experimentally based natural science becomes possible only with the emergence of this essence of technology as *Ge-stell*.

In *Ge-stell* nature comes forth primarily as a source of materials and energy to be integrated into a larger system of utility. In a famous passage Heidegger describes a modern hydroelectric power plant on the river Rhine as having the effect of building the river into the power plant. In this situation the role of humans also obtains a new meaning; they are the ones who have to enact this ordering or commanding, this *Bestellen*, but at the same time are the ones exposed to it, as themselves something commanded and ordered about. It is not incidental that it is in this text that Heidegger makes the only explicit philosophical remark that he ever made concerning the Nazi death camps, whose industrialized disposal of human lives and bodies is likened to the way in which nature is also exploited in modern technological society (GA 79: 27). In the later, published version of the technology essay he took out this remark, for what reason we do not know, but its initial presence in this context indicates that it was through this understanding of *technology* and of the *Ge-stell* that Heidegger, in his own thinking, tried to come to terms philosophically with these unspeakable atrocities executed by a well-organized modern industrial society.

With the forging of the concept of *Ge-stell* as a way to summarize and bring to awareness a whole constellation of phenomena circled around how beings present themselves to humans, Heidegger has thus reached a means with which he can claim to have thought the essence of modernity. It is a concept and a thought that can permit us to see how nature comes forth as a resource to exploit, but also how human beings are conceived as entities that can themselves be reduced to resources. In this instrumentalist paradigm everything is potentially a resource to be used for the benefit of a calculative will. As such, the concept of *Ge-stell* is not only a way to describe a tendency in how things present themselves, but – and perhaps more importantly – a way to describe how human beings for their part are called on to present things to themselves in such a manner. For the *Ge-stell* is not something external to human beings and their free will, but a way in which this will orients itself. It is, as the definition from "The Question Concerning Technology" that was quoted at the outset of this chapter reads, a "challenging claim", a claim that challenges human being to order that which presents itself as standing-reserve (*Bestand*).

The insistence on understanding and experiencing the *Ge-stell* as a claim or demand is crucial. For it is in and through this way of phrasing the analysis that Heidegger also distances himself from, for example, the analyses of Jünger, which are still primarily oriented towards grasping, in a totalizing vision, the essence of modernity: in other words towards bringing it under the mastery of a theoretical gaze. What Heidegger has been working towards, at least from the mid 1930s, and in particular in *Contributions to Philosophy* (*CP* = *GA* 65), but in some ways from the beginning of his path, is a mode of thinking that can somehow incorporate the *how* of thinking into its what: to bring thinking to a thoughtful awareness of what it accomplishes in its very way of conceptualizing being. To think the *Ge-stell* in the way indicated by Heidegger is therefore also to bring to awareness the technological in thinking itself, the inner urge towards mastery, so as ultimately to release us from this urge, and in this way also perhaps to be more free. This strategy is very much present in the opening lines of "The Question Concerning Technology", which begins by saying that the task for thinking in regard to technology is "to build a way toward technology", a way through language that will lead to a new relation to that which is thought, a relation that Heidegger explicitly characterizes as "free". To think technology through the optics of the *Ge-stell* is thus to make us more free *for* and thus in the end also *from* technology.

The way to this realization proceeds by means of addressing the question of the essence of technology in a new way. Rejecting the common approach to this question, Heidegger holds that the essence of something is not simply the answer to *what* it is. In the case of technology the standard answer would be that technology is a means to an end, an instrument for action. But against this standard response Heidegger suggests that we look instead to *how* technology brings about truth. We then ask not simply for the truth about technology, but for the truth of and by technology. And it is at this stage in the analysis that he recalls again the passage from the *Nicomachean Ethics* mentioned at the outset, using it to convey the point that *technē* has to do with bringing about the true, in the sense of disclosing something, letting it come into its appearance. And the way that technology discloses nature is as "exploitation" or "commanding" (*Herausfordern*). It discloses nature as that which can and should be commanded. But not only that; it also discloses the human being to himself as one who is "commanded to command nature", *herausgefordert die Natur herauszufördern* (*BW* 324 = *VA* 21). This is a concentrated formulation of the thought discussed earlier, that *Ge-stell*, as the essence of technology, manifests itself as a demand inherent in the human being himself, as an aspect and a consequence of his freedom. It is not a destiny in the sense of being something ordained by some superior power, by nature or by being itself, but a way in which humans encounter nature, and themselves.

As such a destiny it is not definitive, but something towards which we can establish a freer relation, by listening to its claim (*Anspruch*), permitting it to resonate precisely as such, as a claim, indeed as a "freeing claim" (*BW* 331 = *VA* 29). Precisely for this reason the *Ge-stell* marks in the end a very ambiguous situation. From a superficial perspective the concept and diagnosis may appear as only a dystopian resentment *vis-à-vis* modernity. But Heidegger's point is that it also contains new possibilities. In the obvious danger inherent in contemporary technologically defined modernity, there also lies a saving potential. In his later writings Heidegger would often quote the lines from Hölderlin's "Patmos", "But where danger is, grows the saving power also". In the essay on technology this holds a very special place, for it also summarizes the way in which he wants *Ge-stell* to be understood, namely as an "ambiguous" situation of (manifest) danger and (potential) saving at once. The latter possibility rests, however, on the condition that human being can attain to a thinking, reflective relation to that which is, as it is disclosed in the *Ge-stell*. And at the very end of the essay he explicitly takes up this ambiguity precisely in terms of the aforementioned double inheritance of the Greek *technē*. Once, he says, *technē* also meant the "bringing forth of the true into the beautiful" (*BW* 339 = *VA* 38). To what is hopeful in technology belongs this possibility of bringing it back to a sense of poietic disclosure, first carried forward in the arts, which were also known by the Greeks as *technē*.

References

Jünger, E. [1932] 1981. *Der Arbeiter*. Stuttgart: Ernst Klett.
Sallis, J. (ed.) 1978. *Radical Phenomenology: Essays in Honor of Martin Heidegger*. Atlantic Highlands, NJ: Humanities Press.

Further reading

Primary sources

See Heidegger's *Country Path Conversations*; *Gesamtausgabe*, vol. 79: *Bremer und Freiburger Vorträge*; "The Origin of the Work of Art", in *Basic Writings*, 143–212; and *The Question Concerning Technology*.

Secondary sources

See Davis (2007); Fandozi (1982); Rojcewicz (2006); and Zimmerman (1990). See also N. A. Corona & B. Irrgang, *Technik als Geschick? Geschichtsphilosophie der Technik bei Martin Heidegger: Eine Handlungstheoretische Entgegung* (Dettelbach: Röll, 1999); D. Idhe, *Technics and Praxis* (Dordrecht: Reidel, 1978); and H. Ruin, "Contributions to Philosophy", in *A Companion to Heidegger*, B. Dreyfus & M. Wrathall (eds), 358–74 (Oxford: Blackwell, 2007); and S.-O. Wallenstein, *Essays, Lectures* (Stockholm: Axl Books, 2006).

FOURTEEN

Language and poetry
John T. Lysaker

An orientation

The heart of Heidegger's thoughts on language are gathered in *On the Way to Language*, volume twelve of his *Collected Edition* (GA 12). English translations are distributed among three volumes. Peter D. Hertz translated most of *On the Way to Language* (as OWL) excepting the essay "Language", which appeared in *Poetry, Language, Thought*, translated by Albert Hofstadter (*PLT*). ("The Way to Language" was re-translated by David Krell for the revised edition of *Basic Writings* [*BW*].) Language also arises as a key theme in other published works such as §34 of *Being and Time* (*BT*), "The Origin of the Work of Art" and "Letter on Humanism" (both in *BW*), as well as in many lecture courses and unpublished manuscripts.

Because I regard Heidegger as an unstinting phenomenologist who aims to disclose various phenomena as they show themselves from themselves (as opposed to how they conform to existing knowledge paradigms), I shall not recount these various explorations by way of a chronological textual analysis. Such a reading, while informative, sets aside Heidegger's philosophical project in favour of a historical one that focuses on an evolving "view". This not only diverts attention from the phenomenon of "language", but it also fails to heed Heidegger's own insistence: "The report of a new view about language matters little. Everything depends upon learning to dwell in the speaking of language" (*PLT* 210 = GA 12: 30). Engaging Heidegger on language thus cannot be a matter of tracking views, but of thinking how, in our very approach to him, we might "dwell in the speaking of language",

195

or at least take steps towards accomplishing this task. Said otherwise, in engaging his texts, one should not presume one is already sufficiently attentive to the speaking of language.

In place of presumptions, Heidegger "would like to bring us to the possibility of having an experience with language. To experience something, whether a thing, a human, or a god, means that something befalls us, strikes us, comes over us, overwhelms and transforms us" (OWL 57 = GA 12: 149). I find this passage from "The Essence of Language" instructive.[1] It suggests that we are out of step with regard to language, and to the degree that we need to establish conditions for the possibility of an experience of what seems intimately at our disposal. It is as if, even as words and sentences are written and read, we are not fully attending to what is transpiring, to how we are addressed by and respond to language. And this strikes me as apt. In all but the least likely moments, I address language on the way to something else: sending an e-mail, refining models of self-experience in schizophrenia, letting my wife, Hilary, know that I love her, or trying to provoke students. It is not that my reflective stance towards language is afflicted with infelicities, although it may be. Rather, the charge is that we take language for granted and thus fail to experience its full dimensionality.

Of course, if we take language for granted, being out of step is not a matter of lacking access to some object whose nature lies on the far side of cognition. Rather, language is very much with us. In fact, it seems, "We are always speaking in one way or another" (PLT 187 = GA 12: 9). I note this because exploring the phenomenon of language does not require us to transcend our human situatedness. Rather, the task involves returning to our selves in a more originary manner. In Heidegger's words: "But we do not want to arrive somewhere else. We only would like, for once, just to get to where we ourselves already reside" (PLT 188 = GA 12: 10).

But where do we already reside with regard to language? This is the phenomenon Heidegger seeks to articulate. Recall the remark "We are always speaking in one way or another". The point is not that people chatter on every second of every day. Rather, the speaking Heidegger has in mind need not be verbal. In may involve reflective thinking, reading, writing, and so on. Heidegger's concern is thus: how is it that, when we pause to think, speak or write, language arises, and without our having to summon it? But let us be more concrete. Right now, explain aloud why you are reading this chapter. Did you choose your sentence word by word, or did your thoughts, throat, lungs and mouth find themselves already bound to words and phrases? And as you read this, do you have to decide whether the ink on the page is language, or is it the case that even when a sentence confuses, it confuses as a "sentence"? I hope you now grasp Heidegger's concern. What is our relation to language such that we find ourselves already bound to it by the time we explicitly render a thought, word or sentence?

Although it is not obvious at first, the question of how language claims us is also a question of the essence of language. As I noted before, "essence" concerns the character with which a phenomenon occurs. Heidegger's observation is that language comes to pass by pre-reflectively informing thought and speech. He thus does not render language into an object in order to ascertain its essential features. Rather, he seeks its essence in its occurrence, and he locates that occurrence in how language claims human thought and speech.

Permit me a third thought regarding the passage from "The Essence of Language". In seeking the possibility of an experience with language, Heidegger proceeds with caution. On the one hand, this simply observes the nature of experience. Wanting to have one does not guarantee that one will. I may want to hear fugue structures in Bach, but until I have the ears (and possibly the fingers) for them, I will not. Moreover, fugues need to be available, even if I am prepared to hear them. With regard to an experience with language, the philosophical task is thus one of establishing conditions for the possibility of having an experience with language, not simply willing it to happen. On the other hand, at this point, infelicitous reflective stances may prove a problem. They may establish conditions that render an experience with language unlikely, perhaps even impossible. In preparing us for an "experience" with language, Heidegger thus relies on the term *Erfahrung*, a word he develops in terms of a kind of "suffering" (*Erleiden*) wherein we "comply with/submit to" language (*ihm sich fügen*). In other words, rather than translating things into familiar categories, "experience", in this sense, overtakes us.

But how does one proceed? Heidegger's approaches are multiple. On the one hand, he attempts to displace precisely those intuitions about the nature of language that undermine our ability to have an experience with language. Secondly, through unusual locutions such as "language speaks" (*die Sprache spricht*), he works to attune us to how language addresses us (*PLT* 188 = *GA* 12: 10). And he often engages particular poems and parts of poems on the supposition that the language of the poem addresses us in a particularly rich, even exemplary, manner, at least with regard to how language speaks. In what follows, we shall initially consider some displacements, then one of Heidegger's more unusual locutions, and, finally, we shall explore poetry's place in our effort to learn to dwell in the speaking of language.

Before considering displacements, one more preliminary is in order. According to Heidegger, learning to dwell in the speaking of language is not some avocational pursuit for those curious about esoterica. Rather, it concerns our very nature and the nature of being itself. "Letter on Humanism" opens:

> Thinking accomplishes the relation of being to the essence of human beings. It does not make or cause the relation. Thinking brings this relation to being solely as that which is handed over to thought from being. Such offering consists in the fact that in thinking, being comes to language. Language is the house of being. In language's housing, human beings dwell. Thinkers and poetizers are the guardians of this housing. Their guardianship accomplishes the manifestation of being insofar as they, in their saying, bring this manifestation to and preserve it in language.
>
> (*PM* 239 = GA 9: 313)

This passage raises the stakes marked out by the request that we learn to dwell in the speaking of language. If language is the house of being, then, on Heidegger's terms, learning to dwell in the speaking of language is tantamount to: (i) preparing for or cultivating a kind of thinking and/or poetizing, which (ii) brings being to language and preserves (i.e. houses) it there, (iii) thereby accomplishing the manifestation of being itself, which in turn (iv) engages the essence of human beings. Of course, none of this stands a ghost of a chance if we are unable to find conditions for the possibility of an experience with language. But should that possibility find us, should it steal upon us, then we might be able to come to terms with our relation to being itself, which no doubt includes in some sense our relation with ourselves, one another, with whatever *is* there to be experienced.

Missteps

One key to Heidegger's many responses to the phenomenon of language lies with efforts to displace views that undermine genuine experiences of language. For example, he insists that we should not compile information about language, say through comparisons of various grammars (*OWL* 58 = GA 12: 150). Why not? Heidegger's goal is to think about how we belong to language, and prior to our deciding to speak or read or even reflectively consider something. And no amount of information about various languages will expose the character of that relationship. In fact, such enquiries, in using language to explore language, unconsciously inhabit that relation rather than explore it. Nor will any presentation of features that all languages share, what Heidegger terms a "metalanguage" (in the sense of a universal language), give us what we seek. In focusing on the ways in which languages function and the elements they contain, it too will only enact (rather than explore) how language claims us, thereby leaving the essence of language unthought. That is, in establishing language as an object to be empirically addressed, one looks past the address of language that funds one's own enquiry. Here then is the more general point. What Heidegger seeks is not some fact about language, but our relation to language such that we can propose "facts".

Another displacement expands on a point already ventured. Heidegger is insistent that the essence of language should not be thought in terms of human communication. More specifically, the claim is that language does not originally occur as a medium whereby human beings express something through representations, a phenomenon evident in the following. "I'm furious with you for leaving my MP3 player at mother's". This remark expresses the speaker's anger with a sibling, and with reference to something (an MP3 player) and some action (leaving the MP3 player), which occurs somewhere (their mother's house). The remark is thus an intersubjective action, which expresses a subjective state of affairs (anger), which in turn is explicitly related to worldly affairs (an object, an action, a place).

Now, Heidegger's point, which he offers in "Language" (*PLT* 190 = GA 12: 12), is not that we should not think about language in this manner. Rather, his claim is that such an account misses our basic relation with language. Each of its key notions (expressing thoughts and feelings, representing things and events, and addressing others) evidence a relation with language wherein a feeling, an action and even another appear as already tied to language, namely as "anger", an "MP3 player", and as a "you" that can be addressed. But isn't that relation precisely what we wish to understand? How is it that such phenomena are given to us already bound to language, and without our having explicitly chosen words, grammar, kinds of speech acts or sentences for the purpose of communication? In other words, communication evidences rather than explains our basic relation with language. And that leads me to the more general point of this displacement. Our basic relation to language is not the result of some human decision to represent, express and/or address. Rather, most human decisions presume this relation, and thus Heidegger would prefer to say, it is less that we speak language than that "Language speaks".

A language of essence

Heidegger terms the phrase "language speaks" a *Leitsatz*, a "leading sentence". Its initial work is negative. It leads us to consider that human beings are not the initial speakers, but language. But what could this mean? Let us return to our own speaking. As we have discussed, when we address another or think, we find ourselves already claimed by language, which is to say, we find ourselves thinking with and uttering words, phrases and sentences. As Heidegger writes in "The Way to Language", "Every spoken word is already a response – a reply, a saying that goes to encounter, and listens" (*BW* 218 = *GA* 12: 249). To paraphrase Nietzsche's claim about thinking (*Beyond Good and Evil* §17): it is not that I elect words and phrases but, rather, they come to me. In this sense, human language use is a response to the address of language, which entails the appearing of words and phrases in thought and speech. Not that we ever explicitly observe or even acknowledge this address. Rather, the event of this address and our response has already transpired by the time reflective acts come to pass.[2]

We should now have some sense of why Heidegger says that language speaks. But his claim needs to be heard in a particular manner. If the speaking of language is never present to us as an event, let alone an object to observe, then language comes to pass in a way that cannot stand as a proper subject for conceptual representation. Instead, we have already been addressed by and responded to language by the time we are able to formulate something like a concept of language. The language in which we think the essence of language will thus be unusual. Yes, it might employ concepts, as "language speaks" does, but the phrase itself should not be taken to name some "essence of language". Instead, we need to read it along the lines of a reflective exercise, even a kind of yoga in the sense of a discipline to be practised. Along these lines, "language speaks" works by turning our attention back to what our everyday speaking presumes but overlooks, namely, the fact that in our speaking, language has already addressed us and we have responded.

Here is how Heidegger puts the thought in "The Way to Language".

Speech, taken on its own, is hearing. It is listening to the language we speak. Hence speaking is not *simultaneously* hearing, but is such in advance. Such listening to language precedes all other instances of hearing, albeit in an altogether inconspicuous way. We not only *speak* language, we speak *from out of* it. We are capable of doing so only because in each case we have already listened to language. (*BW* 411 = *GA* 12: 243)

Language speaks in that it addresses us with words and phrases that pre-reflectively claim our thinking and speaking. And so our speaking and thinking is, at the outset, a listening response to the claim of these words and phrases, a claim that indicates or exposes the essence of language.

In trying to make sense of the leading sentence, we have found ourselves thinking about the very language that orients our efforts. In other words, en route to the essence of language, we have been fussing with a language of essence, to employ Heidegger's turns of phrase from "The Essence of Language". And as we have seen, a language of essence can only accomplish its task if it forgoes naming essence, even speaking about it, but works instead to indicate or point out what has always already transpired in its own saying. And in providing us with such a tensely coiled, reflexive indication, it opens us to the manner in which we dwell in language. That is, a proper language of essence accomplishes what Heidegger seeks. "But we do not want to arrive somewhere else. We only would like, for once, just to get to where we ourselves already reside" (*PLT* 188 = *GA* 12: 10).

Now, you might wonder why finding our way into a language of essence requires such a torturous degree of reflexivity. On Heidegger's reading, the riddle lies with the essence of language. In its speaking, language does not simply address us and then supply us with a word, phrase or sentence that allows us to express ourselves to others with regard to things, actions and events. Rather, these events are of a piece. In Heidegger's words, "The essential unfolding of language is saying as pointing" (*BW* 410 = *GA* 12: 242). In short, language addresses us as it provides us with words and phrases in and for our dealings with others, the world and ourselves. The "pointing" of language thus directs us away from language's own initial address, that is, away from a fundamental facet of its essence, and towards what that essence enables, namely, an articulate life. We thus need a language of essence in order to come back to ourselves at the very site where language both situates our factical, particular selves but also turns us away from an essential facet of our selves, namely, our belonging to language.

The house of being

Thus far we have explored how humans belong to language. By indicating aspects of our world (self, other, thing, place, etc.), language claims us prior to any willing or doing on our part. But this means that by learning to dwell in the speaking of language, we are also learning to dwell in the site/event where beings are disclosed or unconcealed, where they appear as something to be desired, known, resisted, worked on, and so on, a site/event that Heidegger recurringly indicates with the word *Sein*, "being". But let us be more precise.

In "Language", Heidegger claims that (a) beings always appear to us within a world, within a context of meanings that wash over things, and (b) a world, while more than the sum of its parts, nevertheless only exists in and through the interrelation of things. In Heidegger's words, "The luster of the world grants to things their essence. Things bear the world. World grants things" (*PLT* 202 = *GA* 12: 21). But that is not all, for in order for the relation of world and thing to come to pass, each must differ from the other, and in a way that nevertheless permits relation. Heidegger names this third the "dif-ference". Now, the *dif-ference* is not itself another thing, nor could it be without yet another world contextualizing it, within which it would come to pass, which in turn would require yet another *dif-ference*, and so on. Rather, the *dif-ference* names the opening of a world wherein beings come to pass (or are gathered) in relation to one another (say a host of eco-social relations in a rainforest or the bustle of bodies along a crowded city street), thus arranging the world or giving it lustre. (Recall or imagine the feel of walking beneath a dense canopy of Douglas Firs or of charging up Manhattan's Fifth Avenue at noon.)

In recalling us to the site/event where thing and world are disclosed or appear, both in their belonging together and their *dif-ference*, language, presuming we have learned to dwell in its speaking, exposes the basic scene of human being-in-the-world. There we find ourselves always ex-sisting, that is, praxically oriented towards beings bound to rich contexts, and in a manner whereby they appear as such, which is to say, they come to pass as the *appearance* of a particular kind of being in a particular kind of way in a world lit with a particular lustre. And in being appearances, these beings bear with them not only the world, but the *dif-ference* that allows things to belong to a world while coming to pass in their own manner (that is, according to an essence of their own).

We are ready to take up Heidegger's claim that language is the "house of being" by way of another passage from "Letter on Humanism": "But the human being is not only a living creature who possesses language along with other capacities. Rather, language is the house of being in which the human being ex-sists by dwelling, in that he belongs to the truth of being, guarding it" (*PM* 254 = *GA* 9: 333). In terms we assumed from "Language", the truth of being is marked by *dif-ference* as it enables (a) beings to appear within a world and (b) worlds to shine with the lustre of interrelating beings. This multi-dimensional site/event is the truth wherein human beings dwell, and this is the truth that language houses in the speaking that pre-reflectively claims us and to which our own words and sentences are responses.

It is crucial that we do not read Heidegger's claim within the confines of social constructivism, which, in this context, would propose that the identity of beings is a result of how they are represented in language. In "Language", Heidegger states that language's "naming does not hand out titles, it does not apply terms, but it calls into the word" (*PLT* 196 = *GA* 12: 18). I take this to mean that in claiming human being, the speaking of language does not construct a thing like some quasi-Kantian category. Rather, in calling a being "to word", language calls it into the scene of worldly appearing that language opens, arranges and thereby indicates. As to its traits (let us say it is smooth, black and more or less round on its top and bottom), or its capabilities (it can glide along ice), or its many possible uses (for example, in a hockey game), none of these are "constructed" by language. Instead, language specifies and preserves the many ways in which things appear, thus allowing them to become explicit or for-us in a conspicuous fashion. This is why Heidegger writes in a relevant page from "The Origin of the Work of Art", "language alone brings beings as beings into the open for the first time" (*BW* 198 = *GA* 5: 61). But language does not somehow manufacture beings, as if words or even entire languages were ideal forms superimposed on the raw materiality of nature.

Let us return to the thought that language is the house of being. In allowing beings to become conspicuous in their appearing, language does not erase the appearance–reality distinction. Instead, language employs it. In giving us the name "hockey puck", language gathers together our experiences of the hockey puck (many of which, e.g. when it strikes my thigh, are more than mere functions of the system of signifiers associated with hockey). And because those encounters are gathered in this manner, each is rendered as an appearance of what is irreducible to any one of them, let us call it the "hockey puck" that can address us in manifold ways, including ways that have little to do with hockey. Language is thus the house of being because, in claiming us, it houses and makes manifest the fact that beings appear to us, engage us. Or, to put the matter more precisely, language is the house of being because, if we attend to its originary speaking, it preserves for us the truth of being, that is, the unconcealment of beings, as the fundamental scene of our existence (see Chapter 8 for an extended engagement with the "truth of being").

The poet as the grounder of being

In "Language", Heidegger claims: "What is purely spoken is the poem" (*PLT* 192 = *GA* 12: 14). "The Origin of the Work of Art" claims that the language of the poem preserves the original essence of language, which is also a kind of poetry, although in a broader sense, namely that of *poesis*, thought in terms of a making (or letting-be) unconcealed (*BW* 199 = *GA* 5: 62). In the text entitled "... Poetically Dwells the Human ..." we find: "But the responding in which human being authentically listens to the appeal of language is that saying that speaks in the element of poetizing" (*PLT* 214 = *VA* 184). Finally, in "Hölderlin and the Essence of Poetry", Heidegger refers to poetry as an *Ursprache*, an "originary language" (*EHP* 60 = *GA* 4: 43). He does so because he believes that poetry, Hölderlin's in particular, provides us with language felicitously attuned to the originary speaking of language, that is, the truth of being and our relation to its disclosures (and concealments). In fact, he claims:

> Poetry is nothing other than the elementary coming-to-word, that is, the becoming uncovered of existence as being-in-the-world. With what is thereby articulated, the world first becomes conspicuous for those who earlier were blind.
> (*BPP* 171–2 = *GA* 24: 244)

> Poetry is founding, the effectual grounding of what endures. The poet is the grounder of being. What we call the real in the everyday is, in the end, unreal. (*GA* 39: 33)

A great deal could be said about (a) how the language of the poem comes to address us in this manner, (b) how one should read poems for founding moments and (c) what Heidegger's poetics have to do with formal analysis, metaphor theory and so on. Here, however, I shall limit myself to a discussion of poetic founding after first providing a brief list of Heidegger's main engagements with poetry.

Heidegger's engagement with poetry spans his career. In many cases, his work explicitly engages a particular poet. In other cases a poet, usually Friedrich Hölderlin (1770–1843) is engaged in order to think through a particular subject, as is the case of "Building Dwelling Thinking", "... Poetically Man Dwells ..." (both in *PLT*), "Language", and "The Essence of Language". Among explicit engagements, the cardinal texts are three lecture courses on Hölderlin (volumes 39, 52, and 53 of his *Gesamtausgabe*, with only volume 43, *Hölderlin's Hymn "The*

Ister", available in English in Will McNeil and Julia Davis's translation [*HHI*]), a collection of essays on Hölderlin (volume 4 of the collected works, translated by Keith Hoeller as *Elucidations of Hölderlin's
Poetry*), an essay on Rainer Maria Rilke (1875–1926) (published in
Holzwege and translated in *PLT* as "What Are Poets For?" and in *OBT*
as "Why Poets?"), another on Georg Trakl (1887–1914) (published and
translated as "Language in the Poem" in *OWL*) and several writings,
most brief, on the poet Johann Peter Hebel (1760–1826) (gathered in
volume 13 of the *Gesamtausgabe*, some of which have been translated
for journals). Heidegger also exchanged letters with the literary critic
Emil Staiger (1908–87) concerning Eduard Mörike's (1804–75) "On
a Lamp" (likewise collected in volume 13 and translated as a journal
article). Volume 13, *From the Experience of Thinking*, also collects short
pieces on poets such as René Char (1907–88) and Arthur Rimbaud
(1854–91), which Andrew Mitchell has translated.

   As noted, Heidegger finds remarkable import in the language of
the poem. Some poems, he holds, unfold an originary language, which
grounds being by figuring the event of unconcealment. They do so with
a language of essence, which dramatizes the event of essence or the
manner in which beings occur. Again, this is not an event of construction. "This never means that language, in any old meaning picked up
at will, immediately and definitively supplies us with the transparent
essence of the matter like some object ready to be used" (*PLT* 214 = *VA*
184). Rather, by way of figures that establish the lustre of the world,
an originary language founds and grounds by exposing us to the *dif-
ferential* dimension of world and thing.

   For example, whereas the lustre of the medieval world bathed everything in the light of a divine creation, such that every being shone as an
ens creatum, a "created thing", Hölderlin, as read by Heidegger, founds
a fourfold world, a dimension marked out by earth and sky as well as
mortals and divinities (the latter present as absent). Such a world is
bound to things, of course, and thus Heidegger refers to figures such as
jugs and bridges, underlining how the fourfold (*das Geviert*) is woven
through the site they inhabit, individually and collectively (see Chapter
15). In other words, as a language of essence the fourfold bathes every
occurrence. One thus never encounters just isolated jugs and bridges,
but rather always encounters them on the earth, beneath the sky, in
relation to one's mortal being and in a presently desacralized (which is
not to say desecrated) milieu.

   Now, poetic founding is a historical event and thus subject to historical decisions that do not flow from individual or aggregate human
choices. In fact, it could very well prove that our world belongs to a

poesis altogether un-poetic in the sense of the language of the poem. Here I have in mind global technology, what Heidegger names *Ge-stell*, the "en-framing" (see Chapter 13). I term it "un-poetic" because, as Heidegger argues in "The Question Concerning Technology", *Ge-stell*, which presents every being as energy to be organized according to productive apparatuses such as the global marketplace, erases its own *poiēsis*. Rather than present itself as a way of revealing, thereby exposing the *dif-ferential* dimension of world and thing and the event of unconcealment in which the whole unfolds, global technology presents itself as the simply real, thus suppressing the truth of being even as it presents beings in manifold ways.

I close with Heidegger's thoughts on technology for two reasons. First, they remind us of the historical struggle to which his work belongs. Many of his engagements with poetry contrast his own poetic thinking with the calculative thinking of global technology, distinguishing them precisely at the point at which each attends to the truth of being. Secondly, the failure of global technology to know itself in a genuine manner underscores precisely what allows the language of the poem (or of certain poems) to offer a language of essence; such language recoils on itself and figures its own essence. In the language of Heidegger's lecture on Hölderlin's poem "The Ister", poetic founding must "poetize the essence of the poet" if it is to enable us to dwell in the speaking of language, exposed to the dif-ferential play of world and thing in the truth of being, a manifold play that is as much a matter of our essence as anything else (*HHI* 165 = *GA* 53: 203).

Notes

1. Hertz translates *Wesen* as "nature", whereas I favour "essence", in the sense of how a being comes to pass or the character of its happening. I prefer "essence" because *Wesen* is historically associated with "essence" and Heidegger is clearly involved in a critical, transformative dialogue with that history.
2. Heidegger uses several different terms to mark the initial address of language, for example *Heißen*, which Hoftstadter translates as "bidding" (*PLT* 206 = *GA* 12: 26), and *Sagen*, which both Hertz and Krell translate as "Saying" (*OWL* 93 = *GA* 12: 188; and *BW* 410 = *GA* 12: 242).

Further reading

Primary sources

See Heidegger's *Hölderlin's Hymn "The Ister"*; *On the Way to Language*; "Language", in *Poetry, Language, Thought*; "The Way to Language" and "The Origin of the Work of Art", in *Basic Writings*; and "Why Poets?", in *Off the Beaten Track*.

Secondary sources

See Bernasconi (1985); F. Dastur, "Language and *Ereignis*", in Sallis (1993), 355–69; Fóti (1992); Lysaker (2002); J. Sallis, "Poetics", in Sallis (1990), 168–89; and Spanos (1979). See also *Research in Phenomenology* **19** (1989); and P. de Man, "Heidegger's Exegeses of Hölderlin", in his *Blindness and Insight*, 246–66 (Minneapolis, MN: University of Minnesota Press, 1983).

FIFTEEN

The fourfold

Andrew J. Mitchell

The fourfold (*das Geviert*) is a thinking of things. The fourfold names the "gathering" of earth, sky, mortals and divinities that comes to constitute the thing for Heidegger. In the late 1940s, operating under a teaching ban imposed by the French authorities in the wake of the Second World War, Heidegger ventures "the boldest statement of his thinking" in announcing the fourfold.[1] First named in the 1949 lecture cycle "Insight Into That Which Is", held at the private Club zu Bremen, the fourfold brings together the poetic sensibility of Heidegger's Hölderlin interpretations with the esoteric quasi-structural concerns of his notebooks from the 1930s, into a new figure of thought: the thing.[2] The simple things around us – indeed, the things themselves – become the focus of his attention and lead him to a phenomenologically more robust sense of world than heretofore found in his work. This world is a world of things, each a cluster of streaming relations reciprocally determinative of world. The fourfold is the key to understanding the utter relationality of worldly existence, for things are now understood to be the gathering points of the fourfold. Only with the fourfold does Heidegger attain the simplicity of vision adequate to a thinking of thing and world.[3]

Things appeared in Heidegger's thinking before the fourfold. Indeed, it would be shocking if they did not. But the notion of the thing that one finds in *Being and Time* is rather slim.[4] We know that there is a scientific approach to the thing that presents itself as objective and regards the thing as something present-at-hand (*vorhanden*). One of the important moments of *Being and Time* is the realization that this presumed objectivity of beings is itself founded on a more primordial lived relationship with these things (see Chapter 3). They are said to be "ready-to-hand" (*zuhanden*). The hammer disappears in use (where it is ready-to-hand), but on the interruption of the work is regarded from a detached perspective (as present-at-hand). Things appear in *Being and Time* in terms of either presence or utility. But by the time of the fourfold, Heidegger sees no real distinction between these alternatives, in so far as the assignment of a use value (of any value) requires a wholly present object available for the assessment.[5] In short, there are no things in *Being and Time*, and this is a problem. For all its transformation of our conceptions of subjectivity, *Being and Time* remains wedded to an inadequate conception of "objectivity" or thinghood. To change our understanding of the subject, it is not enough to rethink human existence as Dasein. Humans do not exist alone, as no one knew better than Heidegger, but exist in a world. To transform the human, to think being-in-the-world, is to transform the world and so long as that additional work of transforming the conception of the thing remains outstanding, the project of *Being and Time* must remain incomplete. To change the subject while retaining the object is to change nothing. The project of *Being and Time* demands more. The thinking of the fourfold provides this rethinking of thing and world and in this regard arguably could be read as the consummation of *Being and Time*'s effort to think the world.

The fourfold is not a passing phase in Heidegger's thinking: references to it are found in the lectures and essays of the 1940s, 1950s, 1960s and 1970s.[6] While the fourfold is often dismissed as an obscure, mystic or overly poetic exuberance of Heidegger's thinking, along its paths Heidegger achieves his most phenomenological thought. Commentators go astray when they try to understand the fourfold as a symbol for something else or a metaphor for a hidden ontological structure or as a reinscription of earlier views: those of Heidegger himself or those of the ancient Greeks, the Taoists, Native Americans, or even Hölderlin.[7] We do best when we take Heidegger at his word and, listening to his thought, let it be as strange, unconventional and thought-provoking as it can be in its evocation of thing and world.

The fourfold and the relational thing

The fourfold is said to be "gathered" (*versammelt*) into things and Heidegger's use of the term warrants comment.[8] As a gathering, the thing is desubstantialized; it is no longer construed as a present and self-enclosed entity, but instead as the intersection of earth, sky, mortals and divinities. Considering the thing a gathering thus precludes any conception of the thing as a steady presence. The fourfold gathers around the thing in a tenuous convergence. There is nothing everlasting or monumental about such things; they tarry ephemerally (Heidegger's term is *weilen*). The thing abides. The same gathering that unites the four in the thing is equally a disaggregation of that thing. What is gathered is not a homogeneity, but a spaced parting of assembled members. The fourfold disaggregates the thing by releasing it from the bounds of an encapsulated self-identity. Heidegger's name for this, not surprisingly, is "thinging" ("The thing things"; *PLT* 176 = GA 79: 17). The thing in its thinging is telescoped out beyond itself. The thing is not only gathered but disassembled at once, and through this disassembly it enters the world. The fourfold delimits and thereby situates the thing in a context of the world. Each element of the fourfold names a limit or interface of the thing whereby it passes into world.

The extrapolated thing extends beyond itself along the avenues of relation presented by the four members of the fourfold. Each of these grants the thing a place within a particular cluster of relations. The particular thing is a node for such relations. The four avenues of relation taken together contextualize the thing. The thing as limited and finite is inherently tied to a world beyond it, "The limit is not where something ceases, but rather, as the Greeks recognized, the limit is that from where something *begins its essencing*" (*PLT* 152 = GA 7: 156, trans. mod.). It begins out beyond itself as led along the pathways of the fourfold. The nature of finitude is to be related to a world extending beyond oneself; it is to be "infinite", properly understood:

> In-finite means that the ends and the sides, the regions of the relation, do not stand by themselves cut-off and one-sidedly; rather, relieved of one-sidedness and finitude, they belong *in*-finitely to one another in the relation which "thoroughly" hold them together from its middle [*Mitte*] ... The in-finity that is to be thought here is abysmally different from that which is merely without end. (*EHP* 188 = GA 4: 163, trans. mod.)

The fourfold names the reverberating extent and radiant fringe of the thing, the way it issues out beyond itself in an infinite belonging to world.

1. Mortals

The mortals are the humans. They are named the mortals, because they are able to die.　　　　(*PLT* 176 = GA 79: 17, trans. mod.)

Death is constitutive for the mortals. The analysis of death in *Being and Time* showed that while death is each time what is most our own, death is nonetheless nothing that any of us might possess (see Chapter 4). What is most our own is no possession and we are no longer its possessors. Mortals are defined by this dispossession, which is only to say that the mortal is defined by something outside it (by what is not its property, by an "improper"). But in so far as I die my death in being-toward-death – and this is as much of my death that I can ever die – then this "outside" is nothing beyond me that I would lack, nothing that eventually could be added to me in order to complete me, but instead a way of naming the inclination of my being into the world. Consequently, "mortals" names those beings defined by exposure and openness to world. But to be open is not to bear a portal within an otherwise closed-off field (existence has no need for such "windows" of openness); it is to be exposed through and through. There is nothing of the mortal that is not opened in this way, for there is no way to construe mortality while retaining a steady conception of pure presence. The "absence" of death that nevertheless determines mortal existence undermines any strict opposition between presences and absence. This death is not an absence at all, but a name for what existence can never possess, which thereby holds existence open, and, in so doing, defines mortal existence as an essential relationship with a world beyond it.

Mortality is nothing other than the ineluctable sharing of such relations, a being-in-community, something made explicit in "Building Dwelling Thinking": "Mortals dwell in so far as, by their own essence, namely, that they are capable of death as death, they accompany [others] in the use of this capability so that there may be a good death" (*PLT* 148 = *GA* 7: 152, trans. mod.). In so far as death demonstrates the role of withdrawal (or dispossession) as constitutive of finite relationality, Heidegger can identify death with a way of being that eludes the oppositional contrariety of presence/absence endemic to metaphysical thinking. Heidegger's term for this way of relationally existing via withdrawal and non-appearance is "essencing": "Death as the shrine of nothingness harbours in itself the essencing of being" (*PLT* 176 = *GA* 79: 18, trans. mod.). Essencing is the entrance to mortal community. Mortals are no longer world-building Dasein, but so thoroughly members of a community as to forego such privilege by participating in the fourfold's play of thing and world.

2. Earth

The earth is the building bearer, the nurturing fructifying, tending the waters and stones, what grows and the animals.

(*PLT* 176 = *GA* 79: 17, trans. mod.)

Heidegger's analysis of earth during the early to mid 1930s informs the conception of earth at the time of the fourfold. With the fourfold the emphasis falls on the earth as "bearer".[9] In "The Origin of the Work of Art", this "bearing" (*tragen*) is associated with ground, but the ground that the earth provides is no stable and present *terra firma*, but always a groundless ground.[10] The earth supports and bears precisely by withdrawing; this is the great insight of the artwork essay. The earth is no substantial ground, but a withdrawal of ground, a remaining away of ground, an "abyss" (*Ab-grund*) as per the first draft version of the lecture, where earth is named "a ground that, as essentially and always self-concealing, is an abyss" (*UKE* 11). The support that the earth provides is the freedom from a substantive basis. The grounding of the earth is a liberating.

But what can such a groundless ground support? Certainly nothing of any substance. The groundless can only support the most superficial: sheer phenomenality. Consequently, the earth is named here a "fructifying", a "nurturing" or "blooming" bringing forth.[11] The earth bears by coming to fruition in phenomenal appearing. If what appears were tied to a substance beneath it, it would never be free to reach out and appeal to us. The earth withdraws ground in order to release the superficial play of appearance, the name for which is shining. Heidegger's earlier analysis of such shining pointed to the way in which the earth receded from every attempt to quantify and capture it (see *OBT* 24–5 = *GA* 5: 33). The earth names uncontained, qualitative appearing. This is the material basis of our existence on the earth: sensible appearance.

As groundlessness that releases appearance, the earth likewise names the register of the natural world and of thriving life. Stones and animals, no longer considered worldless or world-poor, all come to participate in the earthly opening of world.

3. Sky

The sky is the journey of the sun, the course of the moon, the twinkle of the stars, the seasons of the year, light and twilight of the day, dark and light of the night, the favour and the inhospitability of the weather, the drawing of the clouds and the blue depths of the ether.   (*PLT* 176 = *GA* 79: 17, trans. mod.)

The sky is the space of the earth's emergence, the space wherein things appear and through which they shine. The withdrawal of the earth sets things loose to radiate through the air of the sky. But in so appearing, the thing does not enter into an empty vacuum. The sky is no abstract void.[12] Instead, it is a field of movement and alteration, of changing times and changing light. The sky is a medium, an "ether", variegated and diversified, filled with relations across fields of alternating light and time. For what appears phenomenally to reach us and appeal to us, the sky as medium of all appearing is required.[13]

What appears under the sky is affected by so appearing. The medium does not leave the thing untouched. In so far as the thing is exposed under the sky, it enters into a transpirative exchange with what lies beyond it (such is the nature of limit and finitude – it opens relations, wished for or not). What appears under the sky is involved in the world and marked by that involvement. Exposed to the sky, the thing is weathered by it.

While the sky names a region of familiarity, it also points to the unknown. Day follows night and the seasons change in an orderly fashion. But this order is always also an experiential context for the unexpected. The sky allows us to raise our gaze and look up beyond our immediate circumstances, open to the possibility of change. But the grace of the sky is not at our behest and we can only wait for fortunate skies and the passing of inhospitable weather. And yet, whatever change might come could never arrive were there not a medium through which it could destine itself to us.

The blueness of the sky names this mediating, crepuscular character of the sky. Blue is neither the bright light of day nor the black of night.[14] There is no absolute day or night (as already remarked by Heraclitus), only this time of transition. The sky names an inviting space of neither presence nor absence. Clouds are of the essence here. They keep the sky from pure appearing, preserving its distance. In so far as clouds allow something not to appear, they are like poets who remain true to an unsaid: "The clouds poetize" (*EHP* 34 =*GA* 4: 15, trans. mod.).[15]

4. Divinities

The divinities are the hinting messengers of godhood.
(*PLT* 176 = *GA* 79: 17, trans. mod.)

The divinities (*die Göttlichen*) name the fact that godhood (*die Gottheit*) has been sent to us. The divinities are not God or the gods (*der Gott* or *die Götter*), but the god-like: ones sharing in the divine and sharing it further as messengers. Particular gods play no role here and Heidegger makes explicit that the mortals "do not make them [the divinities] into their gods and do not pursue service to them as idols" (*PLT* 148 = *GA* 7: 152, trans. mod.). Rather than such personifications, at stake are the arriving hints of a message of godhood.[16]

The hint (*der Wink*) appears throughout Heidegger's work as a way for what is absent nonetheless to announces itself: "The hint is the message of a lighting veiling [*des lichtenden Verhüllens*]" (*OWL* 44 = *GA* 12: 133, trans. mod.). Such an existence is a showing of concealment, an interruption of the rigid opposition between presence and absence, and hints exhibit the same ambiguity. Hints go unremarked by most, but for those with a sense for them they intimate collusion and clandestine communication. Godhood is sent through messengers who hint in this manner.

But godhood is a strange message, to say the least, and requires that we consider Heidegger's thinking of the holy (*das Heilige*), which he terms the "essential sphere of godhood" (*PM* 258 = *GA* 9: 338, trans. mod.) and understands as the context in which what is "hale" or "whole" (*das Heile*) can appear. What is hale in this manner is a mode of presencing that resists the total availability of the standing-reserve and includes concealment at its essence. For us today, such a mode of being can only be that of the trace: "not only does the holy remain hidden as the trace of godhood, but even what is hale, the trace of the holy, appears to be extinguished" (*OBP* 221 = *GA* 5: 295, trans. mod.). But it only appears to be extinguished; it is "not yet" so. There remains a glimmer of concealment and this is what the divinities signal to us and why they can only hint at it.

To be a messenger is to be defined by something foreign, a message that one harbours without being its source. But the divinities' message is no transmittable content. Instead, they themselves are it. Their belonging in the fourfold, their gathering at the thing, opens the dimension of a beyond in which any decision regarding the otherworldly or divine can first take place.[17] The divinities announce the communicativity of existence, that it is not entirely available, but that there is still a space for decision. This openness is the presupposition for any question concerning God or the gods: "From out of their [the divinities'] holy reign, the god appears in his presence or withdraws himself in his veiling" (*PLT* 148 = *GA* 7: 151, trans. mod.).

Thing and world

There is no fourfold without the things that gather it into place. The elements of the fourfold each articulate a limit of the thing that opens it on to relations. The limits of the fourfold serve to weave the thing into place; they open the register of relations whereby the thing is contextualized within the world. If existence is ecstatic when outside itself, then things, too, exist ecstatically, as each member of the fourfold describes a way for the thing to be outside itself. In so doing, each one exposes the thing through an event of withdrawal that pours the thing out on to the space outside it. Each member forms a bridge by which the thing relates to the world.

This relational limit is what the fourfold share and what gathers them together. Heidegger refers to it as a "mirror-play" (*Spiegel-Spiel*; *PLT* 178 = *GA* 79: 19), which is the essence of each of the four and also what allows them to come together as the fourfold: "The appropriative mirroring sets each of the four free into its own, but it binds these free ones into the simplicity of their essential being toward one another [*Zueinander*]" (*PLT* 177 = *GA* 79: 18). As mirroring, each of the four casts itself out to the others (*Zueinander*) and is likewise cast back from them: "Each of the four mirrors again in its own way the essence of the remaining others" (*PLT* 177 = *GA* 79: 18, trans. mod.). The mirror-play of the four names the way in which the finite always transpires with the beyond (just as an outside is required for mirroring and for the mirror to be what it is). Mirroring thinks the expropriation at the heart of appropriation and belonging ("within their mutual appropriation, each is expropriated into what is its own"; *PLT* 177 = *GA* 79: 18, trans. mod.). It articulates the gathering of the four in the thing and opens the spacing of the world.

This world is a world of things that, according to the lecture "Language", are gestures of world: "The things gesture [*gebärden*] world. World grants [*gönnt*] the things" (*PLT* 199 = *GA* 12: 21, trans. mod.). We might understand gesture here in terms of what Heidegger says of it in the 1953–4 "A Dialogue on Language", where a gesture is "borne along by an appeal from far away calling still farther out, because carried forth out of silence" (*OWL* 16 = *GA* 12: 99, trans. mod.). Things motion beyond themselves in an unfurling of world. But world grants things a reception of their excesses. All this is to say that there is no "world" in the abstract, but always only a populated and articulated one of particular situations at particular times, and likewise no encapsulated things, but always these outpouring gestures of relationality, so many bridges thrown between world and thing. In this thinking of thing and world, what phenomenally appears (earth) does so in a medium (sky) that fosters community (mortals) and communication with a beyond (divinities).

In closing, as a thinking of contextuality, it is worth noting the various contexts in which the fourfold itself is first mentioned in Heidegger's essays and lectures. In the lecture cycle "Insight Into That Which Is" in Bremen, a shipping centre and port city, Heidegger stresses the challenge placed on the fourfold by the ordering and delivering drive of technology; in "Building Dwelling Thinking", a lecture held in the war-bombed city of Darmstadt, Heidegger raises the fourfold in a thinking of place and dwelling; at the Bühlerhöhe sanatorium, Heidegger delivers the lecture "Language" and treats the fourfold in conjunction with poetic language and pain; finally, in the letter to Ernst Jünger, "On the Question of Being", the fourfold names the non-present essencing of being itself (a being that is crossed through) as a response to nihilism. The fourfold addresses all of these major concerns of Heidegger's later work and stands as a crucial turning point along his path of thinking.

Notes

1. Egon Vietta as cited in Petzet (1993: 56).
2. In what follows I shall cite the original lecture version of "The Thing" as published in *GA 79*. The essay was later published in a slightly revised format in Heidegger's 1954 volume *Vorträge und Augsätze* (VA 157–79). Since my English translation of *GA 79* is currently still in preparation, reference will also be made to corresponding passages in the English translation of the published version of the essay in *Poetry, Language, Thought* (*PLT*).
3. In the same lecture cycle, Heidegger's reflections on technology reach their apogee (he first coins the term *"Ge-stell"*, "enframing", there). While it is beyond the scope of this chapter, the fourfold must be understood in conjunction with Heidegger's views on technology (see Chapter 13). The thing is always singularized as unique by its relational existence within a context and this singularity is precisely what is challenged by the circulation of standing-reserve under the aegis of enframing.
4. See also the 1935–6 lecture course *Die Frage nach dem Ding: Zu Kants Lehre von den transzendentalen Grundsätzen* (*GA* 41; translated into English as *WT*), which concludes with a conception of "the between" (*das Zwischen*) quite in keeping with the thinking of the world of the fourfold.
5. The failure to recognize the metaphysical identity of presence and utility is what gives the lie to so many contemporary "pragmatist" accounts of Heidegger, accounts that tend to adhere to *Being and Time* (and often even only Division One). Among Heidegger's numerous charges against pragmatism are the claims that it depends on a traditional understanding of the human as *homo animalis* (*PM* 268 = *GA* 9: 352) and obstructs any real thinking of technology (*MHNS* 61 = *GA* 16: 677).

6. To name only a few, after the 1949 Bremen lectures the fourfold is explicitly named in "Language" (1950, in *BW*), "Building Dwelling Thinking" (1951, in *BW*), "The Question of Being" (1955, in *PM*), "Hölderlin's Earth and Sky" (1959, in *EHP*), "*Sprache und Heimat*" (1960), the "Summary of a Seminar on the Lecture 'Time and Being'" (1962, in *TB*) and the Zähringen seminar (1973).

7. As Heidegger himself points out in "Hölderlin's Earth and Sky", to wit: "This number is never expressly thought or said by Hölderlin. Nevertheless, throughout all his sayings, the four are first caught sight of out of the intimacy of their togetherness [*Zueinander*]" (*EHP* 195 = *GA* 4: 170).

8. See "Building Dwelling Thinking" (*PLT* 151 = *GA* 7: 155), "The Thing" (*PLT* 172 = *GA* 79: 13). The term also plays an important role in the cotemporaneous "Logos" (*EGT* 70 = *GA* 7: 225).

9. See Heidegger's descriptions of the earth as "*die bauend Tragende*" (the building bearer; *PLT* 176 = *GA* 79: 17), "*die dienend Tragende*" (the serving bearer; *PLT* 147 = *GA* 7: 151).

10. There Heidegger speaks of "*der tragende Grund*" (the bearing ground; *OBT* 47 = *GA* 5: 63; on "earth" in the artwork essay, see Chapter 9). *Contributions to Philosophy* articulates a "remaining-away [*Weg-bleiben*] of the ground" (*CP* 265 = *GA* 65: 379, trans. mod.).

11. See Heidegger's descriptions of the earth as "*die nährende Fruchtende*" (the nourishing fructifying; *PLT* 176 = *GA* 79: 17, trans. mod.), "*die blühende Fruchtende*" (the blooming fructifying; *PLT* 147 = *GA* 7: 151, trans. mod.).

12. Technically speaking, this would give the lie to the overt argument of Luce Irigaray (1999), who charges Heidegger with precisely a forgetting of these material conditions of exposure. The world of the fourfold seems the perfect counter to the abstractions that she finds operative in Heidegger's work.

13. The earlier prefigurations of the fourfold found in Heidegger's work throughout the 1930s omit this crucial aspect of the sky and present instead a conjunction of Dasein, gods, earth and world, for instance. Such constructions miss both the weathering aspect of exposure provided by sky as well as the fact that the world of the fourfold is utter relationality born out of the expropriative play of the fourfold, as will be shown.

14. Heidegger's fullest treatment of blueness is to be found in "Language in the Poem: A Discussion of Georg Trakl", delivered in 1953 (included in *OWL*).

15. The "Letter on Humanism" concludes with the thought that "language is the language of being as clouds are the clouds of the sky" (*PM* 276 = *GA* 9: 364).

16. Thus we cannot follow Julian Young's assertion that the divinities would "clearly" be identified with the realm of culture as opposed to "nature" (2006: 375), especially given Heidegger's utter repugnance for anything "cultural" (the Greeks had no culture, we might recall). Nor should the divinities be understood as reinscriptions of the "hero" from *Being and Time*, as he also suggests (*ibid.*: 375). Both attempts miss the divinities' role in a "hermeneutics" of the hale (*das Heile*), as will be shown.

17. Regarding the god who accompanies a metaphysics of presence and absence, the god of philosophy, Heidegger writes, "man can neither pray nor sacrifice to this god … The god-less thinking which must abandon the god of philosophy … is thus perhaps closer to the divine god [*dem göttlichen Gott*]" (*IDS* 72 = *GA* 11: 77, trans. mod.). On the question of god(s) in Heidegger's thought, see Chapters 16 and 17.

References

Irigaray, Luce 1999. *The Forgetting of Air in Martin Heidegger*, M. B. Mader (trans.). Austin, TX: University of Texas Press.

Petzet, H. W. 1993. *Encounters & Dialogues with Martin Heidegger*, P. Emad & K. Maly (trans.). Chicago, IL: University of Chicago Press.

Young, J. 2006. "The Fourfold", in *The Cambridge Companion to Heidegger*, 2nd edn, C. Guignon (ed.), 373–92. Cambridge: Cambridge University Press.

Further reading

Primary sources

See Heidegger's *What Is a Thing?*; "On the Question of Being", in *Pathmarks*, 291–322; "Hölderlin's Earth and Heaven", in *Elucidations of Hölderlin's Poetry*, 175–207; "The Thing", "Language" and "Building Dwelling Thinking", in *Poetry, Language, Thought*, 163–84, 187–208 and 143–59, respectively; and *Insight Into That Which Is: The Bremen Lectures and The Principles of Thinking: Freiburg Lectures*, A. J. Mitchell (trans.) (Bloomington, IN: Indiana University Press, forthcoming).

Secondary sources

See Pöggeler (1987: 200–216); Richardson (2003: 566–94); J. F. Mattéi, "The Heideggerian Chiasmus", in Janicaud & Mattéi (1995), 39–150; and J. Young, "The Fourfold", in Guignon (2006), 373–392. See also F.-W. von Herrmann, "Die vier Weltgegenden als das Geviert", in *Die zarte, aber helle Differenz: Heidegger und Stefan George*, 259–82 (Frankfurt: Vittorio Klostermann, 1999).

SIXTEEN

Ontotheology and the question of god(s)

Ben Vedder

Heidegger's pious origins and his break with Catholic theology

If one wants to understand Heidegger's criticism of "ontotheology" and his thinking about God and the gods, it is important to begin by going back to the young Heidegger and the Christian environment from which he came. An ongoing relationship with theology, faith, the Church and Christianity runs like a thread through Heidegger's life (see Chapter 17). Heidegger was born, so to speak, in the Church. His father was a sexton, living in a house situated next to the church. When he was a young child and schoolboy, the church was always the backdrop for his play. As a young student, Heidegger's intellectual pursuits were inspired by his interest in theology. The relationship that Heidegger maintained with faith, theology and the Church throughout the whole of his work can surely be traced back to this early influence. Heidegger later provided a sketch of this world of his youth in the essay "*Vom Geheimnis des Glockenturms*" (GA 13: 113–16). Throughout his life, he states, the peal of the clock tower of St Martin's Church in Messkirch resounded, a ringing that bears witness to the divine rhythm in which holy days interweave with the course of the hours of the day and year. It is the eternal rhythm that orders daily life.

Despite having giving up his studies in theology in 1911, Heidegger continued to attend the lecture course of one of his professors (Carl Braig) on dogmatic theology (*TB* 74 = *ZSD* 81). As a high school student, Heidegger had already read Braig's book, *Vom Sein: Abriß der Ontologie*. In this book, Braig quotes a passage from St Bonaventure, which states that just as the eye does not see light itself when it is

219

directed towards a manifold of colour, the mind's eye does not see being itself when directed to entities singly or as a whole. And yet it is only by means of being that we can encounter entities in the first place. The mind's eye receives, as it were, an objectless impression, much in the way that one who only sees light sees nothing *per se*. What later emerges in Heidegger's work as the "ontological difference" has its roots in this connection between transcendental philosophy and ontology.

Yet Heidegger's thoughts on religion as such increasingly led away from systematic Catholic theology. In a letter to Engelbert Krebs (a former professor and confidant) in early 1919, he addresses his own development over the previous two years, beginning with his study of Schleiermacher's second address "On the Essence of Religion" (see *PRL* 241–4). It is precisely here that we can discern a significant tie between his thoughts on historicity and religion. Indeed, in his notes on Schleiermacher's essay Heidegger writes: "*History* in its most authentic sense is the highest object of religion, religion begins and ends in it" (*PRL* 244). In his letter to Krebs, Heidegger confesses that epistemological insights concerning historical knowledge made "the system of Catholicism" untenable for him (Ott 1988: 106). This letter bears witness to a decisive religious and philosophical turning point for Heidegger, who was then twenty-nine. Yet most importantly, it marks the end of his career as an aspiring Catholic philosopher, the course he had set for himself since his dissertation in 1913. At this point, Heidegger found himself struggling to develop his own perspective and to free himself from his earlier influences (*ibid.*: 107).

It was not, however, in his efforts to abandon Catholic dogma that Heidegger turned to Schleiermacher, but in his effort to engender a philosophical understanding of religion. The nature of religious experience takes the place of the question of God as the centre of Schleiermacher's thought. What he offers Heidegger, therefore, is a means of overcoming the theological dogmas and metaphysical framework within which he operated as a young student (*PRL* 242).

In order to resist theoretical theology and a theoretical approach in general, Heidegger grounds his thinking in a more personal stance. And in this stance, he finds the means for overcoming the timeless metaphysical framework that governed religious terminology as it had been passed down to him. Such a theoretical treatment was the result of the influence of Platonic–Aristotelian philosophy, which had been taken up into Christianity by Augustine, Aquinas and their successors. Heidegger wants to think out of his own facticity (see Chapter 1). Describing this facticity in an almost confessional manner to Karl Löwith in 1921, Heidegger claimed that it belonged to his facticity that he is a Christian "theo*logian*", and that he is this in the context of the "university" (Papenfuß & Pöggeler 1990: 29). Heidegger therefore seeks to take up an existential relation to himself and a phenomenological approach to religion from the standpoint of this facticity.

Early attempts at a phenomenology of religious life

In 1922 Heidegger writes that "the very idea of philosophy of religion [is] pure nonsense, particularly if it does not take the facticity of the human being into account" (*IHS* 480). Such nonsense evolves out of a merely theoretical approach that fails to attune itself to the facticity of life. Heidegger maintains this precisely because, for him, philosophy must direct itself towards the facticity of human being. The early Heidegger sought in phenomenology a kind of philosophizing that could remain true to life in its factical concreteness, and thus to "primordial Christianity", which "is in factical life experience", or, indeed, which "is such experience itself" (*PRL* 57).

Heidegger's early philosophy of religion then took shape in his lecture courses "Introduction to the Phenomenology of Religion" and "Augustine and Neo-Platonism", which where held in 1920–21, and in his notes from 1918–19 for a lecture that was never given on "The Philosophical Foundations of Medieval Mysticism". His approach in these courses and notes was determined by his adaptations of Husserl's phenomenological method, which he geared towards understanding the facticity of historical life not just in its "content" and "relational" senses, but especially in the sense in which it is "enacted".

As the Winter Semester approached in 1920, Heidegger announced his upcoming lecture course on the phenomenology of religion (Sheehan 1986: 45). In this lecture course, Heidegger presented an explication of the fundamental event of the Christian experience of life as it appears in the letters of Paul. In particular, Heidegger paid special attention to a decisive moment wherein the Christian experience of life becomes manifest in and through the question of the coming of Christ. This coming is described by Paul as a sudden occurrence, like a thief in the night. The suddenness and unpredictability of this moment for which one must solemnly wait was a point of fascination for Heidegger. In order to grasp how "Christian religiosity lives temporality" (*PRL* 55, 73), he focused on Paul's notion of *kairos*, which signifies one's delivery to a *moment of decision*, a moment that cannot be reached through a calculation. The *kairos* does not represent a mastery of time, but rather the uncertainty inherent in the future. This defining characteristic of the *kairos* involves the historicity of life's enactment, which rejects any attempt at objectification. In the moment of *kairos* one's life itself is at stake, not a theoretical grasp of it. Attempts at theoretical mastery or practical control of this moment simply express the wrong attitude for encountering it (*PRL* 4).

The question remains, however, how Heidegger, *as a philosopher*, understood this *kairos* within his phenomenological account of the facticity of life. His response is that, by seeking to give only a "formal indication" (see Chapter 1) of the fundamental Christian experience of life, the philosopher as phenomenologist does not choose a position with respect to the particular content of this experience, but rather limits himself to investigating the sustaining conditions of its possibility.

Drawing a sharp distinction between philosophy and theology

This led Heidegger to later claim, in "Phenomenology and Theology" (1927), that theological concepts are to be examined by the philosopher only with regard to their ontological presuppositions, not to their specific content (*PM* 52). For Heidegger, this has to do with their underlying ontology of temporality. However, the possibility of this specific understanding of being is connected with a certain faith: the expectation of the coming or arrival is connected to the concrete possibility of the coming of Christ. Thus Heidegger uncovers essential structures of Dasein from certain religious phenomena and contexts. The world of the believer offers an expression of fundamental existential structures. In themselves, such structures have nothing to do with religion. This point legitimates Heidegger's entire project. He does not, however, answer the question of whether the ontological implications of these religious phenomena are meaningful for the validity of faith. It is true that Heidegger's philosophy of guilt and future-oriented temporality is essentially developed from out of his interpretation of Christianity, but it is his explicit intention to analyse the philosophical presuppositions of Christian life. His project is not about theology, nor Christian faith, nor religion in general; his references to the religious are always oriented towards, and for the sake of, ontological analysis.

For Heidegger, philosophical concepts can function as a corrective for the understanding of theological concepts. And faith, in its turn, can give direction to empty philosophical concepts. This indicates the specificity of theology with regard to ontology: "that is to say, the ontological concept of guilt as such is never a theme of theology" (*PM* 52). The ontological concept of guilt determines the space in which sin can move in order to be ontologically understandable. For its part, ontological understanding is neutral and atheistic.

Heidegger thus distances himself from religious philosophical approaches in which a religious *a priori* is supposed. He distances himself as well from a reconciliation of faith and reason that would reduce faith to reason, as is the case in the philosophies of Kant and Hegel. Nor does he assume the harmony of faith and reason at which Thomistic philosophy aims.

Heidegger understands faith as the natural enemy, as it were, of philosophy: "This peculiar relationship does not exclude but rather includes the fact that faith, as a specific possibility of existence, is in its innermost core the mortal enemy of the form of existence that is an essential part of philosophy and that is factically ever-changing" (*PM* 53). What we see here is the fundamental opposition of two possibilities of existence, which cannot be realized by one person in one and the same moment. Faith as a possibility of existence implies death to philosophy as another possibility of existence. Heidegger remained resistant to the fusion of theoretical philosophy and theology. As he states in 1935, "A 'Christian philosophy' is a round square and a misunderstanding" (*IM* 8).

This does not mean that philosophers and theologians must behave like enemies; neither position excludes a factical and existentiell attitude of taking the other seriously and of mutual respect. Yet the existentiell opposition between faith, on the one hand, and philosophical self-understanding, on the other, does need to be clearly worked out so that one sees the different points of departure more sharply. Hence, while a "Christian philosophy" may well be a round square and a misunderstanding, theology can have an important role to play in thoughtfully questioning and explicating the world of Christian experience and faith. Nevertheless, in the end Heidegger sees in theology's dependence on philosophy a certain lack of greatness in theology itself (*IM* 8).

The critique of metaphysics as ontotheology

Turning to his later thought, we find that Heidegger develops a critical conception of "theology" as essentially a form of metaphysics. Heidegger sees the continuity of Western philosophy as metaphysics in terms of what he calls its "ontotheological" structure. This structure can be found already in Plato and Aristotle. Indeed, Aristotle not only sees in philosophy a place for theology as well as one for ontology; he also calls the whole project of first philosophy itself a theology. What does this mean? For Heidegger, it means that the question of the divine (*theos*) as a philosophical question is not a religious question to begin with; and yet such a philosophical theology was used as a paradigm for the construction of the theological dogmas of the Middle Ages. This ambiguous connection of the question of God and the question of being was facilitated by Aristotle, who, in the sixth book of the *Metaphysics*, divides first philosophy into two fundamental orientations of questioning – towards the being of beings (ontology) and towards the highest being (theology) – without making their unity itself into a problem (*FCM* 42–3). Heidegger asks about the original unity of both disciplines (*FCM* 34), and he increasingly sees this unity as paradigmatic for the entire tradition of Western philosophy.

The connection between ontology and theology, which determines philosophy as ontotheology, becomes explicit once again in German idealism. Heidegger finds a clear expression of this in Hegel: "For philosophy, too, has no other object than God – and thus is essentially rational theology – and service to God in its continual service to truth" (Hegel 1975: 101; *HPS* 98). In Hegel, according to Heidegger, ontology becomes the speculatively grounded interpretation of being, in such a way that the actual entity (*Seiendes*) is the absolute *theos*. It is from the being (*Sein*) of the absolute that all entities are determined. Heidegger emphasizes the connectedness and unity of ontology and theology especially in his 1936 lecture course on Schelling:

> Theo-logy means here questioning beings as a whole. This question of beings as a whole, the theological question, cannot be asked without the question about beings as such, about the essence of being in general. That is the question about the *on hēi on*, "ontology." Philosophy's questioning is always and in itself both onto-logical and theo-logical in the very broad sense. Philosophy is Ontotheology. (*ST* 51)

Hence, for the later Heidegger, to say that philosophy should not be ontotheological is tantamount to saying that philosophy should not be philosophy. Indeed, in the end (1966) Heidegger announces "the end of philosophy [as metaphysics or ontotheology] and the task of thinking" (*BW* 431–49).

In the "Introduction to 'What is Metaphysics?'" (1949), metaphysics is characterized as "twofold and yet unitary" on the basis of its ontotheological structure.

> Because it represents beings as beings, metaphysics is, in a twofold and yet unitary manner, the truth of beings in their universality

and in the highest being. According to its essence, metaphysics is at
the same time both ontology in the narrower sense, and theology.
(*PM* 287)

Understanding being as a whole presupposes a normative concept of
being, in which an understanding of a highest entity is implied (*PM*
287–8).

By the time Heidegger writes "The Onto-theological Constitution
of Metaphysics" (1959), the insight into this structure is completely
settled. In this essay, he definitely decides that the ambivalent relationship and ambiguous interconnection of ontology and theology are
characteristic of first philosophy. Heidegger refers back to his inaugural
lecture at Freiburg University, "What is Metaphysics?" (1929), which
defined metaphysics as the question about beings as such and as a whole
(see *PM* 93). The wholeness of this whole is the unity of all beings that
unifies as the generative ground. "To those who can read, this means:
metaphysics is onto-theo-logy" (*IDS* 54).

The question, "How does the deity enter into philosophy?" is not
to be answered with the idea of a god that comes from outside. The
god is always already in metaphysics. It belongs to the question of
being, which is characteristic of philosophy as such. While generally
the question about the gods and the godhead is either intentionally or
unintentionally understood within an ontotheological paradigm, by
thinking through the question of how the godhead enters into philosophy, Heidegger makes it possible to isolate the philosophical question of
god from religious speaking and thinking. Hence Heidegger's critique
of ontotheology at the same time enables a reawakening of the question
of god. Indeed he goes so far as to say that the "god-less thinking which
must abandon the god of philosophy", that is, the god of ontotheology,
"is thus perhaps closer to the divine god" (*IDS* 72 = *GA* 11: 77).

On the other hand, the question whether there can be an ontology
without a theology is no longer a question within the domain of philosophy as metaphysics. Rather, with this question we move into what
he calls the domain of "thinking". The original motive of philosophy,
strictly speaking, has disappeared from philosophy as ontotheology;
but it is preserved in the thinking of being. This domain of thinking is,
in a sense, a counterparadigm to philosophy in which the question of
being is not answered with an entity that represents the highest way of
being, the whole of being and the cause of being. In the 1955–6 lecture
course, "The Principle of Reason", Heidegger refers to the mystical
words of Angelus Silesius: "The rose is without why: it blooms because
it blooms, it pays no attention to itself, asks not whether it is seen" (*PR*

35). This "without why" or "without ground" (*ohne Grund*) indicates for Heidegger an a-theological thinking of being as a counterparadigm to metaphysics and its seeking after ontotheological grounds.

The last god

The notion of "the last god" (*der letzte Gott*) runs like a thread through *Contributions to Philosophy* (CP = GA 65), and it may be the most fascinating theme in this pivotal text from 1936–8. The question, "What or who is the last god?" engenders many negative answers, for it is not the "last" in the sense of the "most recent", as one speaks of the latest fashion or the last item in a countable series. Nor can the last god, who is unique, be conceived according to the calculations of monotheism, pantheism or atheism (*CP* 289 = GA 65: 411).

The last god is connected to the experience of being as an event of enowning (*Ereignis*), that is, to the unfolding of the truth of being (see Chapter 10). This bears on the finitude of being, which Heidegger thematized in *Being and Time* in the existential analysis of being-toward-death. Analogous to the manner in which we become aware of the finitude of all possibilities for being in decisive moments of an anticipatory experience of mortality, the radical finitude of being manifests itself in the hint (*Wink*) of the last god, who is only in "passing by". With this, Heidegger continues his polemic against the Christian idea of God, who is seen as infinite in contrast to the finitude of his creation. Indeed the last god is said to be "totally other than gods who have been, especially other than the Christian God" (*CP* 283 = GA 65: 403). To the question of what or who god is, Heidegger answers, in the context of understanding being as an event of enowning, that god is a hint, and nothing but a hint. The last god essentially is as passing by, and thus even the question of its or their number remains essentially undecided (*CP* 308 = GA 65: 437). The last god is not an end but rather a beginning, and this marks its temporal significance. This god *is* only as the decisive moment of its future passing-by (*GA* 39: 111). For this reason the last god does not manifest itself as something present, but is there only as a hint (*CP* 289 = GA 65: 410).

Thus, in talking about the last god, we do not mean the last of a series of gods or a final synthesis. The notion of the last god refers to a moment of decision (*kairos* or *Augenblick*) in which the experience of the last god's passing by makes room for other possibilities of being. Out of this experience, human beings could learn to be open and to look forward to another beginning. However, people do not know what this means, and they are not able to know as long as they are imprisoned – like those held captive by the shadows in Plato's Cave – in a method of calculative knowing through which they understand things, circumstances and themselves.

The word "last" here has no ontic meaning. It indicates something that anticipates very far into the future towards the deepest origin, something that reaches out the furthest and cannot be outstripped. The last god therefore withdraws from every calculation and has to bear the burden of the loudest and most frequent misinterpretations (*CP* 285 = *GA* 65: 405). The hint of the last god springs from a moment that is beyond calculative thinking, and this moment is even more difficult to reach than is the experience of mortality: "Given that as yet we barely grasp 'death' in its utmost, how are we then ever going to be primed for the rare hint of the last god?" (*CP* 285 = *GA* 65: 405). But just as in *Being and Time* death opens the appearance of being as possibility (*BT* §53), so would the passing by of the last god open up the possibility of another beginning for the history of being. Unlike the metaphysics of the first beginning, which understood being in terms of actuality, in this other beginning it would be understood that: "Being is possibility, what is never extant and yet through en-ownment is always what grants and refuses in not-granting" (*CP* 335 = *GA* 65: 475). In this sense, being, as a gathering or "enowning" place for the godhead and humans, is an inexhaustible wealth of possibilities.

The holy as a precondition for the god(s)

For Heidegger the question of the "holy" would be: is an experience of the holy possible within the technological world? It seems that in such a world, the experience of something that shows itself with the quality of the holy is impossible in so far as it is an experience that is only given to acts of worship, and acts of worship are radically other than acts of technological domination, manufacture and consumption. Religious experience as an experience of the holy has become a mere object of anthropological study. Its proper place is, as it were, on a reservation: a private, protected area away from the cultural mainstream. But, in Heidegger's view, the holy is not only a domain of certain protected subjects and objects. As the dimension that makes it possible to worship the divine (*PM* 267), the holy is a dimension that is prior to subject and object, earlier than I and Thou. In this sense, the holy indicates a condition of the possibility for the appearing of the divine.

An understanding of religions always depends first of all on an understanding of the experience of the holy as a fundamental mood. Whether their message will be received by new generations depends on whether this mood is conveyed. If there is no experience of the holy as a whole, the message of the gods in religion will not be understood. Religions have a history because the way the holy appears (*hierophany*) is rooted in the historical situation in which it appears.

Religions are historical because the understanding of being as holy is historical. This cannot be understood ontotheologically, because in that case religious manifestations would be manifestations of an ahistorical highest being that transcends all other beings. Religions and their gods must be understood historically, not as variations of what is eternally the same. As long as there is a forgottenness of the temporality of being in ontotheology, there is also a forgottenness of the historicality of the gods. Ontotheology is an understanding of being in which there is no place for the historical arrival of the god or gods. Such a time needs the poets to regain an entry to the holy as the mood wherein the god(s) can first appear (*EHP* 64).

The holy has to appear as that in which human beings can find their wholeness. The holy is not God or the godhead, much less the highest entity of metaphysics. It is an ontological phenomenon that is expressed in the thinking of being. Nevertheless, the religious human being would not understand himself or herself without the holy. It is precisely where the understanding of the holy has withdrawn that the central place of sacrifice is once again attributed to arbitrariness and barbarian cruelty. Only the holy as an ontological phenomenon can provide an entrance to the religious. Without understanding the holy, we behave with respect to it like tourists or visitors of a museum. Therefore, an understanding of it from the perspective of the historicality of being is an entry to understanding religion and the religions, God and the gods. The gods are in a certain sense on the other side of the holy. This does not mean that they are totally other; but they are other with regard to the modern paradigm of thinking. Modernity is not able to experience the holy in so far as it is not able to experience the wholeness of being.

The role of the gods in the fourfold

After breaking with Catholic theology by way of a phenomenological attentiveness to the facticity and historicity of religious life, and then by way of pursuing an "atheistic piety" of philosophy, and after later recovering a sense of the holy by way of a radical critique of ontotheology, the final chapter of the question of God(s) in Heidegger's thought locates the divine in the "fourfold" of earth and heaven (or sky), divinities and mortals (see Chapter 15). The four of the fourfold are in a certain sense equal to each other. There is no subordination of higher and lower. Although there might seem to be more kinship between heaven and the divinities, on the one hand, and the earth and mortals on the other, these are not two couples that stand against one other and each of the four becomes itself in the coming together of the four. In this way they are connected to each other. "Each of the four mirrors in its own way the presence of the others. Each therewith reflects itself in its own way into its own, within the simpleness of the four" (*PLT* 177).

Sometimes it seems that the divine has a special position. It seems as if the godhead ducks out of the fundamental interdependence of the fourfold, exempting itself from destiny by being the element that rules it. This is suggested, not only in the *Der Spiegel* interview, where Heidegger enigmatically suggests that "only a god can save us" (*HC* 107), but also where Heidegger writes: "the divinities are the beckoning messengers of the godhead. Out of the holy sway of the godhead, the god appears in his presence or withdraws into his concealment" (*PLT* 147–8). Here the divinities, the godhead and the god are spoken of without any explanation of their relations in the fourfold. Yet a certain order is discernible. The godhead seems to be the first by its holy sway. Its beckoning messengers are the divinities, and the god who appears and withdraws, appears only out of the holy sway of the godhead. It seems as though the godhead steps out of the whole of the fourfold, and is not to be found in it, but in the holy. However, the holy does not inhere in the fourfold, nor in the divinities or the mortals. Rather, the holy is the whole relation that comes to be as the fourfold (*EHP* 94ff.). Only in the lightning of the holy can the whole be present. "The holy primordially decides in advance concerning men and gods, whether they are, and who they are, and how they are, and when they are" (*EHP* 97–8). The holy is not holy because it is divine; rather, the divine is divine because it is holy in its way (*EHP* 82). The divine is holy because it participates in the holy, which is the whole of the fourfold.

From the perspective of the notion of the fourfold, it is thus strictly speaking inconsequential to say that the god is nearer to the holy. What is said here is that the god is placed under the holy and that the relation to the holy can only be held in common with human being (*EHP* 90). With this, the mortals as well as the divinities are placed in the fourfold under the holy. The holy indicates the whole of this relation.

The fourfold, as a counterparadigm to the technological world, no longer implies a subjectivistic relation to the divine and the holy. Human beings dwell in so far as they await the divinities as divinities. "They wait for intimations of their coming and do not mistake the signs of their absence. They do not make their gods for themselves and do not worship idols." In misfortune they wait for the salvation that has been withdrawn (*PLT* 148). Under certain conditions one can speak here of theology, but only in a non-ontotheological way. It is impossible to define the holy here ontotheologically, since all ontotheology presupposes a *theos*, or god, as an entity. It does this so certainly that wherever ontotheology arises, the god has already fled (*GA* 52: 132).

References

Hegel, G. W. F. 1975. *Aesthetics*, T. Knox (trans.). Oxford: Oxford University Press.

Ochwadt, C. & E. Tecklenborg (eds) 1981. *Das Maß des Verborgenen. Heinrich Ochsner (1891–1970) zum Gedächtnis*. Hannover: Charis.

Ott, H. 1988. *Martin Heidegger: Unterwegs zu seiner Biographie*. Frankfurt: Campus.

Papenfuß, D. & O. Pöggeler (eds) 1990. *Zur philosophische Aktualität Heideggers*, vol. 2. Frankfurt: Vittorio Klostermann.

Sheehan, T. 1986. "Heidegger's *Introduction to the Phenomenology of Religion*, 1920–21". In *A Companion to Martin Heidegger's Being and Time*, J. Kockelmans (ed.), 40–62. Washington, DC: University Press of America.

Further reading

Primary sources

See Heidegger's "Building Dwelling Thinking", in *Poetry, Language, Thought; Contributions to Philosophy (From Enowning)*, pt VII; *Identity and Difference*; "Letter on Humanism", in *Pathmarks*, 239–76, esp. 258; "Phenomenology and Theology", in *Pathmarks*, 39–62; and *The Phenomenology of Religious Life*.

Secondary sources

See Caputo (1982, 1990), Crowe (2008), Kovacs (1990), Thomson (2005) and Vedder (2007).

SEVENTEEN

Heidegger on Christianity and divinity: a chronological compendium

Bret W. Davis

Heidegger's relation to Christianity and his ideas about divinity are among the most difficult – and, for many, among the most thought-provoking – issues that his readers confront. In fact, these were among the most difficult issues Heidegger personally grappled with, calling "the struggle with the faith of my birth" one of "the two great thorns in my flesh" (the other being his political misadventure; see Ott 1993: 37). This struggle was an ongoing one: over the course of his life Heidegger's thinking underwent significant developments and a number of shifts regarding Christianity, and the *Gottesfrage* (question of God) can be seen as a periodically resurfacing accompaniment to the *Seinsfrage* (question of being) along his entire path of thought.

In compiling this compendium my aim was to glean from the pages of Heidegger's many texts a chronologically ordered selection of passages that exemplify the different phases in the development of Heidegger's thinking about Christianity and divinity. In rough outline, those phases can be described as follows:

1. Up until around 1917 Heidegger exhibits a deep personal faith in Catholicism and a philosophical commitment to Aristotelian–Thomistic scholasticism, which he seeks to defend against "modernism" but also to develop in light of modern logic and medieval mysticism.
2. Between 1917 and 1919 Heidegger undergoes a religious–philosophical conversion from "the *system* of Catholicism" to a non-dogmatic Protestantism or "free Christianity". Inspired by Paul, Augustine, Luther and Kierkegaard, in 1920–21 he seeks to

employ phenomenology to recover an experiential understanding of "primal Christianity".

3. Around 1922 Heidegger begins to strictly separate theology and philosophy (phenomenology), and to identify himself increasingly with the latter. By 1927 he comes to deride the idea of a "Christian philosophy" as a "square circle".

4. Beginning rather abruptly in 1934 with his first lecture course on Hölderlin's poetry, Heidegger's thought undergoes a shift away from *both* Christianity *and* the purported "atheism of philosophy" toward a radical rethinking of the divine. Inspired by the notions of divinity he finds in early Greek thought and above all in Hölderlin's poetic word, Heidegger tends to speak now of *der Gott* (the god) or *die Götter* (the gods) rather than the Creator named *Gott* (God, without an article) in the Abrahamic monotheistic traditions.[1] This final phase in Heidegger's thinking of divinity continues to develop through the inherently enigmatic notion of "the last god" articulated in *Contributions to Philosophy* (1936–8) to his later discussions of "the holy" (*das Heilige*), "the godhead" or "godhood" (*die Gottheit*) and "the divinities" (*die Göttlichen*) of the fourfold (see Chapters 15 and 16). From the middle of the 1930s to the end of his life, these notions of divinity play a crucial – if not always readily apparent – role in Heidegger's thought.

In addition to gathering a thematically focused series of texts, this compendium is also intended to allow readers to conclude their preliminary study (or review) of Heidegger's key concepts with a chronologically comprehensive sampling of Heidegger's own writings, covering a time period extending from his student years up to the final years of his life. (It may be helpful for readers to cross-reference this compendium with the Chronology of Heidegger's Life that follows it.)

1911 Academic lectures on religion instill contemporary ideas: conceived with wide-ranging scope, presented in finely crafted speech, the basic truths of Christianity in their eternal greatness appear before the soul of the Catholic student, arouse his enthusiasm, remind him "what we have" – more precisely put, what the individual *potentially* has. The *actual* self-possession of this treasure of truths does indeed postulate an undaunting, incessant self-persistence, for which merely listening to lectures can never be a substitute. The young mind searches, driven by an inner, magical urge for truth, to secure for *itself* the basic outlines of the necessary pre-knowledge. One can then proceed to take up and think through on one's own the "principal problems of worldviews." One only possesses truth in a genuine sense when one has made it one's own in this way. (*BH* 15)

From one of Heidegger's first publications as a university student, "On a Philosophical Orientation for Academics", which appeared in the anti-modernist Catholic journal *Der Akademiker* just before Heidegger left the seminary and redirected the focus of his studies from theology to philosophy. Theodore Kisiel and Thomas Sheehan comment that the

> young Heidegger's strong commitment to Aristotelian–Thomistic scholasticism nevertheless does not lead him to regard it as a closed and complete textbook system of "doctrinal statements." It is rather an ongoing "struggle after truth" open to advances in more recent philosophy, as in modern logic, which Heidegger will apply to his two still scholastic dissertations. (*BH* 12)

1915 We moderns have in many ways lost sight of the simple, we are fascinated by the complicated, the questionable; thus this dreadful fear of *principles*, which as such are always the simplest; thus the total indisposition toward the grand simplicity and quiet greatness of the Christian worldview and Catholic belief. If we do not want to be conquered by the victory in the future, *we must in principle extricate ourselves from the lack of principles in the most elementary questions of life*.
(*BH* 50)

From a newspaper article, "The War-Triduum in Messkirch", on the occasion of a three-day meditation on the meaning of the war called for by the German bishops.

1916 If we meditate [*sich besinnen*] on the deeper essence of philosophy in its connection with worldview, the conception of the Christian philosophy in the Middle Ages as a Scholasticism standing in opposition to the then-prevalent mysticism must be revealed as fundamentally deficient. For the medieval worldview, Scholasticism and mysticism belong essentially together. ... Philosophy as a rationalistic structure, detached

233

from life, is *powerless*; mysticism as irrational experience is *aimless*.   (*BH* 85; see also *SUP* 68)

From the Conclusion to the published version of Heidegger's post-doctoral dissertation, *The Doctrine of Categories and Meaning in Duns Scotus*.

1917 And dogmatic and casuistic pseudo-philosophies, which pose as philosophies of a particular system of religion (for example, Catholicism) and presumably stand closest to religion and the religious, are the least capable of promoting the vitality of the problem. ... [The] inherent worth of the religion, its palp-able sphere of meaning, must first be experienced through a tangled, nonorganic, dogmatic hedgerow of propositions and proofs which are theoretically wholly unclarified, which as canonical statute with police power in the end serves to over-power and oppress the subject and to encumber it in darkness. In the end, the system totally excludes an original and genuine experience of religious value. ... [S]cholasticism, within the totality of the medieval Christian lifeworld, severely jeopard-ized the immediacy of religious life and forgot religion for theology and dogmas. [In a situation like this,] an experience like that of mysticism is to be understood as an elementary countermovement.

From an unpublished note, quoted in Kisiel (1993: 73–4). Theodore Kisiel estimates that this note was written in early 1917, that is, during the period that he characterizes as "that obscure and virtually unknown Interregnum (1917–19) in Heidegger's development from which he emerges as a 'protestant apostate'" (*ibid.*: 70).

1917 The point is "to get down into the innermost holiness of life," where the original relationship of feeling and intuition is to be found. "But I must refer you to yourselves, to the grasp of a living moment. You must understand, likewise, for your consciousness to, as it were, eavesdrop on, or at least to reconstitute, this state out of the living moment for yourselves." ... The point is to uncover an original region of life and performance of consciousness (or feeling), in which religion alone realizes itself as a certain form of experience. ... Universe – fullness of reality – is uninterrupted flows and operations; all individuals as parts of the whole. Religion is

the specifically religiously intentional, emotional reference of each content of experience to an infinite whole as fundamental meaning. *Devotion*: original streaming in of fullness, without restraint, letting oneself be excited. *To lead back* the respective experience into the inner unity of life. Religious life is the constant renewal of this procedure. ... *History* in its most authentic sense is the highest object of religion, religion begins and ends in it. Humanity is to be seen as a living community of individuals in which isolated experience is to be lost. ... Do all *with* religion and not *from* religion. Religion should accompany, like holy music, all the doings of life.
(*PRL* 243–4 = *GA* 60: 321–2; see also *BH* 86–91)

From notes for a talk, "On Schleiermacher's Second Speech, 'On the Essence of Religion'". The quotations in Heidegger's notes are from Schleiermacher's text.

1918   My husband has lost his religious faith, and I have failed to find mine. His faith was undermined by doubts even when we got married [in 1917]. But I myself insisted on a Catholic wedding, and hoped with his help to find faith. We have spent a lot of time reading, talking, thinking and praying together, and the result is that we have both ended up thinking along Protestant lines, i.e. with no fixed dogmatic ties, believing in a personal God, praying to Him in the spirit of Christ, but outside any Protestant or Catholic orthodoxy.
(Attributed to Elfride Heidegger, quoted in Ott 1993: 109)

From the diary of Father Engelbert Krebs (a theologian friend who performed the Catholic ceremony of Heidegger's wedding), recording the gist of what was said to him in a conversation with Heidegger's wife, Elfride.

1918–19   Sharply divorce the problem of theology and that of religiosity. In theology one must take care to note its constant dependency on philosophy and on the situation of the respective theoretical consciousness in general. Theology has heretofore found no original theoretical basic posture that corresponds to the originality of its object. ... Protestant faith and Catholic faith are *fundamentally different*. Noetically and noematically separated experiences. In Luther an *original* form of religiosity – one that is also not found in the mystics – breaks

235

out. ... The "holding-to-be-true" of Catholic faith is founded entirely otherwise than the *fiducia* of the reformers. ...

... The immediacy of religious experience, the uncontained vivacity of devotion to the holy, godly, does not issue forth the form from out of itself and the contemplation of the genuine performance-character; rather, it emerges as the culmination of a particular historically determined epistemological doctrine and psychology ... One must get clear about this connection in order to really understand Eckhart's mysticism as such ...

... Not the not-yet-determinable and not-yet-determined – rather, that which is essentially without determination in general is the primordial object, the absolute. ... Corresponding to the fundamental principle that the same is recognized only through the same – the same becomes object only *for* the same – the theory of the subject, the soul develops; here also the process of undoing the multiplicity, of the rejection of the individual forces in their individuality and determinate directionality, the return to their ground, origin, and their root. ... Elimination of change, multiplicity, time. Absoluteness of object and subject in the sense of radical unity and as such unity *both: I am it, and it is I*. From this the namelessness of God and ground of the soul. ... Eckhart's "fundamental conception" – "you can only know what you are," becomes conceivable only from out of specific concepts of cognition. Here cognition determines subject and object.
(PRL 235–6, 239, 240 = GA 60: 310, 315, 316)

From Heidegger's notes for a planned – but not given – lecture course on *The Philosophical Foundations of Medieval Mysticism*.

1919 Epistemological insights extending to a theory of historical knowledge have made the *system* of Catholicism problematic and unacceptable to me, but not Christianity and metaphysics – these, though, in a new sense. ... My investigations in the phenomenology of religion, which will draw heavily on the Middle Ages, should show beyond a doubt that in transforming my basic philosophical position I have not been driven to replacing objective appreciative judgment of and deep respect for the life-world of Catholicism with the angry and coarse polemics of an apostate. ... I believe that I have the inner calling to philosophy and, through my research and teaching, to

do what stands in my power for the sake of the eternal vocation of the inner man, and *to do it for this alone,* and so justify
my existence [*Dasein*] and work ultimately before God.

(SUP 69–70; see also *BH* 96)

From a letter to Father Engelbert Krebs.

1920–21   In the following, we do not intend to give a dogmatic or
theological–exegetical interpretation, nor a historical study
or a religious meditation, but only guidance for phenomenological understanding. ... The theological method falls out
of the framework of our study. Only with phenomenological
understanding, a new way for theology is opened up. The
formal indication renounces the last understanding that can
only be given in genuine religious experience; it intends only
to open an access to the New Testament. ... To begin with, it
suffices to seek a general understanding of [Paul's] letter to the
Galatians in order to penetrate therewith into the grounding
phenomena of primordial Christian life. ...
   ... It is a decrease of authentic understanding if God is
grasped primarily as an object of speculation. That can be
realized only if one carries out the explication of the conceptual connections. This, however, has never been attempted,
because Greek philosophy penetrated into Christianity. ...
The awaiting of the *parousia* of the Lord is decisive. ... The
experience is an absolute distress *(thlipis)* which belongs to
the life of the Christian himself. The acceptance *(dechesthai)*
is an entering-oneself-into anguish. ...
   ... "Christian religiosity lives temporality." It is a time without its own order and demarcations. One cannot encounter
this temporality in some sort of objective concept of time. The
when is in no way objectively graspable. ... The present study
takes up the center of Christianity: the eschatological problem.
Already at the end of the first century the eschatological was
covered up in Christianity. In later times one misjudged all
original Christian concepts. In today's philosophy, too, the
Christian concept-formations are hidden behind a Greek view.
... There is no security for Christian life; the constant insecurity is also characteristic for what is fundamentally significant
in factical life. ...
   ... [The] *anamenein* [waiting] is an obstinate waiting before
God. The obstinate waiting does not wait for the significances

237

of a future content, but for God. The meaning of temporality determines itself out of the fundamental relationship to God – however, in such a way that only those who live temporality in the manner of enactment understand eternity. The sense of the Being of God can be determined first only out of these complexes of enactment. To pass through them is the precondition. ...

... There remains a deep opposition between the Mystics and the Christians. The Mystic is, through manipulation, removed from the life-complex; in an enraptured state God and the universe are possessed. The Christian knows no such "enthusiasm," rather he says: "let us be awake and sober." Here is precisely shown to him the terrible difficulty of the Christian life. ... Real philosophy of religion arises not from preconceived concepts of philosophy and religion. Rather, the possibility of its philosophical understanding arises out of a certain religiosity – for us, the Christian religiosity. Why exactly the Christian religiosity lies in the focus of our study, that is a difficult question; it is answerable only through the solution of the problem of the historical connections. The task is to gain a real and original relationship to history, which is to be explicated from out of our own historical situation and facticity.   (*PRL* 47, 67, 73, 83–4, 89 = *GA* 60: 67–8, 97–8, 104–5, 117, 124)

From a lecture course entitled *Introduction to the Phenomenology of Religion*.

1921   Neo-Platonism and Augustine will not become an arbitrary case, but in the study their historicity [*Historizität*] is precisely to be raised into its own, as something in whose peculiar dimension of effect [*Wirkungsdimension*] we are standing today. History hits us, and we are history itself .... The boundaries between the theological and the philosophical are not to be blurred (no philosophical blurring of theology, no "intensification" of philosophy pretending to be religious). Rather, precisely going back behind both exemplary formations of factical life ought to (1) indicate in principle how and what lies "behind" both, and (2) how a genuine problematic results from this; all this not extra-temporal and for the construction of an approaching or not approaching culture, but itself *in historical enactment*. ...

... The curare *(Being Concerned) as the Basic Character of Factical Life: Chapters 28 and 29 [of Augustine's* Confessions] ... My life is "deformis" [deformed]. – Not in order to excuse himself, but indeed to push himself away from himself recklessly, and to gain himself from this severe distance, Augustine now makes it clear to himself, that "life" is no cakewalk [*Spaziergang*] and is precisely the most inopportune moment to assume an air of importance. ... For "in multa defluximus" [we are scattered into the many], we are dissolving into the manifold and are absorbed in the dispersion. You demand counter-movement against the dispersion, against the falling apart of life. ... "Per continentiam quippe colligimur et redigimur in unum [necessarium – Deum?]." [By continence we are gathered together and brought into the One (the necessary One – God?)]. ... In this decisive hoping, the genuine effort at *continentia* is alive, an effort which does not reach its end. (Not "abstinence" which loses precisely the positive sense, but "containment," pulling back from the *defluxio* [dispersion], standing against it full of mistrust.) ... For life is really nothing but a constant temptation. ... "Numquid non tentatio est vita humana super terram sine ullo interstitio?" [Is not human life on earth a trial without intermission?] ...

... The problem of the universal theory of value is connected to Neo-Platonism and the doctrine of the *summum bonum*, in particular, to the conception of the way in which the *summum bonum* becomes accessible. ... [One] cannot simply dismiss the Platonic in Augustine; and it is a misunderstanding to believe that in going back to Augustine, one can gain the authentically Christian.

(PRL 124–5, 151–2, 212 = GA 60: 173, 205–6, 281)

From a lecture course entitled *Augustine and Neo-Platonism.*

1921 I work concretely and factically out of my "I am" – out of my spiritual and thoroughly factic heritage, my milieu, my life contexts, and whatever is available to me from these, as the vital experience in which I live. ... This facticity of mine includes – briefly put – the fact that I am a "Christian theologian." This implies a certain radical self-concern, a certain radical scientificity, a rigorous objectivity [*Gegenständlichkeit*] in this facticity; it includes the historical consciousness, the consciousness of the "history of spirit." And I am all this in the life context of the *university*. (*BH* 99–100)

From a letter to Karl Löwith.

1921–2 My comportment in philosophizing is not religious, even if as a philosopher I can also be a religious person. "The art resides precisely in that": to philosophize and, in so doing, to be genuinely religious; i.e., to take up factically one's worldly, historiological–historical task in philosophy, in action and in a concrete world of action, though not in religious ideology and fantasy. ... Philosophy, in its radical, self-posing question-ability, must be *a-theistic* as a matter of principle. Precisely on account of its basic intention, philosophy must not presume to possess or determine God. The more radical philosophy is, the more determinately is it on a path away from God; yet, precisely in the radical actualization of the "away," it has its own difficult proximity to God.

(*PIA* 148 = *GA* 61: 197–8; see also *BH* 165, 479–80 n.24)

From a lecture course entitled *Phenomenological Interpretations of Aristotle*.

1922 By the beginning of my academic teaching [which, if taken literally, would mean the Winter Semester of 1915–16], it became clear to me that genuine scientific research free from all reservations and covert commitments is not possible along with active adherence to the Catholic faith and its standpoint. This standpoint became untenable for me through my unceasing preoccupation with early Christianity as it is developed by the modern school of the history of religion. My lecture course was forbidden to the theologians. (*BH* 107)

From a *vita* composed in 1922 and sent to Georg Misch as part of an application for a position in philosophy at the University of Göttingen.

1924 The sense and essence of any particular theology can be read off from its view of man's *iustititia originalis* [original right-eousness]. For the more the radicality of sin is underrated, then the more redemption is disparaged and the more God becoming human in the Incarnation loses its necessity. We thus find in Luther's thought the fundamental tendency that the *corruptio* of man's being can never be grasped radically enough. And Luther asserted this particularly in opposition to Scholasticism, which always spoke of *corruptio* with qualification and in extenuation. (*BH* 189–90; see also *SUP* 106)

From a student transcript of a lecture given by Heidegger in Rudolf Bultmann's theological seminar at the University of Marburg.

1927–8 The popular understanding of the relationship between theology and philosophy is fond of opposing faith and knowledge, revelation and reason. ... We, however, see the problem of the relationship differently from the very start. It is for us rather a question about the relationship of two sciences. ... We offer only as a guide the following formal definition of science: science is the founding disclosure, for the sheer sake of disclosure, of a self-contained region of beings, or of being. ... [T]here are two basic possibilities of science: sciences of beings, of whatever is, or ontic sciences; and *the* science of being, the ontological science, philosophy. ... Ontic sciences in each case thematize a given being that in a certain manner is always already disclosed *prior* to scientific disclosure. We call the sciences of beings as given – of a *positum* – positive sciences. ... Ontology, or the science of being, on the other hand, demands a fundamental shift of view: from beings to being. ... Our thesis, then, is that *theology is a positive science, and as such, therefore, is absolutely different from philosophy.* ...

... [W]e maintain that *what is given for theology (its positum) is Christianness* [Christlichkeit]. ... We call faith Christian. The essence of faith can be formally sketched as a way of existence of human Dasein that ... arises *not from* Dasein or spontaneously *through* Dasein, but rather from that which is revealed in and with this way of existence, from what is believed. For the "Christian" faith, that being which is primarily revealed to faith, and only to it, and which, as revelation, first gives rise to faith, is Christ, the crucified God. ... [F]aith is an appropriation of revelation that co-constitutes the Christian occurrence, that is, the mode of existence that specifies a factical Dasein's Christianness as a particular form of destiny. *Faith is the believing–understanding mode of existing in the history revealed, i.e., occurring, with the Crucified.* ... The totality of this being that is disclosed by faith ... constitutes

241

the character of the *positum* that theology finds before it. ...
Theology ... is the science of faith, not only insofar as it makes
faith and that which is believed its object, but because it itself
arises out of faith. It is the science that faith of itself motivates
and justifies. ...

... If faith does not need philosophy, the *science* of faith as
a *positive* science does. ... Every ontic interpretation operates
on the basis, at first and for the most part concealed, of an
ontology. ... All theological concepts necessarily contain *that*
understanding of being that is constitutive of human Dasein as
such, insofar as it exists at all. Thus, for example, sin is manifest only in faith, and only the believer can factically exist as
a sinner. ... But guilt is an original ontological determination
of the existence of Dasein. ...

... *Philosophy is the possible, formally indicative ontological
corrective of the ontic and, in particular, of the pre-Christian
content of basic theological concepts. But philosophy can be
what it is without functioning factically as this corrective.* ...
This peculiar relationship does not exclude but rather includes
the fact that *faith*, as a specific possibility of existence, is in its
innermost core the mortal enemy of the *form of existence* that
is an essential part of philosophy and that is factically ever-
changing. Faith is so absolutely the mortal enemy that philosophy does not even begin to want in any way to do battle with
it. This *existentiell opposition* between faithfulness and the
free appropriation of one's whole Dasein is not first brought
about by the sciences of theology and philosophy but is prior
to them. Furthermore, it is precisely this *opposition* that must
bear the *possibility of a community of the sciences* of theology
and philosophy, if indeed they are to communicate in a genuine way, free from illusions and weak attempts at mediation.
Accordingly, there is no such thing as a Christian philosophy;
that is an absolute "square circle." On the other hand, there
is likewise no such thing as a neo-Kantian, or axiological, or
phenomenological theology, just as there is no phenomenological mathematics.   (PM 40–41, 43–6, 50–51, 53 =
                                            GA 9: 47–9, 52–5, 61–4, 66)

From a lecture, "Phenomenology and Theology". See also the following
relevant notes in *Being and Time*: BTS 404 n.4, 405 n.7, 408 n.6, 410–11
n.2, 416 n.13 = SZ 190, 199, 249, 306, 427 (cf. *BH* 200ff.).

1929 The ontological interpretation of Dasein as being-in-the-world decides neither positively nor negatively concerning a possible being toward God. Presumably, however, the elucidation of transcendence first achieves an *adequate concept* of *Dasein*, and with respect to this being it can then be *asked* how things stand ontologically concerning the relation of Dasein to God. (*PM* 371 n.62 = *GA* 9: 159)

From a footnote to "On the Essence of Ground".

1934–5 One treats Hölderlin "historiologically" and misses what alone is essential, namely that his still timeless and place-less work has already overcome our historiological fuss and grounded the inception of another history, a history which commences with the struggle over the decision about the arrival or flight of the god. (*GA* 39: 1)

From Heidegger's preface to his first lecture course on Hölderlin's poetry.

1935 [Anyone] for whom the Bible is divine revelation and truth already has an answer to the question "Why are there beings at all instead of nothing?" before it is even asked: beings, with the exception of God Himself, are created by Him. God himself "is" as the uncreated Creator. One who holds on to such a faith as a basis can, perhaps, emulate and participate in the asking of our question in a certain way, but he cannot authentically question without giving himself up as a believer, with all the consequences of this step. He can act only "as if" –. On the other hand, if such faith does not continually expose itself to the possibility of unfaith, it is not faith but a convenience. It becomes an agreement with oneself to adhere in the future to a doctrine as something that has somehow been handed down. This is neither having faith nor questioning, but indifference – which can then, perhaps even with keen interest, busy itself with everything, with faith as well as with questioning. ... What is really asked in our question is, for faith, foolishness. ... Philosophy consists in such foolishness. A "Christian phil-osophy" is a round square and a misunderstanding. To be sure, one can thoughtfully question and work through the world of Christian experience – that is, the world of faith. That is then theology. ... Philosophy, for originally Christian faith, is foolishness. Philosophizing means asking: "Why are there beings at all instead of nothing?" Actually asking this means venturing to exhaust, to question thoroughly, the inexhaustible wealth of this question, by unveiling what it demands that we question. Whenever such a venture occurs, there is philosophy.   (*IM* 7–8 = *EM* 5–6)

From a lecture course later published as *Introduction to Metaphysics*.

1936 Schelling ... wants to accomplish precisely this: to bring to a conceptual formulation how God comes to himself, how God – not as a concept thought, but as the life of life – comes to himself. Thus a *becoming* God! ... God as existence, that is, the existing god is this god who is *in himself* historical. For Schelling, existence always means a being insofar as it is *aware of itself* (*bei sich selbst*). Only that, however, can be aware of itself which has gone out of itself and in a certain way is always outside of itself. Only what has gone outside of itself and what takes upon itself being outside of itself and is thus a being aware of itself has, so to speak, "absolved" the inner history of its Being and is accordingly "absolute." God *as the existing one* is the *absolute* God, or God as he himself – in brief: God-*himself*. God considered as the ground of his existence "is" not yet God truly as he himself. But still, God "is" his ground. It is true that the ground is something distinguished from God, but not yet "outside of" God. The ground in God is that in God which God himself "is" not truly himself, but rather his ground for his selfhood. Schelling calls this ground "nature" in God. ...

... God not as an old papa with a white beard who manufactures things, but as the becoming God to whose essence the ground belongs, uncreated nature which is not He Himself. ...

... In philosophy we can no more go back to Greek philosophy by means of a leap than we can eliminate the advent of Christianity into Western history and thus into philosophy by means of a command. The only possibility is to transform history, that is, truly to bring about the hidden necessity of history into which neither knowledge nor deed reach, and transformation truly brought about is the essence of the creative. ...

... At the passage of the transition to the VI section [of Schelling's treatise on freedom] there is the sentence: "In the

244

divine understanding there is a system; God himself, however, is not a system but a life..." Here system is attributed to only one factor of the jointure of Being, to existence. At the same time, a higher unity is posited and designated as "life." ... But when the system is only in the understanding, the ground and the whole opposition of ground and understanding are excluded from system as its other and system is no longer system with regard to beings as a whole. ... That is the difficulty which emerges more and more clearly in Schelling's later efforts with the whole of philosophy, the difficulty which proves to be an *impasse* (*Scheitern*). And this *impasse* is evident since the factors of the jointure of being, ground and existence and their unity not only become less and less compatible, but are even driven so far apart that Schelling falls back into the rigidified tradition of Western thought without creatively transforming it. ... Schelling does not see the necessity of an essential step. If being in truth cannot be predicated of the Absolute, that means that the essence of all being is finitude and only what exists finitely has the privilege and the pain of standing in being as such and experiencing what is true as beings.   (*ST* 109–10, 135, 145–6, 160–62 = *SA* 131–2, 163, 175, 193–5)

From a lecture course later published as *Schelling's Treatise on the Essence of Human Freedom.*

1936 [By] providing anew the essence of poetry, Hölderlin first determines a new time. It is the time of the gods who have fled *and* of the god who is coming. It is the *time of need* because it stands in a double lack and a double not: in the no-longer of the gods who have fled and in the not-yet of the god who is coming.   (*EHP* 64 = *EHD* 47)

From "Hölderlin and the Essence of Poetry".

1936–8 THE LAST GOD ... The totally other over against gods who have been, especially over against the Christian God. ...
   ... But the *last* god, is that not a degradation, nay *the* greatest blasphemy? Yet what if the last god has to be so named because in the end the decision about the gods leads under and among them and so raises to the highest the essential occurrence [*Wesen*] of the uniqueness of the divine essence [*Gottwesen*]?

... If we think calculatively here and take this "last" merely as ceasing and end, instead of as the utmost and briefest decision about what is highest, then of course all knowing awareness of the last god is impossible. ...

... The last god is not the event of appropriation [*Ereignis*] itself; rather, it needs the event of appropriation as that to which the founder of the t/here [*Dagründer*] belongs. ...

... The last god has its most unique uniqueness and stands outside those calculating determinations meant by titles such as "mono-theism," "pan-theism," and "a-theism." "Monotheism" and all types of "theism" exist only since Judaeo-Christian "apologetics," which has metaphysics as its intellectual presupposition. With the death of this god, all theisms collapse. ...

... The last god is the inception of the longest history on its shortest track. Long preparation is needed for the great moment of the passing of the last god. And for this preparation, peoples and states are too small, i.e., already too much torn from all growth and still delivered over to machination. ... Only great and concealed individuals will create the stillness for the passing of the last god, along with the reticent accord among those who are prepared. ...

... [The] god requires beyng, and the human as being-there [*Da-sein*] needs to have grounded the belongingness to beyng. Then, for this moment, beyng as the innermost "between" is like the nothing; the god overpowers the human and the human surpasses the god – in immediacy, as it were, and yet both only in the event of appropriation, which is what the truth of beyng itself is. ...

... All heretofore "cults" and "churches" and such things cannot at all become the essential preparation for the colliding of god and human in the midpoint of beyng. For, the truth of beyng itself must at first be grounded, and for this assignment all creating must take on another inception. ... How few know that god awaits the grounding of the truth of beyng and thus awaits the leap of the human into being-there. Instead it seems as if humans would, and would have to, await the god. ...

... [The] talk of "gods" here does not indicate a decided assertion on the extantness of a plurality over against a singular, but is rather meant as an allusion to the undecidedness of the being of the gods, whether of one single god or of many gods. This undecidedness holds within itself what is questionworthy, namely whether something like "being" [*Sein*] may at all be attributed to the gods without destroying all that is godly. The undecidedness concerning which god and whether a god can, in the most extreme need, once again arise, and [if so] in what way and to what manner of human being – this is what is named with the name "gods." ... Not attributing being to "the gods" initially means only that being does not stand "over" the gods and that the gods do not stand "over" being. But "the gods" are in need of beyng, and in the saying of "the gods" the essential occurrence "of " beyng is already thought. "The gods" are not in need of beyng as their property, wherein they themselves find a standing. "The gods" nevertheless need beyng, which does not belong to them, in order to belong to themselves. ... [The] "gods" are in need of beyng-historical thinking, i.e., of philosophy. "The gods" are in need of philosophy, not as if *they themselves* would have to philosophize for the sake of their godding; but rather philosophy must be *if* "the gods" are again to come into decision and if history is to attain its essential ground. ...

... Beyng essentially occurs [*west*] as the between [*das Zwischen*] for god and human, but in such a way that this between-space first makes room for the essential possibility of god and human ... Beyng essentially occurs as the a-propriating [*Er-eignung*] of the gods and the humans to their en-countering [*Ent-gegnung*].   (*CP* 283, 286, 288, 289, 291, 292, 293, 308–9, 335–6 = *GA* 65: 403, 406–7, 409, 411, 414, 415, 416–17, 437–9, 476–7, trans. mod.)

From *Contributions to Philosophy*.

1937–8 And who would want to ignore the fact that a confrontation [*Auseinandersetzung*] with Christianity silently accompanied me on my entire path hitherto – a confrontation that was and is not a "problem" that was taken up to address, but rather *at once* a preservation of *and* a painful separation from the provenance that is most my own: the house of my parents, my homeland and my youth. Only someone who was likewise rooted in such an actually lived Catholic world may be able to have an inkling of the necessities which, like subterranean earthquakes, have been at work in the pathway of my inquiry hitherto. Moreover, the Marburg period offered an intimate experience of a Protestant Christianity – all of which as what had to be overcome from the ground up, but not destroyed. ... It is not proper to speak of these most inward confrontations, since they do not revolve around issues that concern the dogma of Christianity and articles of faith, but rather only around the sole question: whether or not the god is fleeing from us and whether we ourselves are still truly – and that means as those who create – experiencing this. ... And this has nothing to do with a mere "religious" background of philosophy, but rather with the sole inquiry into the truth of being, which alone decides on the "time" and "place" that is historically preserved for us within the history of the Occident and its gods.   (M 368 = GA 66: 415–16, trans. mod.)

From "My Pathway Hitherto", an appendix to *Mindfulness*.

1938–9 The gods do not create humans; neither do humans invent the gods. The truth of beyng decides "on" both, not by ruling over them, but rather by appropriatively occurring between them such that they themselves first come into an en-counter.
          (M 208 = GA 66: 235, trans. mod.)

From *Mindfulness*.

1939–40 Hölderlin names nature the holy because she is "older than the ages and above the gods." Thus holiness is in no way a property borrowed from a determinate god. The holy is not holy because it is divine; rather the divine is divine because in its way it is "holy" ...
... In its coming, the holy, "older than the ages" and "above the gods," grounds another beginning of another history. The holy primordially decides in advance concerning humans and gods, whether they are, and who they are, and how they are, and when they are.   (EHP 82, 97–8 = EHD 59, 76)

From Heidegger's essay on Hölderlin's poem "As When On a Holiday..."

1942–3 The Greeks neither humanized the gods nor divinized humans; quite to the contrary, they experienced the gods and humans in their distinct essence, and in their reciprocal relation, on the basis of the essence of being in the sense of self-disclosing emergence, i.e., in the sense of looking and pointing. ... The fundamental essence of Greek divinities, in distinction to all others, even the Christian God, consists in their origination out of the "presence" of "present" being. And that is also the reason why the strife between the "new," i.e., the Olympian, gods and the "old" ones is the battle, occurring in the essence of being, that determines the upsurge of being itself into the emergence of its essence. This essential nexus is the reason the Greek gods, just like humans, are powerless before destiny and against it. *Moira* holds sway over the gods and humans, whereas in Christian thought, e.g., all destiny is the work of the divine "providence" of the creator and redeemer, who as creator also dominates and calculates all beings as the created. And so Leibniz can still say: *cum Deus calculat, fit mundus* – "because and while God calculates, the world arises." The Greek gods are not "personalities" or "persons" that dominate being; they are being itself looking into beings. But because being always and everywhere infinitely exceeds all beings and juts forth in beings, therefore where the essence of being has come originarily into the unconcealed, as is the case with the Greeks, the gods are more "excessive" or, spoken in the Christian and modern way, more "ethereal" and more "spiritual," despite their "human qualities." ... Whereas the low-German word *"Got"* signifies, according to its Indo-European root, a being humans invoke and hence is the invoked one, the Greek names for what we call "God" [*Gott*] express something essentially different: *theos–theaon* and *daimon–daion* mean the self-emergent looking one and being as entering into beings. Here God and the gods, already by the very name, are not seen from the standpoint of humans, as invoked by humans. ... Yet the name and the designation of the divinity (*theion*) as the looking one and the one who shines into (*theaon*) is not a mere vocal expression. The name as the first word lets what is designated appear in its primordial presence. The essence of humans, as experienced by the Greeks, is determined on the basis of their relation to self-emergent being, so that humans are the ones who have the word. And the word is in essence the letting appear of being by naming. ... And it is therefore that humans in the Greek experience, and only they, are in their essence and according to the essence of *alētheia* the god-sayers. ... But what if precisely this essence of *alētheia*, and with it the primordial self-manifesting essence of being, are distorted by transformations and because of such

249

distortion are ultimately prey to concealment in the sense of oblivion? ... If the originary divinity emerges on the basis of the essence of being, should the oblivion of being not be the ground for the fact that the origin of the truth of being has withdrawn itself into concealedness ever since, and no god could then appear emerging out of being itself? ... "A-theism" correctly understood as the absence of the gods, has been, since the decline of the Greek world, the oblivion of being that has overpowered the history of the West as the basic feature of this history itself. ... Only when being and the essence of truth come into recollection out of oblivion will Western humanity secure the most preliminary precondition for what is the most preliminary of all that is preliminary: that is, an experience of the essence of being as the domain in which a decision about the gods or the absence of the gods can first be prepared. ...

... If Parmenides names the goddess *Alētheia* at the very outset of his utterance, that is not, as philologists maintain, a kind of poetically fashionable introduction to his so-called "didactic poem," but instead it is the naming of the essential place, where the thinker as thinker dwells. The place is *daimonios topos*.

(*PRM* 110–13, 127 = GA 54: 163–7, 188, trans. mod.)

From a lecture course entitled *Parmenides and Heraclitus* (published in the *Gesamtausgabe* as *Parmenides*).

1943 So long as we understand the word "God is Dead" [in Nietzsche's *Gay Science*, §125] only as a formula of unbelief, we are thinking it theologically in the manner of apologetics, and we are renouncing all claims to what matters to Nietzsche, i.e., to the reflection that ponders what has already happened regarding the truth of the suprasensory world and regarding its relation to the human essence. ... Hence, also, nihilism in Nietzsche's sense in no way coincides with the situation conceived merely negatively, that the Christian God of biblical revelation can no longer be believed in, just as Nietzsche does not consider the Christian life that existed once for a short time before the writing down of the Gospels and before the missionary propaganda of Paul to belong to Christendom. Christendom for Nietzsche is the historical, world-political phenomenon of the Church and its claim to power within

250

the shaping of Western humanity and its modern culture. Christendom [*Christentum*] in this sense and the Christianity [*Christlichkeit*] of the New Testament faith are not the same. Even a non-Christian life can affirm Christendom and use it as a means of power, just as, conversely, a Christian life does not necessarily require Christendom. Therefore, a confrontation with Christendom is absolutely not in any way an attack against what is Christian, any more than a critique of theology is necessarily a critique of faith, whose interpretation theology is said to be. ... In the word "God is dead" the name "God," thought essentially, stands for the suprasensory world of those ideals which contain the goal that exists beyond earthly life for that life and that, accordingly, determines life from above, and also in a certain way, from without. ... The realm for the essence and the coming-to-pass of nihilism is metaphysics itself .... Metaphysics is history's open space wherein it becomes a destining that the suprasensory world, the Ideas, God, the moral law, the authority of reason, progress, the happiness of the greatest number, culture, civilization, suffer the loss of constructive force and become void. ... Unbelief in the sense of a falling away from the Christian doctrine of faith is, therefore, never the essence of and the ground, but always only a consequence, of nihilism; for it could be that Christendom itself represents one consequence and bodying-forth of nihilism. ...

... The ultimate blow against God and against the suprasensory world consists in the fact that God, the first of beings [*das Seiende des Seienden*], is degraded to the highest value. The heaviest blow against God is not that God is held to be unknowable, not that God's existence is demonstrated to be unprovable, but rather that the god held to be real is elevated to the highest value. For this blow comes precisely not from those who are standing about, who do not believe in God, but from the believers and their theologians who discourse on the being that is of all beings most in being [*vom Seiendsten alles Seienden*], without ever letting it occur to them to think on being [*Sein*] itself, in order thereby to become aware that, seen from out of faith, their thinking and their talking is sheer blasphemy if it meddles in the theology of faith. ... The pronouncement ["God is dead"] does not mean – as though it were spoken out of denial and common hatred – there is no god. The pronouncement means something worse: God has been killed. ...

... The uprising of human being into subjectivity transforms that which is into object. But that which is objective is that which is brought to a stand through representing. The doing away with that which is in itself, i.e., the killing of God, is accomplished in the making secure of the constant reserve by means of which humans make secure for themselves material, bodily, psychic, and spiritual resources, and this for the sake of their own security, which wills dominion over whatever is – as the potentially objective – in order to correspond to the being of whatever is, to the will to power. ...

... Perhaps we will no longer pass by so quickly without hearing what is said at the beginning of the passage [from Nietzsche's *Gay Science*] that has been elucidated: that the madman "cried incessantly: I seek God! I seek God!" ... And the ear of our thinking, does it still not hear the cry? (*QCT* 63–5, 105, 107, 111–12 = GA 5: 219–21, 259–60, 262, 266–7, trans. mod.)

From "The Word of Nietzsche: 'God is Dead'".

1943 By using the word "gods" sparingly, and hesitating to say the name, the poet has brought to light the proper element of the gods ...

... The holy does indeed appear. But the god remains distant. ... However, since the find is near, although in a reserved manner, the absent god extends his greeting in the nearing of the heavenly ones. Thereby the "god's absence" is also not a deficiency. Therefore, the countrymen, too, may not try to make themselves a god by cunning, and thus eliminate by force the presumed deficiency. But they must also not comfort themselves by merely calling on an accustomed god. True, on such paths the presence of the absence would go unnoticed. But if the nearness were not determined by the absence, and thus were not a reserving nearness, the precious find could not be near in the way in which it is near. Thus for the poet's care there is only one possibility: without fear of appearing godless, he must remain near to the god's absence, and wait long enough in this prepared nearness to the absence till out of the nearness to the absent god there is granted an originative word to name the high one. (*EHP* 39, 46–7 = *EHD* 20, 27–8)

From Heidegger's essay on Hölderlin's poem, "Homecoming/To Kindred Ones".

252

1944–5 SCIENTIST: The transition out of the will into releasement
[*Gelassenheit*] is what seems to me to be the genuine difficulty.
... GUIDE: And all the more so, when for us the essence of
releasement is still concealed. ... SCHOLAR: And this above all
as a result of the fact that even releasement can be thought of
still within the domain of the will, as happens with old masters
of thought such as Meister Eckhart. ... GUIDE: From whom,
all the same, many good things can be learned. ... SCHOLAR:
Certainly; but what we are calling releasement evidently does
not mean the casting off of sinful selfishness and the letting
go of self-will in favor of the divine will.

(GA 77: 109; see also *DT* 61–2 = G 33–4)

From *Country Path Conversations*.

1947 "Being" – that is not God and not a cosmic ground. Being
is essentially farther than all beings and is yet nearer to the
human being than every being, be it a rock, a beast, a work of
art, a machine, be it an angel or God. ...
    ... [The] holy, which alone is the essential sphere of divinity,
which in turn alone affords a dimension for the gods and for
the god, comes to radiate only when being itself beforehand
and after extensive preparation has been cleared and is experienced in its truth. ...
    ... The statement that the essence of human being consists
in being-in-the-world likewise contains no decision about
whether the human being in a theologico-metaphysical
sense is merely a this-worldly or an other-worldly creature.
... With the existential determination of the essence of the
human being, therefore, nothing is decided about the "existence of God" or his "non-being," no more than about the
possibility or impossibility of gods. ... Only from the truth of
being can the essence of the holy be thought. Only from the
essence of the holy is the essence of divinity to be thought.
Only in the light of the essence of divinity can it be thought
or said what the word "God" is to signify. ... Perhaps what
is distinctive about this world-epoch consists in the closure
of the dimension of the hale [*des Heilen*]. Perhaps this is the
sole malignancy [*Unheil*]. ... But with this reference thinking that points toward the truth of being as what is to be
thought has in no way decided in favor of theism. It can be
theistic just as little as atheistic. Not, however, because of

an indifferent attitude, but out of respect for the boundaries that have been set for thinking as such, indeed set by what gives itself to thinking as what is to be thought, by the truth of being.

(*PM* 252, 258, 266–7 = *GA* 9: 331, 338–9, 350–52)

From "Letter on Humanism".

1950 The default of God and the divinities is absence. But absence is not nothing; rather it is precisely the presence, which must first be appropriated, of the hidden fullness and wealth of what has been and what, thus gathered, is presencing, of the divine in the world of the Greeks, in prophetic Judaism, in the preaching of Jesus. This no-longer is in itself a not-yet of the veiled arrival of its inexhaustible nature.

(*PLT* 182 = *VA* 177)

From "The Thing".

1953 I [Hermann Noack] remarked that [certain] statements [from the "Introduction" to "What is Metaphysics?" and from the "Letter on Humanism"] encourage the interpretation that Heidegger's thinking moves in a dimension which alone makes room for doing genuine theological "thinking" once again – inasmuch as theology at a very early stage fell under the spell of "metaphysics," which is inappropriate for speaking about the truth of revelation. Heidegger did not contest this, but he literally said: "Within thinking nothing can be achieved which would be a preparation or a confirmation for that which occurs in faith and in grace. Were I so addressed by faith I would have to close up my shop. – Within faithfulness one still thinks, of course; but thinking as such no longer has a task." "Philosophy engages in a kind of thinking of which man is capable on his own. This stops when he is addressed by revelation." "Today thinking has taken the most tentative form imaginable." … Theologians, Heidegger continued, have simply too little trust in their own standpoint and have too much to do with philosophy. The impetus from the side of thinking can only be an indirect one. Theologians should abide in the exclusiveness of revelation. For Luther … there was no question of the "claim" (of philosophy). For him Paul's Epistle to the Romans was a revelation from the start; there

254

he heard the word of God. When a thinker listens to a poet like Hölderlin there is something completely different – a listening in another region of "manifestness," the founding of which, in contrast to the already decided revelation of the word of God, the poet himself essentially participates in. The thinker speaks of the "manifestness of being"; but "being" is an untheological word. ... The Christian experience is so completely different that it has no need to enter into competition with philosophy. When theology holds fast to the view that philosophy is foolishness, the mystery-character of revelation will be much better preserved. Therefore, in the face of a final decision, the ways part. ... With respect to the text referred to from the "Letter on Humanism," what is being discussed there is the god of the poet, not the revealed God. ...

... Thinking knows nothing of a "revealed God" and cannot recognize in the Christian proclamation any "historical destining disclosure of being" because the content of revelation consists in statements about "a being" (God as creator and lord of the world). Therefore the "foolishness" of which Paul speaks may be said to be reciprocal for faith and thinking.

(*PT* 64–5, 68)

From "Conversation with Martin Heidegger, Recorded by Hermann Noack". The conversation took place at the Protestant Academy of Hofgeismar.

1954   The divinities are the beckoning messengers of the godhead. Out of the holy sway of the godhead, the god appears in his presence or withdraws into his concealment. When we speak of the divinities, we are already thinking of the other three [members of the fourfold, i.e., earth, sky, and mortals] along with them, but we give no thought to the simple oneness of the four. ... Mortals dwell in that they await the divinities as divinities. In hope they hold up to the divinities what is unhoped for. They wait for intimations of their coming and do not mistake the signs of their absence. They do not make their gods for themselves and do not worship idols. In the very depth of misfortune they wait for the weal that has been withdrawn.   (*PLT* 147–8 = *VA* 144–5)

From "Building Dwelling Thinking".

255

1955–6 [The] most extreme sharpness and depth of thought belong to genuine and great mysticism. ... Meister Eckhart gives proof of this. (*PR* 36–7 = *SG* 71, trans. mod.)

From a lecture course published as *The Principle of Reason*.

1957 Humans can neither pray nor sacrifice to this god [of philosophy]. Before the *causa sui*, humans can neither fall to their knees in awe nor can they play music and dance before this god. ... The god-less thinking which must abandon the god of philosophy, the god as *causa sui*, is thus perhaps closer to the divine god. Here this means only: god-less thinking is more open to him [*freier für ihn*] than onto-theo-logic would like to admit. (*IDS* 72 = *ID* 140–41, trans. mod.)

From "The Onto-theo-logical Constitution of Metaphysics".

1959 Without this theological background I should never have come on the path of thinking. But origin always comes to meet us from the future. (*OWL* 10 = *GA* 12: 91.)

From "A Dialogue on Language between a Japanese and an Inquirer".

1963 With an almost passionate determination, Heidegger then wants to know what the monk [Bikkhu Maha Mani] takes religion to be. Dogmas and doctrines? Or what constitutes their origin? Then he turns to me [H. W. Petzet] and says, "Now you must really try to make clear the difference between Christianity and being Christian (*Christlichkeit*)" – which turns out to be a difficult matter. But a further explanation is not necessary because the monk says quite simply that by religion he understands the teachings of the founders ("sayings of the founders"). ... Excited and very determined, Heidegger responds by turning to me and saying, "Tell him that I consider one thing alone to be crucial – namely, to follow the words of the founder. This alone – neither systems nor doctrines and dogmas are important. *Religion means following*." ...
    ... [The monk asks,] Why does Heidegger never go to the people? ... Heidegger is noticeably affected. He tries to explain that it has primarily to do with the development of thinking, which was addressed earlier in various ways – namely, with how the predisposition of thinking he described makes

people lose their openness to simple hearing (and listening). For instance, if he spoke to Catholics, Catholicism as such would stand in the way (though there are always individuals who, exceptionally, could suddenly be affected). Even the best theologians, Catholic as well as Protestant, take from what he says only what fits their own views. Even they refuse to see the whole of his thinking, of what he says.

(Petzet 1993: 176–7, 179; see *GA* 16: 589–93)

From Heinrich Wiegand Petzet's notes on a conversation held with a Buddhist monk from Thailand.

1964 For in truth this would necessitate that theology once and for all get clear about the requisite of its major task not to borrow the categories of its thinking and the form of its speech from philosophy or the sciences, but to think and speak out of faith for faith with fidelity to its subject matter. ...

... [The] task is for theology to place in discussion, within its own realm of the Christian faith and out of the proper nature of that faith, what theology has to think and how it has to speak. This task includes the question whether theology can still be a science – because presumably it should not be a science at all. (*PM* 55, 61 = *GA* 9: 69, 77)

From "The Theological Discussion of 'The Problem of a Nonobjectifying Thinking and Speaking in Today's Theology' – Some Pointers to Its Major Aspects".

1966 [P]hilosophy will not be able to effect an immediate transformation of the present condition of the world. This is not only true of philosophy, but of all merely human thought and endeavor. Only a god can save us. The sole possibility that is left for us is to prepare a sort of readiness, through thinking and poetizing, for the appearance of the god or for the absence of the god in the time of foundering [*Untergang*]; for in the face of the god who is absent, we founder. ... [The interviewer then asks: "Is there a connection between your thinking and the emergence of this god? Is there in your view a causal connection? Do you think that we can think the god into being here with us?" Heidegger responds:] We cannot think him into being here; we can at most awaken the readiness of expectation. [The interviewer asks: "But are we able to

257

help?" Heidegger responds:] The preparation of a readiness may be the first step. The world cannot be what it is or the way that it is through humans, but neither can it be without humans. According to my view, this is connected with the fact that what I name with the word being ... requires humans for its revelation, preservation, and formation.

(OG 107 = GA 16: 671–2, trans. mod.)

Statements Heidegger made in his interview with the magazine *Der Spiegel*.

1968 [The] poet belongs to the task for which he is needed. For the poet's saying is needed – showing, veiling–unveiling – to allow the appearance of the advent of the gods, who need the poet's words for their appearance, because only in their appearing are they themselves. ... *The* poem, Hölderlin's poem, gathers poesis under a holy compulsion: naming the present gods, gathering them into a saying which is needed by the heavenly ones and ordained by them.   (*EHP* 218–19 = *EHD* 191–2)

From "The Poem".

At the conclusion of his intellectual biography, Rüdiger Safranski writes:

Did Heidegger return to the bosom of the Church? Max Müller reports that, on hikes, whenever they came to a church or a chapel, Heidegger always dipped his finger in the stoup and genuflected. On one occasion he asked him if this was not inconsistent, since he had distanced himself from the dogma of the Church. Heidegger's answer had been: "One must think historically. And where there has been so much praying, there the divine is present in a very special way".   (Safranski 1998: 432–3)

Shortly before he passed away in 1976, Heidegger requested that he be given a Catholic funeral ceremony in Freiburg, that his theologian friend Bernhard Welte speak at his interment in Messkirch, and that passages he had selected from Hölderlin's poetry also be read at his graveside (see Heidegger & Welte 2003: 124–36). It was also apparently Heidegger's wish that his gravestone be marked with a star, rather than a cross.

Note

1. The reader should bear in mind that all nouns, and not just proper nouns, are capitalized in German. Hence *das Sein* can be translated as "Being", although it is most often today translated as "being" in order to avoid connotations of a metaphysical entity. Translators tend to render *der Gott* as "the god", but generally use the capital when the term *Gott* (God) is used as a proper noun without an article, as it is in the monotheistic traditions. In several instances, the use of capitals in the texts reproduced here has been silently modified for the sake of consistency.

References

Heidegger, M. & B. Welte 2003. *Briefe und Begegnungen*, A. Denker & H. Zaborowski (eds). Stuttgart: Klett-Cotta.

Kisiel, T. 1993. *The Genesis of Heidegger's Being and Time*. Berkeley, CA: University of California Press.

Ott, H. 1993. *Martin Heidegger: A Political Life*, A. Blunden (trans.). New York: Basic Books.

Petzet, H. W. 1993. *Encounters and Dialogues with Martin Heidegger: 1929–1976*, P. Emad & K. Maly (trans.). Chicago, IL: University of Chicago Press.

Safranski, R. 1998. *Martin Heidegger: Between Good and Evil*, E. Osers. (trans.). Cambridge, MA: Harvard University Press.

Further reading

Primary sources

In addition to the primary sources listed at the end of Chapter 16, see Heidegger's *Elucidations of Hölderlin's Poetry*; *Mindfulness*, pt XVII; *The Piety of Thinking*; "The Word of Nietzsche: 'God is Dead'", in *The Question Concerning Technology*, 53–112; and *Becoming Heidegger: On the Trail of His Early Occasional Writings, 1910–1927*, chs 1, 2, 5, 9, 10, 11, 12, 15.

Secondary sources

In addition to the secondary sources listed at the end of Chapter 16, see Hanley (2000); Hemming (2002); Kisiel (1993: chs 2, 4); Ott (1993: pt 2); Perotti (1974); Prudhomme (1997); and Van Buren (1994: chs 6, 8, 14). See also N. Fischer & F.-W. von Hermann (eds), *Heidegger und die christliche Tradition* (Hamburg: Felix Meiner, 2007) and W. J. Richardson, "Heidegger and God – and Professor Jonas", *Thought* **40** (1965), 13–40.

Chronology of Heidegger's life

1889[1]   Born on 26 September in Messkirch, a small, predominantly Catholic town in south-west Germany, as the son of Friedrich Heidegger (1852–1924), master cooper and sexton of St Martin's Church, and Johanna Kempf Heidegger (1858–1927).

1895–1903 Attends public schools in Messkirch. Grows up in the sexton's house on the church square; Heidegger later recalls running errands for the priest and ringing the bells in the church tower.

1903–6   Studies on a scholarship at the public Gymnasium in Constance, while residing at a Catholic seminary in preparation for the priesthood.

1906–9   Continues his studies at the public Berthold Gymnasium in Freiburg, residing at the Gsymnasium Seminary. In 1907 receives a copy of Franz Brentano's *On the Manifold Meaning of Being According to Aristotle*. In 1908 reads *On Being: Outline of Ontology* by the speculative theologian Carl Braig. On 13 July 1909 passes his Gymnasium exit examination (*Abitur*) with the highest possible overall grade.

1909–11 In autumn 1909 Heidegger begins a trial period at the Jesuit novitiate in Tisis, Austria, but is dismissed after two weeks on account of health problems. Studies theology and philosophy at the University of Freiburg, residing at the Theological Seminary. Publishes poems, book reviews and articles in anti-modernist Catholic periodicals. Begins study of Husserl and Dilthey.

1911–13 In February 1911 Heidegger breaks off his training for the priesthood and his studies in theology, again on account of health problems (a psychosomatic "nerve and heart condition"). After returning to the university from a period of convalescence in Messkirch, Heidegger redirects his studies, eventually concentrating on philosophy, while also taking courses in mathematics, the natural sciences and the humanities. In 1912 he publishes his first academic philosophical article, "The Problem of Reality in Modern Philosophy" (in *SUP = BH = GA* 1). In 1913 he obtains his doctorate in philosophy, *summa cum laude*, under the direction of Arthur Schneider, with a

260

dissertation entitled *The Doctrine of Judgment in Psychologism* (in GA 1).

1913–18 Initially volunteers for, and is later conscripted into, military service several times, but owing to his health problems is discharged or is enlisted in a limited capacity for postal censorship and meteorological service.

1915 Achieves Habilitation (postdoctoral degree) and *venia legendi* (licence to teach in German universities), under the direction of Heinrich Rickert, with a dissertation entitled *The Doctrine of Categories and Meaning in Duns Scotus* (in GA 1). Begins teaching career as a lecturer (*Privatdozent*) at the University of Freiburg.

1917–18 Marries Elfride Petri on 21 March 1917 with a Catholic ceremony in Freiburg; a week later the couple marry again with a Protestant ceremony in Mannheim in the company of Elfride's family. Around this time Heidegger effectively converts to a non-dogmatic Protestantism ("free Christianity"). In 1919 he announces his "break with the *system* of Catholicism", yet as late as 1921 he still refers to himself as a "Christian theo*logian*". By 1922, however, he begins to sharply separate philosophy – and himself as a philosopher – from faith and theology. Heidegger's complex relation to Christianity and his thoughts on divinity continue to evolve throughout his career (see Chapters 16 and 17).

1919–23 Lectures on phenomenology, Neo-Kantianism, Aristotle and the philosophy of religion as Husserl's assistant. Students during this time include Oskar Becker, Karl Löwith and Leo Strauss. Friendship with Elisabeth Blochmann develops.

1919 Birth of his first son, Jörg. Gives his "breakthrough" lecture course, "The Idea of Philosophy and the Problem of Worldview" (in *TDP = GA 56/57*).

1920 Friendship with Karl Jaspers begins. Birth of his second son, Hermann. In 2005 Hermann Heidegger acknowledged that in 1934 he was informed that Martin Heidegger – whom he characterized in 1999 as a "loving and understanding father and grandfather" (*GA 16: 835*) – was not his biological father. The latter was in fact his godfather, Dr Friedel Caesar, a friend of his mother's from her youth (*LW 317*).

1922–3 Elfride presents her husband with a cabin in the Black Forest mountain village of Todtnauberg, which for the rest of his life Heidegger uses as a retreat from city life and as an undisturbed place to think and write. Heidegger's fame as a lecturer spreads across Germany among university students. Although he had not published anything since his Habilitation thesis, on the basis of a strong recommendation from Husserl and a high regard for his phenomenological interpretations of Aristotle on the part of Paul Natorp and others, Heidegger is appointed associate professor of philosophy at the University of Marburg, where he befriends the Protestant theologian Rudolf Bultmann.

1924 Begins a love affair with a student (and later famous philosopher in her own right), Hannah Arendt. Other students during his Marburg period include Hans-Georg Gadamer, Hans Jonas and Miki Kiyoshi. Father dies. The first article to be written on Heidegger's thought, "A New Turn in Phenomenology: Heidegger's Phenomenology of Life", is published in Japan by Tanabe Hajime after his return from Freiburg.

1927   Heidegger's first magnum opus, *Being and Time* (*BT* = *BTS* = *SZ* = *GA* 2), is published, and his fame rapidly escalates. Promoted to professor in Marburg. Gives lecture course, "The Basic Problems of Phenomenology" (later published as *BPP* = *GA* 24). Mother dies.

1928   Appointed professor of philosophy at the University of Freiburg as Husserl's successor. Students attending Heidegger's lectures at this time include Eugen Fink, Emmanuel Levinas, Herbert Marcuse, Max Müller, Jan Patočka and Karl Rahner.

1929   Presents inaugural lecture, "What is Metaphysics?" (in *BW* and *PM* = *GA* 9). Debates with Ernst Cassirer over Kant and Neo-Kantianism, and publishes *Kant and the Problem of Metaphysics* (*KPM* = *GA* 3).

1930   Declines first offer of professorship at the University of Berlin. Gives first version of lecture, "On the Essence of Truth" (final 1943 version in *BW* and *PM* = *GA* 9).

1933   Elected rector of the University of Freiburg on 21 April. On 1 May becomes a member of the Nazi Party, and on 27 May gives his Rectorial Address, "The Self-Assertion of the German University" (*SU* = *R*; *GA* 16: 107–17). In the summer Heidegger delivers lectures in Leipzig, Heidelberg and Tübingen in support of the National Socialist revolution and makes a number of pronouncements in support of Hitler and his policies. Writes letters in support of some Jewish academics and in denunciation of others. Declines a second offer from Berlin as well as one from Munich. The first book to be written on Heidegger's thought, *The Philosophy of Heidegger*, is published in Japan by Kuki Shūzō, who had studied with Heidegger in Freiburg and Marburg, and who had introduced his thought to Jean-Paul Sartre in Paris.

1934   Owing to disagreements with the faculty and with government and party authorities, resigns as rector on 23 April. Works on plans for a *Dozentenakademie* (academy for university lecturers) in Berlin. Gives first lecture course on Hölderlin's poetry (*GA* 39).

1935   Gives lecture course later published as *Introduction to Metaphysics* (*IM* = *EM* = *GA* 40), as well as the first version of his famous lecture on art later published as "The Origin of the Work of Art" (in *BW*; *PLT*; *OBT* = *GA* 5).

1936   Travels to Rome in April to give the lectures "Hölderlin and the Essence of Poetry" and "Europe and German Philosophy". Meets there with Karl Löwith, who reports that Heidegger was still wearing the swastika, that he still believed in persevering for the sake of the true potential of the National Socialist movement, and that he acknowledged a connection between his philosophical idea of "historicity" and his political "service".

1936–40 In 1936 lectures on Schelling (*ST* = *SA*). In 1936–8 writes what many consider to be his second magnum opus, *Contributions to Philosophy* (*CP* = *GA* 65), the first of a series of manuscripts kept private but intended for later publication. Between 1936 and 1940 gives extensive lecture courses on Nietzsche, later edited and published together with several essays in two volumes as *Nietzsche* (*N1*, *N2*, *N3*, *N4*; *NI*, *NII*). In his private manuscripts and public lecture courses during this time, Heidegger criticizes the will to power and technological machination, as well as the biological racism exemplified by National

Socialism. He is put under surveillance by the Gestapo. The Kyoto School philosopher Nishitani Keiji studies with Heidegger between 1937 and 1939.

1941–3 Lectures on "fundamental concepts" (*BC* = *GA* 51), on Hölderlin (*GA* 52; *HHI* = *GA* 53), on Parmenides (*PRM* = *GA* 54), and on Heraclitus (*GA* 55).

1944–5 Drafted for a time in 1944 into the People's Militia (*Volkssturm*). In January of 1945 goes to Messkirch in order to securely store his manuscripts. In April evacuates with the Philosophy Faculty of the University of Freiburg to Wildenstein Castle, near Beuron, Danube Valley. First edition of *Elucidations of Hölderlin's Poetry* is published in 1944; expanded editions appear in 1951, 1971 and 1996 (*EHP* = *EHD* = *GA* 4). Writes *Country Path Conversations* (*CPC* = *GA* 77).

1945–6 Brought before the denazification committee in July 1945. Jaspers writes a critical letter of expert opinion, which contributes to the decision to ban Heidegger from teaching. (The ban is lifted in 1949.) Suffers a nervous breakdown and recovers for three weeks in a sanatorium. A correspondence with Sartre is initiated by philosophically interested French occupation officers. Friendship with Jean Beaufret begins, which engenders the first publication of a comprehensive statement of Heidegger's later thought, "Letter on Humanism" (in *BW* and *PM* = *GA* 9). Works on a German translation of the *Daodejing* with Paul Shih-yi Hsiao.

1949 Delivers four seminal lectures in Bremen ("The Thing", "The Enframing", "The Danger", "The Turning") under the collective title "Insight Into That Which Is" (in *GA* 79; see relevant essays in *PLT* and *QCT*). Correspondence with Jaspers resumes. Heidegger's older son, Jörg, returns home after being released from a prisoner-of-war camp in Russia; his younger son, Hermann, who had also been taken captive on the Russian front during the war, had been released in 1947.

1950 Publishes a collection of essays under the title *Holzwege* (Wood paths) (*OBT* = *GA* 5). Arendt visits and friendship is renewed.

1951–2 Emeritus status granted. Resumes his university lectures with a course published as *What Calls for Thinking?* (*WCT* = *WhD*). Students at this time include Harmut Buchner, Rainer Marten and Ernst Tugendhat. In Darmstadt gives lecture "Building Dwelling Thinking" (in *BW*; *VA*).

1953 In Munich gives lecture "The Question Concerning Technology" (in *QCT; BW; VA*). Meets D. T. Suzuki. Beginning of friendship with Erhart Kästner.

1954 Publishes *Vorträge und Aufsätze* (Lectures and essays) (*VA*). Tezuka Tomio visits, occasioning the composition of "A Dialogue on Language between a Japanese and an Inquirer" (in *OWL* = *GA* 12).

1955 In Messkirch gives his memorial address for the composer Conradin Kreutzer (entitled *"Gelassenheit"* in German, in *DT* = *G* and *GA* 13). In Cérisy-la-Salle, France, gives lecture "What is Philosophy?" (*WP*). Writes "On the Question of Being" (in *PM* = *GA* 9), addressed to Ernst Jünger on his sixtieth birthday. Gives final lecture course at the University of Freiburg, published as *The Principle of Reason* (*PR* = *SG*).

1957 Lectures in Provence, France, where he makes the acquaintance of poet René Char. Inducted into the Berlin Academy of Arts as well as into

MARTIN HEIDEGGER: KEY CONCEPTS

the Heidelberg Academy of Sciences. Publishes *Identity and Difference* (*IDS* = *ID*).

1958 Participates in a colloquium on "Art and Thinking" with the Zen thinker Hisamatsu Shinichi (*GA* 16: 552–7; see also 776–80).

1959 Named honorary citizen of Messkirch on 27 September. Publishes *On the Way to Language* (*OWL* = *GA* 12) and *Gelassenheit* (translated as *Discourse on Thinking*) (*DT* = *G*). Gives first of a series of Zollikon Seminars with the psychiatrist Medard Boss, which continue to be held regularly until 1966 (the records of which were later published in *ZS* = *Z*). Visits exhibit of Paul Klee's paintings and drawings in Basel with art historian friend Heinrich Wiegand Petzet, and in response considers writing a second part to "The Origin of the Work of Art".

1962 Travels for the first time to Greece (travel reflections published as *SJG*). Subsequent trips are made in 1964, 1966 and 1967.

1963 The first comprehensive studies of Heidegger's thought appear in German and in English: Otto Pöggeler's *Der Denkweg Martin Heideggers* and William Richardson's *Heidegger: Through Phenomenology to Thought*. The latter includes a preface by Heidegger in which he discusses the alleged turn in his thinking (*PMH*). Meets with Bikkhu Maha Mani, a Buddhist monk from Thailand (see *GA* 16: 589–93).

1964 In Paris gives lecture, "The End of Philosophy and the Task of Thinking" (in *BW* and *TB* = *ZSD*). The first conference on Heidegger's thought in North America is held at Drew University; subsequent symposia, also encouraged by letters from Heidegger, are organized at DePaul University and Duquesne University in 1966; in 1967 the Heidegger Circle is formed, with its first annual meeting convened at Penn State University.

1966 Gives the first of a series of seminars with a group of French philosophers in Le Thor, France (in *FS; GA* 15). Gives an interview to the magazine *Der Spiegel,* under agreement that it will not be published until after his death (*OG* = *GA* 16: 652–83). Begins making plans for his *Collected Edition* (*Gesamtausgabe*).

1967 Publishes a selection of key essays from 1919 to 1958 under the title of *Wegmarken* (*Pathmarks*) (*PM* = *GA* 9). Meets for the first time with poet Paul Celan.

1969 Agreement made for the transfer of Heidegger's literary remains to the German Literature Archive in Marbach. Gives television interview to Richard Wisser (*MHC* = *GA* 16: 702–10). Celebration of Heidegger's eightieth birthday in Messkirch; keynote address given by Tsujimura Kōichi. Inducted into the Bavarian Academy of the Fine Arts.

1970 Suffers a minor stroke, but almost fully recovers. Begins to focus his attention on the arrangement of his manuscripts.

1975 The first volume (*GA* 24, translated as *BPP*) of his *Collected Edition* is published.

1976 Dies at home in Freiburg on 26 May and is buried on 28 May in his hometown of Messkirch.

Note

1. Sources consulted for the composition of this chronology include: *GA* 16; *LW*; G. Heidegger, "Life of Martin Heidegger", in *LW*; T. Kisiel & T. Sheehan, "Chronological Overview", in *BH*; J. Van Buren, "Chronological Overview", in *SUP*; Ott (1993); Petzet (1993); Safranski (1998); A. Denker, "Martin Heidegger (1889–1976): Chronology", www.freewebs.com/m3smg2/HeideggerChronology.html (accessed September 2009); M. Geier, *Martin Heidegger* (Reinbek bei Hamburg: Rowohlt, 2005); and R. Mehring & D. Thomä, "Eine Chronik", in *Heidegger Handbuch: Leben–Werk–Wirkung*, 515–39 (Stuttgart: Metzler, 2003).

Bibliography

Texts by Heidegger

"Art and Space", C. H. Seibert (trans.). *Man & World* 1 (1973): 3–8; written 1969.
Basic Concepts, G. E. Aylesworth (trans.) (Bloomington, IN: Indiana University Press, 1993); written 1941.
Basic Concepts of Ancient Philosophy, R. Rojcewicz (trans.) (Bloomington, IN: Indiana University Press, 2008); written 1926.
The Basic Problems of Phenomenology, A. Hofstadter (trans.) (Bloomington, IN: Indiana University Press, 1982); written 1927.
Basic Questions of Philosophy: Selected "Problems" of "Logic", R. Rojcewicz & A. Schuwer (trans.) (Bloomington, IN: Indiana University Press, 1984); written 1937–8.
Basic Writings, 2nd edn, D. F. Krell (ed.) (New York: Harper & Row, 1993); written 1927–64.
Becoming Heidegger: On the Trail of His Early Occasional Writings, 1910–1927, T. Kisiel & T. Sheehan (eds) (Evanston, IL: Northwestern University Press, 2007); written 1910–27.
Being and Time, J. Macquarrie & E. Robinson (trans.) (New York: Harper & Row, 1962); written 1927.
Being and Time, J. Stambaugh (trans.) (Albany, NY: SUNY Press, 1996); written 1927.
Contributions to Philosophy (From Enowning), P. Emad & K. Maley (trans.) (Bloomington, IN: Indiana University Press, 1999); written 1936–8.
Country Path Conversations, B. W. Davis (trans.) (Bloomington, IN: Indiana University Press, 2010); written 1944–5.
Discourse on Thinking, J. M. Anderson & E. H. Freund (trans.) (New York: Harper & Row, 1966); written 1944–55.
Early Greek Thinking, D. F. Krell & F. Capuzzi (trans.) (New York: Harper & Row, 1975); written 1943–54.
Einführung in die Metaphysik, 5th edn (Tübingen: Max Niemeyer, 1987); written 1935.

Elucidations of Hölderlin's Poetry, K. Hoeller (trans.) (New York: Humanity Books, 2000); written 1936–69.

The End of Philosophy, J. Stambaugh (trans.) (New York: Harper & Row, 1973); written 1941–6.

Erläuterungen zu Hölderlins Dichtung, 6th edn (Frankfurt: Vittorio Klostermann, 1996); written 1936–69.

The Essence of Human Freedom: An Introduction to Philosophy, T. Sadler (trans.) (London/New York: Continuum, 2002); written 1930.

The Essence of Reasons, T. Malick (trans.) (Evanston, IL: Northwestern University Press, 1969); written 1929.

The Essence of Truth: On Plato's Cave Allegory and Theaetetus, T. Sadler (trans.) (New York/London: Continuum, 2002); written 1931–2.

Four Seminars, A. Mitchell & F. Raffoul (trans.) (Bloomington, IN: Indiana University Press, 2003); written 1966–73.

The Fundamental Concepts of Metaphysics: World, Finitude, Solitude, W. McNeill & N. Walker (trans.) (Bloomington, IN: Indiana University Press, 1995); written 1929–30.

Gelassenheit, 10th edn (Pfullingen: Neske, 1992); written 1944–55.

Hegel's Phenomenology of Spirit, P. Emad & K. Maly (trans.) (Bloomington, IN: Indiana University Press, 1988); written 1930–31.

The Heidegger Controversy: A Critical Reader, R. Wolin (ed.) (Cambridge, MA: MIT Press, 1993).

The Heidegger Reader, G. Figal (ed.), J. Veith (trans.) (Bloomington, IN: Indiana University Press, 2009).

Heidegger Jahrbuch IV: Heidegger und National Sozialismus, A. Denker & H. Zaborowski (eds) (Freiburg: Alber, 2009).

"Die Herkunft der Kunst und die Bestimmung des Denkens". In *Distanz und Nähe: Reflexionen und Analysen zur Kunst der Gegenwart*, P. Jaeger & R. Lüthe (eds), 11–22 (Würzburg: Könighausen und Neumann, 1983); written 1967.

History of the Concept of Time: Prolegomena, T. Kisiel (trans.) (Bloomington, IN: Indiana University Press, 1985); written 1925.

Hölderlin's Hymn "The Ister", W. McNeil & J. Davis (trans.) (Bloomington, IN: Indiana University Press, 1996); written 1942.

Identität und Differenz, 11th edn (Stuttgart: Nesk, 1999); written 1956–7.

Identity and Difference, J. Stambaugh (trans.) (New York: Harper & Row, 1969); written 1956–7.

Introduction to Metaphysics, G. Fried & R. Polt (trans.) (New Haven, CT: Yale University Press, 2000); written 1935.

Introduction to Phenomenological Research, D. O. Dahlstrom (trans.) (Bloomington, IN: Indiana University Press, 2005); written 1923–4

Kant and the Problem of Metaphysics, 4th edn, enlarged, R. Taft (trans.) (Bloomington, IN: Indiana University Press, 1990); written 1929.

Letters to His Wife: 1915–1970, G. Heidegger (ed.), R. Glasgow (trans.) (Cambridge: Polity, 2008).

Martin Heidegger/Elisabeth Blochmann Briefwechsel 1918–69, J. Storck (ed.) (Marbach: Deutsche Schillergesellschaft, 1990).

Martin Heidegger/Karl Jaspers: Briefwechsel 1920–1963, W. Biemel & H. Saner (eds) (Frankfurt: Vittorio Klostermann, 1990).

Martin Heidegger and National Socialism: Questions and Answers, G. Neske & E. Kettering (eds), L. Harries (trans.) (New York: Paragon House, 1990).

"Mein liebes Seelchen!": Briefe Martin Heideggers an seine Frau Elfride 1915–1970, G. Heidegger (ed.) (Munich: Deutsche Verlags-Anstalt, 2005).

The Metaphysical Foundations of Logic, M. Heim (trans.) (Bloomington, IN: Indiana University Press, 1984); written 1928.

Mindfulness, P. Emad & T. Kalary (trans.) (London/New York: Continuum, 2006); written 1938–9.

Nietzsche: Erster Band, 5th edn (Pfullingen: Neske, 1989); written 1936–9.

Nietzsche: Zweiter Band, 5th edn (Pfullingen: Neske, 1989); written 1939–46.

Nietzsche: Vol. I, The Will to Power as Art, D. F. Krell (trans.) (New York: Harper & Row, 1979); written 1936–7.

Nietzsche: Vol. II, The Eternal Recurrence of the Same, D. F. Krell (trans.) (New York: Harper & Row, 1984); written 1937, 1953.

Nietzsche: Vol. III, The Will to Power as Knowledge and as Metaphysics, J. Stambaugh, D. F. Krell & F. A. Capuzzi (trans.) (New York: Harper & Row, 1987); written 1939–40.

Nietzsche: Vol. IV, Nihilism, D. F. Krell (ed.), F. A. Capuzzi (trans.) (New York: Harper & Row, 1982); written 1940–46.

"Nur noch ein Gott kann uns retten". Interview of 1966, published posthumously in *Der Spiegel* **23** (May 1976), 193–201. Reprinted in *GA* 16: 652–83.

"Of the Origin of the Work of Art (first elaboration)", M. Zisselsberger (trans.). *Epoché* **12**(2) (spring 2008): 329–47; written 1935.

Off the Beaten Track, J. Young & K. Haynes (ed. & trans.) (Cambridge: Cambridge University Press, 2002); written 1935–46.

On the Way to Language, P. D. Hertz (trans.) (New York: Harper & Row, 1971); written 1950–59.

Ontology: The Hermeneutics of Facticity, J. van Buren (trans.) (Bloomington, IN: Indiana University Press, 1999); written 1923.

Parmenides, A. Schuwer & R. Rojcewicz (trans.) (Bloomington, IN: Indiana University Press, 1992); written 1942–3.

Pathmarks, W. McNeill (ed.) (Cambridge: Cambridge University Press, 1998); written 1919–61.

Phenomenological Interpretations of Aristotle: Initiation into Phenomenological Research, R. Rojcewicz (trans.) (Bloomington, IN: Indiana University Press, 2001); written 1921–2.

The Phenomenology of Religious Life, M. Fritsch & J. A. Gosetti-Ferencei (trans.) (Bloomington, IN: Indiana University Press, 2004); written 1918–21.

The Piety of Thinking, J. G. Hart & J. C. Maraldo (trans., notes & comm.) (Bloomington, IN: Indiana University Press, 1976).

Poetry, Language, Thought, A. Hofstadter (trans.) (New York: HarperCollins, Perennial Classics edition, 2001); written 1936–54.

"Preface by Martin Heidegger". In William J. Richardson, *Heidegger: Through Phenomenology to Thought*, 4th edn (New York: Fordham University Press, 2003); written 1962.

The Principle of Reason, R. Lilly (trans.) (Bloomington, IN: Indiana University Press, 1991); written 1955–6.

The Question Concerning Technology and Other Essays, W. Lovitt (trans.) (New York: Harper & Row, 1977); written 1936–54.

Der Satz vom Grund, 7th edn (Pfullingen: Neske, 1992); written 1955–6.

Schellings Abhandlung Über das Wesen der menschlichen Freiheit (1809), 2nd edn (Tübingen: Max Niemeyer, 1995); written 1936, 1941–3.

Schelling's Treatise on the Essence of Human Freedom, J. Stambaugh (trans.) (Athens, OH: Ohio University Press, 1985); written 1936, 1941–43.

Sein und Zeit, 17th edn (Tübingen: Max Niemeyer, 1993); written 1927.

Die Selbstbehauptung der deutschen Universität: Das Rektorat 1933/34 (Frankfurt: Vittorio Klostermann, 1990); written 1933, 1945.

Sojourns: The Journey to Greece, J. Panteleimon Manoussakis (trans.) (Bloomington, IN: Indiana University Press, 2005); written 1962.

Supplements: From the Earliest Essays to Being and Time and Beyond, J. Van Buren (ed.) (Albany, NY: SUNY Press, 2002); written 1910–25.

On Time and Being, J. Stambaugh (trans.) (New York: Harper & Row, 1972); written 1962–4.

Towards the Definition of Philosophy, T. Sadler (trans.) (London: Athlone Press, 2000); written 1919.

"Unbenutzte Vorarbeiten zur Vorlesung vom Wintersemester 1929/1930: *Die Grundbegriffe der Metaphysik: Welt, Endlichkeit, Einsamkeit*". *Heidegger Studies* 7 (1991): 5–12; written 1929–30.

"Vom Ursprung des Kunstwerks: Erste Ausarbeitung", H. Heidegger (ed.). *Heidegger Studies* 5 (1989): 5–22; written 1935.

Vorträge und Aufsätze, 7th edn (Pfullingen: Neske, 1994); written 1936–53.

Was heißt Denken?, 4th edn (Tübingen: Max Niemeyer, 1984); written 1951–2.

What is Called Thinking?, J. Glenn Gray (trans.) (New York: Harper & Row, 1968); written 1951–2.

What is Philosophy?, W. Kluback & J. T. Wilde (trans.) (New Haven, CT: College and University Press, 1958); written 1955.

What is a Thing?, W. B. Barton Jr. & V. Deutsch (trans.) (Chicago, IL: Henry Regency Co., 1967); written 1935–6.

Zollikon Seminars: Protocols – Conversations – Letters, M. Boss (ed.), F. Mayr & R. Askay (trans.) (Evanston, IL: Northwestern University Press, 2001); written 1959–71.

Zollikoner Seminare: Protokolle – Zwiegespräche – Briefe, M. Boss (ed.) (Frankfurt: Vittorio Klostermann, 1987); written 1959–71.

Zur Sache des Denkens, 3rd edn (Tübingen: Max Niemeyer, 1988); written 1962–4.

The individual volumes cited from Heidegger's *Collected Edition, Gesamtausgabe* (Frankfurt: Vittorio Klostermann, 1975–), are as follows:

1   *Frühe Schriften* (written 1912–16)
2   *Sein und Zeit* (written 1927)
3   *Kant und das Problem der Metaphysik* (written 1929)
4   *Erläuterungen zu Hölderlins Dichtung* (written 1936–68)
5   *Holzwege* (written 1935–46)
7   *Vorträge und Aufsätze* (written 1936–53)
8   *Was heißt Denken?* (written 1951–2)
9   *Wegmarken* (written 1919–61)
10   *Der Satz vom Grund* (written 1955–6)
11   *Identität und Differenz* (written 1955–63)
12   *Unterwegs zur Sprache* (written 1950–59)
13   *Aus der Erfahrung des Denkens* (written 1910–76)
14   *Zur Sache des Denkens* (written 1962–4)
15   *Seminare* (written 1951–73)

16 *Reden und andere Zeugnisse eines Lebensweges* (written 1910–76)
18 *Grundbegriffe der aristotelischen Philosophie* (written 1924)
20 *Prolegomena zur Geschichte des Zeitbegriffs* (written 1925)
21 *Logik: Die Frage nach der Wahrheit* (written 1925–6)
22 *Die Grundbegriffe der antiken Philosophie* (written 1926)
24 *Die Grundprobleme der Phänomenologie* (written 1927)
26 *Metaphysische Anfangsgründe der Logik im Ausgang von Leibniz* (written 1928)
29/30 *Die Grundbegriffe der Metaphysik: Welt, Endlichkeit, Einsamkeit* (written 1929–30)
31 *Vom Wesen der menschlichen Freiheit: Einleitung in die Philosophie* (written 1930)
34 *Vom Wesen der Wahrheit: Zu Platons Höhlengleichnis und Theätet* (written 1931–2)
36/37 *Sein und Wahrheit* (written 1933–4)
38 *Logik als die Frage nach dem Wesen der Sprache* (written 1934)
39 *Hölderlins Hymnen "Germanien" und "Der Rhein"* (written 1934–5)
40 *Einführung in die Metaphysik* (written 1935)
41 *Die Frage nach dem Ding: Zu Kants Lehre von den transzendentalen Grundsätzen* (written 1935–6)
45 *Grundfragen der Philosophie: Ausgewählte "Probleme" der "Logik"* (written 1937–8)
46 *Zur Auslegung von Nietzsches II: Unzeitgemäßer Betrachtung "Vom Nutzen und Nachteil der Historie für das Leben"* (written 1938–9)
49 *Die Metaphysik des deutschen Idealismus: Zur erneuten Auslegung von Schelling: Philosophische Untersuchungen ueber das Wesen der menschlichen Freiheit und die damit zusammenhaengenden Gegenstaende (1809)* (written 1941)
51 *Grundbegriffe* (written 1941)
52 *Hölderlins Hymne "Andenken"* (written 1941–2)
53 *Hölderlins Hymne "Der Ister"* (written 1942)
54 *Parmenides* (written 1942–3)
55 *Heraklit* (written 1943–4)
56/57 *Zur Bestimmung der Philosophie* (written 1919)
60 *Phänomenologie des religiösen Lebens* (written 1918–21)
61 *Phänomenologische Interpretationen zu Aristoteles: Einführung in die phänomenologische Forschung* (written 1921–2)
62 *Phänomenologische Interpretationen ausgewählter Abhandlungen des Aristoteles zur Ontologie und Logik* (written 1922)
63 *Ontologie: Hermeneutik der Faktizität* (written 1923)
64 *Der Begriff der Zeit* (written 1923)
65 *Beiträge zur Philosophie (Vom Ereignis)* (written 1936–8)
66 *Besinnung* (written 1938–9)
67 *Metaphysik und Nihilismus* (written 1938–9, 1946–8)
69 *Die Geschichte des Seyns* (written 1938–40)
70 *Über den Anfang* (written 1941)
77 *Feldweg-Gespräche* (written 1944–5)
79 *Bremer und Freiburger Vorträge* (written 1949, 1957)
81 *Gedachtes* (written 1910–75)
90 *Zu Ernst Jünger "Der Arbeiter"* (written 1934–54).

Books in English on Heidegger's thought

Adkins, B. 2007. *Death and Desire in Hegel, Heidegger, and Deleuze*. Edinburgh: Edinburgh University Press.

Adorno, T. W. 1973. *The Jargon of Authenticity*, K. Tarnowski & F. Will (trans.). Evanston, IL: Northwestern University Press.

Allen, W. S. 2007. *Ellipsis: Of Poetry and the Experience of Language after Heidegger, Hölderlin, and Blanchot*. Albany, NY: SUNY Press.

Arendt, H. 1978. *The Life of the Mind*, 1 vol. edn. San Diego, CA: Harcourt Brace.

Babich, B. E. (ed.) 1995. *From Phenomenology to Thought, Errancy, and Desire: Essays in Honor of William J. Richarson, S.J.* Dordrecht: Kluwer.

Babich, B. E. 2006. *Words in Blood, Like Flowers: Philosophy and Poetry, Music and Eros in Hölderlin, Nietzsche, and Heidegger*. Albany, NY: SUNY Press.

Bambach, C. R. 1995. *Heidegger, Dilthey, and the Crisis of Historicism*. Ithaca, NY: Cornell University Press.

Bambach, C. R. 2003. *Heidegger's Roots: Nietzsche, National Socialism, and the Greeks*. Ithaca, NY: Cornell University Press.

Barash, J. A. 1989. *Martin Heidegger and the Problem of Historical Meaning*. New York: Fordham University Press.

Behler, E. 1991. *Confrontations: Derrida/Heidegger/Nietzsche*, S. Taubeneck (trans.). Stanford, CA: Stanford University Press.

Bernasconi, R. 1985. *The Question of Language in Heidegger's History of Being*. Atlantic Highlands, NJ: Humanities Press.

Bernasconi, R. 1993. *Heidegger in Question: The Art of Existing*. Atlantic Highlands, NJ: Humanities Press.

Biemel, W. 1977. *Martin Heidegger: An Illustrated Study*, J. L. Mehta (trans.). London: Routledge & Kegan Paul.

Blattner, W. D. 1999. *Heidegger's Temporal Idealism*. Cambridge: Cambridge University Press.

Blattner, W. D. 2006. *Heidegger's "Being and Time"*. London: Continuum.

Boss, M. 1979. *Existential Foundations of Medicine and Psychology*, S. Conway & A. Cleaves (trans.). New York: Aronson.

Bourdieu, P. 1988. *The Political Ontology of Martin Heidegger*, P. Collier (trans.). Stanford, CA: Stanford University Press.

Bowler, M. 2008. *Heidegger and Aristotle: Philosophy as Praxis*. London: Continuum.

Braver, L. 2009. *Heidegger's Later Writings: A Reader's Guide*. London: Continuum.

Brockelman, T. 2009. *Žižek and Heidegger: The Question Concerning Techno-Capitalism*. London: Continuum.

Brogan, W. A. 2005. *Heidegger and Aristotle: The Twofoldness of Being*. Albany, NY: SUNY Press.

Carel, H. 2006. *Life and Death in Freud and Heidegger*. Amsterdam: Rodopi.

Caputo, J. D. 1982. *Heidegger and Aquinas: An Essay on Overcoming Metaphysics*. New York: Fordham University Press.

Caputo, J. D. 1987. *Radical Hermeneutics: Repetition, Deconstruction, and the Hermeneutic Project*. Bloomington, IN: Indiana University Press.

Caputo, J. D. 1990. *The Mystical Element in Heidegger's Thought*, reprinted with corrections. New York: Fordham University Press.

Caputo, J. D. 1993. *Demythologizing Heidegger*. Bloomington, IN: Indiana University Press.

Carman, T. 2003. *Heidegger's Analytic: Interpretation, Discourse, and Authenticity in* Being and Time. Cambridge: Cambridge University Press.

Cerbone, D. R. 2008. *Heidegger: A Guide for the Perplexed.* New York: Continuum.

Clark, T. 1992. *Derrida, Heidegger, Blanchot: Sources of Derrida's Notion and Practice of Literature.* Cambridge: Cambridge University Press.

Clark, T. 2002. *Martin Heidegger.* New York: Routledge.

Critchley, S. & R. Schürmann 2008. *On Heidegger's "Being and Time".* New York: Routledge.

Crowe, B. D. 2006. *Heidegger's Religious Origins: Deconstruction and Authenticity.* Bloomington, IN: Indiana University Press.

Crowe, B. D. 2008. *Heidegger's Phenomenology of Religion: Realism and Cultural Criticism.* Bloomington, IN: Indiana University Press.

Crowell, S. G. 2001. *Husserl, Heidegger, and the Space of Meaning.* Evanston, IL: Northwestern University Press.

Crowell, S. & J. Malpas (eds) 2007. *Transcendental Heidegger.* Stanford, CA: Stanford University Press.

Dahlstrom, D. O. 2001. *Heidegger's Concept of Truth.* Cambridge: Cambridge University Press.

Dallery, A., C. E. Scott & H. P. Roberts (eds) 1992. *Ethics and Danger: Essays on Heidegger and Continental Thought.* Albany, NY: SUNY Press.

Dallmayr, F. 1991. *Between Freiburg and Frankfurt: Toward a Critical Ontology.* Amherst, MA: University of Massachusetts Press.

Dallmayr, F. 1993. *The Other Heidegger.* Ithaca, NY: Cornell University Press.

Dastur, F. 1998. *Heidegger and the Question of Time*, F. Raffoul & D. Pettigrew (trans.). Amherst, NY: Humanity Books.

Davis, B. W. 2007. *Heidegger and the Will: On the Way to* Gelassenheit. Evanston, IL: Northwestern University Press.

de Beistegui, M. 1998. *Heidegger and the Political.* London: Routledge.

de Beistegui, M. 2003. *Thinking with Heidegger: Displacements.* Bloomington, IN: Indiana University Press.

de Beistegui, M. 2005. *The New Heidegger.* London: Continuum.

de Boer, K. 2000. *Thinking in the Light of Time: Heidegger's Encounter with Hegel.* Albany, NY: SUNY Press.

Denker, A. 2000. *Historical Dictionary of Heidegger's Philosophy.* Lanham, MD: Scarecrow Press.

Derrida, J. 1982. *Margins of Philosophy*, A. Bass (trans. with notes). Chicago, IL: University of Chicago Press.

Derrida, J. 1989. *Of Spirit: Heidegger and the Question,* G. Bennington & R. Bowlby (trans.). Chicago, IL: University of Chicago Press.

Derrida, J. 1993. *Aporias,* T. Dutoit (trans.). Stanford, CA: Stanford University Press.

Dillard, P. S. 2008. *Heidegger and Philosophical Atheology: a Neo-Scholastic Critique.* London: Continuum.

Dreyfus, H. L. 1992. *Being-in-the-World: A Commentary on Heidegger's* Being and Time, *Division I.* Cambridge, MA: MIT Press.

Dreyfus, H. L. (ed.) 2002. *Heidegger Reexamined,* 4 vols. London: Routledge.

Dreyfus, H. L. & H. Hall (eds) 1992. *Heidegger: A Critical Reader.* Oxford: Blackwell.

Dreyfus, H. L. & M. A. Wrathall (eds) 2007. *A Companion to Heidegger.* Oxford: Blackwell.

Edwards, P. 2004. *Heidegger's Confusions.* New York: Prometheus.

Elkholy, S. N. 2008. *Heidegger and a Metaphysics of Feeling: Angst and the Finitude of Being*. London: Continuum.

Emad, P. 2007. *On the Way to Heidegger's "Contributions to Philosophy"*. Madison, WI: University of Wisconsin Press.

Fandozi, P. 1982. *Nihilism and Technology: A Heideggerian Investigation*. Washington, DC: University Press of America.

Farias, V. 1989. *Heidegger and National Socialism*. Philadelphia, PA: Temple University Press.

Faulconer, J. E. & M. A. Wrathall (eds) 2008. *Appropriating Heidegger*. Cambridge: Cambridge University Press.

Feenberg, A. 2005. *Heidegger and Marcuse: the Catastrophe and Redemption of History*. London: Routledge.

Feldman, K. S. 2006. *Binding Words: Conscience and Rhetoric in Hobbes, Hegel, and Heidegger*. Evanston, IL: Northwestern University Press.

Ferry, L. & A. Renaut 1990. *Heidegger and Modernity*, F. Philip (trans.). Chicago, IL: University of Chicago Press.

Fleischacker, S. (ed.) 2008. *Heidegger's Jewish Followers: Essays on Hannah Arendt, Leo Strauss, Hans Jonas, and Emmanuel Levinas*. Pittsburgh, PA: Duquesne University Press.

Foltz, B. V. 1995. *Inhabiting the Earth: Heidegger, Environmental Ethics, and the Metaphysics of Nature*. Atlantic Highlands, NJ: Humanities Press.

Fóti, V. 1992. *Heidegger and the Poets*. Atlantic Highlands, NJ: Humanities Press.

Fried, G. 2000. *Heidegger's Polemos*. New Haven, CT: Yale University Press.

Friedman, M. 2000. *A Parting of the Ways: Carnap, Cassirer, and Heidegger*. Chicago, IL: Open Court.

Frings, M. S. (ed.) 1968. *Heidegger and the Quest for Truth*. Chicago, IL: Quadrangle Books.

Froese, K. 2006. *Nietzsche, Heidegger, and Daoist Thought: Crossing Paths In-Between*. Albany, NY: SUNY Press.

Fynsk, C. 1986. *Heidegger: Thought and Historicity*. Ithaca, NY: Cornell University Press.

Gadamer, H.-G. 1989. *Truth and Method*, 2nd rev. edn, J. Weinsheimer & D. Marshall (trans.). New York: Crossroad Publishing.

Gadamer, H.-G. 1994. *Heidegger's Ways*, J. W. Stanley (trans.). Albany, NY: SUNY Press.

Gasché, R. 2009. *Europe, or the Infinite Task*. Stanford, CA: Stanford University Press.

Gelven, M. 1970. *A Commentary on Heidegger's* Being and Time. New York: Harper Torchbooks.

Gillespie, M. A. 1984. *Hegel, Heidegger, and the Ground of History*. Chicago, IL: University of Chicago Press.

Glazebrook, T. 2000. *Heidegger's Philosophy of Science*. New York: Fordham University Press.

Glendinning, S. 1998. *On Being With Others: Heidegger, Derrida, Wittgenstein*. London: Routledge.

Gordon, P. E. 2003. *Rosenzweig and Heidegger: Between Judaism and German Philosophy*. Berkeley, CA: University of California Press.

Gosetti-Ferencei, J. A. 2004. *Heidegger, Hölderlin, and the Subject of Poetic Language*. New York: Fordham University Press.

Gorner, P. 2007. *Heidegger's Being and Time: An Introduction*. Cambridge: Cambridge University Press.

Gross, D. M. & A. Kemmann (eds) 2005. *Heidegger and Rhetoric*. Albany, NY: SUNY Press.

Groth, M. 2004. *Translating Heidegger*. Amherst, NY: Humanity Books.

Guignon, C. (ed.) 2006. *The Cambridge Companion to Heidegger*, 2nd edn. Cambridge: Cambridge University Press.

Guignon, C. B. 1983. *Heidegger and the Problem of Knowledge*. Indianapolis, IN: Hackett.

Haar, M. 1993. *Heidegger and the Essence of Man*, W. McNeill (trans.). Albany, NY: SUNY Press.

Haar, M. 1993. *The Song of the Earth: Heidegger and the Grounds of the History of Being*, R. Lilly (trans.). Bloomington, IN: Indiana University Press.

Habermas, J. 1987. *The Philosophical Discourse of Modernity*, F. G. Lawrence (trans.). Cambridge, MA: MIT Press.

Hanley, C. 2000. *Being and God in Aristotle and Heidegger*. Lanham, MD: Rowman & Littlefield.

Harman, G. 2002. *Tool-Being: Heidegger and the Metaphysics of Objects*. Chicago, IL: Open Court.

Harman, G. 2007. *Heidegger Explained: From Phenomenon to Thing*. Chicago, IL: Open Court.

Harries, K. 2009. *Art Matters: A Critical Commentary on Heidegger's "The Origin of the Work of Art"*. New York: Springer.

Harries, K. & C. Jamme (eds) 1994. *Martin Heidegger: Politics, Art, and Technology*. New York: Holmes & Meier.

Hart, J. G. & J. C. Maraldo 1976. *The Piety of Thinking: Essays by Martin Heidegger*, J. G. Hart & J. C. Maraldo (trans., notes & comm.). Bloomington, IN: Indiana University Press.

Heine, S. 1985. *Existential and Ontological Dimensions of Time in Heidegger and Dōgen*. Albany, NY: SUNY Press.

Hemming, L. P. 2002. *Heidegger's Atheism: The Refusal of a Theological Voice*. Notre Dame, IN: University of Notre Dame Press.

Hoeller, K. (ed.) 1988. *Heidegger and Psychology*. Atlantic Highlands, NJ: Humanities Press.

Holland, N. J. & P. Huntington 2001. *Feminist Interpretations of Martin Heidegger*. University Park, PA: Penn State University Press.

Hyland, D. A. & J. P. Manoussakis (eds) 2006. *Heidegger and the Greeks: Interpretive Essays*. Bloomington, IN: Indiana University Press.

Inwood, M. 1999. *A Heidegger Dictionary*. Oxford: Blackwell.

Inwood, M. 2000. *Heidegger: A Very Short Introduction*. Oxford: Oxford University Press.

Irigaray, L. 1999. *The Forgetting of Air in Martin Heidegger*, M. B. Mader (trans.). Austin, TX: University of Texas Press.

Jacobs, D. C. 1999. *The Pre-Socratics After Heidegger*. Albany, NY: SUNY Press.

Janicaud, D. & J.-F. Mattéi 1995. *Heidegger From Metaphysics to Thought*, M. Gendre (trans.). Albany, NY: SUNY Press.

Keller, P. 1999. *Husserl and Heidegger on Human Experience*. Cambridge: Cambridge University Press.

King, M. 2001. *A Guide to "Being and Time"*, J. Llewelyn (ed.). Albany, NY: SUNY Press.

Kisiel, T. 1993. *The Genesis of Heidegger's "Being and Time"*. Berkeley, CA: University of California Press.

Kisiel, T. 2002. *Heidegger's Way of Thought: Critical and Interpretive Signposts*. London: Continuum.

Kisiel, T. 2005. "The Demise of Being and Time: 1927–30". In *Heidegger's* Being and Time*: Critical Essays*, R. Polt (ed.), 189–214. Lanham, MD: Rowman & Littlefield.

Kisiel, T. & J. van Buren (eds) 1994. *Reading Heidegger from the Start: Essays in His Earliest Thought*. Albany, NY: SUNY Press.

Kisiel, T. & T. Sheehan (eds) 2007. *Becoming Heidegger: On the Trail of His Occasional Writings, 1910–1927*. Evanston, IL: Northwestern University Press.

Kleinberg, E. 2005. *Generation Existential: Heidegger's Philosophy in France, 1927–1961*. Ithaca, NY: Cornell University Press.

Kockelmans, J. J. 1980. *On Heidegger and Language*. Evanston, IL: Northwestern University Press.

Kockelmans, J. J. 1984. *On the Truth of Being: Reflections on Heidegger's Later Philosophy*. Bloomington, IN: Indiana University Press.

Kockelmans, J. J. 1985. *Heidegger and Science*. Lanham, MD: Rowman & Littlefield.

Kockelmans, J. J. 1985. *Heidegger on Art and Art Works*. New York: Springer.

Kockelmans, J. J. (ed.) 1986. *A Companion to Martin Heidegger's "Being and Time"*. Washington, DC: University Press of America.

Kovacs, G. 1990. *The Question of God in Heidegger's Phenomenology*. Evanston, IL: Northwestern University Press.

Krell, D. F. 1986. *Intimations of Mortality: Time, Truth, and Finitude in Heidegger's Thinking of Being*. University Park, PA: Penn State University Press.

Krell, D. F. 1992. *Daimon Life: Heidegger and Life-Philosophy*. Bloomington, IN: Indiana University Press.

Lacoue-Labarthe, P. 1990. *Heidegger, Art and Politics*, C. Turner (trans.). Oxford: Blackwell.

Lacoue-Labarthe, P. 2007. *Heidegger and the Politics of Poetry*, J. Fort (trans.). Urbana, IL: University of Illinois Press.

Lafont, C. 2000. *Heidegger, Language, and World Disclosure*. Cambridge: Cambridge University Press.

Letteri, M. 2008. *Heidegger and the Question of Psychology: Zollikon and Beyond*. Amsterdam: Rodopi.

Levin, D. M. 1986. *The Body's Recollection of Being*. London: Routledge & Kegan Paul.

Levin, D. M. 1999. *The Philosopher's Gaze: Modernity in the Shadows of Enlightenment*. Berkeley, CA: University of California Press.

Lewis, M. 2005. *Heidegger and the Place of Ethics*. London: Continuum.

Lewis, M. 2007. *Heidegger Beyond Deconstruction: on Nature*. London: Continuum.

Llewelyn, J. 1991. *The Middle Voice of Ecological Conscience: A Chiasmic Reading of Responsibility in the Neighborhood of Levinas, Heidegger, and Others*. New York: St Martin's Press.

Löwith, K. 1995. *Martin Heidegger and European Nihilism*, Richard Wolin (ed.), G. Steiner (trans.). New York: Columbia University Press.

Luchte, J. 2008. *Heidegger's Early Philosophy: the Phenomenology of Ecstatic Temporality*. London: Continuum.

Lyotard, J.-F. 1990. *Heidegger and "The Jews"*, A. Michel & M. S. Roberts (trans.). Minneapolis, MN: University of Minnesota Press.

Lysaker, J. 2002. *You Must Change Your Life: Poetry, Philosophy and the Birth of Sense*. University Park, PA: Penn State University Press.

Ma, L. 2008. *Heidegger on East–West Dialogue: Anticipating the Event*. New York: Routledge.

Macann, C. (ed.) 1992. *Martin Heidegger: Critical Assessments*, 4 vols. New York: Routledge.

Macann, C. 1993. *Four Phenomenological Philosophers: Husserl, Heidegger, Sartre, Merleau-Ponty*. London: Routledge.

Macann, C. (ed.) 1996. *Critical Heidegger*. New York: Routledge.

Macdonald, I. & K. Ziarek (eds) 2008. *Adorno and Heidegger: Philosophical Questions*. Stanford, CA: Stanford University Press.

Macquarrie, J. 1973. *An Existentialist Theology: A Comparison of Heidegger and Bultmann*. Harmondsworth: Penguin.

Macquarrie, J. 1999. *Heidegger and Christianity*. New York: Continuum.

Malpas, J. 2006. *Heidegger's Topology: Being, Place, World*. Cambridge, MA: MIT Press.

Maly, K. 2008. *Heidegger's Possibility: Language, Emergence – Saying Be-ing*. Toronto: University of Toronto Press.

Marion, J.-L. 1998. *Reduction and Givenness: Investigations of Husserl, Heidegger, and Phenomenology*, T. A. Carlson (trans.). Evanston, IL: Northwestern University Press.

Marx, W. 1971. *Heidegger and the Tradition*, T. Kisiel & M. Greene (trans.). Evanston, IL: Northwestern University Press.

May, R. 1996. *Heidegger's Hidden Sources: East Asian Influences on His Work*, G. Parkes (trans.). New York: Routledge.

Mayeda, G. 2006. *Time, Space, and Ethics in the Philosophy of Watsuji Tetsuro, Kuki Shuzo, and Martin Heidegger*. London: Routledge.

McCumber, J. 1999. *Metaphysics and Oppression: Heidegger's Challenge to Western Philosophy*. Bloomington, IN: Indiana University Press.

McGrath, S. J. 2006. *The Early Heidegger and Medieval Philosophy: Phenomenology for the Godforsaken*. Washington, DC: Catholic University of America Press.

McGrath, S. J. 2008. *Heidegger: A (Very) Critical Introduction*. Grand Rapids, MI: Eerdmans.

McNeil, W. 1999. *The Glance of the Eye: Heidegger, Aristotle, and the Ends of Theory*. Albany, NY: SUNY Press.

McNeil, W. 2006. *The Time of Life: Heidegger and Ethos*. Albany, NY: SUNY Press.

Mehta, J. L. 1976. *Martin Heidegger, the Way and the Vision*. Honolulu, HI: University of Hawaii Press.

Milchman, A. & A. Rosenberg (eds) 2003. *Heidegger and Foucault: Critical Encounters*. Minneapolis, MN: University of Minnesota Press.

Mitchell, D. R. 2001. *Heidegger's Philosophy and Theories of the Self*. Aldershot: Ashgate.

Moran, D. 2000. *Introduction to Phenomenology*. London: Routledge.

Murray, M. (ed.) 1978. *Heidegger and Modern Philosophy*. New Haven, CT: Yale University Press.

Nancy, J.-L. 1993. *The Experience of Freedom*, B. McDonald (trans.). Stanford, CA: Stanford University Press.

Neske, G. & E. Kettering (eds) 1990. *Martin Heidegger and National Socialism: Questions and Answers*, L. Harries & J. Neugroschel (trans.). New York: Paragon House.

Nicholson, G. 1992. *Illustrations of Being: Drawing upon Heidegger and upon Metaphysics*. Atlantic Highlands, NJ: Humanities Press.

Nulty, T. 2006. *Primative Disclosive Alethism: Davidson, Heidegger, and the Nature of Truth*. New York: Peter Lang.

Okrent, M. 1988. *Heidegger's Pragmatism: Understanding, Being, and the Critique of Metaphysics*. Ithaca, NY: Cornell University Press.

Olafson, F. A. 1987. *Heidegger and the Philosophy of Mind*. New Haven, CT: Yale University Press.

Olafson, F. A. 1995. *What is a Human Being? A Heideggerian View*. Cambridge: Cambridge University Press.

Olafson, F. A. 1998. *Heidegger and the Ground of Ethics: A Study of Mitsein*. Cambridge: Cambridge University Press.

Ott, H. 1993. *Martin Heidegger: A Political Life*, A. Blunden (trans.). New York: Basic Books.

Parkes, G. (ed) 1987. *Heidegger and Asian Thought*. Honolulu, HI: University of Hawaii Press.

Partenie, C. & T. Rockmore (eds) 2005. *Heidegger and Plato: Toward Dialogue*. Evanston, IL: Northwestern University Press.

Pattison, G. 2000. *The Later Heidegger*. London: Routledge.

Perotti, J. L. 1974. *Heidegger on the Divine*. Athens, OH: Ohio State University Press.

Pettigrew, D. & F. Raffoul (eds) 2009. *French Interpretations of Heidegger: An Exceptional Reception*. Albany, NY: SUNY Press.

Petzet, H. W. 1993. *Encounters and Dialogues with Martin Heidegger: 1929–1976*, P. Emad & K. Maly (trans.). Chicago, IL: University of Chicago Press.

Philips, H. 1998. *Heidegger's Philosophy of Being: A Critical Interpretation*. Princeton, NJ: Princeton University Press.

Phillips, J. 2005. *Heidegger's Volk: Between National Socialism and Poetry*. Stanford, CA: Stanford University Press.

Pöggeler, O. 1987. *Martin Heidegger's Path of Thinking*, D. Magurshak & S. Barber (trans.). Atlantic Highlands, NJ: Humanities Press.

Pöggeler, O. 1997. *The Paths of Heidegger's Life and Thought*, J. Bailiff (trans.). Amherst, NY: Humanity Books.

Polt, R. 1999. *Heidegger: An Introduction*. Ithaca, NY: Cornell University Press.

Polt, R. (ed.) 2005. *Heidegger's "Being and Time": Critical Essays*. Lanham, MD: Rowman & Littlefield.

Polt, R. 2006. *The Emergency of Being: On Heidegger's "Contributions to Philosophy"*. Ithaca, NY: Cornell University Press.

Polt, R. & G. Fried (eds) 2001. *A Companion to Heidegger's "Introduction to Metaphysics"*. New Haven, CT: Yale University Press.

Powell, J. 2007. *Heidegger's Contributions to Philosophy: Life and the Last God*. New York: Continuum.

Prudhomme, J. O. 1997. *God and Being: Heidegger's Relation to Theology*. Atlantic Highlands, NJ: Humanities Press.

Raffoul, F. 1988. *Heidegger and the Subject*, D. Pettigrew & G. Recco (trans.). Atlantic Highlands, NJ: Humanities Press.

Raffoul, F. & E. S. Nelson (eds) 2008. *Rethinking Facticity*. Albany, NY: SUNY Press.

Raffoul, F. & D. Pettigrew (eds) 2002. *Heidegger and Practical Philosophy*. Albany, NY: SUNY Press.

Rapaport, H. 1989. *Heidegger and Derrida: Reflections on Time and Language*. Lincoln, NE: University of Nebraska Press.

Richardson, W. J. 2003. *Heidegger: Through Phenomenology to Thought*, 4th edn. New York: Fordham University Press.

Ricoeur, P. 1984–6. *Time and Narrative*, 3 vols, J. Thompson (trans.). Cambridge: Cambridge University Press.

Risser, J. (ed.) 1999. *Heidegger Toward the Turn: Essays on the Work of the 1930s*. Albany, NY: SUNY Press.

Rockmore, T. 1992. *On Heidegger's Nazism and Philosophy*. Berkeley, CA: University of California Press.

Rockmore, T. 1995. *Heidegger and French Philosophy: Humanism, Antihumanism, and Being*. New York: Routledge.

Rockmore, T. (ed.) 2000. *Heidegger, German Idealism, and Neo-Kantianism*. Amherst, NY: Humanity Books.

Rockmore, T. & J. Margolis (eds) 1992. *The Heidegger Case: On Philosophy and Politics*. Philadelphia, PA: Temple University Press.

Rojcewicz, R. 2006. *The Gods and Technology: A Reading of Heidegger*. Albany, NY: SUNY Press.

Rorty, R. 1991. *Essays on Heidegger and Others*. Cambridge: Cambridge University Press.

Rosen, S. 1993. *The Question of Being: A Reversal of Heidegger*. New Haven, CT: Yale University Press.

Ruin, H. 1994. *Enigmatic Origins: Tracing the Theme of Historicity through Heidegger's Works*. Stockholm: Almqvist & Wiksell.

Sadler, T. 1996. *Heidegger and Aristotle: The Question of Being*. London: Athlone.

Safranski, R. 1998. *Martin Heidegger: Between Good and Evil*, E. Osers (trans.). Cambridge, MA: Harvard University Press.

Sallis, J. (ed.) 1970. *Heidegger and the Path of Thinking*. Pittsburgh, PA: Duquesne University Press.

Sallis, J. (ed.) 1978. *Radical Phenomenology: Essays in Honor of Martin Heidegger*. Atlantic Highlands, NJ: Humanities Press.

Sallis, J. 1990. *Echoes: After Heidegger*. Bloomington, IN: Indiana University Press.

Sallis, J. (ed.) 1993. *Reading Heidegger: Commemorations*. Bloomington, IN: Indiana University Press.

Sallis, J. 1995a. *Delimitations: Phenomenology and the End of Metaphysics*, 2nd exp. edn. Bloomington, IN: Indiana University Press.

Sallis, J. 1995b. *Double Truth*. Albany, NY: SUNY Press.

Schalow, F. 1992. *The Renewal of the Heidegger–Kant Dialogue*. Albany, NY: SUNY Press.

Schalow, F. 2001. *Heidegger and the Quest for the Sacred: From Thought to the Sanctuary of Faith*. New York: Springer.

Schalow, F. 2007. *The Incarnality of Being: The Earth, Animals, and the Body in Heidegger's Thought*. Albany, NY: SUNY Press.

Scheibler, I. H. 2000. *Gadamer: Between Heidegger and Habermas*. Lanham, MD: Rowman & Littlefield.

Schmidt, D. J. 1988. *The Ubiquity of the Finite: Hegel, Heidegger, and the Entitlements of Philosophy*. Cambridge, MA: MIT Press.

Schmidt, D. J. 2001. *On Germans and Other Greeks: Tragedy and Ethical Life*. Bloomington, IN: Indiana University Press.

Schürmann, R. 1987. *Heidegger on Being and Acting: From Principles to Anarchy*, C.-M. Gros & R. Schürmann (trans.). Bloomington, IN: Indiana University Press.

Schürmann, R. 2003. *Broken Hegemonies*, R. Lilly (trans.). Bloomington, IN: Indiana University Press.

Scott, C. E. 1987. *The Language of Difference*. Atlantic Highlands, NJ: Humanities Press.

Scott, C. E. 1990. *The* Question *of Ethics: Nietzsche, Foucault, Heidegger.* Bloomington, IN: Indiana University Press.

Scott, C. E. & E. Ballard (eds) 1973. *Martin Heidegger: in Europe and America*. The Hague: Nijhoff.

Scott, C. E., S. Schoenbohm, D. Vallega-Neu & A. Vallega (eds) 2002. *Companion to Heidegger's "Contributions to Philosophy"*. Bloomington, IN: Indiana University Press.

Shahan, R. W. & J. N. Mohanty (eds) 1984. *Thinking about Being: Aspects of Heidegger's Thought*. Norman, OK: University of Oklahoma Press.

Sharr, A. 2006. *Heidegger's Hut*. Cambridge, MA: MIT Press.

Sheehan, T. 1987. *Karl Rahner: The Philosophical Foundations*. Athens, OH: Ohio University Press.

Sheehan, T. 2009. *Heidegger: The Man and the Thinker*. Edison, NJ: Transaction.

Sluga, H. 1993. *Heidegger's Crisis: Philosophy and Politics in Nazi Germany*. Cambridge, MA: Harvard University Press.

Spanos, W. 1979. *Martin Heidegger and the Question of Literature*. Bloomington, IN: Indiana University Press.

Spiegelberg, H. 1969. *The Phenomenological Movement: An Historical Introduction*, 2 vols. The Hague: Nijhoff.

Stambaugh, J. 1991. *Thoughts on Heidegger*. Lanham, MD: University Press of America.

Stambaugh, J. 1992. *The Finitude of Being*. Albany, NY: SUNY Press.

Stapleton, T. J. 1983. *Husserl and Heidegger: The Question of a Phenomenological Beginning*. Albany, NY: SUNY Press.

Steiner, G. 1987. *Martin Heidegger.* Chicago, IL: University of Chicago Press.

Taminiaux, J. 1991. *Heidegger and the Project of Fundamental Ontology*, M. Gendre (ed. & trans.). Albany, NY: SUNY Press.

Tanzer, M. B. 2002. *Heidegger: Decisionism and Quietism*. Amherst, NY: Humanity Books.

Thomson, I. D. 2005. *Heidegger on Ontotheology: Technology and the Politics of Education*. Cambridge: Cambridge University Press.

Vallega, A. 2003. *Heidegger and the Issue of Space: Thinking on Exilic Grounds*. Univeristy Park, PA: Penn State University Press.

Vallega-Neu, D. 2003. *Heidegger's "Contributions to Philosophy": An Introduction*. Bloomington, IN: Indiana University Press.

Van Buren, J. 1994. *The Young Heidegger: Rumor of the Hidden King*. Bloomington, IN: Indiana University Press.

Van Buren, J. (ed.) 2002. *Supplements: From the Earliest Essays to Being and Time and Beyond*. Albany, NY: SUNY Press.

Vedder, B. 2007. *Heidegger's Philosophy of Religion: From God to the Gods*. Pittsburgh, PA: Duquesne University Press.

Villa, D. R. 1996. *Arendt and Heidegger: The Fate of the Political*. Princeton, NJ: Princeton University Press.

Vogel, L. 1994. *The Fragile We: Ethical Implications of Heidegger's "Being and Time"*. Evanston, IL: Northwestern University Press.

Ward, J. F. 1995. *Heidegger's Political Thinking*. Amherst, MA: University of Massachusetts Press.

White, C. J. 2005. *Time and Death: Heidegger's Analysis of Finitude*. Aldershot: Ashgate.

Wolin, R. (ed.) 1993. *The Heidegger Controversy: A Critical Reader.* Cambridge, MA: MIT Press.

Wolin, R. 1990. *The Politics of Being: The Political Thought of Martin Heidegger.* New York: Columbia University Press.

Wolin, R. 2003. *Heidegger's Children: Hannah Arendt, Karl Löwith, Hans Jonas, and Herbert Marcuse.* Princeton, NJ: Princeton University Press.

Wood, D. (ed.) 1993. *Of Derrida, Heidegger, and Spirit.* Evanston, IL: Northwestern University Press.

Wood, D. 2001. *The Deconstruction of Time*, 2nd edn, with a new preface. Evanston, IL: Northwestern University Press.

Wood, D. 2002. *Thinking after Heidegger.* Cambridge: Polity.

Wrathhall, M. 2006. *How to Read Heidegger.* New York: Norton.

Wrathall, M. & J. Malpas (eds) 2000. *Heidegger, Coping, and Cognitive Science: Essays in Honor of Hubert L. Dreyfus.* Cambridge, MA: MIT Press.

Young, J. 1997. *Heidegger, Philosophy, Nazism.* Cambridge: Cambridge University Press.

Young, J. 2002. *Heidegger's Later Philosophy.* Cambridge: Cambridge University Press.

Young, J. 2004. *Heidegger's Philosophy of Art.* Cambridge: Cambridge University Press.

Zarader, M. 2006. *The Unthought Debt: Heidegger and the Hebraic Heritage*, B. Bergo (trans.). Stanford, CA: Stanford University Press.

Zhang, W. 2006. *Heidegger, Rorty, and the Eastern Thinkers: A Hermeneutics of Cross-Cultural Understanding.* Albany, NY: SUNY Press.

Zimmerman, M. E. 1986. *Eclipse of the Self: The Development of Heidegger's Concept of Authenticity*, rev. edn. Athens, OH: Ohio University Press.

Zimmerman, M. E. 1990. *Heidegger's Confrontation with Modernity.* Bloomington, IN: Indiana University Press.

Index

abyss (*Abgrund*) 28, 78, 120, 127, 162–63, 169, 212
alētheia see truth
analogy 87
Andenken see recollection/remembrance
anticipatory resoluteness 66, 71, 104; *see also* resoluteness
anti-Semitism 109–10
Anwesen (presencing) 15, 134, 160, 214, 254 absencing and 117, 125; *Anwesen-lassen* (letting-come-about) 86; meaning-giving 100; meaningful presence 84
Anwesenheit (presence, coming to presence) 145, 159
Aristotle's *ousia* 15; constant presence 7–9, 25
anxiety (*Angst*) 24, 41, 55–6, 64–6, 143
appearance 37–8, 46, 202–3, 211–12
appropriation *see Ereignis*
a priori 45, 48–50, 84–98, 100, 223
Aquinas, Thomas 98, 117, 220
Arendt, H. 12–13, 161, 261, 263
Aristotle 2, 5, 7, 14–15, 20, 29–30, 34, 36, 38, 80–81, 84, 105, 117, 124, 126–7, 153, 163, 184–5, 223–4, 240, 260–61
art 128–39; *see also* poetry; *poēisis* aesthetics 128–30; a circular movement of questioning 130; of a historical people 135–6; and *technē* 129, 185–8, 193–4 and truth 131–5; work of/artwork 1, 40, 131–4, 187–8, 212, 217, 253
artlessness (*Kunstlösigkeit*) 129
artwork *see* art, work of
assignment (*Zueignung*) 147, 153
assignment (*Verweisung*), assignment-context 50–51, 53, 209
astonishment *see* wonder
atheism *see also* God/gods as the absence of the gods 250; atheism/atheistic piety of philosophy 223, 228, 232, 240; a-theological thinking of being 226; just as little atheistic as theistic 253; and the last god 246
Aufenthalt (sojourn, dwelling) 61, 112–14, 132; *see also* dwelling (*Wohnen*)
Augenblick (moment, brief epiphantic moment) 97, 105, 145, 150, 226
Augustine 12, 80–81, 220–21, 231, 238–9
authentic, authenticity (*Eigentlichkeit*) 23, 30, 54–5, 57–67, 92–4, 97, 100; *see also* inauthenticity
Ereignis 141–4, 146; *Gelassenheit* 168, 176–9; history 111, 220, 235; language 204; religion 220, 235, 237, 239, 243; temporality 71–4, 77, 79; *Volk* 104–6
awareness 45–6, 57, 65, 96, 165, 190, 192, 246; *see also* pre-theoretical self-awareness 45, 55

Baeumler, A. 103, 110
Beaufret, J. 263

beautiful, the 129, 194
Becker, O. 261
Becker-Modersohn, P. 138
beginning/inception (*Anfang*) 75–9; *see also* origin
art 130, 136; *Beginn* versus *Anfang* 76, 162 epochal 145; the first (*der erste Anfang*), Greek 7, 15, 34, 38, 40–41, 106–7, 111, 117, 119, 145, 149, 158–9, 164, 166–7, 173, 226; last god 226; myth of 41; the other/ another (*der andere Anfang*) 41, 103, 105, 110–11, 117, 124–5, 144–5, 147, 150, 153, 158, 166, 226–7, 248; point for "transcendental" analysis 48; wonder/wonderment 106, 124
being (*Sein*) 5–10; *see also* beingness; beyng; beings; *Ereignis*
abandonment of/by 78, 144–7, 149, 168, 171–2; as such 5–6, 8, 12, 77, 142–3, 159, 162–3, 165, 167, 168, 245; of beings 6–7, 10, 38, 83–4, 119–24, 129, 159, 162, 164, 168, 170, 224; belonging *see* belonging, being; forgetting, forgetfulness/forgottenness/oblivion of 5–6, 93, 95–6, 120, 123–5, 144, 147, 158, 163–5, 183, 186, 228, 250; great chain of 6; history of 3, 8, 10, 13, 103, 112, 150–60, 163, 165–8, 170, 173, 227 (*see also* being-historical thinking); house of *see* language, as the house of being; itself 8, 74–5, 83–4, 156, 158–9, 162–3, 166–8, 178, 193, 198, 216, 220, 249–50, 253; meaning of 5, 7, 44, 58–9, 62, 66–7, 178, 184–5; question of 2, 5–10, 59–60, 62, 70, 130, 142, 144, 160, 170–71, 224–5, 231; *qua* being 5; refusal (*Versagung*, *Verweigerung*) 99, 144; relation with human being 8–10, 170 (*see also* being, requirement of human being; *Dasein–Sein* bond; reciprocity; turn, as the reciprocity between being and human being); requirement/need of human being 8, 82, 88, 93, 125, 178 (*see also* being, relation with human being); self-concealing of 120–21, 125, 158 (*see also* concealing/concealment; earth); thinking of 1–2, 4, 7–10, 180, 225–6, 228; and time 7–8, 69–81, 151, 156 (*see also* temporality; time); time as horizon for 70–71, 74–5 (*see also* horizon; horizontal schema); topology of 177; understanding of 7, 19–20 (pre-understanding, pre-predicative understanding), 44–6 (in *Being and Time*), 51, 53, 70, 75 ("from the understanding of being to the happening of being"), 76, 78, 80, 120, 126, 185–8, 222, 225–6, 228, 242; withdrawal of 147, 160, 163–5
being-here, being-there, being-t/here *see* Dasein
being-historical thinking (*seinsgeschichtliches Denken*) 8, 247; *see also* being, history of
being-in-the-world (*In-der-Welt-Sein*) 11, 19, 25, 44–56, 62–6, 71–2, 80, 86, 94, 126, 142, 202, 204, 209, 243, 253; *see also*

the open-region "bethings" things 177;
relational 209; releasement toward 179;
"the thing things" 210; and world 205–6,
208–10, 215–16
thrownness 11, 25–7, 52, 56, 59, 64, 71–3, 76,
82, 88, 92, 96, 98; *see also* facticity
time 28, 69–81 *see also* history; temporality;
time-space
"Am I time?", "I am my time", "we are our
time" 27, 74, 78; being and 7–8, 70–1, 79,
151, 156, 248; Care and the rule of 58; clock
time 73; "Each Dasein is itself 'time'" 70;
ecstases of 74; ecstatic, meaningful 75–6;
elimination of (Eckhart) 236; festal 111;
finite 62, 73; of foundering 257; generation
and "its [Dasein's] time" 24, 26; historical
76 (*see also* historicity; history); Hölderlin's
determination of a new time 245; as the
horizon for being *see* being, time as horizon
for; as an image of eternity (Plotinus) 69;
inception of time 75–8; interpretation of
being in terms of 7 (*see also* being, time as
horizon for); "it gives time" 151; and *Kehre*
92; linear/serial 74–5; natural 75–5; of need
245; originary 77; presence as one mode of
160; Saturn, the god of 57–8, 61; and space
78; true 160; untimely 145, 152
time-space 78, 79, 81, 120
to ti ēn einai 84
tool *see* equipment
transcendence, decision to let happen 29
truth (*Wahrheit*) 1, 7, 13, 74, 77, 79, 109,
116–31, 134–53, 177, 184, 187–8, 193,
233, 243, 245, 257
as *alētheia* (unconcealment, unhiddenness)
9, 15, 20, 34, 36, 92, 106, 112–13, 116–27,
249 (*see also* concealing/concealment; play of
revealing/unconcealment and concealing/con-
cealment); art as the "setting-itself-into-work
of truth" 131; of being 84, 130, 170, 202–4,
206, 224, 226, 228, 248, 250, 253–4; of
beyng 94, 117, 119–23, 125, 127, 143–50,
152–3, 246, 248; as correctness 116–19,
121–2, 124–6, 134; as correspondence
(*adaequatio, homoiōsis*) 92, 106, 116, 118,
124, 126; essence of 93–4, 106, 112–13,
117, 122–4; as *polemos/Aus-einander-setzung*
106; as the process of meaning-giving 100;
and untruth 9, 122–3, 144
Tsujimura, K. 264
Tugendhat, E. 126, 127, 263
turn 1, 82–101
different senses of 82, 100, 181; Heidegger's
"second turn" (from will to non-willing)
8–9, 168–73; in the history of being 112,
146, 168, 170, 173, 175; as the reciprocity
between being and human being (*Kehre*-
1) 87–9, 122, 142–3, 146, 152 (*see also*
Dasein–Sein bond; reciprocity); as the shift in
Heidegger's thinking in the 1930s (*Kehre*-2)
89–93, 103, 140, 142; as the transformation
of human being (*Kehre*-3) 94–5; turn-around
of ontology into a metontology 28

unconcealment (*Unverborgenheit*) *see* truth,
as *alētheia*

understanding (*Verstehen*)
authentic 55; being *see* being, understanding of; categorial versus existential 47;
intuitive 59; phenomenological 237;
preconceptual 19; Schelling's opposition of
ground and 245; self-understanding 2 (of
philosophy), 53, 65
untruth *see* truth, and untruth
Unheimlichkeit (homelessness/uncanniness)
64, 112–13

van Gogh, V. 131, 137–8
Vattimo, G. 13
Vereignung (appropriation/achieving appro-
priation) 148–9
Volk 31, 103–8, 111–13, 171–2, 180
Volpi, F. 13
voluntarism 9, 107, 169, 171–3; *see also*
will/willing

waiting upon 171, 177
Watsuji, T. 14
"ways, not works" 4
will/willing see also *Gelassenheit*; non-willing; will to power
being as will (to power) 10, 163, 168,
172–3, 181, 252; domain of 168, 175–6,
253; as ecstatic-incorporation/being-master-
out-beyond-oneself 173; as evil 173; to
foundation 42; as fundamental (dis-)attune-
ment 168, 174; of God 169, 181, 253;
Heidegger's critique of 173–5; Heidegger's
embrace of 171; Heidegger's turn from *see*
turn, "second turn" from will to non-willing
(*Gelassenheit*); pure 171; in the Rectorial
Address and political speeches 107, 171–2;
and technology 174–5, 191; transcenden-
tal/ontological 171, 174, 176–7; transition
out of 175–7, 253; *Umwillen* (for the sake
of) 170–71; will to will 171, 174
will to power 10, 107, 138, 163, 168, 172–4,
181, 188, 252, 262
wonder/astonishment (*thaumazein*) 66, 86,
106, 108, 124, 127, 145, 201
Wood, D. 13, 81, 263
work *see also* "ways, not works"
of art *see* art, work of; of science versus
philosophical thinking 4–5
world (*Welt*) 8–12, 21–6, 37, 40, 48–54,
58–9, 76, 82, 86, 88–96, 99–100, 180,
186, 201–2, 208, and *passim*; *see also*
being-in-the-world; earth, world and
(strife of); lifeworld; thing, world and;
worldhood; world-formation
and art 131–2; Christian 222–3, 243, 247;
environing/surrounding (*Umwelt*) 19–20,
48, 186; everyday 48–50, 64; fourfold
205, 208–218; historical 12, 28; modern
world picture (*Weltbild*) 189–90; shared
21–2; suprasensory 250–51; technological 99, 177, 227, 229; "the world worlds"
98, 148
world-formation 37, 171
worldhood 48–51, 54, 77

Young, J. 217